T0342095

Harvard Historical Studies • 182

Published under the auspices
of the Department of History
from the income of the
Paul Revere Frothingham Bequest
Robert Louis Stroock Fund
Henry Warren Torrey Fund

# Industry and Revolution

## SOCIAL AND ECONOMIC CHANGE

## IN THE ORIZABA VALLEY, MEXICO

Aurora Gómez-Galvarriato

Harvard University Press

Cambridge, Massachusetts · London, England

2013

Library of Congress Cataloging-in-Publication Data

Gómez Galvarriato, Aurora.
Industry and revolution : social and economic change in the Orizaba Valley,
Mexico / Aurora Gómez-Galvarriato.
pages   cm
Includes bibliographical references and index.
ISBN 978-0-674-07272-5 (alk. paper)
1. Textile workers—Mexico—Orizaba (Veracruz-Llave)—History—19th century.
2. Textile workers—Mexico—Orizaba (Veracruz-Llave)—History—20th century.
3. Textile industry—Mexico—Orizaba (Veracruz-Llave)—History—19th century.
4. Textile industry—Mexico—Orizaba (Veracruz-Llave)—History—20th century.
5. Orizaba (Veracruz-Llave, Mexico)—Economic conditions.   I. Title.
HD8039.T42M6394   2013
338.4'76770097262—dc23          2012038237

*To my parents,*
*Elizabeth and Mario*

# Contents

Industry and Revolution

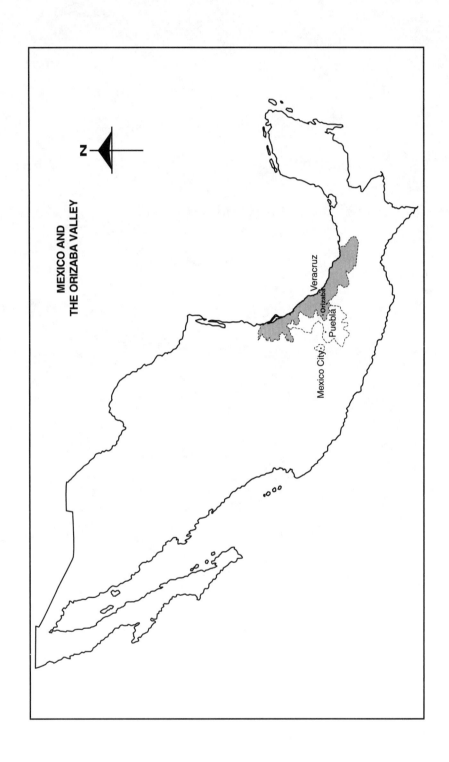

MEXICO AND
THE ORIZABA VALLEY

Veracruz

Orizaba

Puebla

Mexico City

# Introduction

A T THE END THE NINETEENTH CENTURY and the beginning of the twentieth, the Orizaba Valley experienced two major revolutions that would radically transform what had been the way of life in the valley for as long as memory could tell. The first was the introduction of mechanized industries, the railroad, and other innovations that had been developing in the world since the Industrial Revolution. The second was the social revolution that took place during the second decade of the twentieth century in Mexico, which had profound roots and consequences in this region. This book explores how these revolutions came about, how they interacted, and what their impact was in the lives of those who lived through them, dealt with them, and shaped the way these transformations actually took place.

It is important to understand the roles these revolutions played in Mexico's history, and for this the Orizaba Valley is a place clamoring for explanations. Its old factories speak of a past of industrial splendor; its schools, libraries, sports fields, cinemas, and union buildings tell of a time of labor utopia. Nowadays all of them are in decay, all the textile factories have shut down. Unemployment is high, and the once-powerful unions are in disarray. Many workers struggling to find a job must labor without a contract or legal protection; others emigrate. How had the industrial growth and strong labor organizations of the past come about? Why did the industry and its unions decline? Was their present decay inevitable?

The history of the Orizaba Valley is particularly fascinating because the changes it experienced between 1880 and 1930 were not restricted to the valley alone. The revolutions we deal with are the forces that shaped world history during the last two centuries. Looking at the Orizaba Valley during this period gives us a privileged view, because both revolutions manifested themselves forcefully there in a short period of time.

The introduction of the new technologies for communication, transportation, and production that came about as a result of the Industrial Revolution has been one of the major transformations in human history. From its start in Great Britain at the end of the eighteenth century, the Industrial Revolution spread to the rest of the world, and everywhere it reached, life was transformed. Although in one way or another its consequences began to be felt from the beginning all over the world, its impact has varied across the globe according to the timing and strength of the adoption of the new technologies. In Mexico the changes wrought by this revolution began to appear during the second half of the nineteenth century and the first half of the twentieth century, but they were circumscribed to particular regions. One of the places where they had the most dramatic effect was the Orizaba Valley, where the textile industry, one of the sectors crucial to early industrialization, became strongly developed as two of the largest and best-equipped textile companies in Mexico—the Compañía Industrial de Orizaba S.A. (CIDOSA) and the Compañía Industrial Veracruzana S.A. (CIVSA)—were established there during the last decade of the nineteenth century. This book explores how the introduction of mechanized textile industry took place in this region, and the economic and social changes it unleashed.

Social revolutions—violent civil wars that provoked the dramatic collapse of the established sociopolitical orders of property through the widespread rebellion of petty proprietors and the unpropertied— became a major historical feature in the history of the modern world.[1] For the countries where they occurred, these revolutions became the axis around which their postrevolutionary historiography revolved, and historians have often battled over the character of their consequences.[2] For Mexico, where the Mexican Revolution (as myth or reality) has been a source of national identity and pride, and where its legacy has been used both to legitimate and to protest against governments and politicians, the Revolution and the way it is understood still occupies a central place in political discourse. This book, then, also attempts to probe the nature of the Mexican Revolution.

The study of the Orizaba Valley allows us to understand the role that industrial workers played in the Mexican Revolution. At the beginning of the twentieth century, workers from this region created the most powerful labor organization in the country, and gained tragic celebrity as a result of the military repression they suffered in 1907. During the revolutionary years and during the 1920s, they were among of the most strongly unionized workers in the nation. How did Orizaba Valley industrial workers participate in the Revolution and shape it? How did the Revolution change their lives and well-being? How did it transform the economic development of that region?

This book aims to describe the nature and consequences of these two major revolutions in terms of changes in business performance and workers' living conditions. It examines the business and labor history of one textile firm, the Compañía Industrial Veracruzana S.A., and one industrial region, the Orizaba Valley, from the early 1890s to through the 1920s to understand the way these two revolutions shaped the history of modern Mexico.

The type of information required for this kind of analysis is not available in government sources for the period. It can, however, be found in company archives. The historical records of the two major textile companies in the Orizaba Valley still exist. Unfortunately, only a small part of CIDOSA's archive was available for research. However, CIVSA's archive provided a vast wealth information. This was complemented with the many sources at various other archives.

Looking at specific cases provides the richness of vast and detailed information, yet it poses questions about the representativeness of such a study and how its findings can be generalized. The book seeks to put this firm and region in a national and international perspective, something feasible through the vast literature that exists on the textile industry, which is the constant and classic case in any early industrialization experience.

In a major departure from the usual approaches, this book looks at business and labor history together. Sometimes the sources provide important methodological lessons to the historian. In this case, company archives showed that studying labor or business separately would provide only partial answers. Business and labor are both necessary parts of production, so the full story can be obtained only by studying both.

Workers and business carry out twin and competing struggles: the first want to improve their living and working conditions, the second wants to maximize profits and survive in the face of domestic and foreign competition and pressures from labor and the state. This book brings together both stories in order to show the evolution of workers' welfare and the business and productivity conditions of the firm. It shows that the role played by organized workers in the Orizaba Valley was crucial to shaping the path taken by the Mexican Revolution in terms of providing better living and working conditions to industrial workers, in the Orizaba Valley and beyond. It describes how the postrevolutionary state worked with labor and owners to craft a solution in which all won in the short term—but it also shows how that solution was unsustainable in the long run because it stopped technological change in the textile industry and doomed it to inefficiency. When Mexico was forced to abandon protectionism after the economic and financial collapse of 1982, this brought about the collapse of the industry and a great diminishment of its workers' well-being.

Studying business and labor together entailed another major departure from historiography: encompassing as an interrelated and indivisible processes Mexico's industrial revolution and the social revolution that took place in Mexico between 1880 and 1930. To understand the particular ways the worldwide Industrial Revolution settled and evolved in Mexico—how and when new technologies were incorporated—since 1910, it is necessary to take into account the Mexican Revolution and the institutional structures it left in place. Similarly, to grasp the social and economic changes the Mexican Revolution brought about, one must recognize the even greater changes produced by Mexico's industrial revolution. Finally, the long-term consequences of the Mexican Revolution can be understood only by taking into account the forces unleashed by the global Industrial Revolution, which continue to this day.

# CHAPTER 1

# The Mexican Textile Industry

## *An Overview*

T HE LONG AND EXCEPTIONAL HISTORY of Mexico's textile industry winds through a complex and intriguing historical landscape.
Very few countries in the world share with Mexico such a long and continuous history of textile manufacturing. Cotton spinning and backstrap
weaving were widespread in pre-Hispanic America and continued unin-
terrupted after the arrival of the Spaniards. Early in the sixteenth century, a new technology and organization of production was developed
for the manufacturing of woolens: *obrajes,* large workshops that vertically integrated every part of woolen cloth production, employing twenty
to a hundred workers, usually in some form of coerced labor. Mexico is
one of the two present-day Latin American countries where obrajes acquired large economic importance during the sixteenth century, the
other being Ecuador.[1]

Woolen textiles production increased until the end of the seventeenth
century. But by the 1750s its heyday had passed, a result of greater labor
costs and increasingly fierce competition from British and Catalan cloth
and from a growing Mexican cotton textile production. When obrajes
began to falter, a putting-out system, similar to that which flourished in
preindustrial Europe, appeared in Mexico, Tlaxcala, and Guadalajara,
but nowhere on more solid grounds than in Puebla.[2]

Colonial regulations granted substantial protection to New Spain's textile manufacturing. Even after extending to New Spain the so-called free-trade ordinance of 1778, foreign textiles imported via the Spanish ports remained expensive enough to dress only the upper classes. Moreover, the Napoleonic wars in Europe cut off communications between New and Old Spain, encouraging the expansion of textile manufacture in Mexico.[3]

Domestic cotton faced increasing hardship after 1805, when Spanish policy allowed neutral powers to trade directly with the Indies, allowing textile imports to surge. The wars of independence together with greater foreign competition gave obrajes a final blow; whereas there were still nineteen obrajes with 291 looms operating in Queretaro in 1810, only four obrajes were still working in 1812. Cotton textile production was greatly weakened as well. Guadalajara's textile production, which by 1802 was similar in dimensions to that of Puebla, "was virtually eliminated by competition from imports through the newly opened Pacific ports."[4]

The emergence of Mexican Independence did not improve the situation of textile producers. The first Mexican governments adopted liberal policies that were designed primarily to increase government revenue rather than protect domestic manufactures; textiles represented 60% to 70% of total imports from 1821 and 1830, and about 50% of government revenues came from import duties.[5] Despite its wish to implement protectionist policies, the government was prevented from doing this by the loss of revenue that would have resulted.

## The Origins of the Mechanized Mexican Textile Industry

Important changes had been taking place in the world since 1750, to which New Spain became suddenly exposed. European policy moved away from anti-global mercantilism and toward pro-global free trade; a worldwide transport revolution reduced transport costs and integrated world commodity markets; and important technological changes in the manufacturing process, first in England and later in other core economies, led to a rapid expansion of industrial output and productivity, sharply reducing production costs. The price of manufactures relative to agriculture and other natural-resource-based products fell everywhere. The cost of British cottons fell by as much as 70% between 1790 and 1812.[6]

Like the rest of the poor periphery, Mexico had to deal with the deindustrialization forces that resulted from the Industrial Revolution, but it did better on this score than most countries around the periphery. In fact, Mexico's textile industry not only survived but prospered. Five conditions explain Mexico's early industrial growth, relative to other countries in the periphery. (1) Its relatively large population provided the consumer market necessary for industry to develop. (2) During this period, there was a relatively small improvement in Mexican terms of trade, compared to those experienced by most nations in the periphery. (3) Compared to other countries in the periphery, Mexico maintained better wage competitiveness vis-à-vis the core, based on a better relative agricultural productivity performance. (4) A tradition of artisan textile production was able to generate political support for protectionist policies, and Mexico had the autonomy to implement these policies, unlike many other countries in the periphery, which were in colonial status.[7] Finally, (5) the high transport costs resulting from the concentration of population far from the sea in rugged terrain provided additional protection against competition from imports.

Although the cotton textiles sector was heavily damaged, it survived the three decades of foreign competition and *Insurgencia*. Even in the midst of foreign competition some 6,000 looms were in operation in Puebla.[8] Further, in spite of the difficult situation, two Puebla merchants made important investments in the textile business during the 1820s. One of these, the Catalan Francisco Puig, introduced in 1820 the first modern machinery *(brocas)* in Puebla to produce medium-quality cloth *(paño entrefino)*, coarse cloth *(jerga)*, and blankets *(colchas)* in a two-story building. The Casa Puig continued producing until 1850 and became an important supplier of both woolen cloth and cotton yarn for artisan weavers, besides selling its own product. The other merchant was Estevan de Antuñano from Veracruz, who had been involved before Independence in the trade of raw cotton. In 1821 he established modern spinning machinery in a house in the weavers' district of San Francisco, Puebla. But the factory closed in 1824, defeated by cheap foreign imports.

Between 1830 and 1840 the national government, under the influence of statesmen such as Lucas Alamán and industrialists such as Estevan de Antuñano, provided both tariff protection and means of finance through a public development bank, the Banco de Avío para Fomento de la Industria Nacional.[9] Mexico's "industrialists," as they called themselves, established the first mechanized mills in the 1830s, around the same time that the mills were built in Lowell, Massachusetts, and only twenty years after the first mechanized mill was established in the United States. La Constancia Mexicana, established in 1835 by Estevan de Antuñano and financed by the Banco de Avío, was the first enduring mechanized textile mill to operate in Mexico. Mechanized textile mills appeared in Mexico earlier than in any other country outside of Europe and British North America, except for, notably, Egypt.[10] Brazil, the other early industrializer in Latin America during this period, established its first mills in the 1840s. Yet by 1853 it had only eight mills with 4,500 spindles, whereas ten years earlier Mexico's textile manufacture included fifty-nine mills with more than 100,000 spindles.[11]

The Banco de Avío was run by Lucas Alamán (1792–1853), who in 1830 became minister of interior and foreign affairs.[12] Alamán designed a precise and cogent industrial policy. His goal was not merely to protect the inefficient artisan production of colonial times, but to promote a mechanized industry that could produce at a price and quality equal to those of foreign competitors. He believed that by itself the "invisible hand" was not going to lead to industrialization.[13]

Alamán devised a plan whereby one-fifth of the total duties accrued from textile imports would be used to form the capital of the Banco de Avío until one million pesos had been accumulated. The bank would lend money at low interest rates to entrepreneurs proposing to establish modern factories.[14] Although the bank was never able to accumulate the planned capital of one million pesos, it managed to finance industrial projects until 1840, when it ceased to function as an industrial loan agency.

Despite the haphazard way the bank functioned during those unstable years, it was able to implement a machine-purchasing program. Thirteen of the forty loans granted from 1830 to 1840 went to establish cotton textile factories; the rest financed paper mills and iron foundries. Half of the cotton textile mills that opened with Banco de Avío credit were still operating in 1845. Three of those mills—La Constancia Mexicana, Co-colapan, and Industrial Jalapeña—were still functioning in 1893.[15]

The impact of the Banco de Avío on Mexican industrialization must not be exaggerated, however. Of the fifty-nine companies Alamán lists in the 1843 "Report on Industry and Agriculture," only six received a bank loan. Nevertheless, it is possible that the establishment of the first firms, which received loans from the bank, stimulated the creation of firms that came later by showing clearly that the government was committed to industrialization.

Alamán's industrial policy required lasting, stable political conditions based on well-organized public finances, an effective system of tax collection, and a gradual transition to an era of steady economic growth.[16] Unfortunately, political instability, a cause and consequence of a permanent disorder in public finances, made these requirements impossible to attain in Mexico during most of the nineteenth century.[17] Political instability generated institutional frailty under which it was impossible for the government to implement a cogent industrial policy.[18]

In 1836, representatives of the cotton-growing regions of Veracruz and Oaxaca successfully introduced a bill to ban the entry of raw cotton. The textile manufacturers did not oppose the bill at first, but the prohibition of raw cotton imports soon yielded terrible consequences.[19] Within a matter of months the national cotton crop was no longer sufficient to provide the cotton needed by the established factories. From 1838 onward, cotton started to become scarce; and its price, which at that time was only 16 or 17 pesos per quintal, had increased to 40 pesos. The manufacturers had to either stop production entirely or shorten daily production in an effort to continue, waiting anxiously for the arrival of new crop.[20]

In 1843 Estevan de Antuñano wrote several letters to President Santa Anna to explain the problems that the ban on raw cotton was creating for the textile industry. Santa Anna, the political boss of a major cotton-growing region, had too many commitments to cotton growers to relax the ban and the protection it gave them. Instead of lifting the ban, Santa Anna arbitrarily granted special cotton import licenses, which usually ended in the hands of moneylenders *(agiotistas).* One such agiotista was Cayetano Rubio, a man of considerable influence who was both a merchant selling cotton and the owner of a textile mill.[21] It is likely that the government granted the import licenses as part of its negotiations in order to obtain further credits to support their permanent deficit.[22]

Textile industrialists also had to withstand the granting of licenses for the importation of manufactured textiles. The precarious fiscal situation of the Mexican governments made their commitment to protect textile manufactures very vulnerable. In 1841, for example, in order to finance the war against Texas, General Mariano Arista authorized the sale of special import licenses for textile manufactures. Guillermo Drusina and Cayetano Rubio purchased these licenses over the harsh opposition of other textile producers. Furthermore, textile manufacturers often complained of the smuggling that further limited their market.[23]

Another problem the textile industry faced during this period was the backwardness of financial institutions. Apart from the Banco de Avío, which closed its doors in 1840, there was no institutional lending to industry until the 1880s. Only after 1864 did a rudimentary banking system with specialized institutions and stable practices begin to develop in Mexico. Studies of particular mills during this era tell of the serious difficulties business owners faced in obtaining credit, which frequently drove them to bankruptcy.[24] Successful entrepreneurs were those who undertook speculative activities, such as lending money to the government, as part of their businesses. Agiotistas such as Cayetano Rubio, Pedro Berges de Zúñiga, and Manuel Escandón became major textile mill owners by the mid-nineteenth century.[25]

In addition to the problems industrial expansion faced from the supply side, the slow growth of domestic demand must also have placed a considerable constraint on the growth of the textile industry. In the United States, the increase of the domestic demand accounted for more than half the expansion of its textile industry between 1815 and 1833, in which sales rose, on average, by 15.4% per year. This was the result of rapid population growth, averaging 3% a year over the period from 1815 to 1840, rising income levels enjoyed by the growing population, and improvements in transportation.[26] In Mexico, demand remained stagnant as the population grew slowly between 1800 and 1845 at an average annual rate of 0.51%, and income per capita decreased at an average annual rate of 0.6% during that same period.[27]

Despite these difficulties, the cotton industry was still able to grow during this period. Table 1.1 shows a pattern of continuous growth in the textile industry. Cotton textile factory production grew rapidly in the 1830s and early 1840s, rising from less than 30,000 kilos of yarn produced in 1838 to more than 3.5 million kilos in 1843.

The Mexican textile industry of this period was fairly comparable to the British and American industries in terms of efficiency. Between 1841 and 1842, capital–labor ratios in the Mexican textile industry were twenty spindles per worker, about the same as for American workers in 1830.[28] However, the prices of the products were very different from those in the United States. An 1846 U.S. report on the Mexican economy claimed that "cotton goods which sell in the United States for six cents per yard, are worth thirty cents in Mexico."[29] According to the author of that report, "this results from the high price of the raw material, which sells from forty to fifty cents per pound, and from the circumstance that

*Table 1.1*    Growth of the Mexican cotton textile industry, 1837–1879

| Year | No. of factories | No. of active spindles | Yarn (tons) | Cloth pieces (1000s) |
|------|------------------|------------------------|-------------|----------------------|
| 1837 |    |         |       | 45 |
| 1838 |    |         | 29    | 109 |
| 1839 |    |         | 15    | 125 |
| 1840 |    |         | 257   | 88 |
| 1841 |    |         | 467   | 196 |
| 1842 |    |         | 358   | 218 |
| 1843 | 59 | 106,708 | 3,758 | 327 |
| 1844 |    | 112,188 |       | 508 |
| 1845 | 55 | 113,813 | 1,317 | 657 |
| 1853 |    |         | 3,348 | 875 |
| 1850–1857 | 48 | 119,278 | 3,351 | 727 |
| 1862 | 57 | 133,122 | 3,615 | 1,259 |
| 1879 | 89 | 253,594 | 2,925 | 3,255 |

*Sources:* México, Dirección de Agricultura e Industria [Lucas Alamán], "Memoria sobre el estado de la agricultura e industria, México" (Mexico City, 1843), table 5; México, Dirección de Agricultura e Industria [Lucas Alamán], "Memoria sobre el estado de la agricultura e industria, México" (Mexico City, 1845), tables 2, 3, 4; México, Ministerio de Fomento, "Estado de las fábricas de Hilados y Tejidos de algodón existentes en la República Mexicana" (Mexico City, 1857); José Ma. Pérez Hernández, *Estadística de la República Mexicana* (Guadalajara, 1862), 136–139; México, Secretaría de Hacienda [Emiliano Busto], *Estadística de la República Mexicana* (Mexico City, 1880), vol. 1; México, *Anuario estadístico de la República Mexicana* (1894).

all the machinery is imported and transported by land at an enormous cost; and also to the difficulty and delay of repairing it, when it breaks down."[30]

The cotton industry appears to have been profitable. In 1843, profit rates for the industry as a whole were 10% per piece of cloth produced; for La Constancia they were 20% per piece of cloth.[31] However, evidence from the Miraflores mill suggests that the prosperity of a textile mill depended more on its owners' ability to speculate in the cotton market than on its productivity.[32]

Although there was a large degree of political instability in Mexico throughout the first six decades of the nineteenth century, its level was not constant for this whole period. After the Wars of Independence (1810–1821), when violence and political instability were pervasive, there was a period of relative calm between 1821 and 1836. Instability increased as a result of the wars with Texas (1836) and the United States (1846–1848), but it had brief and relatively small consequences when compared with the surge in political instability that took place in 1854–1867.[33] This period of civil war between Liberals and Conservatives increased political instability through its various episodes: the Ayutla Revolution (1854), the war of Reform (1858–1861), the French invasion (1861), and the Second Empire (1864–1867). During some of these years, violence and destruction reached levels similar to those suffered during the wars of Independence.[34]

Yet, as shown in Figure 1.1, Mexican imports of capital goods and machinery from 1845 to 1878 tell a story of relatively high industrialization during these years compared to the period from 1830 to 1845.[35] It appears that there were two periods of relatively high growth: the first in the interval after the war with the United States and before the war of Reform (1849–1857), and the other during the Second Empire (1864–1867). The industry began to grow at a faster and steadier pace after 1870, once the Republic had been restored.

That the textile industry survived these years of foreign invasions, a major civil war, and a slow-growing population was in itself remarkable.[36] Even more remarkable, the industry actually expanded. The total number of looms and spindles increased by 132% and 234%, respectively, between 1843 and 1878. Furthermore, although not at the same pace as in the United States, the average firm grew, increasing its number of spindles by 58% and its number of looms by 126%.[37]

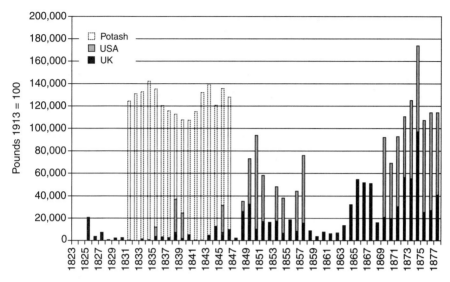

*Figure 1.1.* Mexican imports of manufacturing machinery, 1823–1878. Dotted bars calculated from Robert Potash's estimate of the capital invested during this period. *Sources:* United Kingdom, Parliamentary Documents, *Return to an Order of the Honourable House of Commons* (1823–1879); U.S. Treasury Department, Bureau of Statistics, *The Foreign Commerce and Navigation of the United States* (Washington, D.C.: Government Printing Office, 1835–1877); Robert A. Potash, *Mexican Government and Industrial Development in the Early Republic: The Banco de Avío* (Amherst: University of Massachusetts Press, 1983), p. 151.

During this period the industry successfully integrated spinning and weaving and it completely transformed its sources of power. In 1843, 37% of the firms used men or mules as their source of power; only 3% ran on steam. By 1878 no textile mill operated with animal power. Instead, 64% of factories employed steam power. Of the total common brown sheeting *(manta)* produced, only 2% was made using steam in 1843, but 70% in 1879. In 1843 only 56% of the firms were using water power; by 1879 this figure had risen to 91%. More than half the firms, 55%, combined steam and water power.[38] Technological progress appears to have had a positive impact on mill productivity levels. Measurements of labor productivity and total factor productivity for the period 1850 to 1890 indicate that they increased by 3.3% and 2.6%, respectively, per year when production is measured by physical output.[39]

Industrial growth between 1843 and 1878 is not easy to explain given the difficult economic and political conditions of the time.[40] Moreover, there was a substantial reduction in the tariffs on cotton manufactures in 1856.[41] However, the effect of this reduction was balanced by government's simultaneous decision to lift the prohibition on raw cotton imports.[42] Additionally, the American Civil War had a positive effect on the Mexican cotton textile industry. The blockade of the South by the Union—effective in Texas in mid-1861—forced the Confederates to channel cotton exports through the Mexican border.[43] The increased supply of raw cotton and the rise in demand for cotton manufactures from the embattled American South enabled Mexican textile mills to compete more favorably against foreign imports and even export their products. In 1861–1862, the Ibernia factory in Saltillo produced approximately "11,500 pieces of . . . *manta*, which were sold to the Southerners for $4.50 each."[44] This was a level of foreign trade unheard of before the American Civil War.

Finally, after 1860 domestic demand began to increase, giving an additional boost to textile production. While population grew at an even lower rate from 1845 to 1860 than in the previous forty-five years, its pace of growth rose considerably from 1860 to 1877. In addition, income per capita, which continued to fall from 1845 to 1860, began to recover after that date, growing at an average rate of 1.48% from 1860 to 1877.[45]

The growth of the Mexican textile industry between 1843 and 1879 was accompanied by regional dispersion. In 1843 there were firms in only eight states, and 64% of the firms (57% of spindles and 65% of looms) were located in Mexico City, the state of Mexico, and Puebla. By 1879 almost every state had its own textile mill, and only 33% (46% of spindles, 44% of looms) were located in Mexico City, the state of Mexico, and Puebla.[46]

The high transportation costs in Mexico explain the geographical dispersion of the Mexican textile industry during its early development. Most transportation was by mule and oxcart until the 1880s.[47] In addition to the difficulties of such modes of transport over natural terrain, interstate tariffs—the *alcabalas*—raised transportation costs even more. The owner of La Estrella mill in Coahuila wrote in 1877: "the *alcabalas* are a true gangrene to the social body, even more dangerous than the turbulence to which we are prey so frequently, and if they are not suppressed, they will crush the few industries of some few daring men, who want to see their country full of factories and their fellow citizens employed."[48] Interstate trade barriers were formally abolished by the 1857 Constitution. Yet their great importance as a source of revenues for the states made it impossible to put the law into practice until 1896. High transportation costs and interstate tariffs reduced market size and made for a more dispersed organization of firms.[49]

The geographically scattered nature of Mexico's textile industry contrasted with that of the United States, Great Britain, and Spain, where the industry was more regionally concentrated. Regions with comparative advantages over others in Mexico, in terms of cotton, energy, and labor costs, did not concentrate the industry. Relatively efficient mills coexisted with highly inefficient ones. Furthermore, regional dispersion reduced the externalities; a "big push" might have generated if the industry had concentrated in particular regions.[50]

A more effective government could have allowed a stronger industrialization process in Mexico during the first three quarters of the nineteenth century. However, what Mexico achieved was substantial compared with other countries in the periphery. In 1879 Mexico produced around sixty million square meters of cloth, and imported forty million squares meters. Domestic production thus claimed 60% of the local market, which compares well to other important textile producers at the beginning of the nineteenth century, such as India (which produced only 35% to 42% of its cotton consumption in 1887) and the Ottoman Empire (where domestic supply was only 11% to 38% of total consumption in the 1870s).[51] Mexico also achieved a substantial reduction in its domestic cotton cloth prices. While in 1834–1835 the price of the *vara* (0.836 meters) of cloth was around 0.30 pesos, it had fallen to around 0.12 pesos by 1850 and to 0.11 pesos in 1877.[52]

## The Textile Industry during the Porfiriato

Fundamental changes in the Mexican economic environment took place during the Porfirian regime (1877–1910). After the restoration of the Republic of Mexico in 1867, the calamitous wars that undermined the

Mexican government's capacity to put its finances in order and establish a reliable set of institutions gave way to a more peaceful environment. The Mexican federal government gradually gained control of the whole nation. This objective, more successfully approached by Lerdo than by Juárez, was fully accomplished by Porfirio Díaz's combination of repression and concession toward regional political bosses.[53]

After long, difficult negotiations to settle Mexico's foreign loans and reestablish a schedule of payments, in 1886 the Porfirian government regained access to the international financial system and in just two years negotiated its first foreign loan since 1829. Furthermore, the risk premium the Mexican government paid on its foreign debt diminished considerably from 1893 to 1910, which shows the growing confidence Mexico enjoyed in international financial markets.[54]

The more reliable environment that these post-1867 administrations generated for foreign investment, as well as active policies that granted both concessions and subsidies for railway construction, led to the construction of railway lines. The port of Veracruz was finally linked by rail to Mexico City when the new Ferrocarril Mexicano line was inaugurated in 1873. An important railroad construction spurt took place in the 1880s, so that by the 1890s railroads connected most of the central and northern part of the country. The length of Mexico's railway network rose from 665 kilometers in 1878 to 19,748 kilometers by 1910.[55]

Aided by political stability, effective national government, and access to foreign credit markets, the Porfirian government gradually reorganized its public finances.[56] Greater central government control over state politics and improved finances allowed the government finally to abolish all tariffs in 1896, when states were compensated with income from newly legislated federal taxes.[57] Furthermore, significant legal reforms generated a more favorable and predictable institutional environment. The commercial codes of 1884 and 1889 defined property rights that were more conducive to fostering investment, progressively guaranteeing the operation of joint-stock companies.

By 1883 the stabilization and broadening of short-term money markets had been achieved, and by 1890 the creation of a relatively open internal market for public securities became possible and public bonds began to be sold both nationally and internationally.[58] A banking system began to spread throughout the nation. Whereas until 1880 there had only been one commercial bank operating in Mexico, the Banco de Londres y México, founded in 1864, over the course of the next two years several banks opened.

Tariff protection during the Porfiriato became part of a cogent policy to promote industrialization.[59] After the tariff reform of 1891, tariffs were generally reduced, but selectively changed in order to protect Mexican manufacturing. The tariff schedule gave effective protection to industry through higher rates for finished goods than for the imported raw materials needed to produce them.[60] Nominal duties on cotton cloth were 96% on average in 1890, declining to 65% in 1905. These high rates for cotton cloth combined with lower rates for raw cotton (30% in 1890 and 20% in 1905) provided substantial, effective protection. Protection to the industry was enhanced during most of the period by an important depreciation of the Mexican peso that was not accompanied by an equal rise in domestic prices. Mexico underwent a real currency depreciation of 137% between the mid-1870s and 1902, and a real currency appreciation of 24% between 1902 and 1913.[61]

An important fall in terms of trade that Mexico experienced during the Porfiriato stimulated manufacturing in general, and textile manufacturing in particular because textile goods represented a large share of Mexican imports. In contrast with most countries in the periphery, Mexican terms of trade fell by 37.2% between 1870–1874 and 1910–1913. Moreover, in spite of the decline of the terms of trade, a rapid productivity advance in Mexican mining during this period generated an increase in total export values and foreign exchange earnings, creating an export-led growth.[62] This encouraged manufacturing further by increasing domestic demand and the supply of investment capital. Table 1.2 shows the rapid growth in the cotton textile industry during the Porfiriato, almost tripling the number of spindles, looms, and workers in the industry. Growth came along with a rise in labor efficiency, shown by the growth in the number of loom equivalents and loom equivalents per shift tended per worker through this period.[63]

Despite considerable population and income growth, cloth imports fell at an average rate of 4.3% per year between 1895 and 1908, replaced by domestic production.[64] By 1908 around 78% of cotton textile consumption

Table 1.2   The Mexican cotton textile industry, 1879–1930

| Year | Active mills | Spindles | Looms | Workers | Cotton consumed (tons) | Sales (pesos) | Sales (pesos of 1900) | Loom eq. per worker | Loom eq. per shift | Cotton per worker | Sales per worker (pesos of 1900) |
|---|---|---|---|---|---|---|---|---|---|---|---|
| 1879 | 89 | 253,594 | 8,885 | 12,118 | 12,064 | | | 0.96 | 0.96 | 996 | |
| 1893 | 93 | 355,456 | 11,827 | 19,515 | 21,298 | | | 0.81 | 0.81 | 1,091 | |
| 1895 | 99 | 411,090 | 12,386 | 18,208 | 20,208 | 21,906 | $24,193 | 0.93 | 0.93 | 1,110 | 1,329 |
| 1896 | 101 | 428,560 | 12,974 | 19,575 | 23,771 | 23,658 | $25,338 | 0.90 | 0.90 | 1,214 | 1,294 |
| 1899 | 120 | 479,995 | 14,352 | 22,846 | 26,518 | 29,753 | $32,564 | 0.86 | 0.86 | 1,161 | 1,425 |
| 1900 | 134 | 557,391 | 17,202 | 26,764 | 28,990 | 35,459 | $35,459 | 0.87 | 0.87 | 1,083 | 1,325 |
| 1901 | 133 | 602,223 | 18,885 | 27,663 | 30,262 | 33,877 | $35,553 | 0.92 | 0.92 | 1,094 | 1,285 |
| 1902 | 124 | 575,304 | 17,974 | 25,316 | 27,628 | 28,780 | $27,939 | 0.96 | 0.96 | 1,091 | 1,104 |
| 1903 | 115 | 630,201 | 20,124 | 26,249 | 27,512 | 36,907 | $31,339 | 1.03 | 1.03 | 1,048 | 1,194 |
| 1904 | 119 | 632,018 | 20,326 | 27,033 | 28,841 | 42,511 | $34,646 | 1.01 | 1.01 | 1,067 | 1,282 |
| 1905 | 127 | 666,659 | 21,932 | 29,483 | 31,230 | 51,214 | $46,097 | 0.99 | 0.99 | 1,059 | 1,564 |
| 1906 | 130 | 683,739 | 22,776 | 31,673 | 35,826 | 51,171 | $44,894 | 0.96 | 0.96 | 1,131 | 1,417 |
| 1907 | 129 | 693,842 | 23,507 | 33,132 | 36,654 | 51,686 | $41,326 | 0.94 | 0.94 | 1,106 | 1,247 |
| 1908 | 132 | 732,278 | 24,997 | 35,816 | 36,040 | 54,934 | $45,303 | 0.92 | 0.92 | 1,006 | 1,265 |
| 1909 | 129 | 726,278 | 25,327 | 32,229 | 35,435 | 43,370 | $36,656 | 1.03 | 1.03 | 1,099 | 1,137 |
| 1910 | 123 | 702,874 | 25,017 | 31,963 | 34,736 | 50,651 | $39,119 | 1.02 | 1.07 | 1,087 | 1,224 |
| 1911 | 119 | 725,297 | 24,436 | 32,147 | 34,568 | 51,348 | $39,286 | 1.01 | 1.10 | 1,075 | 1,222 |
| 1912 | 127 | 762,149 | 26,801 | 32,128 | 32,366 | 52,847 | $38,804 | 1.10 | 1.25 | 1,007 | 1,208 |
| 1913 | 118 | 752,804 | 26,791 | 32,641 | 32,821 | | | 1.07 | 1.29 | 1,006 | |
| 1914 | 90 | | | | | | | | | | |
| 1915 | 84 | | | | | | | | | | |
| 1916 | 93 | | | | | | | | | | |
| 1917 | 92 | 573,072 | 20,489 | 22,187 | | 64,130 | $29,974 | 1.21 | 1.70 | | 1,351 |

| | | | | | | | | | | |
|---|---|---|---|---|---|---|---|---|---|---|
| 1918 | 104 | 689,173 | 25,017 | 27,680 | 20,334 | 48,567 | $19,574 | 1.18 | 1.77 | | 707 |
| 1919 | 110 | 749,237 | 27,020 | 33,185 | 31,095 | 69,778 | $25,169 | 1.06 | 1.59 | | 758 |
| 1920 | 120 | 753,837 | 27,301 | 37,936 | 31,694 | 20,492 | $36,890 | 0.94 | 1.41 | 835 | 972 |
| 1921 | 121 | 770,945 | 28,409 | 38,227 | 35,924 | 93,942 | $28,329 | 0.97 | 1.45 | 940 | 741 |
| 1922 | 119 | 803,230 | 29,521 | 39,677 | 34,654 | 85,023 | $26,216 | 0.97 | 1.45 | 873 | 661 |
| 1923 | 110 | 802,363 | 29,668 | 39,629 | 32,344 | 97,490 | $35,882 | 0.97 | 1.46 | 816 | 905 |
| 1924 | 116 | 812,165 | 29,888 | 37,732 | 30,517 | 96,435 | $35,496 | 1.03 | 1.54 | 809 | 941 |
| 1925 | 130 | 838,987 | 31,094 | 43,728 | 40,997 | 108,396 | $38,621 | 0.92 | 1.38 | 938 | 883 |
| 1926 | 138 | 833,388 | 30,597 | 43,776 | 41,522 | 95,437 | $34,782 | 0.91 | 1.36 | 949 | 795 |
| 1927 | 144 | 821,211 | 30,437 | 41,238 | 41,169 | 91,068 | $34,920 | 0.96 | 1.44 | 998 | 847 |
| 1928 | 137 | 836,391 | 30,130 | 39,041 | 39,355 | 96,292 | $37,818 | 1.01 | 1.51 | 1,008 | 969 |
| 1929 | 145 | 839,109 | 30,191 | 39,525 | 39,436 | 97,162 | $38,263 | 1.00 | 1.50 | 998 | 968 |
| 1930 | 148 | 842,265 | 30,625 | 39,424 | 40,582 | 91,145 | $38,857 | 1.01 | 1.52 | 1,029 | 986 |
| **Annual rate of growth** | | | | | | | | | | | |
| 1879–1912 | 1.1% | 3.4% | 3.4% | 3.0% | 3.0% | 5.3% | 2.8% | 0.4% | 0.8% | 0.0% | −0.6% |
| 1912–1925 | 0.2% | 0.7% | 1.1% | 2.4% | 1.8% | 5.7% | −0.04% | −1.3% | 0.8% | −0.6% | −2.4% |
| 1925–1930 | 2.6% | 0.1% | −0.3% | −2.1% | −0.2% | −3.4% | 0.1% | 1.9% | 1.9% | 1.9% | 2.2% |
| **Average values** | | | | | | | | | | | |
| 1879–1912 | 119 | 589,975 | 19,429 | 26,881 | 29,108 | 41,255 | $36,157 | 0.96 | 0.97 | 1,085 | 1,283 |
| 1913–1920 | 101 | 703,725 | 25,324 | 30,726 | 28,986 | 75,742 | $27,902 | 1.09 | 1.55 | 920 | 947 |
| 1921–1930 | 131 | 820,005 | 30,056 | 40,200 | 37,650 | 95,239 | $34,918 | 0.97 | 1.46 | 936 | 869 |

*Sources:* México, Secretaría de Hacienda [Emiliano Busto], *Estadística de la República Mexicana* (Mexico City, 1880), vol. 1; México, Dirección General de Estadística, *Anuario estadístico de la República Mexicana* (Mexico City, 1894); 1895–1911: México, Secretaría de Hacienda y Crédito Público, *Boletín de estadística fiscal,* several issues; México, *Mexican Year Book 1908, 523–531*; Archivo General de la Nación, Departamento del Trabajo, 5/4/4, "Manifestaciónes presentadas por los fabricantes de hilados y tejidos de algodón durante enero a junio de 1912"; 1913: Archivo General de la Nación, Departamento del Trabajo, 31/2/4. "Estadística semestral de las fábricas de hilados y tejidos de algodón de la República Mexicana correspondiente al semestre de 1913"; Stephen Haber, *Industry and Underdevelopment* (Stanford: Stanford University Press, 1989), 124; Secretaría de la Economía Nacional [Moisés T. de la Peña], *La industria textil en México* (Mexico City, 1934); *Boletín de Estadística,* January 1924, 52–55; *Estadística Nacional,* September 30, 1925, 5–17; México, Secretaría de Hacienda y Crédito Público, Departamento de Impuestos Especiales, Sección de Hilados y Tejidos, "Estadísticas del ramo de hilados y tejidos de algodón y de lana," typewritten reports. Prices have been deflated using the textile (gold) index in Aurora Gómez-Galvarriato, "The Impact of Revolution: Business and Labor in the Mexican Textile Industry, Orizaba, Veracruz, 1900–1930" (PhD diss., Harvard University, 1999).

was supplied by domestic production.[65] Furthermore, the new systems of communications and transportation in the country led to a dramatic transformation in both distribution and production of textiles.

## The Porfirian Modernization of the Textile Industry

The coming of modern transportation and communications—the railroad, the telegraph, the steamship, and cable—brought about major changes worldwide in the production and distribution of goods and in firms' strategies and structures. Enterprises grew in size and scope, and they had to adapt both management and finances to the new situation. In the United States, businesses personally managed by their owners gave way to the managerial business enterprise. Ownership and management separated, and the expanded enterprises came to be operated by teams of salaried managers who had little or no equity in the firms. Mass marketing and modern mass production appeared.[66] In other countries, such as Great Britain, there emerged different types of firms and strategies that adapted better to their institutional, social, political, and cultural environments, in contrast to the American large-scale corporate model.[67] One salient characteristic of the transformation of Mexico's business institutions during this period was the important role played by entrepreneurial networks.[68]

In Mexico the revolution in the production and commercial distribution of textiles was carried out largely by French immigrants from several villages of the Ubaye Valley who were called Barcelonnettes. They had established themselves in Mexico in previous decades and developed important companies in the dry-goods trade supported by a network of fellow countrymen, many of whom they had helped travel to Mexico to work in their businesses. By the 1890s many of them had built their own firms and become rich enough to be able to invest important sums of capital. The Barcelonnette network was ruled by strict social norms, reassuring entrepreneurs that their partners, customers, and employees would not defraud them to a much larger extent than formal institutions could. In preindustrial economies "the scarce guarantee that the legal system offered for compliance with contracts gave an advantage to cohesive communities that could exert sufficient internal control so as to dissuade its members from any lack of compliance under the penalty of exclusion from business."[69]

Three types of interrelated investments had to be made in order to benefit from the cost advantages of the new high-volume technologies of production and the facilities provided by the new communication and transportation systems. Production facilities needed to be expanded in order to exploit a technology's potential economies of scale and scope. The national and international marketing and distributing networks had to be modernized so that the volume of sales could keep pace with the enlarged volume of production. Finally, entrepreneurs also had to invest in management.[70]

In the Porfirian textile industry, this three-pronged investment was mainly undertaken within a network of French immigrants from the Ubaye Valley. These businessmen made the major investments in the industry to acquire the new technologies that provided economies of scale and scope. They also established new distribution networks for textile products. Finally, they invested in management, hiring and training personnel almost exclusively within the Barcelonnette community.

The Ubaye Valley, known earlier as the Barcelonnette Valley, is located in southeastern France at the foot of the Alps in the Alpes-de-Haute-Provence department. Its main town is the subprefecture of Barcelonnette. By the end of the nineteenth century it had approximately 17,500 inhabitants and was one of the poorest regions in France. Sheep and cattle raising and the spinning and weaving of wool in family shops were the basis of the economy. From the beginning of the nineteenth century, dry-goods peddling *(colportage)* throughout France, Italy, Belgium, and Holland became an important economic activity in the region during the winter. By 1850 the development of mechanized textile mills made craft production of textiles unprofitable, severely affecting the Ubayen economy and increasing the number of young men ready to migrate. Its population was relatively well educated. Already in the eighteenth century, elementary education was widespread throughout the Ubaye Valley and literacy had reached 100%.[71]

The first immigrants from the Ubaye Valley, the Arnauds from Jausiers, came to Mexico in 1821 and opened a dry-goods shop, Las Siete Puertas, retailing imported French textiles in Mexico City. Gradually other young men from the valley followed in their wake. By 1850 there were already nine dry-goods shops in the country owned by Barcelonnettes.[72] A crucial factor in French commercial preeminence was the establishment of a direct transatlantic steamship line between Veracruz and Saint Nazaire in 1865, during Maximilian's empire. The steamers of the Compagnie Générale Transatlantique that sailed from Saint Nazaire to Veracruz were the fastest connection between European ports and Mexico.[73] This line reduced transportation costs for merchandise to 6% of what they had previously been.[74] After the establishment of this line, French merchants in Mexico began to import directly from Europe, instead of buying from German merchants as they had done previously.

This process gained strength during the Franco-Prussian War in 1870, when Barcelonnettes boycotted German wholesale stores. Several Barcelonnette companies established their own export houses in Paris and Manchester. Of over forty German wholesale import stores in Mexico in 1870, only one-third were left by 1889. In 1892 the last one closed.[75] By 1890 there were already 110 Barcelonnette commercial houses established in Mexico, in 1910 there were 214.[76] From textiles, the Barcelonnettes moved into other lines. By the end of the nineteenth century, Barcelonnettes had become major stock owners and top managers of the most important banks and manufacturing companies in Mexico.

Through ethnic cohesion the Barcelonnettes built a bridge from the Basses Alpes to Mexico, crossed by two thousand young men from the mid-nineteenth to the mid-twentieth century. Letters from several young Barcelonnette immigrants tell the story. Their trips were paid for by fellow countrymen who had already established some sort of business in Mexico. Normally the businessman financing the trip was well known to the family of the person who made the trip, but not necessarily a relative. Young men were housed and fed by their employers in Mexico. By the turn of the century, there was a well-established recruiting system, as revealed by letters from several of the French immigrants. The incoming immigrants started out spending at least a year doing the shop's packaging, sweeping, and other menial tasks. They worked at those chores seven days a week for very low wages, at the same time also working hard to learn Spanish, become knowledgeable about business practices, and prove themselves trustworthy to their employers. When they had accomplished those tasks, they were promoted to working at the shop's counter and then eventually to working as an accountant or a traveling salesperson. After another four to six years they might become partners in the business or set up businesses for themselves—often regional branches of the company they worked for. The luckiest ones were able to return to France after fifteen or twenty years, marry a French woman, and live off their savings.[77]

The importance of reputation and business networks is clear in the writings of Chabrand, a Barcelonnette merchant. He wrote that "a Barcelonnette last name was equal, in a wholesale house, to a credit eight or ten times higher than normal," and that when Barcelonnette young men were introduced by agents *(couriers)* to wholesale merchants, many of whom were not Barcelonnettes themselves, the merchants would say, "it is enough that you introduce him and that he is a Barcelonnette for our house to be at his service."[78] Within the Barcelonnette community strict rules had to be complied with, but this had its rewards. "No Barcelonnette could buy supplies from anyone outside the commercial networks of the colony, [but] as a counterpart the suppliers gave them good facilities for payment and helped them to enlarge or open new commercial houses."[79] This type of behavior can be explained as a form of relational contracting, in which "the relation takes the form of a minisociety with a vast array of norms beyond those centered in the exchange and its immediate processes."[80]

## From the "Cajones de Ropa" to Department Stores

In Mexico the expansion and modernization of the textile industry during the Porfiriato occurred both after the transformations in commercial distribution and as a result of them, for the capital required to expand and modernize the mills came from commercial undertakings. Dry-goods commerce evolved into department stores, which acquired a major share of the retailing and wholesaling textile business and later became founders and major shareholders of the most important textile manufacturing firms in Mexico.

In preindustrial economies with underdeveloped markets, accumulated knowledge in the areas of distribution and commercialization were even more important than technical knowledge for the creation of modern industrial enterprises.[81] In the case of Mexico's textiles, this network was the Barcelonnettes.

During the second half of the nineteenth century in North America and Western Europe the new instruments of transportation and communication transformed the way manufactured products were distributed. In the 1870s and 1880s the modern mass retailer—the department store, the mail-order house, and the chain store—appeared.[82] In Mexico, railroads and telegraph also brought about significant changes in the way commerce operated at the end of the nineteenth century.

Most Barcelonnette textile business until the 1870s was undertaken by small retail stores located all over the country. Each of them bought directly from textile mills spread throughout Mexico and from traveling salesmen who worked on commission.[83] Around 1880 the stores still followed old-fashioned practices for management and accounting. The store itself would be just one large open room with a large counter running down the middle. "In front, the boiling and chirping crowd of Indians. . . behind, the salesmen *(les commis)*, busy, always in a hurry." Cloth was displayed on shelves, without being fronted by protective glass doors, and the businesses themselves were conducted without much organization. "There were no accounting books that recorded the sales of the day, or any control; there was total trust, which rarely, very rarely, was disappointed."[84]

By 1904 Mexican stores had been greatly transformed. A French journalist wrote that if a Parisian were suddenly transported Mexico's biggest department store, El Palacio de Hierro, he would not believe that he was so far from the Seine. "The astonishment . . . would be greater if he could have an idea of what the commercial houses in Mexico had been like thirteen years before. . . . They were small shops without air or light . . . where clients in semi-darkness spent two hours to buy the article they desired, having frequently to come back five or six times in order to get it."[85]

But in Mexico, just as in Paris, progress arrived. "Those old shops were progressively transformed, when they did not disappear completely, in order to give way to the new establishments."[86] Old-style retail continued to exist, but by the last decade of the nineteenth century, in larger cities, it disappeared into department stores similar to those in Europe and the United States—Bon Marché, Harrods, Macy's. (Most of the early Mexican companies are still the dominant department stores in Mexico.) Department stores thus evolved from small retail shops *(cajones de ropa)* that had been founded decades before and gradually entered the wholesale trade. All of them were owned and run by Barcelonnettes (see Table 1.3).

In Mexico City, which then had over 300,000 inhabitants, El Palacio de Hierro, El Puerto de Liverpool, Las Fábricas Universales, El Puerto de Veracruz, El Correo Francés, and El Centro Mercantil changed the commercial and even architectural scene. They were the highest buildings in Mexico City in that era. Around the turn of the century, department stores also opened in other Mexican cities, such as Guadalajara (Las Fábricas de Francia and La Ciudad de Londres), San Luis Potosí (La Ciudad de Londres), and Puebla (Nuevos Almacenes de la Ciudad de México).[87]

The creation of El Palacio de Hierro was very influential in the evolution of commerce in Mexico City, as others soon followed in its path. El Palacio de Hierro was founded in 1888 as a joint-stock company *(sociedad anónima)* by Joseph Tron, who had owned a novelty store in the Portal de las Flores. At first it operated on a small property, but very soon the company began the construction of a huge building, of dimensions previously unknown in Mexico, designed by a French architect. Its name, "the Iron Palace," was a consequence of the deep impression that the first building constructed in Mexico on a steel framework made on the public. Its construction lasted from 1888 to July 1891, and once its doors opened, it was a highly profitable enterprise. In 1904, for example, the Societé Financière pour l'Industrie du Mexique, one of its major shareholders, reported that it had generated a profit of 15% (although most of this was reinvested, so the dividend paid was only 6%).[88]

At first El Palacio de Hierro's directors wanted to organize the company exactly according to the practices followed by the most important department stores in Paris. However, they later decided that it was not a good idea to break so drastically with Mexican traditions. Thus, they

Table 1.3  From "cajones de ropa" to department stores

| Company name | Owner | Type | Founded | Capital (pesos) |
|---|---|---|---|---|
| El Palacio de Hierro | J. Tron & Co. | Dry-goods store | 1888 | |
| | J. Tron & Co. | Dry-goods store | 1892 | 100,000 |
| | El Palacio de Hierro S.A. | Dept. store | 1898 | 4,000,000 |
| | El Palacio de Hierro S.A. | Dept. store | 1908 | 5,000,000 |
| El Puerto de Liverpool | Jean-Baptiste Ebrard | Dry-goods store | 1847 | |
| Cajón del Puero de Liverpool | J. B. Ebrard and F. Fortolis | Clothing and lingerie | 1851 | |
| El Puero de Liverpool | Eduard Ebrard & Co. | Dry-goods store | 1887 | 5,000 |
| | J. B. Ebrard & Co. | Dry-goods store | 1894 | 20,000 |
| | J. B. Ebrard & Co. Sucesores | Dry-goods store | 1896 | 20,000 |
| | J. B. Ebrard & Co. | Dept. store | 1907 | 935,000 |
| Las Fábricas Universales | A. Reynaud & Co. | Dry-goods store | 1896 | 45,000 |
| | A. Reynaud & Co. | Dry-goods store | 1906 | 40,000 |
| | A. Reynaud & Co. | Dry-goods store | 1910 | 102,000 |
| | Compañía Comercial e Industrial | Dept. store | 1909 | 967,500 |
| El Centro Mercantil | S. Robert & Co. | Dry-goods store | 1897 | 150,000 |
| | S. Robert & Co. | Dry-goods store | 1899 | 240,000 |
| | S. Robert & Co. | Dry-goods store | 1905 | 300,000 |
| | S. Robert & Co. Sucesores | Dry-goods store | 1908 | 2,000,000 |

| | | | |
|---|---|---|---|
| El Nuevo Mundo | | | |
| Max Ma Chaubert | Clothing and lingerie | c.1867 | |
| Max Chauvert & Co. | Dry-goods store | 1889 | 30,000 |
| Max Chauvert & Co. | Dry-goods store | 1893 | 222,422 |
| Hijas de Max Chauvert | Dry-goods store | 1908 | 150,000 |
| El Nuevo Mundo S.A. | Dept. store | 1910 | 2,000,000 |
| La Ciudad de Londres | | | |
| Jauffred, Ollivier & Co. | Dry-goods store | 1863 | 10,000 |
| Ollivier & Co. | Dry-goods store | 1872 | 50,000 |
| J. Ollivier & Co. | Dry-goods store | 1875 | 70,000 |
| J. Ollivier & Co. | Dry-goods store | 1889 | 40,000 |
| J. Ollivier & Co. | Dry-goods store | 1894 | 81,000 |
| J. Ollivier & Co. | Dry-goods store | 1898 | 166,000 |
| J. Ollivier & Co. | Dry-goods store | 1904 | 170,000 |
| El Puero de Veracruz | | | |
| Signoret, Honnorat & Co. | Dry-goods store | 1888 | 12,000 |
| Signoret, Honnorat & Co. | Dry-goods store | 1892 | 100,000 |
| Signoret, Honnorat & Co. | Dept. store | 1907 | 250,000 |

*Sources:* México, Secretaría de Hacienda y Crédito Público, "Noticia de las Sociedades que se han registrado en la Oficina del Registro Público de la Propiedad y del Comercio, desde el 15 de enero de 1886 hasta el 31 de diciembre de 1910" (Mexico City, 1911), 46–287; Eugenio Maillefert, *Directorio del Comercio del Imperio Mexicano* (Mexico City, 1867); *Almanaque Bouret* (Mexico City, 1897); Patrice Gouy, *Pérégrinations des "Barcelonnettes" au Mexique* (Grenoble: Presses universitaires de Grenoble, 1980), 135.

decided to keep a counter that separated the employee from the client on the ground floor. But one important innovation was introduced: the fixed price, "a system that was applied and maintained with rigor."[89] Despite the modernizing spirit of El Palacio de Hierro's businessmen, they maintained the old recruiting procedures, almost exclusively employing young Barcelonnettes, who were housed and fed on the fourth and fifth floors of the building.

In the center of the building, in a huge hall enclosed in glass, all the operations of receipt and delivery of merchandise were undertaken. Hundreds of packages arrived each day. The reception department took note of the arriving merchandise and sent it immediately to the various floors and departments by elevator. The delivery department organized the orders placed by merchants from all over the country and quickly packaged the products and sent them off. The company owned several horse-pulled wagons that took goods from the store to the railway station, or any other place in Mexico City, on the day of purchase.[90]

In addition to the main department store building, El Palacio de Hierro owned four other buildings in Mexico City for its workshops. El Palacio de Hierro vertically integrated the production of many kinds of articles. Women's clothing and lingerie, ties, shirts, parasols, umbrellas, and furniture were manufactured on its own premises. Furthermore, in 1889 El Palacio de Hierro became the major partner of the Compañía Industrial de Orizaba S.A. (CIDOSA), Mexico's largest textile firm, which owned four textile mills in the Orizaba Valley.

Following the example of El Palacio de Hierro, another major department store, Las Fábricas Universales, opened. It was established in 1887 in Mexico City by Alejandro Reynaud as a wholesale and retail store *(grandes almacenes)* of clothes and novelties, but was not fully transformed into a department store until 1909, when its new building was inaugurated. As business expanded, it vertically integrated both its imports and several of its national supplies. In 1896 Alejandro Reynaud became the major partner in the creation of the Compañía Industrial Veracruzana S.A. (CIVSA) to supply the store with several lines of cloth. In 1896 A. Reynaud & Cia opened a trade business *(maison d'achats)* to export directly from France to Las Fábricas Universales in Mexico City. This export company later expanded to supply several stores in the

Mexican provinces and in other Latin American countries. It was also crucial for supplying CIVSA with machinery, chemicals, and even personnel from Europe. It also facilitated the placement of CIVSA bonds on the European market.

In January 1909, Las Fábricas Universales inaugurated its new six-story building, designed by a French architect, "with all the improvements that experience has suggested to the architects of department stores in Europe and the United States."[91] A detailed description of the organization of Las Fábricas Universales shows how closely it followed the pattern set by El Palacio de Hierro. Like El Palacio de Hierro, the higher floors of Las Fábricas Universales housed bedrooms for the companies' employees, as well as a dining room, a library, a bowling hall, and other rooms for their leisure and recreation.[92]

## The Modernization of Production

By the end of the 1880s it had become clear that the Mexican textile industry was operating with such outdated technology and organization that those who modernized it would reap great profits. In 1888 the magazine *Le Courier Français* described the situation of the industry and made an appeal to textile manufacturers from Alsace and Lorraine to come to Mexico to install an industry with the perfection and economic organization that existed in France. "We can predict a prosperity greater than they had before the annexation to Germany," it said, because "it would not be difficult to rival the old mills that seek only to survive through merging."[93]

Thus it was clear that investing in more up-to-date textile mills could yield high profits. The problem, as it often is in underdeveloped economies, was to raise the capital to make the new investments.[94] Barcelonnette immigrants, owners of important commercial enterprises, had not only the liquidity necessary to make such investments, but also the right connections with banks to obtain credits.[95] Although it appears that Porfirian banks did not finance major textile mill investments, they were important for loosening liquidity constraints on day-to-day operations. The capital necessary for the modernization of textile production came mostly from the profits Barcelonnette dry-good merchants had accumulated from their commercial businesses. Thus, the Barcelonnette network helped ease capital constraints, both through combining resources with Barcelonnette partners at a lower risk and through easier access to bank credits. Several wholesale stores joined as partners to create textile mills large enough to take advantage of economies of scale.[96]

In 1884, attempting to establish a monopoly on purchases and distribution, the most important French dry-goods warehouses in Mexico formed a syndicate to buy the totality of the production of the country's textile mills. Soon after, in 1886, three smaller French companies (Signoret, Honnorat & Co., Lambert, Reynaud & Co., and Garcin, Faudon & Co.), unable to supply their stores, broke the monopoly, buying the Cerritos mill in Orizaba and establishing the Compañía Manufacturera de Cerritos S.A.[97]

The success of the strategy followed by these companies of getting directly involved in textile production interested the owners of the largest commercial companies, who soon joined them as partners in the creation of CIDOSA in 1889. These were J. Ollivier & Co., J. B. Ebrard & Co., and J. Tron & Co. They invited the Escandón Arango family and Thomas Braniff into their partnership in order to incorporate the two other mills that operated in the Orizaba Valley—Cocolapan and San Lorenzo. The Escandóns did not accept, but Thomas Braniff, a Welsh North American who was one of the richest men in Mexico, did, and San Lorenzo became part of CIDOSA. Braniff's entry into the partnership was very valuable to the company because he was also the president of the Ferrocarril Mexicano, the railway line that connected Orizaba to the port of Veracruz and Mexico City.[98] In 1900 CIDOSA acquired Cocolapan from the Escandóns for 670,000 pesos. In the following years CIDOSA invested a further 489,167 pesos in rebuilding most of the factory, acquiring new machinery, and adapting the mill to the use of hydroelectric power.[99]

The objective of CIDOSA was not only to acquire and modernize mills already in place, but also to build a new and large one with state-of-the-art technology. The Río Blanco mill was inaugurated in October 1892 by President Porfirio Díaz. Its dimensions dwarfed all other existing companies. The waters of the Río Blanco river provided hydraulic power for the mill. The company also obtained a concession to use the nearby Rincón Grande waterfall, where it built a hydroelectric power plant, which opened in 1897.

Just as El Palacio de Hierro set an example in commercial practices, so did CIDOSA in production. After CIDOSA was created, several owners of dry-goods stores decided to enter textile production by becoming partners of manufacturing companies. The Compañía Industrial Veracruzana S.A. (CIVSA), a company we shall analyze in more detail in Chapter 2, was founded in 1896 by another set of important Barcelonnette dry-goods firms. CIVSA built a new factory, the Santa Rosa, inaugurated in 1898. Santa Rosa was then the second largest mill in the country, and, like Río Blanco, had the latest technology, including hydroelectric power. Several other similar textile companies were formed in the following years (see Table 1.4).

Textile firms profited from economies of scale and scope. They integrated spinning, weaving, and finishing, often specializing each of their mills in certain parts of the production process and in the production of specific types of cloth. Their mills ran on hydroelectric power, and produced on a larger scale than the country's average mills. They acquired an important share of the market, which they supplied through their associate commercial companies, which in turn distributed their products on a national scale. They produced a wider variety of cloth than older mills. Whereas until 1878 Mexican mills manufactured almost exclusively yarn and coarse cloth *(manta),* these new firms introduced the production of higher-quality, bleached and printed cloth, such as percale, cretonne, muslin, organdy, drill, and flannel.[100]

The new industrial firms were limited-liability joint-stock companies *(sociedades anónimas,* or S.A.), not family enterprises like the mills they acquired. Companies of this type were considerably larger and used more modern machinery than those owned by individuals.[101] They were operated by managers under the close supervision of a board of directors formed by the leading executives of the commercial companies that were their major shareholders. Because stockholders, leading executives, and managers were mostly Barcelonnettes, ethnic ties and family kinship bound them together. An important share of the Porfirian textile industry's growth took place as part of this process of organization. The companies listed in Table 1.4 were responsible for 81% of the national growth

*Table 1.4*  Major textile companies, 1912

| Company | Year founded | Textile mills | Stores owned by associates | Associates |
|---|---|---|---|---|
| Compañía Industrial de Orizaba S.A. | 1889 | Cerritos<br>Cocolapan<br>San Lorenzo<br>Río Blanco | El Palacio de Hierro<br>El Puerto de Liverpool<br>La Ciudad de Londres<br>Francia Marítima<br>El Gran Oriental<br>El Puerto de Veracruz<br>El Correo Francés | Tomás Braniff, J. Ollivier y Cía., J. B. Ebrard y Cía., J. Tron y Cía., Signoret, Honnorat y Cía., Lambert, Reynaud y Cía., Garcin, Faudon y Cía., Juan Quinn. |
| Compañía Industrial Veracruzana S.A. | 1896 | Santa Rosa<br>El León (1920) | Las Fábricas Universales<br>La Ciudad de México<br>El Centro Mercantil<br>La Reforma del Comercio | A. Reynaud y Cía., S. Robert y Cía., F. Manuel y Cía., P. y J. Jacques y Cía., Paulino Richaud. |
| Compañía Industrial de San Antonio Abad S.A. | 1892 | San Antonio Abad<br>La Colmena<br>Barrón<br>Miraflores | La Reforma del Comercio | Iñigo Noriega, Adolfo Prieto, Agustín Garcin, Enrique Monjardin. |
| Compañía Industrial de Atlixco S.A. | 1902 | Metepec | La Reforma del Comercio | B. Rovés y Cía, A. Richaud y Cía., S. de Juanbelz y Cía, Solana Barreneche Cía, Antonio Basagoiti, Luis Barroso Arias, Agustín Garcin, Leopoldo Gavito, Felix Martino, Benjamín Ochoa, Iñigo y Constantino Noriega, Sotero de Juanbelz, Emilio André, Eduardo Vega y Santiago Aréchaga. |

| Compañía Industrial Manufacturera S.A. | 1896 | Hércules<br>San Antonio<br>La Purísima<br>La Sultana<br>La Teja<br>Río Grande | Las Fábricas Universales<br>La Reforma del Comercio<br>La Ciudad de Londres (Guad.) | Agustín Garcin, Joseph Signoret, Brun, Lerdo de Tejada.<br>(1905) Cuzin, Fortuol Bec, Lèbre and Brun. |
|---|---|---|---|---|
| Compañía Industrial de Jalisco/Compañía Industrial de Guadalajara S.A. | 1899 | Río Blanco (Jalisco)<br>Atemajac<br>La Escoba | La Ciudad de Londres (Guad.)<br>Las Fábricas de Francia (Guad.) | Fortoul Chapuy y Cía., Gas y Cía., Laurens Brun y Cía., Bellón Agoneca y Cía., E. Lèbre y Cía. |
| Compañía Industrial de San Ildelfonso S.A. | | San Ildelfonso | El Puerto de Liverpool<br>Francia Marítima | J. B. Ebrard, H. Reynaud and E. Pugibet. |
| J. y L. Veyan y Co. | 1898 | La Magdalena<br>Santa Teresa<br>Río Florido | El Centro Mercantil<br>La Valenciana | Meyrán Donnadieu & Co.<br>(1912) Adrien Jean and Luis Veyan. |

*Sources:* Jorge Durand, *Los obreros de Río Grande* (Zamora, 1986), 54–55, 62; Guillermo Beato, "Loa grupos, las relaciones familiares y la formación de la burguesía de Jalisco durante el siglo XIX" (mimeo, 1982), 48; Mario Trujillo, "La fábrica la Magdalena Contreras (1836–1910)," in Carlos Marichal and Mario Cerutti, comps., *Historia de las grandes empresas* (Mexico City, 1997), 265–270; Luis Everaert, *Centenario 1889–1989* (Querétaro, 1990), 59–67; CIVSA, Actas de la Asamblea General, November 24, 1896.

in the number of spindles from 1878 to 1893, and for 46% from 1893 to 1912. CIVSA and CIDOSA alone accounted for 45% of the growth in spindles from 1878 to 1893, and 18% of growth from 1893 to 1912.

In the textile industry in the north of Mexico, a similar process seems to have taken place. Modernization, both in terms of an increase in scale and in the formation of limited-liability companies, was important there. But in this region, where Barcelonnettes had no influence, a commercial network centered in Monterrey was formed by Mexicans and Spanish immigrants. In Coahuila, both industry growth and increase in scale were accompanied by the creation of several joint-stock companies—the Compañía Industrial de Parras S.A. and the Compañía Industrial Saltillera S.A.[102]

In the South and in states such as Colima, San Luis Potosí, and Aguascalientes, where the scale of production was small and no joint-stock companies were formed, textile mills practically disappeared. However, in the states of Puebla and Tlaxcala, many old-style textile mills survived. Every mill in those states, with the exception of Metepec (owned by the Compañía Industrial de Atlixco S.A. [CIASA]), continued to be family-run businesses, and this remained true until the 1920s. Even when mills in this region became joint-stock companies, in the early 1930s, it was more a formal than a real change, because they continued to be family-run.[103] Their size, in terms of spindles per mill, grew modestly. Nonetheless, the industry in the Puebla-Tlaxcala region was able to modernize its machinery and acquired an increasing share of the national industry.[104]

Labor productivity and total factor productivity in the cotton textile industry substantially increased in the last two decades of the Porfiriato. According to some estimates, labor productivity grew by 5.5% per year when output is measured in real value, and by 2.6% when measured by physical units of output. Total factor productivity increased by 4.5% and 1.5% per year, respectively. The fact that productivity estimates are higher when measured by the value of production rather than by meters of cloth or kilos of yarn show that companies were improving both the quantity and the quality of their products per unit of input.[105]

The Porfirian modernization of textile production had three major characteristics: an increase in scale; modernization of machinery and utilization of electricity as a major source of power; and a merger of mills into joint-stock companies owned by major textile distribution companies, generally the property of Barcelonnettes, except in the northern states.

Greater mill scale was concomitant with the reduction in transportation costs brought about by the railroad and the abolition of tariffs. In the 1890s, for the first time in Mexico it became possible to produce for a national market. As a direct result, Río Blanco, Santa Rosa, and Metepec almost tripled the size of the largest mills that existed in 1878. While the number of mills increased, average mill size grew even more.

In 1880 the average number of spindles per mill in the United States was 14,092, while in Mexico it was 2,918, a small figure even when compared with that of the southern United States (3,367).[106] In order to produce with technology like that used in the United States and profit from economies of scale, mills had to increase their size. In 1878, 33% of mills had fewer than 1,000 spindles, a figure that declined to 21% by 1893 and to 2% by 1912.[107]

Mills not only grew in size, but also modernized. Whereas in 1893 new spindles represented only 37% of total spindles in the industry, by 1913 they accounted for 96% of them. For looms, these proportions were 43% and 93%, respectively.[108] Furthermore, they underwent a transformation in their power source, changing from water power to electricity. Given the scarcity of coal in the country, hydroelectric power produced important savings and was therefore rapidly introduced.

At first electricity was used in the mills only for lighting; by 1889 there were already several mills in Mexico using electricity for this purpose. Then mills started using electricity for power. In 1894, only two years after the installation of the first electric generators to power textile mills in the United States, San Ildefonso in Mexico City began to move its machinery using electric power. Two years later, CIDOSA supplied electric power to its four mills. In Puebla, the San Antonio Abad mill and CIASA began to run on electricity in 1896 and 1899, respectively. In 1898 a hydroelectric power plant was built to provide electricity for La Magdalena Contreras, La Hormiga, and La Alpina textile mills, and for the Loreto paper mill. CIVSA worked from the beginning in 1898 using hydroelectric power. Textile mills soon became a major producer of electricity in the country.[109] By 1900 textile mills owned 44% of the country's total installed capacity in electricity, which was 22,340 kilowatts. The Orizaba Valley textile industry alone owned 29% of this capacity (6,530 kilowatts).[110]

Modernization and an increase in scale followed the merging of textile mills into conglomerates and concentration in the industry's structure. The eight textile conglomerates founded by the turn of the century owned only 12% of the mills but 41% of the spindles, 45% of the looms, and 60% of the printing machines of the entire industry.[111] These companies employed 38% of the labor force in the industry, and paid 40% of the taxes. CIDOSA and CIVSA alone accounted for 20% of the total sales in the industry and employed 18% of the labor force. Barcelonnettes held the majority of the shares in most of these. By 1901 the Barcelonnettes owned 28 out of a total of 125 mills (19%) and paid more than a third of the industry's taxes.[112] Mexico's textile industry concentrated from 1878 to 1902. Whereas in 1879 the four biggest mills produced 16% of total sales, by 1902 this figure had risen to 38%.[113]

During the Porfiriato the textile industry also began to concentrate geographically. In 1879, 59% of the spindles were located along the corridor that encompassed the state of Mexico, Mexico City, Puebla, Tlaxcala, and Veracruz, and this figure increased to 70% by 1912. However, compared to its American counterpart, the Mexican textile industry continued to be relatively dispersed.[114] The relative concentration of the industry in terms of industrial structure makes its regionally dispersed nature even more remarkable.

Reduction in transportation costs generated a more radical transformation in cotton production than in textile manufactures in terms of geographical distribution. After 1892, 80% to 90% of cotton produced in Mexico was grown in La Laguna district, a region located in the states of Durango and Coahuila, linked to the rest of the country in 1888 by the Mexican Central Railway.[115]

Data on imports of manufacturing machinery to Mexico from the United States and Great Britain tell of an extraordinary growth of industrial investment in Mexico during the Porfiriato, compared to the other major Latin American countries. The pace of Mexico's industrial growth was faster than that of Brazil, Argentina, and Chile up to 1902; after that year Mexico's growth rate of imports of manufacturing machinery became negative, while it rose in the other three countries. This resulted from various events in the national sphere—the end of the secular depreciation of the price of silver in 1902, the adoption of the gold standard in 1905, the 1907 financial crisis, and political troubles starting in 1906, turning into a civil war by 1910.[116] In Brazil the 1907 crisis produced only a small downturn in imports of manufacturing machinery, but in Mexico it marked the beginning of a long decline in such imports (see Figure 1.2).[117] The different investment trends (proxied by machinery imports) explain why Mexico's cotton textile industry, which was the most important in Latin America until 1905, was after 1905 surpassed by that of Brazil.[118]

Textile manufacturing developed more widely in Mexico than in the rest of Latin America and most of the periphery from colonial times to

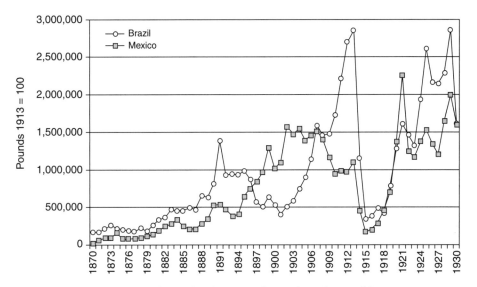

*Figure 1.2.* Mexican and Brazilian imports of manufacturing machinery, 1870–1930. *Sources:* Wilson Suzigan, *Indústria Brasileira: Origem e desenvolvimento* (Sao Paulo: Editora da Unicamp, Editora Hucitec, 2000), 372–383; U.S. Department of Commerce and Labor, *The Foreign Commerce and Navigation of the United States;* United Kingdom, *Annual Statement of the Trade of the United Kingdom with Foreign Countries and British Possessions, Parliamentary Papers.* Prices deflated using the "Whole Sale Price Index" in Brian R. Mitchell, *European Historical Statistics, 1750–1975,* 2nd rev. ed. (New York: Facts on File, 1980).

the end of the nineteenth century, despite the great difficulties Mexico faced as a consequence of political instability during most of the nineteenth century. After 1880, when Porfirio Díaz's regime of "order and progress" fostered the expansion of financial institutions, railroads, and foreign investment and trade, the textile industry grew and modernized. This is the period where our exploration into Orizaba textile firms and its workers begins.

# CHAPTER 2

# CIVSA

## *The Nature of the Firm*

THE COMPAÑÍA INDUSTRIAL VERACRUZANA S.A. (CIVSA) is an excellent example of those companies that experienced the Porfirian revolution in distribution and production. On November 24, 1896, several Barcelonnette entrepreneurs—Alejandro Reynaud, Eugenio Signoret, Sebastián Robert, Fermín Manuel, Paulino Richaud, and José Jacques—met in Mexico City, under the leadership of Alejandro Reynaud, to sign the articles of incorporation of the Compañía Industrial Veracruzana S.A., a joint-stock limited-liability corporation. The corporation's purpose was the creation and operation of a factory for the spinning, weaving, and printing of cotton and other fibers near the city of Orizaba. The corporation also dealt with commerce in regards to the factory's products.[1]

Just as in the case of CIDOSA, created five years earlier, CIVSA's founding associates were not individuals but commercial firms—A. Reynaud & Co., S. Robert & Co., F. Manuel & Co., and J. and P. Jacques & Co. These firms owned important dry-goods stores in Mexico City (see Table 1.3). The only individual shareholders in the firm's formation were Alejandro Reynaud, a major partner of A. Reynaud & Co., and Paulino Richaud, also the owner of a dry-goods store.

Originally the company's capital totaled 1,200,000 pesos ($14,357,606.23 in 2007 U.S. dollars), divided into 12,000 shares of 100 pesos each. One year later, in the stockholders meeting of July 1897, shareholders agreed upon the issue of 10,000 additional shares, so the company's capital was increased to 2,200,000 pesos.[2] Another capital-stock increase was decided at the extraordinary general stockholders meeting of July 1899, bringing CIVSA's capital to 3,350,000 pesos. At this time, 11,000 additional shares were offered to the existing stockholders of the company and 500 additional shares were sold to M. Bellón & Co., the owner of another dry-goods store. An additional firm joined the company in 1900, Desdier, Sibilot & Co., in Puebla.[3]

A. Reynaud & Co. was the major stockholder of the firm, with 25% of the shares in 1896. This figure increases to 48% when shares owned personally by Alejandro Reynaud and other members of the Reynaud family are added. S. Robert & Co. was the second largest stockholder with 12.5% of the company's stock. Manuel F. & Co., J. and P. Jacques & Co., and Paulino Richaud owned only 4.17%, 1.83%, and 2.5% of the shares, respectively. Among these partners 68.9% of the company stock was distributed. The remaining shares were divided among another twenty-eight partners, all but five of whom had Barcelonnette family names.[4]

There was great continuity among CIVSA shareholders until 1930, especially if they are thought of in terms of families. The Reynaud holdings remained important in 1930, when A. Reynaud & Co. and its members owned 38.9% of all stock.[5] Yet there was certain mobility among them. Exchange of CIVSA stock became important during the Revolution, and even more so in the 1920s. During this later period, several of the founding associates sold their shares to persons not originally related to the company, such as J. B. Ebrard & Co. (a major partner of CIDOSA and El Puerto de Liverpool). Two banks, the Compañía Bancaria de París y México and the Banco Nacional de México, became CIVSA shareholders in the 1920s, perhaps acquiring their shares as payments for debts original shareholders owed them.

Although a minority, many shareholders lived abroad, particularly in France. In 1920, 13.2% of CIVSA's shares were held in foreign countries. In shareholders meetings these foreign investors often allowed themselves to be represented by other Mexican companies that they controlled or owned. However, some did not have businesses in Mexico, and carried out transactions with CIVSA through its company agents in Europe, such as A. Reynaud & Co. in Paris, or Gassier Frères in Barcelonnette.[6]

CIVSA's investment capital came from the sale of shares rather than from bank financing. Debt over total capital was always very low. However, short-term bank loans were useful for providing the firm with the necessary liquidity for current expenses, such as buying cotton and other inputs.[7] Although fluctuations in the exchange rates made foreign credit risky, CIVSA obtained credit from foreign sources on several occasions. A. Reynaud & Co. of Paris granted loans to CIVSA from 1908 to 1910 for more than 80,000 pesos, and Henry Reynaud, also of Paris, lent CIVSA 60,000 pesos from 1901 to 1907.[8] CIVSA also accepted credits from associates and friends in Barcelonnette, such as the Gassier Frères.

Two years after the company was founded, the factory of Santa Rosa began to operate. It was inaugurated on May 15, 1899. The mill's main engine was stopped to allow President Porfirio Díaz to restart it as part of a huge celebration. More than 100 nationally renowned guests attended the banquet, among them the governor of Veracruz, Teodoro Dehesa, several ministers of the federal and state governments, the political chief

The Santa Rosa factory, ca. 1900. (Collection du Musée de la Vallée, La Sapinière à Barcelonnette, France. Fonds Mémoire de l'Emigration ubayenne aux Amériques.)

of the Orizaba district, the French ambassador to Mexico, and several of Mexico's most important bankers and industrialists. Workers were given the day off and 2,000 liters of *pulque* to join the celebration. The factory had been operating for at least six months before its inauguration, yet several of its departments were still unfinished, and construction of the mill continued for several years.[9]

## The Barcelonnette Network in Operation: CIVSA's Shareholders

CIVSA's major shareholders were companies, not individuals. Yet the individuals behind these companies had a significant role in how CIVSA was run. The most important of these company owners was Alejandro Reynaud, under whose leadership CIVSA was created. He was the founder of the dry-goods store Las Fábricas de Francia, a major partner of A. Reynaud & Co., and the owner of the important store Las Fábricas Universales. He left Mexico for Paris shortly after founding CIVSA in 1896. From then on, he was in charge of A. Reynaud & Co. in Paris, which did all the foreign purchases and transactions for the company's branch in Mexico and for CIVSA, as well as for other important businesses in Mexico and South America.

Other Reynaud family members, including Honorato, Alberto, Alfredo, Antonio, Francisco, and Paul, were CIVSA shareholders. Honorato Reynaud was president of CIVSA's board from 1908 to 1914, and was also a board member of the Compañía de San Ildefonso, a wool textile mill.[10] Antonio Reynaud was general director of CIDOSA from 1905 to 1917.

Paul Reynaud, the son of Alejandro Reynaud, would become the most notable member of the family. He did not follow his father's career, but went into politics. In 1919 he was elected deputy in France, representing the Basse-Alpes district. Between 1928 and 1940 he served as France's minister of finances, colonies, and justice. He was president of France from March 20 to July 17, 1940, just before Marshal Pétain came to power.[11]

The Reynauds were closely related to the Signorets, another prominent Barcelonnette family. The two families had several businesses together, such as the Reynaud & Signoret Company, which by 1912 owned the El León mill at Puebla.[12] Eugenio, Gustavo, José, Léon, and Pablo

Signoret were CIVSA shareholders. It is difficult to think of a family with better relations in the Porfirian regime than the Signorets.

José Signoret was an important partner of A. Reynaud & Co. and, as such, a co-owner of Las Fábricas Universales, of which he was director. In 1897, 1906, and 1907 he was president of CIVSA's board of directors and a member of the board of the knitwear Factory La Abeja. Deeply involved in banking, he was a founder and board member of the Banco Central Mexicano and of the Banco Agrícola e Hipotecario, and sat on the boards of the Banco Nacional de México and the Banco Peninsular.[13] He was also in the railway business as board member of the most important railroad company in Mexico, Ferrocarriles Nacionales de México.[14] Eugenio Signoret was the first president of CIVSA's board, and after a brief period of absence held this position from 1898 to 1905.

Through S. Robert & Co., Sebastián Robert was the second most important partner in CIVSA. A nephew of Joseph Ollivier, he was first an employee and later a partner in and director of J. Ollivier & Co., owner of the La Ciudad de Londres store.[15] In 1884 he left J. Ollivier & Co. and established his own trading company *(maison de commission et d'achats)* in Paris. Some years later he created S. Robert & Co., with Fermin Manuel and his cousin José Pinoncely, to operate the La Valenciana dry-goods store in Mexico City. Under another partnership he also opened the dry-goods store La Ciudad de México in Buenos Aires, Argentina.[16] In 1896 S. Robert & Co. was reestablished with new associates, including Emile Meyran, Santiago Arechederre, and Pedro A. Chaix.[17] When CIVSA was created, Sébastian Robert was vice president, but because he lived in France, Emile Meyrán represented him in that position.[18]

S. Robert & Co. was an important partner of El Banco Central Mexicano and owner of the textile mill La Hormiga in Tizapan, Federal District, and the hydroelectric company La Luz Eléctrica, which supplied energy to the mill and light to the southern part of the federal district. In 1900 La Valenciana was destroyed by fire, so S. Robert & Co. opened the El Centro Mercantil department store and three years later another department store, La Ciudad de Bruselas. The firm also owned stock in several industrial and financial enterprises. In 1904 its total investment in Mexico was calculated by the credit research company R. G. Dunn at some 2 million pesos, although the firm's declared capital was only 300,000 pesos.[19] Sebastian Robet was a councilor in France to the Banco Nacional de México and an agent of the Compagnie Générale Transatlantique. In Paris he was "favorably spoken of and regarded as a shrewd and careful buyer with wide experience in his line."[20]

P. and J. Jacques & Co., formed in 1893, was composed of Pablo and José Jacques, both Barcelonnettes who had been in Mexico for several years and were "well and favorably spoken of in trade circles throughout the country."[21] They were for many years salesmen on commission and from the 1890s they acted as local representatives of a limited number of merchants in the interior of the Republic. They carried no stock of goods on hand, but bought direct for their customers from manufacturers and jobbers. Besides CIVSA, Pablo and José Jacques owned and managed a woolen mill, San José de Silva, located near Celaya, Guanajuato. They were also owners of several buildings in Mexico City. "Opinions vary somewhat as to the capital they may possess, but estimates range between 200,000 and 300,000 pesos and some even higher. Personally they bear a good reputation in every respect, are regarded as capable business-men, of correct business principles," R. G. Dunn & Co. reported.[22]

M. Bellón & Co. owned the dry-goods store El Progreso in Mexico City. The firm was founded in 1883 by Mariano Bellón and Enrique Jean, and later reorganized under the name of M. Bellón & Co. with Enrique Monjardin, Alfredo Brun, and Luis Sicard as new partners. "The several partners of the firm," explained R. G. Dunn & Co., "while reported to be of but little initiative and not credited with more than fair business capability, are said to be industrious and well meaning, . . . [and] will doubtless endeavor to protect the credit stand-ing of the house and not assume obligations lightly."[23] In 1903 El Progreso carried nearly 400,000 pesos in stock, and its building was worth 60,000 pesos. The firm owned shares in the Compañía Destiladora S.A., and in the Compañía Industrial Veracruzana S.A., La Abeja S.A., and the San Antonio Abad cotton mills. Moreover, the firm was one of the founders and stockholders in the Banco de Morelos, of Cuernavaca, established in 1902. "From investigation in the local trade it would appear that the af-fairs of the firm are in fairly good satisfactory condition," concluded R. G. Dunn & Co.'s report.[24] In the late 1910s the company also owned and operated the La Moderna brick factory in Mixcoac.[25]

Less is known about CIVSA's other partners. In the early 1900s E. Manuel and Brother and E. Manuel & Co. owned two dry-goods stores with a reported capital of 5,000 and 16,137 pesos, respectively. Yet, because it appears that underreporting capital was then a common practice, it could have been much larger.[26] By 1906, P. Richaud & Co. owned a clothes warehouse.[27] Eugenio Caire and Amado Aubert, members of the CIVSA board, must have been related to Caire, Aubert & Co., owners of El Puerto de Tampico, one of the largest dry-goods store in Mexico City in 1897.[28]

Other CIVSA shareholders were companies that provided services to the firm, such as Jauffred & Gariel, a company in Manchester that made all purchases of machinery, spare parts, and raw materials for CIVSA, and recruited technicians in England for the company. Gassier Frères of Barcelonnette and Gap in France were bankers who financed the company on different occasions, besides serving as CIVSA's agents to make dividend payments to shareholders in Europe.

## CIVSA's Organizational Structure

In a traditional capitalist firm, owners manage and managers own. Capital stock stays in the hands of a few individuals or families, who rarely hire more than two or three managers. These firms are defined as personal enterprises. In contrast, in modern business enterprises ownership becomes widely scattered. Stockholders do not have the influence, knowledge, experience, or commitment to take part in top management. Salaried managers determine long-term policy as well as manage short-term operating activities, and dominate top as well as lower and middle management. These are defined as managerial enterprises.[29]

CIVSA's structure was halfway between a personal and a modern managerial enterprise of the kind described by Alfred Chandler. Although the Reynaud family owned a majority of the company's shares throughout the period studied, CIVSA was not a family business. The Reynauds did not run CIVSA; instead, the board, representing the various commercial firms that owned CIVSA, managed the company. Yet A. Reynaud & Co. controlled the board's presidency for most of the period studied. Members of the board often contested the president's opinions. However, although every board member had a vote, when positions about any issue were divided, the president's vote had extra weight and determined the course of action to be taken.[30] Thus, in practice, A. Reynaud & Co. exercised greater control over CIVSA than any other partner.

Nonetheless, there was some distance between ownership and management in CIVSA's operation. Commercial firms participated in CIVSA's board as business associations, not through the personal involvement of their major owners.[31] CIVSA board meeting minutes were signed until 1910 with the names, not of the individuals who attended, but of the companies they represented. In 1896 these were: A. Reynaud & Co., president and treasurer; S. Robert & Co., vice president; F. Manuel & Co., secretary; and P. and J. Jacques & Co., members of the board (vocal). In April 1900, M. Bellón & Co. became a member of the board (vocal), and in September 1902 so did Desdier Sibilot & Co. In order to comply with the Mexican Code of Commerce after 1911 members of the board signed the minutes with their own names, but they continued to represent the commercial firms they worked for.[32]

While smaller companies such as F. Manuel & Co. appointed family members to the CIVSA board, larger firms were generally represented on the CIVSA board by the general directors of those companies in Mexico, who also managed the department stores, or by persons closely related to them.[33] With very few exceptions, board members were part of the tightly knit Barcelonnette network. Indeed, all company correspondence and minutes of the board were written in French until 1905. Beginning in that year, the board decided to use Spanish in these documents, although a large part of the correspondence continued to be in French.

CIVSA's board of directors was located in Mexico City, the site of the company's headquarters. Until 1911 the Mexico City offices were managed by the president of the board of directors. And the Santa Rosa mill was overseen by a general manager, appointed by the board of directors, who lived on the mill's premises. Early on, the board agreed that when board members visited Santa Rosa they should not interfere in the manager's duties "and leave to him the complete administration of the factory, even when they are informed of complaints or demands of the employees."[34] Daily correspondence went back and forth between the board's president in Mexico City and Santa Rosa's manager; thus railroads and the telegraph were crucial to CIVSA's management.

In 1911 the general manager moved to Mexico City and assumed most of the managerial duties previously held by the president of the board. The position of assistant general manager was created to replace the general manager in his responsibilities for the technical administration of the mill.[35] This reform allowed for a further separation between entrepreneurial decisions and actions taken by the board, and operating decisions and actions assigned to the general manager and assistant manager.[36]

From the outset the mill's organization was divided into several departments, corresponding to the various production processes, management, reception of inputs, distribution of finished products, and the workshop that was responsible for repairs and improvements. Santa Rosa's major departments, spinning and weaving, were run by heads of department. Between them and the workers there was a technician *(maestro)*, more than a dozen clerical and staff employees, and several foremen. The printing department was under the direction of a chemist, who enjoyed the highest salary in the mill after the assistant general manager. He also supervised the finishing, bleaching, and dyeing departments. In 1926 there were six technicians and 16 clerical and staff employees under his control. In all, 165 clerical and staff employees and 3,267 blue-collar workers were employed by CIVSA that year.[37]

Most high-level employees were foreign and hired directly from Europe. They lived on the mill premises in elegant houses built for them by CIVSA, or, if they were single, in a hotel also located on the mill premises. The factory also owned a recreational area with a bar, billiard tables, bowling courts, tennis courts, and a swimming pool, all for the use of high-level employees and the directors when they visited Santa Rosa.

The board held weekly meetings at which most of the company's strategy was devised.[38] In these meetings members decided all matters regarding input purchases, allocation of financial assets, recruitment and appointment of Santa Rosa's employees, sale policies, negotiations with unions, and the company's relations with federal, state, and municipal governments and with other companies or industrial associations. Reports of production and costs were sent weekly from Santa Rosa to the Mexico City offices. The board analyzed them and sent alarm signals to the mill whenever it found unexplained changes in the accounts, demanding solutions to the problem.

At almost every meeting the board spent some time deciding the quantities of each type of fabric that should be produced for the following week. Because the members of the board were also managers of the dry-goods firms they represented, they had an accurate idea of the kind of fabric in greatest demand and of the general market trends that would be of use for CIVSA. The board of directors also spent some time every week analyzing trends in the cotton market in Mexico and abroad. The board also frequently compared CIVSA's prices with those of their competitors, mostly those of CIDOSA, of which they were always aware.[39] During the first ten years of CIVSA's operation a member of the board traveled weekly to Santa Rosa, and all board members met at Santa Rosa during the last week of December.[40] After 1911, visits of board members to the mill, although still frequent, became less regular.

CIVSA's accounting and sales were conducted directly in Mexico City offices. The company held warehouses in Mexico City and later in Puebla from which a large part of the mill's production was distributed to customers. Payments by customers were also made directly to Mexico City, with few exceptions. Mexico City offices made all purchases of cotton, raw materials, and machinery. Every week CIVSA's offices in Mexico City sent the cash to pay workers and employees at the mill.

This way of conducting business was disrupted temporarily during the Revolution when railway and even telegraph lines between Mexico City and Orizaba for civilian use were cut for long periods of time. On those occasions Santa Rosa made sales and purchased inputs directly. Strangely enough, information traveled between Santa Rosa and Mexico City by cable via New York, with the aid of CIVSA's bankers in the United States. When the situation was pressing, messengers were sent from Mexico City to Orizaba by horse.[41]

In 1911, because several of CIVSA's founding associates or former board members had left Mexico for Paris, under the proposal of A. Reynaud & Co. in Paris the Paris Advisory Committee (Comité Consultatif de Paris) was created.[42] The Advisory Committee was formed in June 1911 with the following members: Alejandro Reynaud, Alberto Reynaud, Fermin Manuel, Paulino Richaud, Pablo Jacques, Eugenio Signoret, Desiderio Signoret, Eugenio Zivy, León Audiffred, José Pinoncely, and Juan Derbez.[43]

The Paris Advisory Committee was constantly in contact with the board and with the general manager of CIVSA. It received weekly reports on production, costs, and sales, and on the firm's financial standing, as well as letters explaining the general situation of the firm. Periodically it received a set of the company's accounting data, including balance sheets, reports on profit and loss, and minutes of the board of directors meetings and of the general shareholders meetings. Formally the Committee's role was merely advisory, but in practice it had great influence over the major decisions taken by the board of directors, such as the setting of dividends, capital increases, the purchase of other mills, and the general strategy to be followed with regard to government and labor.[44] Furthermore, it had a prominent role in the firm's financial management.

The Committee's residence in Paris facilitated CIVSA's operations by providing a close link with Europe. It assisted the firm's search for technicians and executives, the purchase of chemicals, machinery, and other inputs, and the acquisition of funds and the allocation of assets in foreign capital markets. Before the Advisory Committee was created, A. Reynaud & Co. in Paris had served as CIVSA's link in Europe, and the CIVSA board's major decisions were only taken after A. Reynaud & Co. in Paris had approved them.[45]

In 1919 CIVSA's operations expanded with the lease of La Covadonga, and in 1920 with the acquisition of El Leon. Both were mills in the state of Puebla. Like CIDOSA, CIVSA became a multiplant firm, and consequently the firm's accounting and administration procedures became more complex.[46] Routine procedures previously developed in Santa Rosa were established for all mills. These included standardized forms, to be filled out weekly and submitted to the board in Mexico City, giving detailed information on production, costs, and sales at each mill. Accounting procedures were also standardized in all mills.

When operations at Covadonga started, the board explained that "hiring highly skilled personnel is very difficult, especially because of the economic situation, so we cannot expect to hire first-class personnel."[47] Thus it decided to hire less-qualified managers for these two mills, and put them under the supervision of Santa Rosa's personnel.

The various production stages were distributed among the three plants. Cloth from El León was finished at Covadonga along with Covadonga's own cloth, and production from this mill was sent to Santa Rosa when the fabric produced required more-sophisticated finishing processes. Inputs, when in large stock, were generally located at Santa Rosa, or in the warehouse the company owned in Puebla. Thus production in the three mills had to be synchronized. The general manager controlled communication links between factories from Mexico City, but there was also continuous contact between these mills and Santa Rosa.

## Making the Link between Production and Distribution

CIVSA never developed sales or advertising departments because the commercial firms that owned and managed CIVSA carried out these duties. Most of CIVSA's sales (93% in 1905 and 91% in 1925) were made to its board member companies, which sold both wholesale and retail from stores located mostly in Mexico City to different regions throughout Mexico.[48] Yet CIVSA also had customers in several other cities, some as far away as Chihuahua or Mérida. Through both direct sales and indirect sales, CIVSA served an extensive interstate, if not national, market.

Because the cotton textile market was highly protected from foreign competition, imported cloth represented around 12% of total Mexican consumption from 1890 to 1930.[49] Imports set an upper limit on prices to compete with similar goods in Mexico, but Mexican firms were well aware that they had plenty of maneuvering room and a decided commercial advantage over their international competitors.

CIVSA and CIDOSA together accounted for almost 20% of total sales in the Mexican cotton textile industry.[50] However, this figure disguises the larger control these companies held in the market of higher-quality products, such as colored, finished, and printed cloth, in which they specialized. Between 1916 and 1926 colored cloth represented 70% of CIVSA's sales, while sales of unfinished cloth and yarn were negligible.[51] A comparison of CIDOSA price lists with those of CIVSA show that CIDOSA had a distribution of sales among different types of cloth similar to that of CIVSA. Very few firms in Mexico besides CIVSA and CIDOSA produced high-quality printed cloth in Mexico, because only 15 mills out of 148 factories had printing machines by 1912.[52]

Collusive agreements between CIVSA and CIDOSA were common. On several occasions CIVSA board members held meetings with their CIDOSA counterparts to set prices.[53] In April 1918, for example, because of increases in cotton prices the CIVSA board announced higher prices, "a decision taken in common agreement with the majority of mill owners, and especially the Managing Committees *(Comités Directores)* of CIVSA and CIDOSA, in order to standardize prices of similar articles."[54]

## Sales Policies

At the beginning of the year CIVSA established sale contracts with the customers, to whom most of its production was allocated. It was difficult to purchase goods from CIVSA without a yearly contract. In February 1900, for example, CIVSA's director wrote to A. Lions that CIVSA could not sell him the merchandise he required because all CIVSA's production was already committed to those customers who had a yearly contract. Moreover, it was not possible for everyone to obtain an annual contract. In January 1913, Caledonio Alvarez S. en C. in Puebla and Víctor Audiffred wished to make yearly contracts with CIVSA for purchases of 30,000 and 25,000 pesos, respectively, but CIVSA answered that this was impossible because all its production for that year was already committed.[55]

Every year the board of directors set a scale of discounts to be given to customers with an annual contract, depending on their annual purchases, and reimbursed to them at the end of the year.[56] Given that the commercial houses represented on CIVSA's board all made substantial purchases, general discounts set for amounts above a certain level (50,000 in 1905 pesos, or $100,000 in 1925 U.S. dollars) were, in fact, distributed exclusively among board members. Discounts provided a significant income for board members, and thus debates among them before setting the annual scale were often recorded in the minutes of board meetings.[57]

Discounts for board members increased substantially after 1910. Perhaps because of harsher economic conditions, the scale of discounts was replaced by a flat rate along with the commitment of board members to reach a minimum volume of purchases. This discount policy prevailed from 1910 to 1915, and again from 1927 to 1930. In these later years the general discount policy was explained in the board meeting minutes but specific discount rates were no longer recorded.[58]

CIVSA's discount policy was partly pursuing the objective of minimizing administrative and other transaction costs by supplying a wholesale market. However, the increase in discounts for board members after the Revolution most likely had the objective of hiding profits from workers and government authorities as relations with them deteriorated. At the same time, this policy distributed profits from CIVSA's minor shareholders in favor of those who sat on the board. Greater discounts for board members promoted noncompetitive practices in the textile distribution market. It allowed the stores represented on the board to gain an edge in their sales over stores that were not important shareholders of a mill. This is why after the foundation of CIDOSA so many dry-goods stores wanted their own mills.

CIVSA set lists of retail prices that its customers had to charge. In 1899 it specified that customers had the obligation to sell at least at those prices plus a surcharge of 1%.[59] However, it was not always easy for CIVSA to make customers comply with their price lists. By 1918 many immigrants from the Ottoman Empire had established important dry-goods commercial houses that rivaled those belonging to the Barcelonnettes, something the textile firms had to accommodate.[60] CIVSA and CIDOSA had troubles with "Turkish and other Arab customers" because they sold at prices below those established by the firms.[61] However, afraid to lose these customers, they could not do much to change this practice.[62]

CIVSA sales policy was described by its board as "common practice throughout textile mills in Mexico."[63] This policy corresponds to a market where collusive arrangements were the norm in production and distribution.

## CIVSA's Strategy and Structure in Perspective

CIDOSA's capital formation, structure, and organization paralleled CIVSA's in almost every aspect. Once CIDOSA was formed by several major dry-goods stores, it prompted the formation of other companies with similar characteristics, including not only CIVSA, but also the Compañía Industrial de Atlixco, the Compañía Industrial de Jalisco, the Compañía Industrial de San Ildefonso, the Compañía Industrial Manufacturera, and others.[64]

In terms of organization, the main difference between CIDOSA and CIVSA was that CIDOSA soon controlled several mills: Cocolapan, Cerritos, San Lorenzo, and Río Blanco. Thus, it developed the practices adopted by CIVSA in the 1920s. From CIDOSA's creation there was a general manager resident in Mexico City, and a manager at the Río Blanco mill. The other mills were run by less-qualified managers, and although they were under the direct control of the general manager in Mexico City, they often were supported by the Río Blanco staff. In 1908, many years before CIVSA, CIDOSA created an Advisory Committee in Paris, with the same role as CIVSA's. Both firms differed greatly from the Puebla textile mills analyzed by Leticia Gamboa, which were always family-run businesses and on a much smaller scale.[65]

A comparison of CIVSA's and CIDOSA's structures shows that CIVSA profited from CIDOSA's organizational experience and adopted its practices. Thus, an inter-institutional learning experience seems to have taken place, where innovations made by one firm were rapidly adopted by others. Similarities between CIVSA and CIDOSA, whether the result of CIVSA's imitation or independent parallel developments, also indicate that the strategy and structure they followed were organizational innovations well adapted to Mexico's economic, social, and political environment.

Industrial enterprises of the size of CIVSA and CIDOSA required more capital than a family business firm could provide. Furthermore, they were too large for a single entrepreneur (or family) to manage. If capital could not be raised through financial institutions, and the capital required for such enterprises was too large for a single family to supply, the solution was the strategy CIDOSA and CIVSA followed. Basically this was to join the capital of several commercial firms, and divide management responsibilities among them. These firms were already well acquainted with the textile distribution business, so their partnership served yet another purpose. It guaranteed sales and provided the textile mills with the necessary knowledge of the market for its products from the outset.

In order for this type of firm to succeed, an additional ingredient was necessary: trust. Mexico's institutional development had improved by leaps and bounds during the Porfiriato. Nonetheless, it still left much to be desired. Business or commerce in Mexico was still filled with legal holes accompanied by very little protection for the unwary or unlucky. Doing business within the Barcelonnette ethnic network, ruled by rigid social norms, offered a way of avoiding many of these traps or unsafe negotiations. The Barcelonnettes provided entrepreneurs with the necessary trust that their partners, customers, and managers would not defraud them and create costly legal difficulties.[66]

Mexico's institutional development favored those few entrepreneurs who were able to fulfill the necessary requirements to create businesses of the kind described above. These requirements included not only owning large amounts of liquid assets, but also belonging to a tightly knit social network that provided the necessary trust. This social networking within business is one of the reasons behind the very concentrated industrial structure Haber has found.[67]

## Technology

Santa Rosa was built and equipped according to the latest advances in mill technology.[68] Miguel Angel de Quevedo, a well-known Mexican engineer educated in Europe, directed the construction of the mill buildings and its system, following plans from Pott Sons & Hodgson from England, to which he made several improvements.[69] In nationality de Quevedo was an exception to the rule, since all other engineers and highly skilled personnel who erected CIVSA were of foreign origin.[70]

CIVSA acquired most construction materials and machinery in Europe through its agents, Jauffred & Gariel Co. in Manchester and A. Reynaud & Co. in Paris, because very few of the materials required for mill construction were available in Mexico. Even glass sheets had to be brought from Europe.[71] English houses, such as Mather & Platt, Musgrave & Sons., and Dobson & Barlow, supplied most of the machinery and equipment.[72] Some purchases were also made from French, German, and American companies.[73]

Santa Rosa vertically integrated spinning, weaving, and finishing. In 1912 it had 40,184 spindles and 1,380 looms, which made it the second largest mill in Mexico after Río Blanco.[74] Though it was a large mill relative to other Mexican mills, it was not large compared to mills in the United States.[75] The information collected by the Tariff Board of the United States in 1911 shows that in its size Santa Rosa was within the range that was most commonly chosen by U.S. mills; 22% of the 74 mills studied had 40,000 to 50,000 spindles, and 39% had 1,000 to 2,000 looms. No other size range had a larger percentage of mills. Several mills were even larger.

Santa Rosa integrated spinning and weaving as 90% of the American mills surveyed did and used ring spindles as 85% of the American mills studied did.[76] Vertical integration of spinning and weaving made the choice of ring instead of mule spinning optimal.[77] Ring spindles were a more advanced technology than the mule spindles, which were still operating in several parts of the world. Ring spinning frames were purchased from Dobson & Barlow Ltd. in Lancashire. In 1908 the average number of spindles per warp frame at Santa Rosa was 380.27, which was a large figure compared to the number of spindles per frame in several countries in 1910, and also larger than the Mexican average of 348 spindles per frame. Only France, Italy, and Spain were using larger spinning frames than Santa Rosa.[78]

The scale of production of Santa Rosa was large, but it was not obstructed by a lack of technological choices in the international markets of machinery. On the contrary, CIVSA seems to have chosen the factory's size based on its being the optimal scale internationally adopted by the end of the nineteenth century. Lack of demand was not a constraint for CIVSA because it normally faced more demand than it could supply, with the exception of years of economic crisis, when oversupply is a normal problem everywhere. However, the lack of skilled technical labor in Mexico appears to have been an important problem that inhibited CIVSA's capacity to absorb the newest foreign technology.

When CIVSA was being established, the company at first hesitated to buy American Northrop looms. These looms were the utmost novelty in the market. The manufacturers compared their invention to the Eli Whitney cotton gin invented 100 years before: "nothing devised in the years between has sufficient relative importance in the art."[79] Typical power looms achieved high speeds but at low efficiency, because the machine had to be stopped each time the weaver manually replaced a full weft pirn in the shuttle. The Northrop was the first system to replace the weft automatically without stopping the loom.[80] By reducing the weaver's duties, it allowed for an increase in the number of looms each weaver tended, reducing the usual force of weavers to less than half.[81] Moreover, Northrop looms stopped instantly when a thread was broken, thereby reducing imperfections in the cloth.[82] The Northrop also consisted of standardized parts, whereas most British machines, such as Keighly looms, were produced in hundreds of variants as models were updated regularly, making it difficult to obtain spare parts for older machines.[83] According to Geo. Draper & Sons, there was no possible doubt for a new textile mill about the convenience of acquiring Northrop looms, "unless the style of goods demands modifications in the present mechanism not yet designed or invented."[84] Nevertheless, Santa Rosa preferred to acquire traditional Keighly looms. Why?

Alejandro Reynaud visited the United States in 1896 to become acquainted with the Northrop looms and considered they had several disadvantages but suggested that CIVSA buy a few to test them.[85] In 1898 CIVSA acquired eight Northrop looms, but being quickly dissatisfied with them, decided to buy the rest of its looms from George Keighly Ltd. By April 1899 Santa Rosa had 640 Keighly looms and only the initial eight Northrop looms operating in the mill.[86]

Northrop looms offered substantial savings in labor costs in spite of CIVSA's lower wages because of the larger increase in looms per weaver it could have generated. In the United States, as Geo. Draper & Sons advertised, the extra US$80 that Northrop looms cost would have been paid off in 2.84 years, considering that the number of looms tended per weaver increased from eight to sixteen, at a wage of US$9 per week. At CIVSA weavers earned only US$2.24 weekly in 1900 but they tended only 2.3 looms on average. If the looms tended per weaver at CIVSA doubled, the extra cost of the Northrop looms would have been paid off in 3.28 years, but if they increased to sixteen, it would have been paid off in just 1.92 years. Considering interest rates of 4.5% for the United States and 8% for Mexico, it would have been 13.6% more expensive for CIVSA than for American firms to buy such machinery in the first case and 2.2% more expensive in the second case. However, it still would have made good economic sense for CIVSA to acquire such machinery.[87] The reduction in cloth imperfections gained by using Northrop looms could have provided additional savings to even out their extra cost.

Yet Northrop looms had other drawbacks. The manufacturers pointed out that "on account of the novelty, they required more fixers and more repairs."[88] This appears to have been a problem for Santa Rosa. In April 1899, Mr. Anderson, Northrop's agent in Mexico, visited the mill in order to examine the difficulties Santa Rosa was experiencing with its Northrop looms. He suggested that the technicians who had installed them go back to the mill for two or three days to solve the problems. There was a discussion over whose fault it was that the looms were not working correctly and who should pay for the technicians' expenses.[89] Skilled technicians were far more expensive in Mexico than in the United States, and this may explain why CIVSA decided to acquire traditional looms.

Another problem with Northrop looms was that they were more suitable for producing plain cloth than fancy fabrics. This was apparently why the British textile industry did not welcome the Northrop system.[90] Perhaps this was another reason why Santa Rosa preferred traditional looms. Although it seemed reasonable not to acquire Northrop looms when CIVSA was established, it was a decision that marked the fate of the company two decades later when Northrop automatic looms became the dominant international technology and CIVSA was no longer able to acquire them, as will be explained later.

## Costs and Productivity Comparisons

CIVSA's cloth prices were 64% higher than American prices and 28% higher than English prices, on average (see Table 2.1). However, once the tariff is added to foreign prices, CIVSA's prices were only 1% higher than American prices and 14% below British prices, on average. Taking transportation costs into account, CIVSA's prices would have been even lower in a relative comparison. Foreign competition, tariffs included, seems to have been an important benchmark for defining CIVSA's prices, which were basically the same as those of its domestic competitors (such as CIDOSA).

Table 2.1 also shows that CIVSA required much lower tariffs than those established to compete with American competitors and practically

*Table 2.1* Tariffs, prices, and production costs of cloth: CIVSA, England, and the United States, 1911

| Cloth | CIVSA prices/costs | CIVSA U.S. prices | CIVSA English prices | Tariff CIVSA required relative to the United States (pesos) | Tariff CIVSA required relative to England (pesos) | Actual tariff (pesos/m²) |
|---|---|---|---|---|---|---|
| Dril necoxtla blanco (denim) | 137% | 173% | 136% | 0.08 | 0.00 | 0.14 |
| Franela velours (canton franel) | 156% | 179% | 131% | 0.04 | −0.05 | 0.11 |
| Dril kaki (brown drills) | 136% | 261% | 192% | 0.18 | 0.11 | 0.17 |
| Dril palmita blanco (white drills) | 116% | 153% | 113% | 0.07 | −0.01 | 0.10 |
| Toile sublime (shirting) | 134% | 163% | 138% | 0.04 | 0.01 | 0.11 |
| Bramante 7/4 (table damask) | 147% | 110% | 123% | −0.08 | −0.04 | 0.10 |
| Santa rosa 1 (madras) | 118% | 131% | 101% | 0.02 | −0.03 | 0.10 |
| Flor de lys 1 (madras) | 114% | 118% | 92% | 0.01 | −0.05 | 0.10 |
| Tela francesa 1 (madras) | 130% | 257% | 122% | 0.04 | −0.01 | 0.11 |
| Nansu mulhouse (calico print) | 133% | 217% | 129% | 0.09 | −0.01 | 0.14 |
| Percal un color (printed percale) | 108% | 138% | 123% | 0.04 | 0.02 | 0.11 |
| Cotelina fantasía (printed lawn) | 118% | 173% | 133% | 0.06 | 0.02 | 0.11 |
| Average | 129% | 164% | 128% | 0.05 | 0.00 | 0.12 |

*Sources:* For England and United States: U.S. House of Representatives, *Cotton Manufactures: Report of the Tariff Board* (Washington, D.C., 1912), 1:443–444; for Mexico: Archive of the Compañía Industrial Veracruzana S.A., Libros de Precios y Costos, January–December, 1911; for tariffs: Aurora Gómez-Galvarriato, "The Impact of Revolution: Business and Labor in the Mexican Textile Industry, Orizaba, Veracruz, 1900–1930" (PhD diss., Harvard University, 1999), appendix 8, table A8.1. For further detail, see Gómez-Galvarriato, "The Impact of Revolution," chap. 8, tables 1 and 2.

none to compete with the British for most of the types of cloth in the sample. Assuming a return on capital of 8%, in 1911 several of the types of cloth shown in Table 2.1 could have competed with English imports, but practically none with American imports. However, it can be speculated that much lower tariffs than those established would have sufficed to enable CIVSA to compete with foreign imports (on average only 41% of the tariff was necessary for CIVSA to compete with American cloth and no tariff was necessary to compete with English weaves). Because during the 1900s Mexico imported around 70% of its fabrics from England, and only about 15% from the United States, English prices were more relevant for the Mexican industry.[91] Thus a great part of the tariff served merely to provide CIVSA with higher profit margins.

Although the Mexican cotton textile industry enjoyed high protection levels during the Porfiriato, they were not higher than those of the United States. A comparison of Mexican and American tariff levels indicates that levels of protection for cloth in Mexico were actually lower than in the United States in 1911, which was one of the highest in the world.[92] In that year the simple average of all duties for coarse unbleached cloth in the United States was 34.9%, and for fine unbleached cloth was 41.8%.[93] In Mexico the comparable ad valorem equivalent tariffs for 1911 were 20.1% and 26% respectively. Because raw cotton was tariff-free in the United States, effective protection rates were even higher in that country with respect to Mexico than the difference suggested by their ad valorem tariffs.[94]

The difference in prices between Mexico and the United States resulted partly from the cost of raw cotton, which was on average 20% more expensive at CIVSA than in the United States during the Porfiriato.[95] Because cotton represented between 57% (shirting) and 79% (brown drills) of the cost of cloth in the United States, the extra cost of cotton would have represented an additional cost of 11% to 15% in these fabrics.[96]

CIVSA also faced additional costs for machinery because it had to import it from abroad. Transportation costs increased the cost of equipment at Santa Rosa by 4% to 43%, depending on the cost per unit of weight.[97] The cost of looms at Santa Rosa was approximately 20% higher than that in Burnley, Lancashire. Interestingly, except for very heavy equipment, railroad transportation costs from Veracruz to Nogales were almost as high as the steamship fare from Liverpool to Veracruz. An extra 4% over equipment costs was paid for consular charges, for insurance, and for commissions to the company's agent in Manchester and to banks.

Because machinery costs were approximately 20% higher in Mexico due to transportation costs, and because depreciation and return on capital (of 8%) were 12% of the cost of cloth per yard in the United States, the extra cost of the mill would represent an additional 2.4% over the American cost of cloth production.[98] Together the extra cost of cotton and mill construction would have accounted, at most, for an extra cost of 17.4%. Yet CIVSA's costs to produce these fabrics were on average 28% above U.S. prices for such fabrics. An important part of the difference was the result of labor productivity, partly determined by technology.

As Table 2.2 shows, the low wages in Mexico relative to those in the United States and the United Kingdom allowed CIVSA to enjoy lower costs of labor per pound of yarn spun than American or English mills.[99] CIVSA produced a considerably lower quantity of yarn per spindle than its American counterpart, but a similar figure to those produced by the mule-spinning English mill, in spite of using ring spindles.[100] CIVSA's larger production of yarn per cotton inputs indicates that CIVSA was saving on cotton, which was relatively more expensive than in the United States and England.[101]

A comparison of the employees necessary to operate a 40,000-spindle spinning mill in the United States and Japan with the workers employed in CIVSA's spinning department (40,184 spindles) explains how CIVSA paid lower labor costs than U.S. mills in yarn manufacturing (see Table 2.3). Although the number of workers employed by CIVSA was almost twice (183%) that for U.S. mills, labor costs were only 70% of those in the United States. However, the Japanese industry, paying even lower wages but not competing with Mexican mills, had lower labor costs than CIVSA (94%), in spite of employing more than twice as many workers as CIVSA (240%).

In weaving, however, lower wages at CIVSA were not enough to counterbalance the extra labor it employed relative to the U.S. industry. CIVSA (with 1,380 looms) employed almost seven times (676%) the number of workers employed in U.S. mills to tend a 1,000-loom weaving mill, and paid more than twice the wages (219%). Because wages per worker were

Table 2.2  Pounds per spindle and cost of labor per pound: CIVSA, the United States, and the United Kingdom

| Yarn | CIVSA (ring spindles) | | U.S. (ring spindles) | | U.K. (mule spindles) | | CIVSA vs. U.S. mill. | | CIVSA vs. U.K. mill. | |
| --- | --- | --- | --- | --- | --- | --- | --- | --- | --- | --- |
| | Pounds per spindle (11 hours) | Cost of labor per pound (US$) | Pounds per spindle (10 hours) | Cost of labor per pound (US$) | Pounds per spindle (10 hours) | Cost of labor per pound (US$) | Pounds per spindle | Cost of labor per pound | Pounds per spindle | Cost of labor per pound |
| Warp 29 | 0.1951 | $0.0080 | 0.2440 | $0.0151 | 0.1940 | $0.0126 | 80% | 53% | 101% | 64% |
| Warp 36 | 0.1339 | $0.0106 | 0.1730 | $0.0212 | 0.1440 | $0.0170 | 77% | 50% | 93% | 62% |
| Weft 30 | 0.1673 | $0.0088 | 0.2590 | $0.0142 | 0.1810 | $0.0135 | 65% | 62% | 92% | 65% |
| Weft 36 | 0.1121 | $0.0098 | 0.2060 | $0.0178 | 0.1370 | $0.0168 | 54% | 55% | 82% | 58% |

*Sources:* Archive of the Compañía Industrial Veracruzana S.A., Payrolls 1911 (Week 6); U.S. House of Representatives, *Cotton Manufactures* (Washington, D.C., 1912), 1:410–412. For further detail, see Aurora Gómez-Galvarriato, "The Impact of Revolution: Business and Labor in the Mexican Textile Industry, Orizaba, Veracruz, 1900–1930" (PhD diss., Harvard University, 1999), chap. 8, table 5.

*Note:* Costs presented here are the costs per pound of yarn as spun, excluding spooling or other processes beyond spinning. Data from England and the United States were taken from the most efficient mill in each country on which the Tariff Board had information.

*Table 2.3*  Employees necessary to operate textile mills in the United States, Japan, and CIVSA, 1911

|  | Spinning | | | Weaving | | |
| --- | --- | --- | --- | --- | --- | --- |
|  | Number of workers | Total daily earnings | Daily earnings per worker | Number of workers | Total daily earnings | Daily earnings per worker |
| United States | 180 | $211.51 | $1.18 | 123 | $180.24 | $1.47 |
| Japan | 794 | $139.57 | $0.18 | 850 | $151.56 | $0.18 |
| CIVSA | 330 | $148.87 | $0.45 | 832 | $395.31 | $0.48 |

*Sources:* U.S. House of Representatives, *Cotton Manufactures: Report of the Tariff Board on Schedule I of the Tariff Law* (Washington, D.C., 1912), 524, 526; Archive of the Compañía Industrial Veracruzana S.A., Payrolls, 1911 (Week 6). See Aurora Gómez-Galvarriato, "The Impact of Revolution: Business and Labor in the Mexican Textile Industry, Orizaba, Veracruz, 1900–1930" (PhD diss., Harvard University, 1999), chap. 8, tables 6 and 7.

*Notes:* Daily earnings are in U.S. dollars. Ten-hour work shift in the United States, and 11-hour shift in Japan and CIVSA. 40,000 spindles in the United States and Japan; 40,184 spindles in CIVSA; 1,000 looms in the United States and Japan; 1,380 looms in CIVSA.

higher in Mexico than in Japan, CIVSA paid more than twice the total wages Japanese mills did (261%), although it employed almost the same number of workers (98%). While American weaving mills required only 53 weavers to tend 1,000 looms, Japanese mills required 700 weavers, and CIVSA 613 weavers (to tend 1,380 looms). Thus, although American weavers earned $1.59, weavers at CIVSA $0.45, and Japanese weavers $0.19 per day, their daily cost to the mill was $84.27, $274.08, and $129.50, respectively. Labor costs at CIVSA's weaving department were far higher than in the United States or Japan.

The crucial difference between the American mill compared here and the Japanese and Mexican mills, is that the U.S. firms used Northrop automatic looms. When tending power looms, "the most time-consuming tasks of the weaver were, first, to keep looms supplied with weft shuttles and, second, to piece together broken threads. Both these operations required that the machine be stopped."[102] The Northrop system replaced the weft automatically without stopping the loom, allowing for an increase in the number of looms tended.[103]

While American weavers were tending on average of 18.87 automatic looms each, CIVSA's were tending only 2.24 power looms, and Japanese weavers 1.43. At CIVSA, as in the English mills, weavers working with plain power looms seldom tended more than four of them, while in the

United States a weaver working on automatic looms generally tended twenty of them.[104] In the United States, however, weavers working with plain power looms rarely tended fewer than six looms, more often eight.[105] A U.S. weaver tended so many looms because he (or she) tended strictly to the skilled work of weaving, and all the other work was performed by other, less-skilled workers; this way of operating was called the "American System."[106] Unskilled workers helping weavers at CIVSA and the Japanese textile mill represented only 26% and 18%, respectively, of the total labor force in the weaving department, compared to 57% in the American mill. A significant part of the difference between the number of looms tended in the United States and CIVSA may also have been due to the fact that CIVSA's weavers were not relieved of unskilled chores to the same extent American weavers were. CIVSA also produced a broader range of fabrics than American mills, which usually specialized in only certain brands. CIVSA payrolls indicate that the same weaver could produce as many as four kinds of different fabrics in a single week, which implied much additional work in resetting the loom for the different types of weave.

Overall, one can conclude that in 1911, CIVSA was less productive than the best American textile mills but not so far behind the English mills, and more productive than the Japanese mills. Lower wages for spinning helped CIVSA offset its greater labor and machine requirements per pound of yarn, but this was not the case for weaving, particularly when compared with the American industry. This, together with its greater cotton and machinery costs, made CIVSA's production costs higher than those of the American industry. Its higher labor costs compared to Japan made it less competitive than mills in that nation. Yet CIVSA's production costs were fairly similar to the sales prices of English cloth of similar kinds.

Through the study of the birth and operation of CIVSA we have analyzed how the Barcelonnette network allowed CIVSA's shareholders to build and manage a textile mill of a size and technology equivalent to the best in the world at that time, in a country with still underdeveloped financial and legal institutions. CIVSA's competitive levels were much better than the historiography on Mexico's industrialization suggests.

Perhaps there was even a chance that Mexico's Porfirian infant industry could eventually have made it to adulthood.[107] But future events in Mexico would pose serious problems for CIVSA's ability to compete internationally by creating greater disadvantages in both real wages and CIVSA's ability to introduce new technology and devise changes in the organization of labor on the shop floor.

CHAPTER 3

# The Nature of the Labor Force

INDUSTRIAL PRODUCTION REQUIRES more than businesspeople and investors. It needs labor. "The human engagement with machinery gives both labor and the machine their meaning, . . . [and] they are incomprehensible except together and historically."[1] Who were the workers who provided labor for the cotton textile mills of the Orizaba Valley?

Porfirian publications show the perceptions held about workers during that period, including the elite's stereotype about Mexican workers—as uneducated, irrational, irresponsible, and prone to alcoholism. Even the articles that defended workers shared this view. One of them explained, for instance, that the reason company stores were harmful to workers was because credit "was very dangerous when given to individuals not very reflective and of a light temperament, as our workers frequently are."[2]

Similarly the renowned intellectual Andrés Molina Enriquez considered that giving credit to workers favored their "lack of foresight and spendthrift attitude, stimulating their vices and tolerating their dissolute customs."[3] An article in the *Semana Mercantil* explained that although cooperative societies could be a good alternative to company stores, they were unlikely to appear in Mexico because they were not within "the possible personal effort that the majority of our workers can exert . . .

because of the vice of drunkenness that has them shackled, in it they spend most of their wage, [thus] they get on credit the food for them and their families."[4]

Porfirian scientists and journalists constructed a discourse that linked class and morality by conceptually isolating the illness of alcoholism and criminality from the "good" or "high" parts of Mexican society.[5] Workers' penny journals had a clear awareness of the prejudices and scorn with which the well-to-do regarded workers, and they protested against such negative preconceptions. *La Cagarruta* noted, for instance, that "those who wear shirts and have calloused hands" were called "drunkards of *pulquerías*," while "those who wear suits and frock coats, whose artistic heads are well combed and perfumed," were termed "decent people."[6] *El Diablito Bromista* complained that the subsidized press usually depicted workers as "drunkards," "lynchers," and "debased," and *El Papagayo* complained that the worker was considered "[not] a rational being, but a beast of burden."[7]

In 1907 José Neira, a prominent labor leader of the Orizaba region, wrote a letter from prison to President Porfirio Díaz in which he presented his view on industrial workers, arguing against the misconception that all workers were ignorant, lazy drunkards.[8] Like other Orizaba labor leaders of the period, he belonged to the Methodist congregation and the Mexican Liberal Party. His letter, although full of his own prejudices, is an excellent point of departure to draw a picture of the Orizaba labor force.

According to Neira there were three classes of textile workers in Mexico. The first was "workers who know how to read and write, do not drink alcohol; never miss work; and when they have a woman and children, their woman is legitimate; their children wear shoes and socks, and go to school. Their house is clean, has chairs, table, bed, and all the necessary house wear, that although humble, form part of the civilized life; they read the daily press, and they are aware of the world in which they live."[9]

Workers from the second class were those who "do not know how to read and write, or if they do it is hard to tell, because they never read or write anything; they get drunk on Saturday nights and all day on Sundays." Nevertheless during the week, according to Neira, they were judicious and hardworking; their women legitimate or not, were generally good, and helped them to work and took care of those children who were younger than 7 years old, since older children went to work as well.[10] They could be at the same time anticlerical and superstitious. They did not know the laws, and would rather take justice into their own hands than file a legal claim. If they faced any injustice, they blamed on the rich. Finally, workers from the third group were those who always drank a lot; Neira believed that these, fortunately, were very few. It is clear from his descriptions that Neira linked morality to both education and higher economic status within the three classes of workers, which was a common point of view among Porfirian intellectuals.

However, Neira's analysis of the mills' social structure included also a fourth group—white-collar employees, supervisors, and all workers whose duties involved overseeing and management, such as *revisadores* (those who inspected the quality of the goods produced), *apuntadores* (note-takers), *correiteros* (loom-fixers), *cabos* (foremen), *maestros* (masters), *rayadores* (payers), and managers. Although the employees and workers from this group generally got better wages, he did not consider them morally superior to the other workers, but quite the contrary. According to Neira the members of this fourth group, placed between the workers and industrialists, were the sole communication channel between the two, and frequently exploited and deceived both. He considered this group of workers an important source of disputes between labor and capital.

Neira tried to convey the idea that an important objective of labor organization was to encourage the passage of workers from the third and second groups to the first. He shared the ideas of other Protestant Liberals, such as journalist Simón Loza, who named tyranny, Catholicism, and alcoholism as the obstacles to the creation of new democratized citizens.[11] The great importance that unions would give to the promotion of education and the fight against alcoholism in the following decades shows that these ideas prevailed for a long time. How accurate was Neira's view?

## Origin

In contrast with most Mexican rural workers, and even some industrial workers, who lived and worked within their traditional communities, or in haciendas, mines, or factories close to their pueblos, alongside fellow laborers of similar origin, workers from the Orizaba Valley during the Porfiriato were mostly immigrants coming from many different places. Their history must therefore be thought of as the history "of *déraciné* workers, of new social formations, of improvised *compañeros* (mates), of a new sense and loyalty of class, of a new Mexico fighting to preserve the useful relations of the past, but at the same time forging new values that the workers were by themselves creating."[12] Orizaba Valley workers lacked a history as a group and were unfettered by "traditional" authority such as common moral codes or methods of organization.[13] Hence, trust, alliances, leadership, organization, and community had to be built up from scratch.

At the turn of the century, when the Río Blanco and Santa Rosa mills were founded, manufacturing workers were not readily available in the Orizaba Valley. The companies looked for them over a wide area, mostly across Mexico's central plateau. Sometimes CIVSA practiced outright recruitment, as in 1897 when it sent Alvarez to Pachuca to hire workers for its tunnel works.[14] Yet most of them came by their own means, as word of mouth spread about job opportunities in the new mills.

At first the scarcity of labor posed problems for the companies. In 1899 at the annual shareholders meeting, the CIVSA board reported that production in that year had been scarce "because, among other things, they had faced great difficulties in finding workers capable of running the machinery."[15] Yet CIVSA was gradually able to hire enough workers—1,441 by 1900, 2,112 by 1906, and by 1913, 2,311, the highest number ever. From 1893 to 1912, in Río Blanco the number of workers rose from 1,220 to 2,575, in San Lorenzo from 470 to 642, in Cocolapan from 450 to 602, and in Cerritos from 190 to 465. The number of textile workers in the Orizaba Valley cotton textile mills almost tripled from 1893 to 1912.[16]

The most highly skilled personnel came from Europe, at great cost. The first were technicians to erect the machinery acquired in Europe. Then, when the mill was ready to work, superintendents of weaving, spinning, bleaching, printing, and engraving arrived, mostly from France although some English technicians were also hired.[17] This practice was the result more of need than of chauvinism, given the great scarcity of such skills in Mexico. Whenever CIVSA found capable personnel in Mexico, it hired them. Only after the CIVSA board was certain that the required skilled employees could not be found in Mexico did it search for them in Europe.[18] In 1897, for instance, CIVSA wrote to its shareholders in Paris that workers from Europe were not needed to install the iron structures because in Mexico good workers could be found to do the job.[19] More commonly, however, CIVSA had to hire technicians in Europe. This happened in 1899, for example, when Signoret told the board that in spite of having placed several advertisements in the most important Mexican newspapers, he had not been able to find workers to run the printing machines, so he considered it necessary to bring them from Europe.[20] Foreign employees were generally paid by the month under special contracts that included paid visits to Europe every couple of years.

A large share of Neira's fourth group was made of foreigners, which must have generated a stronger aversion to them. At CIVSA, most heads of departments and superintendents were foreigners. In 1919, twenty of the twenty-eight technical and clerical employees working at Santa Rosa had non-Hispanic last names. In 1920 there were thirty-eight foreign employees working at CIDOSA's four mills.[21] However, just one echelon down all personnel were Mexican. Even highly skilled jobs, such as that of loom fixer *(correitero)*, were held entirely by Mexicans.

A list of 625 weavers from the Santa Rosa mill who were working at the mill in 1906–1907 shows that most came from the neighboring states of Puebla (40%), Oaxaca (20%), and Mexico (10%).[22] Only 14% of the weavers were originally from the Orizaba Valley, and 2% were from other regions of Veracruz. The rest came from other states, some as distant as San Luis Potosí or Jalisco.[23] Many workers came by train, such as Ernesto Palacios Garcés, who came from Apizaco, Puebla. However, several others arrived walking, such as Gonzalo San Juan Hernández, who in 1907, at the age of 9, walked with his family through the mountains for seven days (from 4:00 a.m. to 8:00 p.m.) to get from Tlaxiaco, Oaxaca, to Orizaba.[24]

Some of the workers who came to the Orizaba Valley were peasants without land, perhaps driven away from their small plots as the result of the expansion of haciendas. This was the case of Delfino Huerta's father, who worked as a peasant in the Ranch García in the state of Puebla. Around 1893 someone told him that they were hiring country people in

Río Blanco, and because his living conditions were terrible, at the age of 20 he decided to migrate together with his wife, and got a job at the mill.[25] Others, such as Gonzalo San Juan's family, had experience with textile production working as artisan woolen weavers in the small town of Santa Cruz Acayaca, Oaxaca. Just like the mill owners' Barcelonnette ancestors, they had been displaced by mechanized textile production, but in contrast with them, their alternative was to find a job as industrial workers in the new mills.[26]

Many others came from other textile mills, attracted by the region's higher wages or simply because they faced problems in the mills where they worked. By 1890 the long tradition of the mechanized textile industry in Mexico had created a pool of textile workers from which the new Porfirian mills of the turn of the century could draw. At least 41% of weavers in the sample of weavers studied came from cities and towns that had textile mills at the turn of the century, such as Etla (Oaxaca), Querétaro, or Tlalpan (Mexico).[27] This means that many of the workers hired by CIVSA already had industrial socialization and skills.

Gonzalo García Vargas is an interesting case. He had been a weaver at the San Bruno mill in Xalapa, Veracruz. His father had also been a weaver and had become the master of weaving of that mill, but because Gonzalo García Vargas liked the "free life," he left San Bruno to go to work at the Metepec mill in Atlixco, Puebla. After becoming involved in a strike there, he moved with his wife and children to work at the Santa Rosa mill, and had more children there. But he did not stay for long at Santa Rosa; soon he moved to the Cerritos mill in Nogales and later to Río Blanco. The children started working in the mills, so they stayed in the Orizaba valley together with their mother. Their father left once again, to work in first Atlixco, then at the Hormiga mill near Mexico City, and later at the Covadonga mill in Puebla. "My father went through all the mills in the Republic," recalled his son Gonzalo García Ortiz. Apparently the itinerancy of workers between mills was very common. According to him, it was usual to see people coming up and down the Camino Real, the street that joins the different mill towns in the Orizaba Valley, carrying their belongings in pillowcases, their common substitute for suitcases.[28]

Several workers in the Orizaba Valley were the sons of recent immigrants (from within Mexico), who either arrived as young children to the region or were born there. It was common for children to begin working at an early age, they soon became part of the labor force. Gonzalo García Ortiz, born in Santa Rosa in 1905, started working when he was only 7 years old as weaver helper at the Santa Rosa mill. Gonzalo San Juan, born in Tlaxiaco, Oaxaca, in 1896, got a job as doffer *(mudador)* in Nogales upon his arrival to the region, at the age of 9. Ernesto Palacios Garcés, born in Felipe Angeles, Puebla, in 1900, started working at the age of 14 in a mill in Apizaco, Tlaxcala, and after six months he moved together with his uncle to work at the Santa Rosa mill. Delfino Huerta, born in Río Blanco in 1901, got a job in the Río Blanco mill when he was 13 years old as the helper for a weaver who was a friend of his father.[29]

Immigration to the region was so large that in the period 1900–1910, when in Mexico the population increased by 11%, in Santa Rosa (Necoxtla) it increased by 37%, in Nogales by 48.5%, and in Río Blanco (Tenango) by 47%.[30] "Immigrants came carrying almost nothing material, except their own willingness to work and their blanket at the shoulder. They arrived carrying as well a lot of their own local culture, yes, but each of them their own culture, trusting in everything and for anything in their *paisanos* (their fellow countrymen), with whom they met, but untrustworthy of all the rest."[31] Workers from the same region formed networks that gave support to newcomers and established links of information and solidarity that ran from their towns of origin to the several textile mills where their *paisanos* labored. In the Orizaba Valley workers even grouped together in distinct quarters of the towns according to their regions of origin.[32]

Several studies confirm the large nomadism present among textile workers during the Porfiriato.[33] Migration was partly due to the large demand for workers in the growing textile industry combined with the lack of any formal contract between laborers and employers. Because there were no labor regulations, workers were hired without signed contracts and could be dismissed without previous notice; the firm's only responsibility was to pay their due wages. Therefore, workers changed jobs often. After 1915, as unions and labor laws began to appear, jobs became more permanent. Workers and their families increasingly began to settle down in the region, developing a new sense of belonging both to a particular town in the Orizaba Valley and to an exceptionally proud, organized, and combative Mexican working class.

Workers in the Orizaba Valley labored in the mill full-time year-round, and usually for several years. If they changed jobs, they did so within the textile industry. This contrasts with workers in other regions, who shared their time between the mills and agriculture. CIVSA employers considered mill hands at Santa Rosa less rustic than their counterparts in the Puebla mills of El León and La Covadonga, which they felt made them more belligerent. In 1921 CIVSA's general manager explained: "In spite of the constant agitation that can be observed in the state of Puebla, caused by workers from Mexico and Orizaba, life in the mills [of Puebla] is still bearable. . . . Workers there are very different from those in these two cities, given that most workers [in Puebla] are mill hands during the night and peasants during the day or vice versa, and they own or rent land in the surrounding towns, something that makes them less susceptible to red doctrines."[34] Likewise, in 1924 CIVSA's manager observed that the situation in El León and La Covadonga was "much more satisfactory than in the region of Orizaba, in spite of the intense agitation to which the working class is being subjected. Since, in general, mill hands are both factory workers and owners of a small plot which they tend by themselves, they easily refuse to use the double-edged sword that is being offered to them."[35]

## Age and Education

Youth was another trait of Orizaba Valley textile workers. At Santa Rosa, 41% of the mill's weavers in 1906–1907 were less than 20 years old; almost 60% were under 25. There were more workers under 16 than over 30. There were also many children working in the mill, 8% of the workforce in the weaving department were children under 12.[36] In 1893 children constituted 10% of textile mill workers in the state of Veracruz and 12% in the country. This figure is similar to that of children working in the U.S. South, but much larger than in New England, where children were only 4% of the workforce.[37]

The youth of CIVSA's workers appears to have been a common trait of mill workers at that time. There is an appalling similarity between the age structure of Santa Rosa workers and that of the mills in Atlixco, Puebla.[38] In age, the workers at Santa Rosa, and at textile mills in general, were closer to our present-day high school or college students than what we now would usually think of as a factory workforce.[39]

However, as the workforce of the region gained stability in the following decades, the average age of workers gradually increased. In 1900 the population in Nogales, Tenango (later named Río Blanco), and Necoxtla (later named Santa Rosa) was largely people under 30 years old. The largest age groups were young adults between 26 and 30 years old and children younger than 10 years old. These were towns with very few people above 50 years old. In contrast, by 1910 the population of these towns had aged and looked more like the national age structure; the population older than 51 increased by 261% between these two dates.[40]

Mill hands in the Orizaba Valley had a higher educational level than was common in Mexico in those times. In Mexico 78% of the population was illiterate in 1900. In contrast, in Orizaba illiteracy rates were 51%, at Río Blanco 50%, at Nogales 55%, and at Santa Rosa 62%.[41] Illiteracy rates declined considerably nationwide from 1900 to 1930, but they decreased further in the Orizaba Valley. However, the decline in illiteracy was substantially stronger for men than for women, so the gap between both increased.[42] The relatively high literacy levels in the mill towns indicate that a considerable percentage of Orizaba Valley workers would have belonged to what Neira defined as the first class. It also explains the great importance of the workers' penny-press during this period.[43]

Although several letters and articles written by workers for *El Paladín* and other workers' publications show poor spelling and a low level of education, many others tell of highly cultivated workers. Interviews with several elderly former workers in the 1970s also indicate that many workers were more well-read and sophisticated than their elementary school degrees would suggest. For example, Cocolapan weaver Rafael Mendoza, who studied until fourth grade, was an avid reader of Mexican literature and history. He was particularly fond of historic novels such as *Martín Garatuza* by Vicente Riva Palacio, and *Los Bandidos de Río Frío* by Manuel Payno. He also had read the main works of Fray Servando

Teresa de Mier, José Joaquín Fernández de Lizardi, and Rafael Delgado. He had learned English while working on the railroads; later he founded a school of languages. When he was old he wrote his memoirs, which dealt thoroughly with the Mexican Revolution in the state of Veracruz, reflecting not only his remembrances but also a good knowledge of the historiography on the subject.[44]

Gonzalo San Juan, a Cocolapan spinner, was more inclined to political writings. He recalled having read *La Conquista del Pan* by Piotr Kropotkin and the writings of the Spanish communist libertarian Federico Urales (Juan Montseny Carret), from which he took names for his daughters. He was knowledgeable about the Catalan libertarian pedagogue Francisco Ferrer Guardia, whom he admired. At his youth he received from Spain the journals *La Tiniebla*, *La Madre Tierra*, and *Ideas*, and from the United States he got *Solidaridad*.[45]

## Gender and Marital Status

Textile workers in the Orizaba Valley were mostly male. At CIDOSA, only 6% of its workers were female in 1893 and only 2% in 1920.[46] At Santa Rosa, 4% were female in 1900, and this figure increased to 5.4% in the 1920s.[47] As Table 3.1 shows, the percentage of women working in the mills differed by region (north, west, and center). Puebla and Tlaxcala had even fewer female workers than the Orizaba valley mills. In the rest of Mexico, particularly in Mexico's Northern and Western states, textile companies hired a higher percentage of women.[48] The female-to-male ratios in the west and north of Mexico were closer to those in the New England and southern mills of the United States than to those in Veracruz, Puebla, and Tlaxcala (see Table 3.1).

An econometric analysis of the Mexican textile industry using state data for the period 1925–1934 indicates that women tended to be a smaller part of the labor force in larger, higher-paying mills.[49] Given that both variables were strongly related to the level of unionization, this result could suggest a negative relationship between unions' strength and female participation in the industry. However, it could also indicate that when wages were high enough to support the family, women ceased to work in the mills. The econometric analysis indicates that in the west of

*Table 3.1*   Age-sex composition of the cotton textile labor force

|  | 1893 | | | 1925 | | |
|---|---|---|---|---|---|---|
|  | Female | Children | % of total workers | Female | Children | % of total workers |
| Puebla-Tlaxcala | 1.5% | 13.9% | 16.9% | 3.5% | 11.5% | 33.9% |
| Veracruz | 6.3% | 9.5% | 14.4% | 3.6% | 5.2% | 17.1% |
| Federal District | 19.2% | 7.6% | 10.2% | 27.2% | 6.8% | 16.3% |
| State of Mexico | 22.0% | 12.0% | 9.0% | 11.4% | 3.3% | 4.3% |
| Coahuila | 30.7% | 14.6% | 7.4% | 25.8% | 7.3% | 5.5% |
| Querétaro | 18.5% | 7.4% | 5.6% | 33.5% | 5.7% | 2.9% |
| Jalisco | 34.0% | 8.2% | 5.0% | 49.6% | 5.3% | 5.9% |
| Guanajuato | 26.5% | 8.5% | 4.9% | 34.0% | 0.0% | 1.2% |
| Chihuahua | 32.8% | 15.8% | 4.6% | 22.3% | 7.5% | 0.7% |
| Durango | 44.5% | 23.5% | 3.1% | 35.3% | 6.5% | 1.6% |
| Nuevo León | 29.8% | 8.5% | 2.4% | 46.8% | 0.0% | 2.6% |
| Mexico total | 18.9% | 11.9% | 100% | 16.4% | 7.8% | 100% |
| U.S. South | 49.9% | 12.4% | | 36.7% | 2.5% | |
| New England | 50.1% | 3.5% | | 45.9% | 2.5% | |

*Sources:* México, Secretaría de Hacienda y Crédito Público, Dirección General de Estadística, *Anuario estadístico de la República Mexicana,* 1894; México, Secretaría de Hacienda y Crédito Público, Departamento de Impuestos Especiales, Sección de Hilados y Tejidos, "Estadísticas del ramo de hilados y tejidos de algodón y de lana," typewritten reports, 1925; Gavin Wright, *Old South New South: Revolutions in the Southern Economy since the Civil War* (New York, 1986), 139.

*Notes:* Children in Mexico means younger than 12 years old; in the U.S. means younger than 15. Data for the U.S. corresponds to the years 1890 and 1920.

the country, when men's wages in alternative jobs increased, women tended to replace them at the mills. In contrast, in the center an increase in male wages meant a decrease in female labor participation in the mills, perhaps because as family incomes were larger, female labor became less necessary to the family's subsistence. This must have been the result of a more negative social stigma against women working in the industry in these latter regions, and underlines the importance between material conditions and the discourse of female honor and sexual morality.[50]

In Mexico's cotton textile industry, as a whole, the percentage of female workers declined between 1893 and 1925 from 19% to 16%. This declining trend continued through the following decades, until the percentage of women in the textile workforce was only 2.5% by 1965. According to Dawn Keremitsis, the decline was a result of the introduction of paternal welfare legislation and of increased protectionism, which reduced factories' need to reduce labor costs.[51] However, at least from 1893 to 1925 it was also the consequence of an increase of the share of the labor force employed in the textile industry in those states such as Puebla and Veracruz, with a lower participation of women in the labor force.

Neira's view on wage-earning women helps explain these findings. According to him the wives and children of what he called the second and third class of workers needed to work to complement the families' incomes. But women and children who had husbands and fathers who belonged to the first class of workers could stay at home or go to school because the family income was enough to support them. Thus, according to him, the ideal situation was for women and children to not work outside their homes. This suggests that in the Orizaba Valley, just as in Medellín, Colombia, prevailed a similar "idealized image of a woman who depended on the benevolent protection of a male provider."[52] Yet in the Orizaba Valley it was not the result of mill-owner paternalism influenced by social Catholic teachings. In contrast, this way of thinking, already present in the Protestant-Liberal labor leaders of the first decade of the twentieth century, was prevalent in the ideology and practices of the Orizaba Valley's textile unions, as we will see.

Women who worked at Santa Rosa concentrated in a few positions. In 1905, the 70 female mill workers were in mixed-sex occupations. They were half of the drawing machine tenders, 23% of the spooling machine tenders *(cañoneros)*, and only 3% of the weavers. In contrast, by 1928 the 113 women working in the mill concentrated in a smaller number of occupations that were female-dominated. Almost 60% of them were now spooling machine tenders and 20% were drawing machine tenders. These occupations had almost completely feminized, 97% and 72% of workers in each of these jobs, respectively, were women.[53] Gonzalo García Ortíz considered that "there was a lot of respect for women in the spooling machine tenders department, since there were only women in it, and the department was separate and surrounded by a wall so men could not get there to interfere, only the overseer *(cabo)* was a male because there were no women who could do that job, since they were only occupied in making knots." According to him there were only a few women in the mill who liked to joke with men, most of them were submissive, modest, and shy.[54]

The evolution of female chores at Santa Rosa contrasts with what happened in Mexico City between 1879 and 1930, where the variety of industries in which women worked increased to include more mixed-sex occupations. Female-dominated industries were understood as conducive to protecting female morality, so the widening of occupations for women in Mexico City has been interpreted as a change in the cultural understanding of working women.[55] The ways women's occupations evolved in Santa Rosa tell that views on female labor did not change in the Orizaba Valley at the same pace as they did in Mexico City. This could have been partly a consequence of the supremacy of the Confederación Regional Obrera Mexicana (CROM) in the Orizaba Valley textile unions during the 1920s; in Mexico City in those sectors where the CROM prevailed, such as the cigarette industry, women were kept out of skilled positions and gradually dismissed. In addition, women who joined the CROM were less likely to serve in leadership positions than they had in other worker confederations such as the Confederación General de Trabajadores (CGT).[56]

For women, working in the Orizaba mills, in an environment where there were so few of them, must have been very difficult. They often suffered sexual harassment from their bosses. A 1906 letter to *El Paladín* told of a foreman in Río Blanco's spooling department who "tormented and besieged with fines and fired" those women (whether single or married) not willing to accept "certain propositions" from that man who "attempts to become a Sultan with his respective harem."[57] A 1907 letter to *El Paladín* reported that a foreman in Nogales shoved away a woman who did not want to "correspond to his attentions" and spoke obscenely to her. This young woman, the letter continued, "had the civic courage to protest to the authorities against him, but [they] only advised the enamored foreman *(cabo enamorado)* to abstain from doing it again."[58] In 1908 a Mrs. Marín, a doorkeeper in Río Blanco, was fired and evicted from her house "because she did not agree with the bad customs of a certain individual."[59] This man, Manuel, hit her with a mallet, kicked her, and insulted her. The letter to *El Paladín* explained that the foremen's favorites were allowed to lend money inside the mill at a 25% interest rate, all of which was forbidden, and that he received a share of the profits. The other women received a scolding and were threatened with dismissal. Moreover, the foreman deliberately undercounted the number of meters in their rolls, keeping the pay difference to himself.[60]

Unionization does not appear to have improved the female workers' situation. In 1916 the labor inspector, the manager of Río Blanco, and the president of the labor union decided to fire four women because their behavior "was unsuitable both for the internal order of the department in which they labored, and for the interests of the company." According to their report, "[as] a result of certain intimacy [between them and their superiors], they did not follow orders any more, and their work was deficient."[61] To prevent similar problems in the future, the committee held a meeting at which they agreed to dismiss the other eight women who worked in that department and to replace them with men.[62]

As for marital status, because of their youth, most CIVSA workers in 1907 were single (59%). However, relatively fewer women in the weavers sample were married (17%) than men (29%). In contrast, the percentage of widows (9.4%) was three times higher than that of widowers (3.1%). There were many fewer girls (1.9% of female workers) than boys (8.8% of male workers) employed at the mill. Some women with small children worked at the mills and were given permission to go to the door twice a day (at 10:00 a.m. and 5:00 p.m.) to breastfeed their babies.[63]

Women in the Orizaba Valley mill municipalities of Nogales, Tenango, and Santa Rosa married when they were between 22 and 23 years old, on average. Men married when they were 27 to 28 years old, on average. Ages of marriage both for men and women were a little bit lower than those in more urban Xalapa, where men's average age of marriage was 30 and that of women 24, but higher than in Tepetzintla, a rural town in the north of Veracruz, where men married, on average, when they were 24 years old, and women when they were 18. From 1880 to 1940 there is not a significant change in these figures.[64]

Most people, however, did not marry before forming a family. Between 1900 and 1930 in Necoxtla (Santa Rosa) and Tenango (Río Blanco), 78% of the children born were born out of wedlock. In contrast, in the municipalities of Veracruz and Tepetzintla the percentage of illegitimate children between 1900 and 1930 were 62% and 41%, respectively.[65] Even though so many people were born out of wedlock in the Orizaba mill towns, workers' interviews show that there were strong prejudices against it, because they referred to their half-siblings as "bastard" brothers or sisters.[66]

Getting married was related not only to holding more traditional values, as the low figure of Tepetzintla suggests, but also to being more educated and wealthier. In the Orizaba Valley textile towns the percentage of parents who were able to sign the birth certificate averaged only 57% for the fathers and 15% for the mothers between 1900 and 1930. In contrast, the percentage of husbands and wives who could sign their marriage certificate was 83% for the first and 56% for the second.[67] Gonzalo San Juan Hernández recalled that he was planning to marry his fiancé in 1919, but after several years had gone by, he had been unable to gather the money for the wedding. Thus he talked to her and they decided to live together without getting married.[68] If Neira considered it a requirement for workers to have legitimate children in order to be part of the first class, then very few would have belonged to it.

Because most of the mill towns' populations were factory workers, and most of them were young and single, one would expect the towns' population to be also mostly male. However, this was not the case. The percentage of Santa Rosa's population that was female was 49.2% in 1900 and 49.6% in 1910, and similar rates prevailed in Nogales and Veracruz. In Tenango, where the Río Blanco mill was located, 46.5% of the population was female in 1900 and 48.5% in 1910.[69] The increase in the percentage of female population between 1900 and 1910 indicates a tendency for workers to live in families as the towns matured.

Young, single workers in the Orizaba district mill towns generally lived not on their own but with their families, and families usually had several members working at the mills. This was the case of Gonzalo García Ortiz's family; in 1909 his father was as a weaver at Cerritos, his brother Angel and his sister Herlinda were weavers at Río Blanco, and his brother Félix was a weaver at Santa Rosa. After a couple of years, when his father left, one of his brothers died, and the other brother joined the Revolution, Gonzalo and his sister Isaura had to start working as weavers' helpers.[70]

In 1900, 73% of the male population of Santa Rosa worked at the mill, whereas only 5% of the female population did, and in 1910 these figures were 83% and 2%, respectively.[71] Although relatively few women worked in the mills, many more worked outside their homes. Several women in the Orizaba Valley worked as seamstresses for two garment workshops, La Suiza and El Castillo, making shirts and trousers.[72] La Suiza, which by 1915 was already an important establishment, hired at its peak in the mid 1920s between 150 and 175 seamstresses.[73] El Castillo, founded in 1925, was smaller, perhaps half the size of La Suiza. Seamstresses from La Suiza organized a union by 1915, and in 1925 they invited the seamstresses from El Castillo to form part of the same union.[74] There were also several smaller workshops, such as the one established by the Spaniard Don Mauricio Cuervo, and the one owned by "the Arab" Jacobo Diff, each of which employed around 35 seamstresses, and another one called El Punto specialized in underwear. Several women worked at the workshops the whole day (eight hours), but because they were paid by the piece, they often carried home some of their chores to finish them during the night. Others, particularly married women, went to the workshops only to get the materials required, worked at home with their own sewing machine, and handed the finished work back on the next morning.[75]

During the 1920s a considerable number of women from the Orizaba Valley also worked as coffee sorters. In 1930, 515 women worked at the three coffee mills in the region: Guillermo Boesch Sucs. S en C., Desmanche de Café Hard y Band, and El Modelo, Beneficiadora de Café. Two of these Orizaba coffee mills had unionized by 1936, and they had 400 women working in them.[76] Finally, other women worked as merchants in the municipal markets, established small diners in their homes for workers, worked as cookers, cleaners, or wet nurses in rich people's homes, washed and ironed cloth for a fee, made tortillas and *gorditas*[77] for sale, or used their Singer machines at home to sew dresses and other "made-to-measure" garments for their family and for sale.[78] Many women raised chicken and pigs at their homes to eat or sell, an important form of family savings.[79]

Although many women worked outside their homes, none of the 1,436 birth certificates and only one of the 228 marriage certificates collected between 1870 and 1930 from the Orizaba textile towns indicates an occupation for the mothers or wives, while most of them do for the fathers or husbands.[80] This reflects a social perception of working women (and particularly of working mothers or wives) as something not wholly natural or socially accepted. It also indicates that statistics on working women during the period could be seriously biased downward.

Women at the Santa Rosa mill earned an average of 48% less than males.[81] Part of the wage difference was due to the fact that women generally were assigned to lower positions than men, such as spooler machine tenders. Yet there was also an important wage difference for men and women working in the same positions. Male weavers earned on average 18% more than women weavers between 1900 and 1930. Most of the difference in earnings (78%) can be attributed to the lower number of looms women were given to tend.[82] However, women's per-loom wages were still below men's. Women could have been given lower-quality cloth to weave or older or narrower looms to tend, or they could have worked less intensively or effectively. Further research is necessary to disentangle this issue.

The difference in male and female wages diminished over time, but it did so most from 1926 to 1927, when the male-to-female wage gap went from 42% to 18%, remaining at a low level of around 23% in the following years. This was the result more of a leveling of male and female wages working in similar positions, than of a change in the jobs generally carried out by women.[83] This might have been the result of the implementation of the wage list established by the Workers' and Industrialists' Convention of 1925–1927.

## Income Levels, Job Tenure, and Labor Mobility

It would be wrong to think of Santa Rosa's workers as an aggregate with similar income levels, as Neira well understood. Workers at CIVSA earned very different wages. Average weekly wages from a sample of selected positions ranged from 1.63 to 30 pesos in 1905. Higher wages implied hierarchy levels, and/or greater skills, as the posts of foreman and loom fixer exemplify, respectively. Lower wages went to jobs generally carried out by boys, such as that of doffer. In between there were two ranges of salaries, one at 3 to 6 pesos and the other at 6 to 9 pesos. The difference had to do with skill and seniority. For example, the first range would include the carpenter's helper *(peón)* and the second would include the carpenter *(oficial)*. Almost half the weavers—those who tended more than two looms—earned more than 6 pesos. Those who tended four looms earned more than 9 pesos, although very few weavers made more than 15 pesos weekly.

There were considerable differences in the weekly earnings of workers whose names appeared on the payroll lists. In 1905, 14% of workers earned less than 3 pesos per week, 44% earned 3–6 pesos, and 42% earned more than 6 pesos per week; half of the latter earned 6 to 9 pesos weekly. Differences between wages increased from 1905 to 1925.[84]

From the available sample of workers, we know that in early 1907 the average number of years workers had been at the mill was four. In 1923, average job tenure had doubled, and 27% of mill hands in the sample had worked in Santa Rosa for over twelve years. The increase in job tenure in the 1920s is partly explained by the longer time Santa Rosa had been in operation, but it was also a consequence of the larger role of unions and the implementation of labor laws that gave workers greater stability in their jobs.

The stories of the Orizaba Valley workers who were interviewed in the 1970s indicate that they progressed to higher-paying occupations in the mills as they aged. If they entered the mill young and did not know a trade, they first worked in low-skilled chores and found ways to learn the skills required for advancement to a better-paying job, which meant finding a worker who would take them on as helpers or apprentices. Many of them also attended night school for some years to learn reading, writing, arithmetic, and other skills, such as drawing, that would help them get a better job.

Ernesto Palacios Garcés, who attended school only until the second grade, started working at the age of 14 as a peon at the San Lorenzo mill, carrying material from the weaving department to the boilers. After three years he became a weaver, and he remained on that job until he retired at the age of 60. He tended three looms at first but later he tended four.[85] Gonzalo San Juan started working as doffer *(mudador)* at the San Lorenzo mill when he was 9, then later became an apprentice of *engomados* (slasher sizing) at Colcolapan. Then he joined the Revolution. When he returned, he got a job as a floor sweeper, then as a peon, and then as a spinner. When he was around 30 years old he attended night school for several years and learned typewriting and shorthand. Finally he became a second master of spinning.[86] Macario Ventura Ochoa began to work as a spinner helper when he was around 15 years old, and after a few years he became a spinner. Then at the age of 20 he started to learn about machinery transmissions and cables, working as the helper of a cable fixer *(cablero)*; after some years he became a cable fixer himself, and he remained in that position for forty-eight years.[87] Valentín Cueto began to work at selling newspapers and carrying baskets when he was a child. Then at the age of 15, his mother, who had also worked in the factory, got him a job as doffer. After some time he became a cloth folder *(doblador textil)*, then a cloth arranger *(acomodador)*, and finally, after having attended night school, where he learnt linear drawing, he became an engraver *(grabador)*.[88] Luis Garcés Velázquez began to work at the age of 16 at Santa Rosa as a peon, then he became a spinning helper, then a helper of a spinning machine mechanic *(armador de trócil)*, and finally a spinning machine mechanic himself.[89]

Climbing to better positions had to do with hard work, learning new skills, and having a higher level of education. It also depended on knowing the correct people in the mill and having good relations with overseers and directors—and, after 1915, also with the union representatives. It was as well a matter of time, because once the echelon system was established by the unions, workers had to wait their turn to climb to the next level within their trade.

The analysis of the information available on 135 weavers working at the Santa Rosa mill in 1923 shows that workers who remained in the job for several years gained higher wages because they tended more looms and were given finer cloth to weave. It was extremely unusual for a worker who had been at the mill for over seven years to tend fewer than three looms, and those who tended four looms had been at the mill at least three years. In 1923 only workers with five years at the mill earned more than 3 pesos a day (167 pesos in 2010, or \$14 in 2010 U.S. dollars) and workers who had been in the mill for over eight years earned more than 4 pesos a day (222 pesos in 2010, or \$18 in 2010 U.S. dollars).[90] These figures would amount, respectively, to three and four times the 2010 daily minimum wage in Veracruz.

Gonzalo García Ortiz provides a good example of how promotions in the weaving department worked out. When he was around 7 years old, his brother-in-law, Crisóforo Carrillo, who was a loom tender, arranged for a weaver to teach Gonzalo to work with the looms at the Santa Rosa mill. He first worked as a helper, then as first apprentice, and then as apprentice helper. During his three years as apprentice Gonzalo worked for four weavers earning 10 cents a week. Apprentices wages were paid by the weavers, not by the company, and sometimes were severe. He recalled that with one of his masters, the "Chino Ortega," he got, besides the 10 cents, a thousand kicks every week. Finding the situation unbearable, he convinced his brother-in-law to talk with Mr. Guillermo Brom, the mill's director, to give him one loom to tend. He showed good abilities at work, so after only a week he was given two looms to tend. By then he earned 7.20 pesos a week. Soon after, a law was passed that forbade children to work, and he had to stop working. To solve the problem, his mother went to see Mr. Facundo Hernández, the first secretary general of the union, and convinced him that the family needed Gonzalo's wage. Gonzalo was allowed to continue working, and after some time his turn in the echelon list arrived and he began to tend three looms. At this moment, when he was 15 years old, he joined the night school, where he studied up to the third grade of elementary school. Later, through the echelon process, he was given four looms to tend. Then he became interested in being a loom fixer, and he registered in the echelon list to get a position as a loom fixer helper. He recalled that he had to wait for fourteen loom fixer helpers to die or leave the mill to get the job. After some more years he became a loom fixer.

## Behavior

The list of weavers of Santa Rosa kept after 1907 had a line on which the superintendent wrote down some notes on the workers' behavior, similar to a school report card. They wrote down if the workers' conduct was very good, good, regular, or bad, and if the workers were drunkard, violent, disdainful, coarse, troublemakers, or often absent. Those reports indicated that 87.6% of workers were considered to have good or very good behavior and only 5.5% were reported to have been violent or troublemakers; 95.6% of women rated as well or very well behaved, compared to 86.5% of men. Against the common notion at that time that alcoholism was prevalent among lower-class Mexicans, only 2.8% of workers were reported to have been drunkards.[91] In four of those cases, annotations in the margin read "drunkard but works well."[92] This suggests that very few workers belonged to what Neira defined as the third class, and against the Porfirian common held notion that workers were prone to alcoholism.

The picture given by these reports must be complemented by comments sometimes written about the workers. These annotations tell of a violent climate in Santa Rosa between 1906 and 1916. Some of these annotations seem to have been taken from the sensationalist press, rather than from a report on workers. By 1916 nine workers from the list had been caught stealing cloth from the mill and were fired, and some of them were imprisoned.[93] Seven workers from the list were reported to have killed or seriously injured someone, and twenty-eight workers were reported to have been killed (4.5% of total workers in the sample), a figure that contrasts with only ten who died because of disease (1.6%).

Some of the murders appear to have been the result of disputes between workmates. In 1910 José Ma. Luna killed Andrés González, whose name also appeared on the list. Enrique Cortés killed Eduardo Beristain in Santa Rosa by stoning him. Sacramento Rodríguez killed Aniceto García alias "El Magistrado." In 1908 Pedro Osorio killed Joaquín González, from Mexico City. Luis Guerrero injured José Ma. Navarro with a knife. Other cases appear to have been the result of family disputes; Arturo Alarcón killed his wife, Concepción Corona, in 1908 at a town festival *(feria)*. Dominga Santiago killed her husband, Paulino Castellanos, with nine stabs, aided by her mother and sister. The fact that names of the victims were provided indicates that these events must have been well known in the Orizaba region. Simón Feria, whom the report described as "hardworking but brave *(trabajador pero valiente),*" was killed by Pedro Guzmán with twelve stabs in 1909. The Orizaba Valley seems to have been violent, but workers appear to have been no safer elsewhere. Two workers were killed when visiting their native regions; Prisciliano Aquinas from Tuxtepec, Puebla, was murdered in "San Andrés Cacalsupan [*sic*]," Puebla, and Sixto Galván from Oaxaca was killed in his hometown.

Other workers died because of government repression. The list reported that Mariano Vallejo, aged 27, was "killed on the 7th of January

1907 by the 13th battalion," and in the margin next to Justo González's name, aged 20, it said, "killed rebel." José Ríos, aged 20, was "sent to Quintana Roo on September 17, 1907" together with the two brothers Enrique and Mauro Manzano, aged 29 and 16, respectively. Being sent to Quintana Roo's working camps was almost the same as receiving the label "killed," because few survived the experience. Dolores Juárez, aged 35, was also made prisoner in September 1907.

As we have seen, the workers of the Orizaba Valley mill towns were mostly immigrants who had recently arrived from many different parts of the country. Some of them had been agricultural workers, but a large share of them had already an experience working in a textile mill. They were more educated than the average Mexican, and they were relatively young. Most of them lived with their families, and although not many women worked in the mills, a large share of them worked outside their homes. Most couples did not marry before forming a family, a larger share than in traditional towns. There were important differences between workers in terms of income, skills, and education. Yet it was possible for workers to improve their status as time went by acquiring new skills and attending formal schooling. Most workers were considered well behaved and hardworking by their supervisors, and very few were alcoholics. Putting together all these characteristics we get a picture of the Orizaba Valley mill towns as vibrant, young, educated, and nonconformist working communities.

# CHAPTER 4

# Labor Organization during the Porfiriato

Textile workers from the Orizaba mills began to organize and attempt to change their working and living conditions almost as soon as the regions' looms began running. Because many of the workers who came to the Orizaba Valley had previously been employed in manufacturing jobs, they brought with them an organizational experience that quickly bore its first fruits. Thus factories started experiencing strikes very shortly after opening. A strike broke out in San Lorenzo in 1881, the year of its inauguration, in Cerritos in September 1884, in Río Blanco in 1898, and in Santa Rosa in 1899, when the factory had been in operation for only three months.[1]

In 1898 José Rumbia, a Methodist priest and radical Liberal, arrived in Orizaba and started organizing a Methodist congregation that became a unique space where workers talked about the problems that affected their daily lives and about their labor relations in the factories. He soon gained a reputation among workers as someone they could count on. That year Río Blanco strikers named him, together with Manuel Avila, a Methodist worker, as their representatives to voice their complaints against an increase in the fines for cloth defects that the company wanted to impose. In 1900 Rumbia established a school for workers' children at Río Blanco and a night school at the public jail. He also encouraged workers to celebrate civic liberal festivities, such as the thirtieth anniversary of Benito Juárez's death on July 18, 1902, where he gave a speech praising the democratic rights that the 1857 Constitution guaranteed. The Methodist congregation, which by 1905 had around sixty active members and many more sympathizers, became one of the few places where workers could talk openly about their collective problems in the mills and in their community.[2]

Companies were confident of government support against worker protest. In 1884 the army expediently arrived at Cerritos to repress the strike.[3] For Díaz's government, industrial companies brought prosperity to the nation and its workers, and therefore deserved its assistance. For Porfirio Díaz, harmony should exist between capital and labor, because, as he said in CIVSA's inaugural speech, companies "provide jobs, and make the happiness of many families, by giving the proletarian class the means to defend themselves from the greater instigators of vice that are idleness and misery." He praised the foreigners who had built enterprises in Mexico, saying they should be considered "apostles of labor," and expressed the hope that the day would come when entrepreneurial workers would establish factories of their own.[4]

## The Revolution of 1906: From "Operarios" to "Obreros"

It appears that total calm had reigned in the Orizaba Valley between its early strikes and 1906, when an outburst of workers' discontent took several forms: strikes, newspaper articles, and the formation of a powerful organization, the Gran Círculo de Obreros Libres (GCOL). Furthermore, this phenomenon appears to have taken place not only in the Orizaba Valley but also in such distant regions as Cananea, Sonora, and San Luis Potosí. Why did so much opposition break out at the same time after so many years of apparent calm? Although economic growth began to slow down in 1906 relative to the previous year, there was not a clear economic downturn until the following year, when the economic crisis began. Political factors, more than economic, must explain the surge in the labor movement, especially when considering that the Mexican Liberal Party (Partido Liberal Mexicano, PLM), founded in 1905 by a group of intellectuals against the Porfirian Regime, was a catalyst in the organization of the strikes.[5]

Through their clandestine newspapers—*Regeneración, El Colmillo Público, El Hijo del Ahuizote, El Paladín,* and others—the PLM and the Liberal clubs that preceded it had been able to exert an important influence on the working class. Moreover, several of the leaders of the labor movement throughout the country had joined the PLM's ranks, sent it monetary support, and presented the party's program, published in July 1906, as part of their labor objectives.[6] Whether or not these strikes were part of a revolution planned by the PLM leaders from their exile in the United States, as the government believed, they spread throughout the country in 1906, like a contagion, making it "the year of strikes," as Rodney Anderson called it.[7]

In the early 1900s several liberals from Orizaba, mostly professionals from the middle class, formed the Liberal Mutualist Circle. Among its founders were Rafael Tapia, a saddler, Gabriel Gavira, a carpenter, Sánchez Gutiérrez, a lawyer, Miguel Atienza, a notary, Manuel O. Nieto, Angel Juarico, and three physicians, Carlos Ramírez, Nicolás Valerio Lara, and Manuel Puga. Its objectives were to "fight ignorance and vice, and to exalt patriotism among the people by celebrating festivities in honor of the heroes of the motherland."[8] They founded a free night school for workers and a library, and organized yearly festivities to celebrate the birth of Benito Juárez.

Between 1903 and 1908, many letters were sent by workers from the Orizaba district to *El Paladín,* a radical newspaper in Mexico City, complaining about working conditions. This newspaper even opened a special column devoted to labor issues in the Orizaba Valley factories.[9] In these letters, workers wrote about the Círculo Liberal Mutualista in Orizaba, showing that in spite of its middle-class origin, the liberal circle had built an important base among workers. Letters also talked about the liberal Club Melchor Ocampo, formed by "a group of honest and honorable workers."[10]

In spite of strict government control, dissident voices started emerging from these groups. A letter from workers of Río Blanco to *El Paladín* reported that, as part of the celebrations for the centennial anniversary of Benito Juárez, the Club Melchor Ocampo organized a soirée at the Plaza Theater in Orizaba. When the club asked local authorities for permission to use the theater, they were asked to submit in advance copies of all the speeches that were going to be given there. Members of the club gave them false copies, then made uncensored speeches at the meeting.

"How the innate eloquence of the oppressed burst forth!" The official representatives who attended the meeting "were in the rack; they twisted as if their seats were full of needles, and sweated as if they were in the anteroom of Satan." According to this account, one of the speakers, "a patriot named Aguila . . . asked in the name of Juárez, what we all ask, justice! He demanded that the laws of the Reform (the 1857 Constitution) be fulfilled, and that small children of 8 to 9 years old, who are admitted to work in the mills, not be deprived of instruction." "Of course," the report continued, "several of these self-sacrificing and determined citizens, lovers of their sacred doctrines, paid for their boldness by being expelled from the mill on the following day. Only by a miracle were they saved from being imprisoned as rebels by Don Carlos Herrera [the political chief of Orizaba] following the inveterate custom of the *caciquillos* [petty chiefs]."[11]

From Aguila's speech, it is clear that the Club Melchor Ocampo was one of the hundreds of liberal clubs that had been created after the Liberal club Ponciano Arriaga, which had been founded in San Luis Potosí in 1900 by Antonio Díaz Soto y Gama, Camilo Arriaga, and Juan Sarabia, and later joined by Jesús and Enrique Flores Magón. This was to become the origin of an important movement of opposition to Díaz's government that crystallized in the creation of the PLM.[12]

Writing or reading *El Paladín* was considered a serious offense, yet many workers committed the offense readily, as the frequent letters sent to it indicate. Letters were signed with pseudonyms because, as "those who do not crumple" *(los que no se arrugan)* expressed, "if we do not sign letters it is for the simple reason that in current times there is no respect for the freedom of thought." It is impossible to "attack the petty sultans *(sultancillos)* without being exposed to multiple vexations," but "between anonymous and pseudonymous there lies an abysm."[13]

Sunday meetings in the Methodist congregation for Río Blanco were a point of reunion between workers and PLM affiliates such as José Neira, who had met Camilo Arriaga in Mexico City in 1904. In April 1906 in one of these meetings a group of workers decided to organize a workers' association.[14] From the beginning they were divided about the objectives the organization should have. José Rumbia and Andrés Mota, the owner of the house where workers met, wanted it to be a reformist organization similar to other mutualist societies, arguing that otherwise they would soon face government repression. But Manuel Avila, Genaro and Atanasio Guerrero, and José Neira wanted it to be more radical and oppose the abuses of the employers. To resolve the issue, a vote was taken, and a majority voted in favor of an association with a more combative character. The association was named Gran Círculo de Obreros Libres (GCOL), a name that recalled the Gran Círculo de Obreros that, thirty-four years earlier, had been created in the Valley of Mexico, and thus showed the sense of continuity in the Mexican labor movement that its founders wanted to impart to the public and its members.

To protect the organization, they decided that it should have two programs: one public, one secret.[15] The public GCOL program set the following goals: (1) establish a newspaper; (2) establish a system of independent cooperative societies in all the factories that would jointly make merchandise purchases; (3) create a central administration of the GCOL in Mexico City formed by a representative from each of the ten factories; (4) establish a system of compulsory savings among all its associates; (5) found a school and a library in every factory; (6) establish baths, gyms, and parks in the factory towns; (7) establish in Mexico City an asylum for workers who could not work any longer because of their age or a disability caused by a labor accident; (8) establish in Mexico City a hospital to treat all diseases, including alcoholism.[16] In contrast, the secret program, which was known only within the GCOL's closest circle, called for maintaining relations with the PLM and defined as its main objective the organization of workers against capitalism and against the dictatorship of Porfirio Díaz. The GCOL maintained close clandestine relations with the Revolutionary Junta of the PLM in exile in the United States.[17] Manuel Avila was elected president of the first GCOL board and José Neira, the leading advocate of the more radical position, was elected vice president. However, the sudden death of Manuel Avila a month later left José Neira as its president.[18] Soon the GCOL established branches in the nearby mills of San Lorenzo and Santa Rosa and at El Dique in Jalapa, the state capital.

The GCOL achieved its first victory in May when through its intervention an unpopular supervisor of the Río Blanco mill was reprimanded by the mill's administrator for intentionally injuring a worker. In the following months several strikes broke out in the Orizaba Valley. From the descriptions of these strikes, they seem to have been spontaneous outbursts of unorganized workers' discontent. But because so many strikes occurred right after the GCOL was formed, this organization must have had an influence on them.

On May 17, workers at San Lorenzo struck when employers tried to impose on them the task of cleaning machinery three times a day. Workers were paid by piece, so spending time cleaning the machinery reduced their income. During the same month, workers at the Santa Gertrudis jute mill struck because the factory wanted to reduce their wages. On June 1, workers in the spinning department of Santa Rosa also struck. They claimed that they were given very poor material to work with, and that despite this, superintendents wanted superior quality thread from it, as if they could become "silk worms." Ten of these spinners were imprisoned for refusing to return to work.[19]

Early in June, fulfilling the first objective the GCOL had established in its program, the first issue of the association's newspaper, *La Revolución Social,* appeared.[20] Neira ran the paper, assisted by Porfirio Meneses and Juan Olivares. Its main articles, written by Meneses and Neira, denounced working conditions in the mills and placed the blame not only on industrialists but also on the government, and did not reject violence as a means to end the injustice.[21] "El Corresponsal" (another anonymous worker) reported to *El Paladín* that this new journal "presented a picture of all the inequities that reign inside the mills [and] expressed the aspirations of the people."[22] The newspaper obviously aroused fears among the mill's managers and the government.

On June 4 another strike broke out at San Lorenzo. Ropiot, the superintendent of the weaving department, closed one of the two doors at the entrance to the department when the whistle blew, leaving several workers outside. The weavers who were able to enter protested, stopped the looms, and walked out of the mill down to Río Blanco where CIDOSA's central offices were. Soon the *rurales* (mounties) arrived to dissolve the protest. Workers appointed a commission to talk with Mr. Harrington, the manager of CIDOSA. Neira, GCOL's president, and Carlos Herrera, Orizaba's political chief *(jefe político),* joined the commission, and after difficult negotiations Mr. Harrington promised that no worker would be fined as a consequence of that day's incidents.[23]

On June 14, one day after workers had come back to work, the government sent the 4th, 6th, and 9th Corps of rurales to apprehend the GCOL's board while they held a secret meeting.[24] The government ordered the arrest of José Neira, Porfirio Meneses, J. A. Olvera, Juan Olivares, and Anastasio Guerrero, who had been the authors of several of the "seditious" articles. All but Porfirio Meneses fled before being caught, because information "filtered in" from police forces. Nine more workers were imprisoned because they belonged to the Club Melchor Ocampo or were considered suspects, but all were soon freed because the district judge could find no legal charges to make against them.[25] Soon companies adopted policies to purge from their mills any workers considered rebels *(revoltosos).* They made lists of rebellious workers and sent them to Orizaba's political chief. These workers were immediately laid off.[26]

The confiscation of the printing shop where *La Revolución Social* was produced was no easier for the government authorities attempting to silence the growing discontent. The judge of the district of Mexico City decreed an order of confiscation of the "Phillips" shop, where the newspaper apparently had been printed. Yet the government soon found out that such a shop did not exist. When the third issue of *La Revolución Social* came out, the government of Veracruz tried to find out whether it was printed in Orizaba, but confirmed that it came from Mexico City by mail. Police arrested Jesús Martínez Carreón and Federico Méndez, charging them with printing the journal. A day later Governor Dehesa still guessed that perhaps the *La Revolución Social* was printed on the same press that published *El Colmillo Público,* because several articles from that newspaper had been reproduced in *La Revolución Social.*[27]

A few days later, a handful of Santa Rosa workers refused to work at night for three days in a row ("and we should note what working three nights in a row besides working the day means," the letter declared). "El Coyote" immediately went to Spitalier to inform him about this "rebellion," and very soon policemen and rurales with orders from the municipal president (who was also the mill doctor) came to apprehend them "with machetes and guns in their hands."[28] Santa Rosa, Río Blanco, and Nogales were plunged into a state of siege. As "Rómulo and Remo" wrote, "All this . . . just because of the small newspaper *La Revolución Social,* that . . . was denounced by the powerful industrial companies, Veracruzana and Orizaba."[29]

Through the end of June and the beginning of July, houses were searched with or without a search warrant, and all correspondence was scrupulously checked. Independent newspapers circulated with difficulty because the police expelled the newspaper vendors who came into the towns.[30] And yet "Rómulo and Remo" and others continued to send letters to *El Paladín.*

Also in June, in the northwestern corner of Mexico, in Cananea, Sonora, miners from the Cananea Mining Company struck when they received notice that several of them were going to be laid off and that the workload was going to increase for those remaining, without an increase in wages. Strikers marched through the streets of Cananea, recruiting workers from various company installations and workshops. Two American supervisors of the company lumberyard met them with rifles, and the enraged workers killed the supervisors and set fire to the structure. "Throughout that day and the next, confrontations between the workers and the armed American guards of the mines, as well as town police, resulted in at least eighteen Mexican dead and a number of wounded. The workers were, for the most part, unarmed."[31] On the second day of the unrest, 300 American volunteers arrived to restore order, something that was viewed by many as a violation of Mexico's sovereignty. Although there were also links between some Cananea workers—Manuel M. Diéguez and Esteban Baca Calderón—and the PLM, the strike was not organized by this party, but was the reaction of workers against an unfair policy, which they resented further given the disparity between the wages of Mexicans and Americans in that mine.[32]

"Rómulo and Remo" commented to *El Paladín* on the repression suffered by miners at Cananea from "the military forces of Uncle Sam who invaded national territory." They regarded the recent imprisonment of Santa Rosa workers as another example of the same policy, and concluded from these events that workers should not strike, because "it only opens up the opportunity for savage attacks to be made upon workers and to worsen their situation. Peaceful strikes could provide some results when enough money and solidarity, which unfortunately is yet unknown, are available. . . . To strike without a cent and without thinking of the terrible consequences that it inflicts upon the poor, is craziness that cannot be countenanced. The fifteen Mexicans dead in Cananea are testimony to it."[33]

Animosity and tension between workers and employers escalated. In early July the superintendent of weaving at San Lorenzo, Miguel Ramos, insulted the worker Garfias, one of the writers for *La Revolución Social,* and shot him, although not fatally.[34] But by the end of July, government, companies, and workers began to pursue a more conciliatory strategy. It appears that the Díaz government had mixed feelings with regard to the workers' newspaper. Although repressive measures against the paper were immediately ordered, Porfirio Díaz also sent a letter to Governor Dehesa asking him to find out whether it was true that mills in Veracruz were working fifteen-hour shifts, as the workers' newspaper claimed, and whether the industry would be hurt if the shift was reduced to twelve hours. A full inquiry of the issue was begun immediately.[35]

After long interviews between governor Dehesa and the district judge, and the GCOL leaders during their arrest, Dehesa concluded that the GCOL was quite harmless. He wrote to Porfirio Díaz, "those who preside over the Gran Círculo de Obreros Libres, . . . are poor ignorant men, and well intentioned since, from what appears, they only pursue philanthropic goals." Dehesa even asked the political chief of Orizaba, Carlos Herrera, to intervene to get the mills to rehire the workers they had fired the previous month. Dehesa wrote to Díaz, "Those workers, who do not seem to have evil intentions to me, promised . . . that they will never use violent means, which they have always condemned."[36]

This was not the first occasion when Dehesa intervened in favor of workers. A year earlier he had negotiated the end of a strike in the cigars-manufacturing company Valle Nacional, of Jalapa, obtaining a 20% wage increase. Later in that year, through the deputies of Veracruz, he proposed a national labor law, which did not pass because of the opposition of the *científicos,* a group of functionaries close to Díaz who favored laissez-faire economic policies.[37]

In July, workers also resorted to a more cautious and appeasing strategy. "Varios Trabajadores" (several workers) from Santa Rosa wrote in a letter to *El Paladín* that they did not want strikes. They felt that disunity among workers made it very difficult for them to protect their rights. Those who led any commission to favor workers soon found themselves alone and were either imprisoned or fired and "well recommended" to other mills as *revoltosos.* The way out was to found workers' leagues *(ligas)* to help each other. Workers would then be able to get lawyers to defend them against arbitrary fines and obtain compensation for unlawful damages inflicted upon them. They proposed to form a Workers' Association in each mill that would establish a small library, a night school, and a savings cooperative *(caja de ahorro).* "What do we want?" they wrote, "to set fire, destroy, kill, spread a 'suicidal-strike,' spread anarchy and a revolution that so worries our government? Or to try something rational, which with constancy and faith can be achieved?"[38]

The change in the government's and employers' attitudes started to have an impact in small but significant aspects of working conditions. In late July, workers wrote to *El Paladín* that they were beginning to be heard, and were grateful to the newspaper for that. Carlos Herrera had recently ordered authorities from the surrounding municipalities to take children out of the mills and to oblige their parents to register them in schools, the workers applauded.[39]

In early August the complaints of Santa Rosa workers about the on-site physician, Dr. Ambrosio Vargas, also began to be heard. Vargas's monthly payment came from discounts from workers' wages, and he was indolent and despotic, forcing most Santa Rosa workers to visit Dr. Garza in Nogales, for which they had to pay extra fees. Moreover, they considered it grossly unfair that Vargas should be an employee of the mill and at the same time Santa Rosa's municipal president.[40] In January a worker who attempted to gather signatures against the doctor was fired, but in August workers were able to collect "more than one thousand five hundred signatures" in a letter that asked for the doctor's dismissal. As a result, CIVSA replaced Dr. Vargas and eliminated the contribution workers had to pay for medical services. From then on the company paid the on-site doctor with its own resources.[41]

That same month the federal government sent an officer from the 9th Battalion of rurales to find out if it was true that rurales forced workers to go to work. Although "Varios Trabajadores" wrote to *El Paladín* that, given the current repression, collecting signatures was obviously not the right way to find out what rurales were up to, at least it showed that the federal government had begun to worry about the issue. Soon the commander of the rurales stationed in Orizaba was sent away from the valley, to the delight of workers.[42]

In August, when "the authorities became perfectly persuaded of the kind of union that they (the GCOL) wanted there to be from the beginning," a truce between the "authorities" and the CGOL was reached.[43] Some former GCOL leaders had fled. Some were captured, including Rafael Valdez, president of the Río Blanco GCOL branch, who was taken to the terrible San Juan de Ulúa prison.[44] The more moderate José Morales, who was not involved in the PLM, became the CGOL's president.[45] He thought that the labor movement should concentrate exclusively on the fight against employers, leaving aside political struggle. He was a loom fixer *(correitero)* in Río Blanco and had a reputation of being responsible and diligent.[46] His status as a highly skilled worker and his less radical attitude made it easier for government and mill authorities to accept the GCOL.

No longer afraid of persecution, the association called upon all its members to attend its inauguration, which finally took place in a large hall in Nogales on August 12. Morales gave an opening speech, and many others also spoke and recited poetry. The speeches emphasized that the GCOL sought "to look out for the interest of its compatriots, and to defend them within the bounds of the law." The new CGOL set as its first goals the abolishment of arbitrary fines that mills imposed, as well as ending the mistreatment that workers often suffered from superintendents. According to workers' accounts, everything took place in the greatest order, "with not even a single outcry against anyone."[47]

At that moment the feeling that prevailed in the Orizaba Valley was one of "the calm that comes after a storm," as "Un Grupo de Trabajadores" (a group of workers) wrote to *El Paladín*. They considered that the events of the recent months, which they called "a revolution," had led to "a better understanding by the workers that their only salvation was to unite in order to resist the several abuses that were still there to redress."[48] It had also heightened awareness among the authorities of the children working in the mills.

More benefits were achieved. By the end of the month, fines were abolished in the Nogales mill.[49] The GCOL also began to place limits on foremen's mistreatment of workers. According to a GCOL member's letter to *El Paladín,* one of the "bosses" of Santa Gertrudis hit a worker with a sack *(un costalazo).* This worker went discreetly to the president of the GCOL, and the association managed to get the authorities to "severely reprimand the foreigner *(gabacho)* who had perpetrated the fault." He was not punished, but he was warned that he would be if this happened again. Workers appear to have been content with this. "At other times," said the letter, "we would have never hoped that our MASTERS *(AMOS)* would have attended immediately to a summons (by the authority). That was left only to the lower classes *(los NACOS)* like us. . . . At other times, who among us would have had the courage to stand up to the bosses and the authorities?"[50]

Changes were evident even in language. Whereas before 1906 manufacturing workers were generally referred to by newspapers, companies, and even themselves as operators *(operarios),* gradually and almost unconsciously they became "workers" *(obreros).*[51] This in itself reflects their empowerment. The word *operario* connotes a passive creature who does not create but only operates machinery. This concept reflects the idea that it is the machine, not the worker, that produces. In contrast, the word *obrero* implies someone who actively creates, because the word comes from *obra,* the piece created.

Between 1898 and August 1906 the CIVSA board minutes contained only two references to workers, and in both cases referred to them as "operarios."[52] After mid-1906 the board frequently talked about the "workers movement" *(movimiento obrero)* and the "obreros," and after May 1907, weekly reports from Santa Rosa on the "obreros" were read in every board meeting.[53] The same is true of workers' letters to *El Paladín,* which from 1903 to 1904 always refer to workers as "operarios" and from 1906 on as "obreros."[54]

## The Expansion of the Gran Círculo de Obreros Libres

As soon as the CGOL emerged from its clandestine existence, it founded locals at every mill in the Orizaba Valley.[55] It then expanded into the rest of the country, aided by the acquaintances that immigrant workers from Orizaba had left behind.[56] By the end of 1906, in addition to Veracruz where CGOL was based, it had branch organizations in the states of Puebla, Jalisco, Oaxaca, Tlaxcala, Mexico, the Federal District, Querétaro, and Hidalgo.[57]

In Puebla, the Liga de Obreros Esteban de Antuñano, created in early 1906 and headed by Pascual Mendoza, joined the CGOL and became its second largest branch.[58] According to government sources, at its apex the CGOL had 9,000 to 10,000 affiliates.[59] The Orizaba GCOL created a new journal, *La Unión Obrera,* to replace the defunct *Revolución Social.* The GCOL's Puebla branch published another journal, *La Lucha Obrera,* directed by Pascual Mendoza, with similar characteristics. The watchword of these weekly journals was borrowed from the *Revolución Social:* "a journal written by the workers and for the workers."[60]

The solidarity that the GCOL had established began to show its strength in two strikes that broke out in the Orizaba Valley over the following months. On September 19, workers from Santa Gertrudis struck because the mill wanted to reduce piece rates by five cents a roll. A commission from the GCOL went to Puebla and persuaded workers in those branches to give financial support to Santa Gertrudis workers. They gathered enough funds to pay strikers 50 cents per day. On October 1, the strike ended with a victory for the workers, no reduction in rates.[61]

In October another strike broke out, this time among Santa Rosa workers who demanded a wage increase, the abrogation of fines, and the rehiring of several workers, including Manuel Juárez, vice president of the GCOL in Santa Rosa. Rafael Moreno, a weaver who was the president of the GCOL in Santa Rosa, headed the movement. A strong nationalist sentiment was expressed in a letter written by various workers to Ramón Corral, the minister of the interior *(gobernación),* in which they argued that foreign capital violated the Constitution and imposed fines erasing their rights and guarantees.[62]

The GCOL supported the strike by distributing flyers throughout mills in the country that explained the objectives of the strike and asked workers to abstain from coming as strike-breakers to the mill. It warned workers to be aware of Angel W. Velasco, who was hiring mill hands throughout the republic for that purpose.[63] Furthermore, the GCOL obtained contributions of corn and beans to support the strikers.[64]

On November 10, after negotiations between the GCOL leaders, the company's manager, and Carlos Herrera, the strike ended successfully for the workers. Fines were suppressed, and wages increased.[65] However, in the course of the strike bitterness arose between Santa Rosa workers and José Morales, whom they considered too close with Herrera and with the Orizaba district judge, Ramón Rocha. Samuel Ramírez, a Santa Rosa worker who had recently arrived from Atlixco and was apparently linked to the PLM, accused Morales of indecisive leadership and of betraying his comrades to the government for personal gain.[66] The old disputes between GCOL moderates and radicals revived. Santa Rosa workers, who according to Rocha had always been the most unsubordinated, supported Ramírez to replace Morales as GCOL's president in a meeting held on November 23. Ramírez sent a letter to Díaz, signed by all the presidents of the Orizaba Valley GCOL branches, explaining that he would respect law and order just as his predecessor had done, but the authorities did not believe him.[67] Morales went to Puebla to ask for the support of Pascual Mendoza, and came back with him to hold a meeting at the Gorostiza Theater, where he was reinstalled.[68] The workers who supported Ramírez did not accept this imposition and refused to pay the GCOL quotas. Later, on December 12, they organized a protest of about 800 workers in front of Herrera's office, but the political chief told them they could choose anyone as their president except Ramírez. This opened a wound in the GCOL that would not heal easily, precisely when it needed to be as strong as possible, as the events of the following weeks would show.

While the GCOL was facing these internal quarrels, industrialists began to organize a strong offensive. In November mill owners joined together in the Centro Industrial Mexicano (CIM) "in order to counteract the labor movement," as the CIVSA board put it, and secondly, to maintain "the object of defending our common interests and the well-being and *moralization* of the workers *(obreros)*."[69] This organization published factory regulations (a *reglamento*) on December 2 that were meant to prevail in all mills in Puebla and Tlaxcala. The *reglamento* was hard on the workers and was immediately rejected.

The leaders of the GCOL's affiliated organizations in Puebla and Tlaxcala revised the regulations and presented them to the CIM. They proposed a *reglamento* strikingly similar to that of the employers but with two significant differences. The GCOL's proposal eliminated from the CIM's regulations the prohibition against workers receiving guests in the houses that they rented from the companies, and added an article by which mills should accept a representation of two workers from the CGOL to negotiate with the company.[70] The CIM would not accept any modification of its regulations, which it tried to impose unilaterally.

On December 4, 1906, GCOL's Puebla and Tlaxcala affiliated organizations coordinated a general strike, shutting down thirty mills in Puebla and ten mills in Tlaxcala. Workers on strike received support from the other Gran Círculo branches, particularly the one in Orizaba, which increased dues from 15 to 25 cents a week in order to raise funds to support strikers. This was the first strike to take place in so many textile mills and also to channel funds to strikers that could make them stronger in their claims. The government and the textile companies felt so threatened by the CGOL that they opposed it with all their strength.

Industrialists of the Centro Industrial Mexicano, with government support, decided in a *tour de force* to put an end not only to the strike but also to the Gran Círculo, by shutting down all textile mills in order to stop the flow of resources to the strikers. They wanted to show workers that it was mills, and not unions, that held the ultimate power. CIVSA's council reported on November 30:

> In order to counteract the workers' organization, and to end the strike at Puebla, it being recognized that workers who continue working support the strikers, it has been considered that the only remedy is the general lockout of all textile mills. This extreme measure has been suggested by the government, which has taken the necessary precautions, sending troops to the industrial centers.[71]

On December 14, Pascual Mendoza and José Morales sent a telegram to President Porfirio Díaz asking him to arbitrate the dispute.[72] Díaz accepted on December 21, but the CIM refused his arbitration, as part of what appears as a well-planned scheme of which Díaz was part. They felt that it was necessary to weaken workers' strength before Díaz could give any acceptable arbitral decision *(laudo)*.

On December 24, 93 of the nation's 150 mills joined the lockout in twenty states of the Republic, leaving more than 30,000 workers without a pay.[73] The federal government sent 2,000 troops to strategic points in order to suppress any possible revolt. A commission from the GCOL asked for an audience with President Porfirio Díaz, which took place in December 26. In the meeting, José Morales from the Orizaba GCOL, Pascual Mendoza from the Puebla GCOL, Antonio Hidalgo, Adolfo Ramírez, and Santiago Cortés from Tlaxcala, and Antonio Espinoza from Atlixco expressed their demands to Díaz. They included a differentiated wage scale based on job difficulty and skill, the elimination of fines and other discounts on wages, an agreement that workers should not have to pay for parts and equipment broken through normal usage, and the freedom to have visitors in mill housing.[74]

Although some employers were willing to make some concessions to workers, others, particularly the French industrialists, opposed them. Throughout the weekend major stockholders and company lawyers held a meeting, and on December 31 they voted to accept Díaz's arbitrage. On Tuesday, January 3, 1907, Díaz met with workers' and industrialists' representatives and listened to their complaints in silence, as was his custom. On the following day both groups went to the president's office to hear Díaz's arbitral decision. He promised workers that a uniform wage list would be established, so that similar jobs received similar payments (but not the differential wage scale they had demanded), and that new factory regulations would be studied by the mills in order to improve working conditions. Fines were not going to be abolished, but such funds were going to be channeled to support widows and orphans. Doctors were going to be paid by the companies, no longer through discounts from workers' wages. Mills would not hire children younger than 7 years old, and would establish or improve schools. Workers were allowed to receive guests in the houses they rented from the companies.

On the other hand, several parts of the arbitral decision gave a direct blow to workers' chances for organization and protest. Each worker would carry a notebook where his behavior would be written down. This notebook would be checked by a mill before hiring anyone, and would thus damage any worker regarded as a rebel. The editors of the workers' newspapers would be appointed by the political chiefs in their regions, so that no "subversive doctrines" were published. Furthermore, workers had to commit not to strike. If they had any complaint, they should personally submit it in writing to the mill's manager, who would need to answer it within two weeks. The worker would continue working until the manager's answer was given, and if finally they did not agree with the manager's answer, they could then leave the job.[75]

Puebla and Tlaxcala workers accepted the *laudo* with few protests. However, in spite of José Morales's efforts to convince the workers in Orizaba to accept it, many refused to do so. On Sunday, January 6, when workers met at the Gorostiza Theater to learn about Díaz's *laudo,* spontaneous cries arose against it, and Rafael Moreno and Manuel Juárez, leaders of the Santa Rosa branch of the GCOL, still resenting Morales, organized the opposition.[76] That afternoon many workers tried to convince other workers not to return to work on the following morning.

## The "Río Blanco Strike"

As is the case with most episodes in which government forces massacre civilians, it is virtually impossible to know the true story of what happened. Countless different versions of the events are built up from the beginning by different actors, with varied intentions, making it difficult to tell true from false, much like Gabriel García Márquez's inquiries into the massacre of the banana plantations of Aracataca.[77] Unable to find the true number of workers killed, he raised it to 3,000 in order to give it epical proportions for his novel. After some time, in a ceremony commemorating the event, he realized that 3,000, the number he had invented, had become the official figure; "real life ended making me justice," he wrote. Studying the "Río Blanco strike" raises similar problems.

Even the way the episode has been described in the historiography is faulty, because the so-called "Río Blanco strike" was not a strike but the end of a company lockout.[78] Its framing as a strike began with all the newspapers that reported on the event in the days following January 7 and was then taken over by the historiography.

On January 7, according to the *laudo,* workers had to return to work, but in the Orizaba Valley very few did. Workers and women from their families gathered at the mill entrances to discourage others from entering.

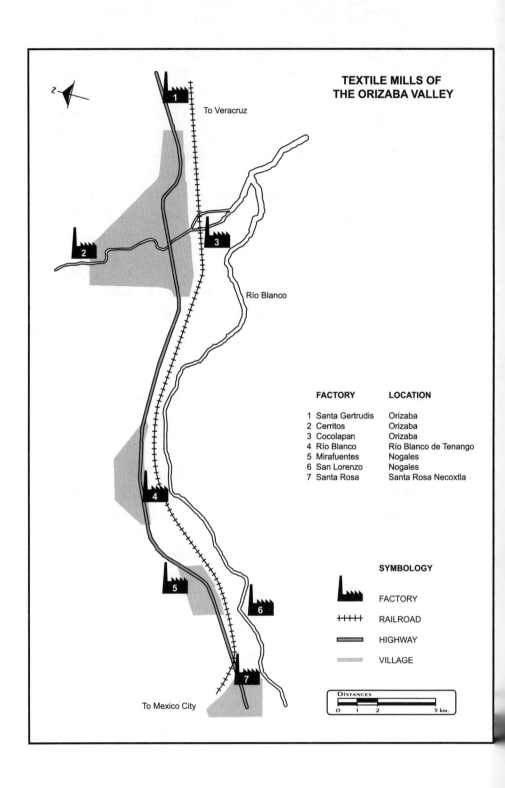

TEXTILE MILLS OF
THE ORIZABA VALLEY

To Veracruz

Río Blanco

| FACTORY | LOCATION |
|---|---|
| 1 Santa Gertrudis | Orizaba |
| 2 Cerritos | Orizaba |
| 3 Cocolapan | Orizaba |
| 4 Río Blanco | Río Blanco de Tenango |
| 5 Mirafuentes | Nogales |
| 6 San Lorenzo | Nogales |
| 7 Santa Rosa | Santa Rosa Necoxtla |

SYMBOLOGY

FACTORY

RAILROAD

HIGHWAY

VILLAGE

To Mexico City

DISTANCES

0   1   2        5 KM.

A crowd in an increasingly angry mood gathered outside the entrance to Río Blanco that morning. As this happened, some women who had been denied credit and perhaps insulted by the clerks of the company store, owned by Víctor Garcín, harangued the crowd around the area. Workers stormed toward the store, and the store's employees, when they saw the crowd descending on them, fired several shots, killing one worker. Enraged, the people ran to the store, broke some of the windows, sacked the place, and set fire to it.[79]

Then the crowd of more than 1,000 people marched to Nogales, where they looted two pawnshops and freed prisoners held in the municipal jail. Finally workers looted and burned the Centro Comercial store, in front of the San Lorenzo mill. Troops of the 13th Battalion, who had been posted in the region for several days, encountered the crowd there and opened fire, killing six workers and wounding several others.[80] Nonetheless, the crowd continued marching, and looted and burned another store, El Puerto de Veracruz, also in Nogales. Finally, workers walked to Santa Rosa, where they sacked and burned the El Modelo store.[81]

The next morning General Rosalino Martínez, then undersecretary of war, arrived with orders to replace the political chief of Orizaba, Carlos Herrera, who was considered too soft to deal with the situation. In the same train arrived federal troops under the command of Colonel Francisco Ruiz, a former police director of the Federal District.[82] That morning the soldiers immediately began killing protesters, and later that day, and on the following day, the killing continued. Some workers were hunted down in the hills nearby, others were executed in full view of their comrades.

On Wednesday morning, exemplary executions of the GCOL's most important leaders were carried out on the ruins of every burned store, in front of hundreds of workers who were waiting to enter to work. Among those executed were Manuel Juárez, vice president of the GCOL, and Rafael Moreno, president of the Santa Rosa branch of the GCOL. After analyzing several documents, Rodney Anderson concluded that 50 to 70 workers were killed, but most of the literature puts the number killed at over 300 workers—the exact number will never be known. Over 200 were put in prison.[83] In May 1907 many workers were still awaiting trial in the Orizaba jail. According to José Neira, who was among them, many innocent people had been apprehended, including several children 8 or 9 years old, as well as some street vendors who had nothing to do with the conflict.[84] Many of the workers convicted were taken to work camps in Quintana Roo.[85] According to a newspaper report, from a total of 6,138 workers who labored at CIVSA and CIDOSA in the days previous to the lockout, only 4,818 came back to work after January 9, 1907. This means that more than a thousand workers either fled the region or were killed or imprisoned.[86]

Workers' attacks particularly targeted stores belonging to Víctor Garcín, such as the Río Blanco company store, the Centro Comercial, at Nogales in front of the San Lorenzo mill, and El Modelo at Santa Rosa.[87] Other stores that were burnt included El Puerto de Veracruz at Nogales, owned by some Spaniards, and the Singer sewing machine agency in Santa Rosa, both destroyed as fire spread from El Modelo to the whole block. Pawnshops, such as those of Rafael Mateos and Lauro Machorro in Santa Rosa, were also sacked.[88] Workers burned down the house of José Morales, the president of the CGOL, on the belief that he had betrayed them.[89]

It has generally been assumed that the stores burned down on January 7, 1907, were all company stores.[90] From CIVSA company documents we know that El Modelo, the store burned down in Santa Rosa, was not a company store. The company store of Santa Rosa, leased at that time to José Fuentes, was neither looted nor burned down.[91] However, Garcín's Río Blanco store was in fact a company store. The minutes of the CIDOSA General Assembly held in March 1907 reported that workers "burned down the store of Río Blanco, which building belonged to our Company."[92] A week after it was burned down, the company's board decided "to rebuild the store exactly as it had been previously."[93] Most probably his Centro Comercial store at Nogales was also a company store, because the Cerritos and San Lorenzo factories in that town also belonged to CIDOSA.

Why did the rioting workers of January 7, 1907, almost exclusively target stores, particularly Garcín's businesses? As of January 7 they had not been paid since December 24, when the factories started the lockout, and families suffered from hunger. In the days workers went unpaid, which included Christmas, a bitter relationship must have developed between workers, stores, and pawnshops. Stores were vulnerable spots, whereas factories were impregnable fortresses. Because workers from the Orizaba region had been supporting Puebla workers on strike for the first two weeks of December, the GCOL of Orizaba had few funds saved for the lockout. Workers from other regions could not give them support as industrialists consciously planned the lockout to be general in order to prevent gestures of solidarity. Given their low wages, most families did not have enough savings to outlive the lockout.

In December 1906, *El Cosmopolita,* a newspaper from Orizaba, reported that many textile workers were fleeing the region, indentured *(enganchados)* to work on the haciendas of Tierra Blanca and those along the Pacific railroad, while others had gone back to their villages. The article reported that between two and three hundred were leaving within the next few days to the town of Zongolica, where labor was needed to cultivate vast areas of virgin land. Aware of their desperate situation, Francisco I. Madero, who later would be the leader of the revolution to depose Díaz, as a first gesture of his concern about industrial labor offered textile workers jobs in his properties in Coahuila.[94] Workers were obtaining money from any possible source in order to be able to leave the Orizaba region. "Many workers who had bought sewing machines on credit, had returned them to the agencies they had got them from, and with the money they got back, as well as that from articles pawned or sold, they have undertaken the exodus."[95] "Stores, had stopped lending workers the merchandise they had previously allowed them to pay for in short terms of between a week and a fortnight."[96] The CIVSA's board, aware of this situation, before the reopening of the mill wrote to the mill's manager: "Because we assume that workers are at the bottom of their resources, it would be good if from Tuesday you gave them some advances of one or two *piastres* or more for food."[97]

Workers asked merchants, and the population in general, for donations of food. Precisely on January 7, a petition of this kind appeared in the *Tipografía del Comercio,* asking for bread for their "adored children" who "suffer the terrible consequences of the caprice of industrialists who have become executioners of the worker."[98] In a letter sent to *El Diario,* Garcín argued that on the Friday before the massacre he was visited by a workers' commission that asked for cereals and other foodstuffs, and that given that his business was more important than the rest, and since all the other merchants had given a contribution, he decided to give 20% more than the largest contribution.[99] It is impossible to know whether this was true, but in any case it was not enough to meet workers' needs or to suppress their anger.

Moreover, Lucas Rex's study of a 1970s Canadian company town suggests that the relationship between the storekeepers and the customers in these environments are always problematic. He explains that "whatever the community or the industry, there is a great deal of manifest hostility on the part of the employees of the single industry toward those who supply the goods and services in the community. The hostility is greatest in those areas where the shopkeepers have the greatest power, and where the customer has the fewest alternatives, basically in day-to-day grocery shopping."[100]

Garcín was the most important merchant in the region, and his business developed a difficult relationship with workers both before and during the lockout. The fact that one of his employees killed a worker opened Pandora's box.

## The "Germinal" and the Birth of a Myth

On the days following the massacre of Río Blanco a heated debate began over the causes of the terrible episode. The not very impartial newspaper *El Imparcial* rapidly blamed the tragedy on the leaders of the labor movement and the publishers of radical newspapers, who, it claimed, had deceived the uneducated workers and instigated violence in order to pursue their own selfish interests.[101] *El Imparcial* argued that the workers had become criminals, and it demanded for them "not in the name of the employers and of those directly affected by the violence, but in the name of society as a whole . . . the most severe punishment."[102]

The industrialists were not to blame for the events: "The brief conflict between workers and employers—that arose from a disagreement over issues regarding the interior administration of the factories—had been solved on 'the basis' that had been approved by the representatives of the workers on strike."[103] This was apparently proved by the fact that the Puebla workers had peacefully resumed work.

Porfirio Díaz should not be blamed either: "as an arbiter to resolve the differences, he received on several occasions the workers' representatives and listened, with his usual attention, to their aspirations," which were incorporated in the new factory regulations, which were favorable to the workers.[104] The only fault of the government, if any, according to *El Imparcial,* was that it had not acted earlier to suppress the radical newspapers, such as *La Revolución Social* and *La Unión Obrera,* which disseminated subversive socialist doctrines and planted the seeds of rebellion in the workers' minds.[105]

Other newspapers took a similar stance. According to *El Tiempo* the workers' leaders who opposed Díaz arbitrage decision had become "the Judas . . . , present in every strike, who pursue their self profit without considering the grave damage that their criminal acts could carry to others."[106] This perspective completely justified the brutal military repression that had been taking place in Orizaba.

*El Diario,* the journal that gave the widest coverage to the event, offered a different explanation of the tragedy that provided some justification to the workers' acts, without having to blame the industrialists or Porfirio Díaz. The blame fell on Víctor Garcín, the greedy owner of the Río Blanco company store, and more generally on the existence of company stores. This enabled it to defend a more moderate policy against the workers. *El Diario* openly criticized those newspapers that without any evidence had put the blame on "agitators" they could not even name. What those newspapers had written, *El Diario* claimed, could only be the result of either a "systematic spirit of distorting the truth or the hope of receiving payment from those . . . who had vested interests in distorting it."[107]

According to *El Diario,* the deplorable events of Río Blanco could have been precluded if only Víctor Garcín had read *Germinal,* a novel by Émile Zola published in 1885 that narrates a similar episode in which a greedy storekeeper who monopolized commerce in a mine in France caused great violence in a strike and generated workers' outrage by not giving them the bread they needed. The article claimed that more than a violent strike, what happened in the Orizaba Valley was a vengeance against Víctor Garcín, given that the attacks were targeted at his stores. "As to the immediate cause of the violent protest, that is the strike, we are convinced that it should not be considered but in second place."[108]

Another article in the same issue of the newspaper explained that the riot started because Garcín, "who had the trust of commerce in Río Blanco, Nogales, and Santa Rosa, denied giving workers 30 of the 5,000 cargas of corn that he had."[109] A day later the newspaper reported that its journalists had tried to interview Víctor Garcín on the previous afternoon, but that he refused to talk to them. The article gave a detailed description of his rich house and dress, and was accompanied by a cartoon of Garcín.[110]

*El Diario*'s view prevailed, and gradually most newspapers started incorporating it in their articles. Even *El Imparcial,* which at first depicted Víctor Garcín as an innocent victim whose employees had only deployed a defensive attitude against the mob, began to put some responsibility on him for monopolizing trade in the region, and for denying aid to the strikers.[111] It even revised Garcín's losses from a million pesos, claimed in its first articles, to 200,000.[112] The triumph of this perspective, although helping Díaz and the industrialist save face, ended up moving public opinion against company stores *(tiendas de raya).*

*La Semana Mercantil,* a business journal, took a similar stance blaming the company stores for the violence that took place in January 7 at Orizaba. The source of the conflict, claimed the journal, was not the differing "interests of the industry and the worker" but the abuses inflicted upon workers by the company stores. "The company stores . . . are harmful to workers . . . by negotiating the values of credit . . . they open the way for squandering and vice, and these same evils are the foundation of their prosperity and profits."[113]

Francisco I. Madero was aware of the politics behind the way the press reported the Río Blanco events, which he considered a "bloody hecatomb." In a letter to a friend, the journalist Francisco Sentíes, he complained, "The press, gaged by its fear, did not give responsibility to whom it corresponded."[114] Even *El Diario* had not been frank enough. "Although it is true that it is not convenient [for the newspaper] to attack the true guilty party [Díaz], at least it should not contribute to misleading the public, making him appear immaculate in this tragedy."[115]

Madero was well aware of the importance of giving publicity for the truth in order to bolster the opposition movement. By making the names of the victims known to everyone, their spilled blood could "water the tree of freedom." He asked Sentíes to make a careful study of the events and publish it in a pamphlet he would help pay for.[116] Madero wrote also to the historian and journalist Fernando Iglesias Calderón to complain about his attitude toward the Río Blanco events, saying that the journalist had been too passive and that he "should not hesitate to help with his name, his pen, and his energy" the cause that his father (the famous liberal José María Iglesias) had served all his life. Madero believed that Río Blanco's painful events showed the urgent necessity of starting their political campaign. It would be foolish not to grasp the political opportunity that this tragic event offered to dissidents of the regime "because it is not likely that what took place in Orizaba, which has left so deep an impression all over the country, will happen again soon."[117]

The newspapers' interpretations of the Río Blanco events placed the *tiendas de raya* at the top of the list of the problems affecting workers, a problem that needed to be solved in order to avoid similar violence. At this moment in public policy theory "the situation" of the company store began to be generally understood as "a problem." At the same time, in spite of the care the press took to make Díaz's government appear innocent, January 7 changed the way the regime was perceived both nationally and internationally. "The painful events of Orizaba have caused a deep and sad impression in all the Republic. Everywhere it is clear that the brave Mexican people are full of indignation," wrote Madero in January 1907.[118]

John Kenneth Turner's famous book *Barbarous Mexico* (1910), which included a chapter on the "Río Blanco strike" and on the working conditions in that mill, shows how the power of a single episode can shape the way a regime is perceived internationally. It can be argued that the strike had consequences for the Porfirian regime similar to the effects that, sixty years later, the student massacre of October 2, 1968, would have on public perception of the Partido Revolucionario Institucional regime.[119]

## The Demise of the GCOL

After January 1907, the CGOL was disbanded and its major leaders had been either killed or arrested.[120] The mills suffered from lack of hands for some months, but by April they were again operating with all the labor required.[121] From early on, Díaz sought to gain a tighter grip over the region to pursue stronghand policies. On January 7 he ordered the governor to suspend Carlos Herrera and to replace him with Colonel Ruiz, judging that Herrera's "benevolent character is not suitable for the energetic measures that will be necessary to repress the commotion in such a way that it will not be repeated."[122] In February Colonel Miguel V. Gómez, former political chief of Córdoba, was named political chief of Orizaba. Díaz reached an agreement with the governor of Veracruz, Teodoro Dehesa, so that Gómez reported directly to him and his minister of the interior, Ramón Corral, in order to have a closer supervision of the region.[123] The political chief, the chief of the Orizaba military district, and the head of the rurales all watched the workers and reported regularly to Díaz. The military chief of the zone of Veracruz, General Joquín Maass, kept secret watch over the sale of arms and ammunitions while the 26th Battalion of the federal army remained posted at Orizaba.[124]

After January 1907 CIVSA and CIDOSA followed different strategies. Whereas CIVSA granted certain concessions besides those established in Porfirio Díaz's *laudo,* CIDOSA seems to not have even fulfilled what the *laudo* ordained. In January CIVSA's company store stopped operating as before—CIVSA stopped charging a commission on workers' purchases in the store, and by 1908 the company ended the practice of deducting workers' debts to the stores directly from their pay. In February, CIVSA workers received a 10% wage increase and fines disappeared from Santa Rosa's payrolls.[125]

In May 1907 new strikes broke out in the Orizaba Valley, and the way the government dealt with them made clear what Díaz had in mind when he wrote to Dehesea about the "energetic measures" that he deemed necessary. Now the government was much more inclined to repression than it had been during 1906, although it still pursued some negotiation and accommodation. On April 22, workers from the jute bag factory of Santa Gertrudis at Nogales went on strike because a weaver was expelled for attempting to injure another worker. "To prevent the scandalous scenes of early January from being repeated," reported *El Imparcial,* "federal forces headed by Colonel Mier immediately arrived to the mill." The municipal president of Nogales ordered the capture of five workers who were claimed to be the instigators, and sent them to the Orizaba jail, to the further discontent of workers. Finally, the political chief settled the problem by negotiating with both the industrialists and the workers.

The strike ended on May 6 when the five imprisoned workers were freed and the company accepted their return to employment; however, the company did not comply with the workers' petition that the originally expelled worker regain his job.[126]

Then, on April 31, about 750 workers from Río Blanco left the mill, demanding that the promises made to them in January by Porfirio Díaz's *laudo* be fulfilled. According to a Río Blanco's employee who sent a letter to *El Imparcial,* those promises included a raise in wages, the regulation of child labor, shorter working hours, and an end to company store script and the hated fines. They wanted to get at least the same benefits that CIVSA had granted its workers. As in the Nogales strike, Colonel Mier arrived to the factory premises as soon as he was notified. All the bars *(pulquerías)* of the region were ordered to shut down and all stores were forbidden to sell any alcohol.[127] This measure stemmed from the belief among authorities that the events of January 7 had been a consequence of workers' drunkenness, an idea the newspapers had spread and that fit the higher classes' beliefs about workers.

Before this strike was settled, a larger strike broke out at Río Blanco, this time because workers opposed a new *reglamento* that the company wanted to impose. This set of rules was written up by the Comisión Industrial de México, presided over by Mr. Henry Tron. Although according to *El Imparcial* this new *reglamento* was more liberal than the one included in Díaz's *laudo,* Orizaba's political chief, Miguel Gómez, considered it "deficient, badly written, and containing clauses that were inadequate for workers."[128] Apparently Gómez tried to convince the industrialists to modify it but he was not heard. When interviewed by journalists, he explained that he had signed the *reglamento* only because in his view he had no legal capacity to oppose to what was a set of private rules of purely administrative character. Workers considered it tyrannical.[129]

*El Diario* reported that on May 27 some 1,500 workers went to the gates of several of the mill's departments to instigate other workers to join the strike, carrying knives and threatening the superintendents, while others threw stones at the factory. According to that account, rioting was crushed by 100 troops from the 26th Battalion with the support of 25 more from the 9th Battalion of cavalry and ten rurales. General Maass arrived to the region to supervise the military operations. One hundred more troops from the 26th Battalion were later sent as reinforcements. Two workers were injured and eighteen were arrested for carrying arms or shouting in protest.[130]

On May 30 the *reglamento* was posted in all the CIDOSA factories and on the corners of several streets close to the mills, stating that those workers who did not come back to work on the next day and accept the conditions that the *reglamento* established would be replaced by new workers. Those who did not attend work would have to vacate the company dwellings within six days. Rumors spread that 1,500 workers from Oaxaca that CIDOSA had hired at double pay would soon arrive to the Orizaba Valley. That day, 175 troops from the 26th Battalion, headed by Captain Montes de Oca, remained at the workers' district of Santa Catarina, nearby the Río Blanco mill. Military forces were posted at Nogales and Santa Rosa to prevent workers from the other mills from joining the strike to support their fellow workers.[131]

As if the situation was not already bad enough, on the afternoon of May 31 a large storm hit the region and the water channel that served the Río Blanco and Cocolapan mills overflowed, flooding many factory dwellings. The rain fell all day, and during the night hail fell over the valley. The next morning, before sunrise, at 4:00 a.m., as workers were struggling to rescue what they could from their flooded houses, 22 workers were lined up with their hands tied, led by an escort from the 26th Battalion, to be sent to the work camps of Quintana Roo. Among them was a 15-year-old boy whose mother and sisters cried desperately by his side. Two hours later most CIDOSA workers went back to work, and by their reentry they tacitly accepted all the *reglamento's* articles. The strike had ended with no gain for the workers.[132]

As a response to the May disturbances, Díaz ordered governor Teodoro Dehesa to draw up a set of new regulations to rule in the state of Veracruz mills. Dehesa worked on them in close cooperation with the president and then submitted them to CIDOSA's directors for comments, who reluctantly accepted them. The new regulations were more generous to workers than the *laudo* in several ways. Child labor minimum age was raised to 10, instead of 7 as the *laudo* specified, and an arbitration committee would be established, at a worker's request, to judge cases of defective materials. Complaints submitted by workers to company management had to be replied to within eight days, instead of fifteen days, and the regulations prohibited foremen from taking money from workers on any pretext, providing for the expulsion of foremen in the case of noncompliance.[133]

During the Porfiriato, albeit at a high cost, workers from the Orizaba Valley had obtained some improvements in their working conditions, as a result of the "revolution" of 1906–1907. Several mills in the Orizaba Valley had abolished fines in the course of the second part of 1906. Yet it seems that only after "the sad events of January 1907" did fines disappear completely from mills in the region.[134] In August 1910, Santa Rosa workers went on strike to reduce their working hours. They won, and the shift was reduced from twelve to eleven hours. This was the first of a series of reductions in the hours of work that took place during the following years.

However, the increase in real wages, one of the most important gains obtained, would be diluted in the following years by rising inflation. In addition, the economic crisis of 1907 reduced workers' employment opportunities. The crisis hit Orizaba textile mills hard. Santa Rosa cloth sales decreased in 1907 and remained low in 1908, at levels below the cloth produced. Although sales improved in 1909, and the problem of overproduction disappeared, sales would not reach the precrisis levels until 1912. Profitability also declined. As a consequence of the economic crisis, between 1907 and 1911 almost 17% of Santa Rosa's labor force was laid off. A similar situation prevailed in the CIDOSA mills. Moreover, the evolution of events during 1906–1907 had made clear to Orizaba textile workers that their aspirations could not be fulfilled within the boundaries imposed by the Porfirian regime.

# CHAPTER 5

# Textile Workers and the
# Mexican Revolution

T HE FINAL YEARS of the decade of 1900 were marked by the political problem that the elections of 1910 posed. The question of presidential succession took an unexpected turn when, in an interview with
James Creelman in 1908, Díaz promised that he would not stand for reelection and would support free elections instead, opening the way for
the rise of political opposition movements. When it became clear that he
would not keep his word about leaving the presidency, the crucial issue
in dispute became who was going to be the vice president, since he would
most likely succeed the 80-year-old president. The quarrel between the
*científicos,* the group of Porfirian politicians close to big business and
foreign capital, and the *reyistas,* a group that supported Bernardo Reyes,
the former governor of Nuevo León and a former minister of war, became intense. In September 1909, when it became evident that Reyes was
not going to be the vice president, the Anti-Reelectionists, those who opposed the reelection of Porfirio Díaz, headed by Francisco I. Madero,
gained increasing strength.

Industrial workers in general, and Orizaba textile workers in particular, would play an important role in this contention. Francisco I. Madero
dedicated several pages of his book *La Sucesión Presidencial de 1910,*
published in 1909, to the Río Blanco strike, placing the blame of the

massacre on Díaz. Madero thought that, given the economic crisis, Díaz was in no position to demand industrialists to pay higher wages. However, he argued that the president would have prevented violence if he had demanded that the mills treat workers with equity, support schools for their children, provide hygienic housing, and not allow them to be exploited in the company stores, by unjustified fines, or under any other pretext. Instead, according to Madero, Díaz's *laudo* gave almost nothing to workers and restrained their freedom. In a subtle manner Madero suggested in these pages the kind of policies toward labor that he would pursue if he were elected.[1]

## The Maderista Revolution

In spite of repression, workers' organization survived in the Orizaba Valley after the GCOL was dismantled, providing a ground base for the growing support Madero gained in the region. From letters to *El Paladín* in 1908, it appears that GCOL former leaders and supporters, now under ingenious new pseudonyms, continued to carry on a lower-profile struggle. Gradually new organizations were built, although of a narrower and more moderate character than the former GCOL, and the authorities had to tolerate them. In October 1908 Miguel Gómez, the new political chief of Orizaba, recognized the new workers' organization, La Alianza Obrera, at the Río Blanco mill but told workers that although they had a right to associate under Article 9 of the Constitution of 1857, they should also respect Article 3, the right of the community to tranquility and peace, and in case they violated the public order the government would severely punish them. In 1909 Orizaba workers founded the Sociedad Mutualista de Ahorros "Ignacio Llave," which, although of a mutualist character, was led by Andrés Mota, the worker in whose house the GCOL had been founded in 1906.[2]

The Orizaba Mutualist Liberal Circle had radicalized since January 7, 1907. On that day, General Rosalino Martínez caught three members of the Liberal Circle, Gabriel Gavira among them, who were barely saved from being executed. Although many of its members left the organization, afraid of the repression, those who remained decided to remove the word "mutualist" from its name as well as the article of the association's bylaws that forbade it to get involved into politics. By then, Camerino Z. Mendoza, Heriberto Jara, and Ricardo Sentíes had joined the Circle. Mendoza and Jara had met as employees at Río Blanco, where they worked as assistant bookkeepers. Mendoza had later founded a general store in Santa Rosa and helped workers during the factory lockouts. As a member of the PLM, Jara had participated in the Río Blanco strike, and later was an employee in the *pulque* business. Under the leadership of Dr. Carlos Ramírez, a *Magonista,* and Gabriel Gavira, they joined the Anti-Reelectionist movement and founded the "Liberal Anti-Reelectionist Club of Orizaba" in May 31, 1909, the first to have been established in the Republic.[3]

Manuel Alonso, the president of the Club, tried to make a deal with Governor Teodoro Dehesa, who was his friend, so the Club would support his candidacy as vice president. When the rest of the members found out, the Club split and most of its members, under the leadership of Gavira, Tapia, Jara, and the hatmaker Francisco Camarillo, organized the Club Ignacio de la Llave de Orizaba. Within a few months thousands of workers from the surrounding mills joined the club, and other clubs were founded in Río Blanco, Nogales, and Santa Rosa under its leadership.[4]

These organizations served as a platform for the rapid formation of six Anti-Reelectionist clubs in the region between 1909 and 1910, five of them in the mill towns outside the city. In April 1910 the Club Anti-Reeleccionista de Santa Rosa Necoxtla had 489 members, about one-fourth of the total workers employed by the mill.[5] In the nearby town of Atoyac, near Córdoba, Cándido Aguilar led the creation of another Anti-Reelectionist club.[6]

Miguel Gómez, the Orizaba political chief, became uneasy about the growing Maderismo among workers, fearing that the labor conflicts would become linked to political movements. The officers of the clubs were under constant surveillance. Several leaders were fired from their jobs and some of them were arrested. Rurales were put on guard at the Río Blanco mill entrance to make sure that workers were not carrying "subversive literature."[7]

Díaz and Corral were aware of the problem that industrial workers posed to their election, so at some point in 1909 they tried to win the favor of labor. This policy was most clear in Mexico City, where the governor, Guillermo Landa y Escandón, opened a mutualist organization and intervened on the side of workers to resolve labor conflicts.[8] In the Puebla-Tlaxcala region Díaz could count on the support of former GCOL's Puebla branch president, Pascual Mendoza, who had become an unconditional ally of the reelectionist cause. In April 1909 he arranged a pro-Díaz and Corral rally in Mexico City attended by 3,000 workers, mainly from Puebla and Tlaxcala mills.[9]

In the Orizaba Valley, Díaz's government also tried a similar policy. In May 1909 an unpopular rurales officer in the mill town of Río Blanco was fired, to the satisfaction of workers. And in January 1910, when a strike broke out in the Santa Gertrudis jute mill, Miguel Gómez met with workers and administrators to try to arrange a solution. In spite of his efforts, Gómez did not achieve much; hatred was too deeply entrenched. While on the 1909 Cinco de Mayo celebration many workers marched in front of the balcony of the Mexico City's National Palace, in Orizaba, where a similar demonstration had been planned, no workers appeared.[10]

Instead, workers were eagerly reading the Constitution of 1857, of which one million copies had been printed and sold at 10 cents each as part of the Anti-Reelectionist campaign. The Club Ignacio de la Llave organized meetings in which Gavira, Jara, and Ramírez explained and discussed with the workers the articles of the Constitution. On April 1910, Gavira, Mendoza, and Jara went to Mexico City to attend the Anti-Reelectionist Convention, representing about 3,000 members, to support the candidacy of Madero for president and Emilio Vázquez Gómez for vice president.[11]

When Madero visited Orizaba on Sunday, May 22, 1910, as part of his campaign, around 20,000 people came to meet him at the train station and gathered in front of the Hotel de France, where he was staying.[12] According to Roque Estrada, his trip companion, Madero was welcomed as a hero in his passage through Orizaba mill towns, people threw gardenia flowers to his train car window, and schoolchildren lined up by the railway to honor him.[13] From the balcony of the Hotel de France he gave a famous speech in which he vividly remembered the events of January 1907, saying that such a tragedy was one of the bloodiest dramas of the dictatorship, and that the red stain it had left needed to be washed with a democratic demonstration. Madero proclaimed that in order to remedy the workers' situation it was necessary to recognize that the enemy was the dictatorship, and be alert. "It does not depend on the government to raise wages and reduce working hours," he said, "so we do not come here to offer you that, because that is not what you want. What you want is that your rights are respected, that you are allowed to gather in powerful associations, so that united you can defend your rights."[14] Workers interrupted the speech at this moment with a prolonged applause.

Some historians have inferred that in this speech Madero denied the need for governments' intervention in labor questions and favored a laissez-faire policy.[15] However, the history of workers' organizations in the Orizaba Valley shows that many Orizaba workers shared Madero's view of the labor problem. They did not want the paternalism that Díaz's offered them, because they had learned—the hard way—that it was unreliable, shallow, and ultimately fruitless. What they wanted was the freedom to organize that Madero offered, because they knew that through their organization they could fight to win better working and living conditions. Contrary to most Mexican workers, they had experienced what an independent and powerful labor movement could do. Orizaba workers were as confident as Madero was about their own strength, if only they could win the freedom to pursue their goals.

During the spring of 1910, Porfirio Díaz became increasingly worried about Madero's popularity and decided to repress his movement; on June 4, Madero and his closest allies were jailed in San Luis Potosí. Also during the early days of June several leaders of the Orizaba Anti-Reelectionist group were arrested on charges of fomenting rebellion in the mills.[16] While Madero was in prison, the elections were carried out without freedom or fairness and Porfirio Díaz and Ramón Corral won. In October Díaz's government felt strong enough to free Madero, who fled to San Antonio, Texas, and issued the Plan of San Luis, calling for an armed revolution that should start on November 20.

The newspapers reveal that there was great apprehension about the possibility of a massive rebellion starting on that date. There was particular concern about the course of action that the nearly 18,000, mostly Maderista, workers of the Orizaba Valley would take.[17] The crucial insurrections that ignited the Mexican Revolution in November 1910 were taking place very far away from Orizaba, in the distant mountains of Chihuahua. However, the newspaper headlines on the following week to November 20 focused on Orizaba.

On November 21, *El Diario*'s front-page headlines read, "The Workers of Orizaba Rose Yesterday in Arms" and "Orizaba Seized with Panic Gets Ready for Its Defense" while the headline of *El Imparcial* said, "In Río Blanco Near Orizaba There Was Some Disorder" and its second line read "A Group of Workers Armed the Scandal."[18] Soon it became clear that the situation in the Orizaba Valley was not as grave as it was at first believed to be, and that workers had not massively supported the revolt. "In Orizaba Tranquility Has Reigned and It Seems the Mutiny Has Been Crushed" read *El Diario's* headline on the next day, dissolving the evident anxiety over the impact that Maderos's call for a revolution could have had in the region.

As in Puebla, Tlaxcala, and several other places, preparations for rebellion in the Orizaba mill towns were discovered by Díaz's intelligence, and the instigators were apprehended. An informer had warned Díaz that workers from the Cocolapan and Cerritos mills would attack the barracks of the 15th Battalion on the evening of November 20, so they were set in alert and the 6th Cavalry was sent as reinforcement.[19] On November 18, seven people were captured by the secret police in the Orizaba mill towns; among them were three workers from the Río Blanco, Nogales, and Santa Rosa mills. Arms and documents that linked them to the Maderista sedition were found at their homes. The house of Gabriel Gavira was searched and several boxes of explosives were found. Gavira had fled earlier, but his family was apprehended.[20] Camerino Mendoza and Rafael Tapia also fled.

According to their original plan, Tapia was going to capture the church of San Antonio, and Vivanco, Juarico, and Gavira were going to attack the barracks of San Antonio, where they expected to encounter around 400 soldiers; Camerino Mendoza was going to lead the rebellion in Santa Rosa. However, once the main leaders fled and several rebels and armaments were captured, the insurrection was seriously weakened and without direction. Independently from Gavira and Tapia, Samuel Ramírez, a former Santa Rosa GCOL representative, had also been organizing clandestine meetings with workers to plot a revolt for November 20.[21] Although the coup appeared to have been suppressed, in the following days Miguel Gómez organized the military and the rurales troops to resist any possible attack. As rumors of the rebellion spread, families were desperately buying food supplies. On Sunday, November 20, the political chief ordered all the bars and *pulquerías* closed and ordered the police watch over any gathering of workers.[22]

The plans for rebellion in Orizaba, Santa Rosa, and Nogales were aborted. However, in Río Blanco, in spite of the odds against them, on the evening of November 20, at 7:00 p.m., around 200 workers and townspeople rose in arms. One group attacked the barracks of the rurales and the Muncipal Palace in Río Blanco and as they were pursued the fight continued in the Río Blanco market. Others captured the jail and set free the nine prisoners to join them in battle.[23] Apparently Camerino Mendoza joined this group led by Inés Olaya, a Río Blanco worker.[24] Another group cut several light, telephone, and telegraph lines, but they did not have enough time to cause serious damage because they were immediately pursued and fled. A band of around fifty rebels came down from the hills and fought in the Nogales surroundings. Gavira arrived at the San Antonio barracks in Orizaba with around thirty poorly armed Indians he had recruited in Santa Ana Atzacan, but finding that the others had not been able to get to the appointed place, and that Orizaba was well guarded by the soldiers and police, they fled, pursued by about twenty rurales. He managed to reach Veracruz, and from there he fled to Cuba with Camerino Mendoza.[25]

The rebels were outnumbered and poorly armed, and the dynamite bombs they used failed to explode, but most of them managed to escape to Nogales and from there to the mountains. According to *El Imparcial*, as a result of the mutiny, twelve soldiers and guards were killed and five were injured while seven rebels were killed and two were captured, both of them Río Blanco workers.[26]

That night Miguel Gómez called Mexico City for further reinforcement and at 1:00 a.m. the 10th Infantry Battalion, under the command of General Gonzalo Luque, boarded a military train to get there as soon as possible. That day around 100 workers were missing at the Río Blanco mill, but on the following days most of them were back at work. Around 1,000 men from the 10th, 16th, and 15th Battalions of the federal army and the 9th Battalion of rurales stayed in the Orizaba Valley through the following months to preclude any further insurrection.[27] This was an important portion of the federal army, considering that it had only around 18,000 soldiers and 2,700 rurales.[28]

The search of houses and the nearby mountains continued, and more explosives and arms were found.[29] In total, from November 18 to December 10, fifty people presumably related to the rebellion were captured and sent to Mexico City.[30] Although the newspapers claimed that the mutineers were outsiders—rancheros, said *El Imparcial,* drunkards, remarked *El Diario*—among those caught there were several workers and some local people who belonged to the middle class.

It appears that the leaders of the revolt were the shoemaker Ricardo Sentíes, the saddlemaker Rafael Tapia, the carpenter Gabriel Gavira, and the Santa Rosa shopkeeper Camerino Mendoza.[31] Miguel Gómez believed that Diódoro Batalla, a liberal lawyer from Veracruz and a founder of the National Anti-Reelectionist Party, was also involved in the rebellion, having a close relation with Tapia, whom Gómez considered the main instigator of the revolt.[32] All of them managed to escape. In the following months Gavira, Tapia, and the Córdoba Anti-Reelectionist Cándido Aguilar led some revolts in Córdoba, Huatusco, Xalapa, and the Orizaba area.[33] Their recruits were mostly peasants, but several industrial workers also joined them.[34] Among them was Rafael Mendoza, a weaver from Cocolapan who had studied in the night school of the Liberal Club with Gavira and Jara as teachers. He joined Gavira's army in 1910 together with thirty-three other men, presumably workers as well.[35]

The Maderista leaders of Orizaba were more successful at carrying out a guerrilla war in the countryside than they had been in their attempt at an urban insurrection. The steep mountains between the states of Veracruz and Puebla became their territory, and they indiscriminately attacked positions in both states.

In Puebla and Tlaxcala, the participation of industrial workers in the revolutionary armies was even more pervasive than in Orizaba. Several hundred workers from the textile mills of Los Molinos, Metepec, La Carolina, and La Covadonga joined the Maderista revolution under the leadership of Juan Cuamatzi. Rafael Tapia, working with other rebels from the border between Veracruz and Puebla, by the end of 1911 had collected a force of around 3,000 men. Camerino Mendoza also played an important role in the Maderista revolution in Puebla. Together with Prisciliano Martínez, he took the city of Tehuacán, the second largest city of Puebla, on May 13, and was named provisional governor of Puebla by Madero.[36]

In Mexico City, former Orizaba GCOL leaders Porfirio Meneses, José Neira, and Samuel Ramírez, who had emigrated there, also formed part of the Maderista revolution. In March they participated in a pro-Madero uprising centered in Tacubaya, Federal District, led by Camilo Arriaga. Among the conspirators were several workers from La Hormiga mill in Tizapán, Federal District, and other shops and factories.[37]

Those workers who stayed at work struck with greater frequency in the first months of 1911 than at any time since 1906; there were eight textile strikes from January to May 1911. Río Blanco workers struck on February 28, and as they left the mill, cries of "Viva Madero!" were heard. Two days later, a group of workers broke into the company store. When the rurales arrived to crush the rebellion, shots were exchanged. Thirty-six workers were taken prisoner by the rurales. Río Blanco workers struck again in April, staying out until June.[38]

Although the role of industrial workers in the Maderista revolution was limited and by no means crucial to its success, it was important in distracting a large number of troops from going to fight rebels in the north, where the revolution finally triumphed.[39] Moreover, the fact that most of Puebla was controlled by rebel forces appears to have played an important role in Díaz's decision to surrender.[40] At the same time, it is very likely that the revolt in the Orizaba Valley starting on November 20, 1910, would have had important dimensions, if the conspiracy had not been discovered and so many troops sent to guard the region.

After a major defeat in Ciudad Juárez, Chihuahua, led by the revolutionary generals Francisco Villa and Pascual Orozco, Díaz decided to leave office and signed a peace treaty with Madero on May 21, 1911. The treaty established that Díaz's former minister of foreign affairs, Francisco León de la Barra, would remain as interim president until elections were held. The army, the rurales, and most of the bureaucracy remained in place. On October 1, 1911, elections were held, the Madero–Pino Suárez slate won, and on November 6 Madero became president.

Once the revolution triumphed, the most important leaders of the revolutionary guerrillas of Puebla and Veracruz lost the political battle against more moderate and upper-middle-class Maderistas. In Puebla, Madero supported Rafael Cañete to become governor, instead of Camerino Mendoza, whom Madero had named provisional governor of the state during the May combats. Cañete was a 55-year-old lawyer who had been president of an Anti-Reelectionist club in 1910, but he had also worked for the Porfirian regime as a district judge. This produced conflict and division among the Puebla revolutionaries. When Emilio and Francisco Vázquez Gómez distanced themselves from Madero, Mendoza was accused of rebellion and sent to prison, but he was later liberated under Madero's orders and put in charge of a force of rurales.[41] In Veracruz, Madero supported Francisco Lagos Cházaro instead of Gabriel Gavira in the 1911 elections for governor of that state. Cházaro had been a member of the Anti-Reelectionist Party in 1909, but was deemed too close to the former Porfirian governor of the state, Teodoro Dehesa. Gavira, who had led the Maderista revolution in the state, resented Madero's decision. According to him it was based on Madero's preference for a lawyer over a carpenter. Deciding that the elections were fraudulent, Gavira decided to rebel.[42] Thus, the triumph of the Maderista revolution did not mark the radical turn in the states of Puebla and Veracruz that had been expected by the revolutionaries who had been backed by many industrial workers. Yet some important changes did take place.

## Labor Organization under Madero

The new political climate opened the way for the formation of new workers' organizations. Through 1911, workers' "societies" or "clubs" were formed within each mill; these included the Mártires de Santa Rosa from Santa Rosa, the Solidaridad Obrera from Río Blanco, and the Unión y Progreso from Cerritos. These societies had close links of solidarity with each other, at least within the Orizaba Valley.[43]

During the second half of 1911 the number of strikes continued rising. On June 6, 1911, more than 1,000 workers struck in Río Blanco, asking for the dismissal of two foremen. Santa Rosa workers and those of other mills joined the strike in solidarity.[44] Some days later, over 500 workers from all the mills in the region marched to Orizaba to ask the political chief of Orizaba to intervene in their favor. The demonstration turned violent when the chief of the armed forces of Santa Rosa ordered his soldiers to shoot into the crowd. Fortunately no one was injured. After several days of striking, the two foremen were fired and the Río Blanco workers' society was officially recognized.[45] When another strike broke out at Río Blanco on September 11, *El Imparcial* reported that a workers' club preached seditious doctrines in that mill.[46] From September 28 to October 16, Santa Rosa workers struck, asking for a 20% wage increase, a reduction in the number of daily working hours, and the removal of the chief of the weaving department.[47]

The government had to devise a cautious policy toward workers because they could pose a serious threat to stability. In October 1911 *El Demócrata* reported that Emiliano Zapata had been in Río Blanco recruiting workers for his army and offering very high pay. According to that report, "the Head of the Security Commissions" immediately went to Orizaba, Río Blanco, and Santa Rosa.[48] In fact, some workers of the Orizaba textile mill, such as Acisclo Pérez Servín, who would later become municipal president of Santa Rosa and a prominent promoter of education in the region, joined Zapata's Liberating Army of the South, attaining the rank of colonel.[49]

To cope with labor unrest, Interim President de la Barra proposed on July 24, 1911, the creation of a Department of Labor within the Ministry of Development (*Fomento*), so that the more troublesome and contentious labor issues could be dealt with on a daily basis. He sent the proposal to Congress in September, but it was not approved until December 18, after Madero had assumed the presidency.[50] The Department of Labor was to act as a mediator, facilitate negotiations between labor and capital, and resolve conflicts. Porfirio Díaz had intervened in conflicts between capital and labor when asked to by the disputing parties. During his regime, however, it was not considered the government's responsibility to undertake that role, nor was there any official agency specifically designed for this purpose. The Department of Labor therefore marked a turning point in the Mexican government's involvement in capital–labor relations.[51]

The creation of the Department of Labor was more a reaction to the threat that the labor movement posed to the new government, than a favor granted to workers. One of its first challenges was to negotiate the end of a general strike in the textile industry that broke out in December 1911. This strike caused great commotion; in January, 5,000 to 7,000 textile workers demonstrated in the streets of Mexico City demanding higher wages and a reduction in working hours.[52] All mills in Puebla and in the Orizaba Valley joined the strike.[53]

Workers from the Orizaba mills sent representatives to talk with government officials. Pánfilo Méndez and Lauro F. Luna, representing CIVSA and CIDOSA workers, met on January 8 with the minister of development.[54] On January 20, the Department of Labor called several employers and workers' representatives to Mexico City, and they agreed to a reduction in daily work hours to ten, and a 10% wage increase. They also agreed to organize a "Workers' and Industrialists' Convention" to negotiate a general wage list for the textile union and a set of regulations for all mills.[55] By then, the Department of Labor had already opened offices for the National Convention of Workers in Mexico City to provide workers with the space and necessary resources to prepare the proposal they would submit to the Workers' and Industrialists' Convention.[56]

These agreements did not put an end to increasing labor unrest; from January to September 1912, forty major strikes took place in the nation, four of them in the textile district of Atlixco.[57] New problems also arose in the Orizaba Valley. In February, CIDOSA fired a worker named Francisco Palafox because he had commissioned one of his fellow workers from San Lorenzo to collect funds for a mutualist society, Solidaridad Obrera, inside the mill's premises, which went against factory regulations. Workers protested and struck.[58] Antonio Ramos Pedrueza, director of the Department of Labor, went to Orizaba to talk to workers and employers and negotiate a solution. The conflict was solved, but Francisco Palafox was not readmitted to the mill.[59]

From July 2 to August 1, 1912, the Department of Labor held the Workers' and Industrialists' Convention in Mexico City. Textile mill owners showed great interest in participating in it; 98 of Mexico's 133 textile mills sent representatives.[60] Employers' and workers' committees held separate meetings. Then both positions were negotiated between the employers' representatives and the Department of Labor officials, who represented labor.[61]

The results of the convention were new factory regulations *(reglamento)* and a detailed wage list *(tarifa mínima)* for the textile industry throughout the country.[62] "This labor contract, the first in Mexico which had even a semblance of collective bargaining, seemed very radical in its provisions at the time."[63] Corroborating the January agreements, it limited the workday to ten hours, set the minimum wage at 1.25 pesos per day, abolished fines, and obliged employers to answer their workers' grievances within ten days.[64] A Workers' Standing Committee was created, with headquarters in Mexico City and branch committees in the various textile centers. These committees were to report infringements of the convention, and the Central Committee was to represent workers in any dispute that arose.[65]

These concessions did not come free to Orizaba workers. On July 3, when the first session of the Workers' and Industrialists' Convention had just started, a strike broke out in Cocolapan. The manager there had fired a worker, Angel Pérez, who was a member of the board *(vocal)* of the workers' Cocolapan association. Soon all the other mills in the region joined the strike, which meant, according to press reports, approximately 12,000 strikers.[66]

The government's new attitude toward workers did not prevent another massacre. Once again it happened at Río Blanco, although this time it was not government forces that fired against workers, but security personnel hired by the mill, the so-called group of volunteers.[67] According to *El Imparcial,* approximately thirty workers were killed, and many more were injured.[68]

According to CIDOSA a group of violent workers had tried to prevent other workers from entering the mill at the 2:00 p.m. call and they were opposed by the company's armed forces, which tried to reestablish order and liberate an officer who had been captured and injured by the crowd.[69] Several workers sent a letter to the Veracruz state attorney general, demanding justice. They explained that the "group of volunteers," which was paid by the company and under the orders of the mill's manager, had killed and injured several workers "whose only crime was to strike peacefully."[70]

The government's response was definitely different from how it had dealt with the strikes of 1906–1907. Manuel Castelazo Fuentes, the federal attorney general, immediately went to Orizaba to clarify what had happened. He learned that the volunteers were drunk, and that after shooting workers at the mill entrance, pursued those who had fled to the surrounding mountains, killing several others.[71] Colonel Rodríguez Malpica, Madero's chief of the presidential guards military unit (Jefe del Estado Mayor Presidencial) and a candidate for governor of Veracruz, visited Orizaba under Madero's orders to solve the conflict. He organized a meeting in Orizaba's Theater of the People attended by over 3,000 workers. Workers asked for the dismissal of the volunteers and of Río Blanco and Cocolapan's managers, José Reynaud and Herrechs, respectively. Rodríguez Malpica agreed to the first point; but explained that the government could not dismiss company managers.[72]

The assistant director of the Department of Labor also traveled to Orizaba to gather information on the conflict. According to him, Reynaud, Ollivier, and Levalois ordered the volunteers (approximately ninety) to attack the workers. From the factory windows, several shots were fired into the crowd and these three employees were identified as among those who shot from the mill.[73] Several witnesses identified them, and ballistic tests were carried out.[74] To the astonishment of the region's elite, Orizaba's penal judge ordered the arrest of Reynaud and Ollivier.[75] They were immediately detained but released the same night on 10,000 pesos bail.[76]

Madero's ambivalent attitude toward workers was clearly expressed in a message he sent to Río Blanco strikers. He told them the government could by no means support them financially, because that would be equivalent to acknowledging that justice was on their side. He considered the strike to be unjustified because their own representatives had already agreed with both the government and industrialists that any differences would be submitted to the Workers' Committee. However, he said that the government was doing everything within its means to punish those responsible for the bloodshed.[77]

All workers, except those from Río Blanco, returned to the mills on July 22. Yet when they reached the mill doors, they found lists posted with the names of over 100 workers who had been expelled. Santa Rosa's manager reported internally "that they were able to expel some pernicious elements."[78] The assistant director of the Department of Labor went to Río Blanco to negotiate with employers to reduce the number of expelled workers, but his efforts were to no avail. He returned to Mexico City with six workers to meet with the president.[79]

The workers proposed to President Madero that if the conflict was not solved, the government could give expelled workers vacant public lands and the means to cultivate them. Madero offered instead to find them jobs in other factories, but demanded that the rest immediately return to work.[80] The minister of the interior tried to obtain land in Chiapas for them, but the project meant great expense and was canceled.[81] On August 12, eighty-seven of the expelled workers arrived in Mexico City and were received by the Labor Department director, Antonio Ramos Pedrueza, who found them jobs in several Mexico City factories.[82]

On August 1, the Workers' and Industrialists' Convention ended its sessions. Despite its efforts, the Department of Labor had very little power to enforce the Convention's agreements. The regulations and the minimum tariff were never compulsory. To provide an incentive for their adoption, the Department of Labor arranged with the Ministry of Finance for a 50% discount on the "special tax" on the textile industry to be granted to those mills that complied with the regulations and the tariff.[83] By August 1914, the Department of Labor reported that only 42 out of 146 factories had not complied with the minimum tariff, but it based its report on information from the mills themselves, which it rarely inspected.[84]

Although the Convention's agreements generally benefited workers, it did not improve the situation much for those who had previously enjoyed higher than average wages, such as those in Orizaba, and for whom fines had long been abolished.[85] Workers from Santa Rosa struck for twelve days against the wage list approved by the Convention, because it barely increased spinners' wages.[86] Workers from other mills in the region joined the strike, while those from Río Blanco continued the strike that had started in early July.[87] Eventually workers accepted the new factory regulations and wage list. By August 12 all Orizaba mills were working.

From 1911 to 1912 several labor organizations were formed, mainly in Mexico City.[88] In May 1911 the Spaniard Amadeo Ferrer organized the Confederation of Graphical Arts, which later became the Typographers Union, headed by Antonio Díaz Soto y Gama. Its weekly, *El Tipógrafo Mexicano*, was circulated throughout the country.[89] This organization was important in the shift from mutualist societies to unions.[90] Also that year, the Union of Stonemasons of Mexico City (Unión de Canteros del Distrito Federal) and the Grand Labor League were founded. Soon other groups, such as the shoemakers, tailors, and bakers, followed their example.[91]

Most of these organizations were of a loose and casual character.[92] Some were mutualist, others professed syndicalist, socialist, anarchist, or communist doctrines. However, they were crucial to the formation of the Casa del Obrero, or House of Workers, in September 1912, conducted by disciples of Pedro Kropotkin and Max Simón Nordau, including Antonio Díaz Soto y Gama and Manuel Sarabia.[93] The word "Mundial" (World) was added to the Casa del Obrero's name a year later.[94] The Casa del Obrero Mundial (COM) lent coherence to the labor movement, becoming the headquarters of radical labor militants of the time.[95]

From 1912 to 1916, the COM was the most important workers' organization in Mexico. Conceived as a "Center of Doctrinaire Dissemination of Advanced Ideas," it was not a union, "but a meeting place where ideas were exchanged, compared and developed, where propaganda was prepared, and from which it was disseminated to all parts of the country."[96] From its inception, it was dominated by anarcho-syndicalist beliefs, and dedicated to a policy of nonpolitical, direct, even violent action, with an emphasis on general strike and sabotage. In order to pursue the education of workers, a "Rationalist School" was established in the COM, following the ideas of the Spaniard anarchist Francisco Ferrer Guardia, with the financial support of the Union of Stonemasons.[97] Madero feared its radicalism and opposed it but did not forbid it.[98] Instead, government strategy was to restrain its power through the Department of Labor and to place a limit on its most radical aspects. But in September 1912 Madero's government closed the Rationalist School, imprisoned the anarchist group "Luz" that published a workers' journal of the same name, and expelled the Spaniard Juan Francisco Moncaleano, founder of the Union of Stonemasons and one of the intellectual leaders of the COM.[99]

## A Labor-Constitutionalist Alliance

Madero's policies soon generated dissatisfaction. Some revolutionary groups, such as those led by Emilizano Zapata and Pascual Orozco, considered Madero had betrayed the Revolution and rebelled against him.

On the other side, members of the Porifiran elite deemed Madero's policies too radical and chaotic. Bernardo Reyes, former minister of war,
and Félix Díaz, Porifirio Díaz's nephew, organized two rebellions to
fight for a restoration of the status quo of Díaz's regime. They were defeated and imprisoned, but together with Victoriano Huerta, Madero's
minister of war, and the aid of the American embassy, they organized a
plot to overthrow Madero. In February 9, 1913, a group of rebels led by
General Mondragón freed Reyes and Díaz from prison. Together they
attacked the Maderista forces led by Huerta in a fake war, the "Tragic
Ten Days," that took many lives and caused much destruction in Mexico
City. On February 22, Madero and his vice president, José María Pino
Suárez, were first imprisoned and then assassinated. Reyes was killed in
the assault, and Huerta became the new president. This marked a new
episode of the revolutionary war, because several former revolutionaries
did not recognize Huerta and, under the leadership of Venustiano Carranza, governor of Coahuila, they formed the Constitutionalist army to
oust Huerta and reestablish the Constitution.[100]

Victoriano Huerta's coup d'état did not mark an end to the labor reforms of his predecessor. Huerta did not want to alienate labor, fearing
that masses of workers would support the Constitutionalist cause, but
neither did he want to support its more radical elements. Huerta appointed two brilliant reformers, Andrés Molina Enríquez and Rafael
Sierra, to direct the Department of Labor and doubled the department's
budget. He asked Congress to give the Department of Labor a ministe-
rial rank by transforming it into the Ministry of Industry, Commerce,
and Labor, as well as to decree the equality before the law of workers and
employers. Huerta's government also requested that Congress pass laws
to protect workers from accidents. However, Huerta's regime collapsed
before these reforms could take place.[101] The Department of Labor under his regime helped certain unions gain recognition from their employers, and approved the organization of the Confederation of Unions
of the Mexican Republic in Veracruz.[102] It also supported the agreements
of the Workers' and Industrialists' Convention and tried to ensure its
fulfillment.

On the other hand it led a purge of Maderistas that included many
industrial workers. On March 8, 1913, Huerta's forces under the com-

mand of Colonel Gaudencio de la Llave attacked Camerino Mendoza's house in Santa Rosa under the claim that he was planning an insurrection, and killed him and his two brothers. Later they summarily executed on the factory yard at least fifteen workers from Santa Rosa accused of being involved in the insurrection.[103] Among them was Esteban Zúñiga, who had been dismissed in November for being the vice president of the workers' association of that mill.[104] In May, Rafael Tapia was imprisoned under similar charges and assassinated by Huerta's police.

On May 1, 1913, Mexican workers publicly commemorated for the first time the Chicago massacre of 1886. Over 12,000 workers from the COM and several unions, workers' leagues, and mutualist societies marched through the streets of Mexico City demanding the eight-hour work shift and the Sunday rest.[105] This event must have increased the fears of Huerta's administration regarding the COM and workers' radicalism and made it ready to act against them on the next possible occasion. On May 25, the COM organized a meeting in which several speeches against Huerta's tyranny were proclaimed. Some hours later the government arrested several COM leaders together with everyone known to be influential in the labor movement—a total of twenty-two persons, including the deputy, Serapio Rendón, who was murdered.[106]

The COM was not closed down until a year later. It continued organizing its Sunday meetings, and its members kept writing articles for workers' journals, the *Emancipación Obrera* and the *Tinta Roja* being the most important at that time. The ideology of the COM further radicalized, as is clear from the speeches given at a meeting to commemorate the birth of the Commune of Paris that the COM organized in March and others that followed.[107] On May 27, 1914, Huerta sent the police to close the COM, and approximately twenty workers were imprisoned.[108]

Meanwhile, revolutionary armies trying to oust Huerta fought to gain control of strategic regions of the country, from which to expand in order to restore a constitutional national government. The corridor from the port of Veracruz to Mexico City was crucial. It was the main commercial route that linked the capital to foreign nations, and the port of Veracruz collected the major share of import and export duties, a substantial part of Mexico's fiscal income. Textile workers did not have the strategic importance that electricity or transport workers had in terms of the disruptive capability that their ceasing production could create.[109] However, the fact that textile workers were the largest organized group in the labor movement and that their clusters were precisely along the Veracruz–Mexico City corridor made them an important potential ally or enemy whose favor the revolutionaries were willing to gain.

Between April 1914 and April 1915, Mexico took a very sharp turn. On April 21, 1914, the U.S. navy occupied the port of Veracruz, blocking Huerta's access to imports and revenue, and reducing his military power to fight against the Constitutionalist army that wanted to depose him. On May 18, the Constitutionalist Cándido Aguilar took Tuxpan, where he became provisional governor of Veracruz. On August 20, major Constitutionalist military advances drove Huerta into exile. However, the revolutionary armies' attempt to negotiate an accord at the Convention of Aguascalientes, to create a united revolutionary government, failed, and instead war broke out between the revolutionary groups led by Pancho Villa and Emiliano Zapata, called the Conventionists, and those who followed Venustiano Carranza, who kept the former name "Constitutionalistas." On October 20, the Conventionists elected Eulalio Gutiérrez as provisional president, but Carranza did not recognize him and moved his government from Mexico City to Orizaba. On November 23, the United States evacuated the port of Veracruz. Three days later Aguilar occupied it, and Carranza moved his government there. Meanwhile, Villista and Zapatista forces occupied Mexico City. The Convention established its government there until January 28, 1915, when the Constitutionalist general Alvaro Obregón reoccupied the city. In March, Obregón evacuated Mexico City, and the Convention reoccupied it. In August, after Villa's defeat at the Bajío and his retreat north, Carranza moved his government to Mexico City.[110]

Orizaba industrial workers were geographically at the juncture of these great political and military movements, and became a valuable strategic resource for them. They played a minor role as soldiers in revolutionary armies. However, this would have been different without the intricate policy Constitutionalists devised to keep them calm working in the mills.

In October 1914 Governor Cándido Aguilar issued decrees no. 7 and 11 to improve the conditions of workers. They made Sunday a compulsory day of rest, reduced the workday from ten to nine hours, required double pay for night shifts, and obliged owners to provide medical assistance and pay to sick or injured workers.[111] These decrees indicate how far the revolutionary government in Veracruz was willing to go to obtain labor support.

However, its ability to enforce the new laws was limited. The government left it to workers to seek compliance with the new laws. Thus, the reduction of the workday, established by the October 1914 decree, was not carried out in Orizaba until 1915, after several workers' protests. Following Aguilar, in December 1914 Carranza issued a famous decree in which he promised that as soon as he became president his government would expedite and implement "the laws, dispositions, and measures necessary" to improve the conditions of the working classes.[112]

When Carranza entered Mexico City in August 1914, after defeating Huerta, the COM was reopened.[113] The Federation of Workers' Unions of the Federal District (FSODF) had been formed by then and became the Casa's most important affiliated union.[114] In late 1914, when the Constitutionalists controlled Mexico City, General Alvaro Obregón approached certain influential members of the COM, asking them to take an active part in the struggle, and giving the Casa a generous and politically important amount of money to distribute among workers to alleviate their penury.[115] The Casa soon held a meeting with the FSODF where members voted to support the Constitutionalist army.[116]

The Casa entered into an agreement with Carranza and his government, represented by Rafael Zubarán Capmany, in which were stipulated the practical rewards that the workers would expect to receive as payment for their entry into the war.[117] On February 17, 1915, Carranza reluctantly signed the pact, on Obregón's insistence. It stipulated that the Constitutionalist government pledged to fulfill the decree of December 12, 1914. Furthermore, the Constitutionalists agreed to back the "just claims of the workers in any conflicts which may arise between them and employers, as a consequence of the labor contract" and to offer all possible aid in the formation of new unions.[118] Workers from every branch of the COM were to hold the territory conquered by the Constitutionalist army, and act as reserves.[119]

In February 1915 approximately 8,000 persons, including COM workers and their families, moved to Orizaba to join Carranza's forces there.[120] They were received by a crowd of workers who were waiting for them, and were given several churches for housing, to the outrage of the city's religious citizens. Carranza sent one of his colonels to give workers military instruction, and six groups with 600 to 1,000 workers each, known as Red Battalions, were formed and sent to different parts of the country.[121]

While in Orizaba, COM workers conducted a powerful propaganda campaign to recruit industrial workers from the region into their ranks. A few days after arrival they marched up the valley's main street from Orizaba to Santa Rosa to pay homage to the martyrs of January 7, 1907. In April they organized several labor unions in shoe and cigar factories and in the important Moctezuma brewery.[122] Yet among textile workers they were not very successful, as these workers were no amateurs in labor organization. Textile workers from the Orizaba Valley had had at least eight years of organized labor struggle by then, and two months before the COM's arrival they had formed "resistance associations" sponsored by the Department of Labor of the Constitutionalist government.

When Carranza established his government in Veracruz in November 1914, the Department of Labor moved along with him.[123] Because its lack of resources and infrastructure prevented it from doing very much, it decided to focus its energies on the most important strategic target, Orizaba. In January 1915, the Department of Labor installed local offices in Orizaba and appointed two inspectors to monitor compliance with the 1912 Convention.[124] Moreover, Marcos López Jiménez, then director of the Department of Labor, personally went to Orizaba to promote the foundation of resistance associations (known as *mesas de resistencia* or *agrupaciones de resistencia*) in each factory. He did not wish to alienate employers, so he sent letters to all mill managers informing them that he was in the city to exchange ideas with workers of the region and solve any outstanding difficulties. He invited them to talk with him, if they wished, at the Grand Hotel de France where he was staying.[125]

Between January 11 and 17, López Jiménez organized workers' assemblies in San Lorenzo, Cerritos, Santa Gertrudis, San Lorenzo, Cocolapan, Santa Rosa, and Río Blanco, in all of which resistance associations were created. Under his auspices, workers elected the boards of their associations, and at solemn ceremonies, attended by officers of the Constitutionalist army, inspectors of the Department of Labor, and municipal presidents, the boards were officially appointed.[126] The resolute and expeditious election of these associations' boards indicates that what actually took place was not the creation of new organizations but the formalization of previously existing ones. The minutes of the organizations' meetings suggest that the elections to choose the members of their directive boards were carried out democratically.[127]

Some weeks later, the San Lorenzo resistance association invited others to form a regional association. On February 27 it was formally constituted, and its board, the so-called Central Board, was elected.[128] Textile firms did not readily accept the resistance associations. Even with the government's patronage these organizations faced great difficulties in being recognized by the mills' management as representatives of workers.[129] In July 1915, for example, workers from the Santa Gertrudis jute mill sent a letter to Governor Cándido Aguilar complaining that the managers of the mill did not recognize their association and had fired several of the members of its board without pretext.[130] The lack of recognition of workers' associations by the firms, together with the urgent need to obtain a raise in wages, given the rising inflation, convinced the Central Board of the need to go to Veracruz to negotiate a general wage increase with Carranza. In Veracruz, the Central Board also sought an interview with Zubarán Capmany, minister of the interior, because he was working on a project for a labor law.

In March, while the Central Board was in the port of Veracruz, the COM arrived in Orizaba. Several letters between them and the leaders of the mills' resistance associations tell of the anxiety the arrival of the COM provoked. They feared that all their members would join the COM and that their organizations would disappear. Members of the Central Board wrote to the government that the COM held socialist ideas to which they objected.[131] According to them, the COM was telling workers that the Department of Labor was useless and that workers were not going to obtain what they wanted through legislation, but would have to achieve it through use of arms instead.[132]

The COM's first target was Río Blanco, where on March 15 there was a brief strike, caused by "elements alien to the locality."[133] According to members of the resistance association, a majority of workers from Río Blanco apparently decided to join the COM, take arms, and forget about their jobs.[134] In fact, despite opposition from the resistance associations, several workers did follow this course.[135]

Faced with the option of supporting either the COM or the more moderate leaders of the resistance associations, Carranza, who always had strong doubts about the convenience of recruiting industrial workers into the revolutionary army, found it opportune to support the latter.[136] On March 21 Carranza decreed a wage increase of 35% to day workers and of 40% to pieceworkers for the textile industry.[137] This decree gave great leverage to the resistance associations to convince their members of the advisability of staying on the Department of Labor's side and keeping the COM away from the mills.

The temporary consensus that the COM had achieved at Río Blanco was broken.[138] Only at Cocolapan was the COM able to convince the majority of workers to establish a union in that mill. However, López Jiménez, using coercive measures, soon deposed the COM's leaders there and replaced them with workers who supported the Department of Labor.[139]

Gonzalo San Juan Hernández was one of the Cocolapan workers who joined the Red Battalions. He explained that he enlisted with the Third Company of the Great Powers that were recruiting workers at Río Blanco because the mill had practically stopped working after most of the workers from the mill left to join the revolution. Moreover, he would be paid 2 pesos daily, plus rations of corn and beans, while in the mills he could get only 70 to 80 cents daily. Though he did not seem to have had any ideological reasons to join the Red Battalions, once there he became acquainted with the anarcho-syndicalist doctrine, he learned about Miguel Lacurín, Carl Marx, Becker, and Francisco Ferrer Guardia, and later became a libertarian syndicalist and an important leader of the Cocolapan labor movement.[140] The ideological influence of the COM seems to have been considerable for the Orizaba labor movement. According to Gonzalo García Ortíz, a Santa Rosa worker, many workers from Santa Rosa joined the Red Battalions, and when they returned they came back with more awakened ideas.[141]

However, most workers from the Orizaba Valley kept working in the factories, as Carranza had advised the first COM commission that visited him as to what workers should do, "because working is one way of helping the Revolution."[142] Moreover, of those workers who decided to take up arms, only one part joined a Red Battalion, while the other remained in the valley under the orders of an officer loyal to Carranza.[143]

Having the backing of the Department of Labor had its rewards. In the following months, its inspectors proved very helpful in solving several conflicts between mill hands and employers in favor of the former.[144] However, the Department of Labor had no legal power to demand compliance of Aguilar's decrees because they were state regulations. It was therefore necessary to involve the government of Veracruz. In September 1915, the interim governor, Agustín Millán, created an Industrial Commission with three branches: one to inspect compliance with Aguilar's decrees, known then as the Labor Law; another to inspect health and hygiene; and a third to inspect commercial and accounting matters regarding taxation and prices. The governor appointed the chief of the State Bureau of Development and Agriculture in Veracruz, the engineer Victorio E. Góngora, as head of the commission.[145]

In the following months, numerous letters from the inspectors of the Industrial Commission flooded companies' correspondence. Health inspectors visited the mills to see if the companies had applied the necessary precautionary measures to reduce accidents.[146] They also required companies to compensate workers who had suffered accidents or became sick. From then on, the companies reluctantly began to provide payments to sick and injured workers, and to the relatives of workers who died as a result of accidents or job-related diseases.[147] However, companies rejected most of the requests, alleging that the diseases were not of an occupational nature.[148] Commercial inspectors were less effective. Their duties required information from the companies that firms felt no obligation to provide. No regulations legally bound them to do so, and companies always denied their requests.[149]

The Labor Law Commission was the one with the greatest impact, because it could exact fines. In September and October it penalized companies on several occasions for failure to comply with the Labor Law's regulations on working hours and payment for night work.[150] The reduction of the workday to nine hours was not carried out until companies received signed petitions from the mill's workers' associations, backed by the Department of Labor, in August 1915. CIVSA's manager explained that the company had been able to defend itself against workers' requests to comply with Aguilar's decrees by explaining that the company remained subject to the agreements of the 1912 Convention.[151] In those days when several regulations coexisted, this was an easy way out. However, in September 1915 the state government informed companies that they had no excuse for disregarding the Labor Law, because it voided all previous regulations.[152]

Concerned by the inspectors' frequent visits and fines, CIVSA and CIDOSA sought an interview with Governor Aguilar to talk about his October 1914 decrees. They were especially worried about having to pay night work and overtime at a double rate since they were currently paying only 10% extra. The companies explained that these regulations caused them enormous problems. Governor Aguilar advised them to pay at piece rates, because in that case workers could labor all the time required to finish their tasks without extra payment.[153] Aguilar's response shows that from the beginning Constitutionalists sought a middle path between employers and workers in order not to alienate either. It also shows that government decrees and legislation were more radical than those who decreed them. Therefore, lack of enforcement, and ways around the law, were due not only to a lack of resources but also to a clever strategy.

During the second half of 1915, upon the advice of the Industrial Commission, mills' resistance associations became labor unions *(sindicatos)*.[154] This change probably came from Góngora's attempt to fit Mexican labor regulations to the standards in Europe and the United States, of which he was very aware.[155] Furthermore, it would give the unions a stronger position to fight against the COM, whose associations had been labor unions from the beginning.

In May 1915 San Lorenzo workers sent a letter to Governor Cándido Aguilar to inform him that the union of workers of spinning and weaving of the San Lorenzo mill had been established, "accepting the modern means of struggle suggested by the painful experience acquired, to oppose a check against the injustices that until today have been inflicted upon us."[156] The articles of incorporation of Santa Rosa's union explain that on September 21, 1915, most workers from the mill attended a meeting at the Juárez Theater where summoned by a "Delegate of Labor" they unanimously voted to become a union. They then elected the union's secretary general, secretary of the interior, secretary of the exterior, secretary of minutes *(Actas),* and secretary treasurer.[157]

Although apparently created by the government, the names, emblems, and slogans chosen by the unions tell of the living memory of the Gran Círculo de Obreros Libres among workers and of its organizational experience. Río Blanco and Cocolapan workers included the term "Free Workers" (Obreros Libres), which recalled the GCOL into their unions' names. They were the Sindicato de Obreros Libres de Río Blanco and the Sindicato de Obreros Libres de Hilados y Tejidos de la Fábrica de Cocolapan.[158]

The emblem of San Lorenzo's union was written over the face of Juárez, bringing to mind the admiration that the Club Melchor Ocampo, the PLM, and the GCOL had for him, and for the 1857 Constitution. On the other hand, liberal praise for progress appears to have been part of the San Lorenzo and Santa Rosa workers' beliefs. Their unions should be a step for progress and "progressive workers." Thus they called themselves the Sindicato de Obreros Progresistas de San Lorenzo and Sindicato de Obreros y Artesanos Progresistas de Santa Rosa.[159] Cerritos workers, for their part, preferred to be "evolutionary" workers, naming their union Sindicato de Obreros Evolutivos de Cerritos, recalling positivist praise for evolution.

These "free," "progressive," and "evolutionary" unions met later that month to form the Chamber of Labor of Orizaba, which replaced the Central Board of Resistance Associations. The patronage of the Veracruz state government was evident. The inspector of the Labor Law, Domingo A. Jiménez, came to the region to give a talk on the chambers or federations of labor. The creation of the Chamber of Labor responded to the challenge posed by the recently created COM's Federation of Workers of Orizaba, which grouped seamstresses, masons, and beer, tramway, and tobacco workers.[160]

In October, interim governor Millán issued a decree by which labor unions acquired civil status and federations or labor chambers were legally recognized. As a consequence of this decree the function of the inspectors of the Labor Law acquired legal status.[161] In December 1915, he decreed the Law of Professional Associations, which specified the requirements unions should fulfill in order to be recognized. The law established that labor unions had to register at the Juntas de Administración Civil (Civil Administration Boards), and submit to them their objectives and regulations. Unions should explain their means of obtaining resources, the use to which they would be put, the conditions of admission and separation of their members, and the way their executive committees were chosen. They must submit to the *Juntas* a biannual report of their financial operations.[162] When Aguilar returned to the governorship of Veracruz a month later, he again issued this law, with basically the same wording.[163]

Legalization of unions meant that for the first time they could legally deal directly with the mills' management, and make petitions and demands in their own names. Before 1914 there were practically no letters in companies' correspondence files that dealt with labor conditions. Only very sporadically did managers receive petitions signed personally by workers. Then, in the first semester of 1915, companies began to receive several letters from the Department of Labor. During the second semester of 1915, more letters came from inspectors from the Commission of Industry. After 1916, unions' letters replaced those of the former agencies, which, although they continued to write, did so less frequently. It was not only the correspondents but also the quantity of correspondence that changed. Unions' communication with the firms from 1916 on was much more abundant than that from the government agencies, even at their height.[164] In 1915 there were also plenty of letters sent from the unions to Governor Cándido Aguilar asking his support for their organizations or for his intervention in specific disputes against the companies, which he often answered favorably.[165]

On January 13, 1916, Orizaba textile unions took a decisive step toward gaining control over hiring and firing. The Orizaba unions, the companies' managers, and governor Aguilar signed an agreement giving unionized workers preference in filling vacancies and management power to fire workers who refused to join the union. It also established that no worker could be fired without justified cause. In case of conflict, the Arbitration Committee, formed by the secretary general of the union, the factory manager, and the Labor inspector, had to make the final decision. In practice, according to the CIVSA board, this meant that in order to fire any worker, the company had to pay him a three months' wage.[166] On the strength of this agreement, most day-shift workers at Orizaba mills became union members under a collective contract.

Orizaba unions were able to offer powerful resistance to the constant deterioration of real wages that workers faced as a result of rising inflation in 1915–1916, through several general strikes. Most important were the strikes that took place in May, October, and November 1916 demanding payment of wages in gold. As a consequence of rising inflation, "all over the country, during the latter part of 1915 and the first months of 1916, workers were exceedingly restless, and strike followed strike in swift succession."[167] As long as they were against private concerns, Carranza's government did not actively interfere, "but when the depreciated currency of the country became the principle causes of discord his action was both prompt and drastic."[168]

When unions of the Tampico oilfields struck against low wages in April 1916, with the COM's support, Carranza sent the army to repress the strike and imprison its leaders.[169] Similarly, a strike by railroad workers in early May demanding that wages were paid in gold was declared illegal by Minister of War Alvaro Obregón and some of its leaders were arrested.[170]

From May 20 to May 26, 1916, Orizaba workers joined a strike that reached national levels. On May 23, bakers, electricians, and tramway, telephone, and water workers in the national capital struck. While Orizaba workers suffered no repression from the government, the situation in Mexico City turned out differently. The military commander of Mexico City, Benjamín Hill, ordered strikers to return to work, arresting those who did not comply with his orders.[171] With the government's intervention, the strike ended with a compromise by which wages were raised by 400%.

Yet as inflation kept rising and real wages deteriorated, on June 31 the FSODF organized another general strike in Mexico City, joined by more than 30,000 workers.[172] All public services—water, light, telephone, and transport—were paralyzed. "Labor, which had served Carranza's purpose, now threatened to become a menace," and Carranza's government reacted harshly to it.[173] Troops led by General Pablo González occupied the headquarters of the COM and of the Mexican Electricians Union

(SME), the most important member of the FSODF, as well as the shop of the workers' weekly *Acción Mundial.* Carranza declared the COM illegal and, based on a law passed by Juárez in 1862 that ordered death to traitors, he decreed the death penalty for those who remained on strike.[174] This was a hard blow against Mexico's labor movement.

After closing the COM in Mexico City, Carranza launched a campaign against COM branches in the states. He ordered governors to close the COM's offices, arrest their leaders, and confiscate their propaganda. Because the COM and the Orizaba Labor Chamber shared offices in the Dolores parish church, both were ousted from the church. After several days of negotiation, the Orizaba Labor Chamber headquarters reopened on condition that the COM could no longer share its offices.[175]

In July 1916, while these events were taking place, the Chamber of Labor of Orizaba decided to pursue the ambitious objective of organizing a National Textile Convention to revise the agreements of the 1912 Convention.[176] If it had been organized, it would have marked a major turning point in Mexican labor history, showing workers' ability and power to organize such an event. Labor's role in shaping "the Revolution" would have been different and greater. Even after the COM's demise, the "moderate" branch of the labor movement, which Orizaba textile workers then represented, could have stood on more independent ground and would have been able to frame more powerfully its conditions to support the revolutionary governments. Unfortunately the Textile Convention of 1916 remained an unfulfilled dream.

The plans for the Convention were the following. First delegates from the Orizaba Chamber of Labor would study the working conditions at Orizaba and draft a document that would express Orizaba workers' position in the Convention. It would then appoint commissions to visit textile workers throughout Mexico, to encourage them to help organize the Convention. Finally all workers' delegates would meet in Mexico City to elaborate a national platform and press the Ministry of Development to invite industrialists to the Convention.[177]

In accordance with the strategy of cooperation with the government that the Orizaba Chamber of Labor had pursued, it sought the support of Veracruz's interim governor, Heriberto Jara, and of the Ministry of

Development. Carranza was not convinced that a national convention was a good idea and proposed that the Orizaba delegates organize it at a regional level instead. He reluctantly accepted the Chamber's plans, perhaps because after crushing the COM he could not afford to alienate the less radical workers. Funds for the national tour were provided mostly by the Orizaba textile unions (2,500 pesos), but some funds also came from the Veracruz government (1,000 pesos), and from the Ministry of Development, which gave them railway tickets.[178]

The first part of the Convention plan was carried out successfully. Chamber delegates presented a technically elaborate proposal of the wages to be paid at each job and of the working conditions that should prevail in the mills. However, the second part of the project, which required the existence of a well-organized labor movement throughout the nation, proved to be too difficult.

From October to December 1916, delegates from Orizaba's Chamber visited 43 mills in Puebla, Tlaxcala, Mexico City, the state of Mexico, Michoacán, Guanajuato, Jalisco, Nuevo León, and Coahuila. In Puebla they reached twenty-five additional mills through the National Confederation of Labor, which represented them.[179] But they were not very successful.

If the Revolution provided an opportunity for the labor movement to organize projects such as the Textile Convention, it also created tremendous hardships. Given the rising inflation the country faced during this period, the paper money in which resources for the trips were given depreciated daily, and became totally insufficient for travel expenses. Workers in Orizaba, who also were suffering from the deterioration of their real wages, could not offer more support to the Chamber delegates. Thus, the commissions endured great privations. Their travels were cut short when they realized that they only had enough money left to get back to their homes. Moreover, a third of the mills the commission planned to visit were closed. Others were in such a precarious situation that it was impossible for their workers to collect funds to send delegates to the Convention.[180]

Orizaba's chamber delegates found on their trip that textile labor was less organized than they expected. Sixteen of the mills they visited lacked any form of workers' association. With the efforts of Orizaba delegates, unions were formed in ten of them. However, these unions were too poor to support the Convention. Orizaba's Chamber of Labor did, however, manage to organize a meeting in Mexico City in March 1917 attended by over sixty delegates from several mills throughout the country. This encounter was meant to delineate the proposal on wages and regulations that workers would submit to the Workers' and Industrialists' Convention to be held on May 1. Industrialists were also preparing for the Convention and several inspectors from the Department of Labor were visiting the factories in order to report on the prevailing conditions there. However, Carranza's government adamantly opposed the Convention, proposing instead that conferences be held separately in each state.[181]

In the local arena Orizaba Valley textile workers were more successful. After 1916, Orizaba's unions played an active role in the election of its members as municipal presidents. Until that year, municipal presidents of the various mill towns in the Orizaba Valley had normally been white-collar employees from the factories. This gave companies direct power in these towns. Workers considered this power equivalent to "including justice in the company's inventory and making authority a blind instrument to quiet the voice of those workers who had the energy to complain against daily abuses."[182] When Santa Rosa had its first worker elected as municipal president in 1916, the situation inverted and CIVSA's board complained: "we have a weaver as municipal president and only one gendarme for police, it is not from respect for these authorities that workers will stop stealing."[183]

## Labor and the Constitution of 1917

Soon after Carranza's Constitutionalist forces took control of the country, they began to organize the process for the writing of a new Constitution. In September Carranza issued a decree establishing the rules for the election of the deputies of a Constitutionalist Congress that should meet in Querétaro between December 1916 and January 1917 to design a new Constitution.[184]

Although the Constitutionalist deputies were mostly middle-class professionals, there were also some workers among them, such as Héctor

Victoria, a railroad worker from Yucatán, Nicolás Cano, a miner from Guanajuato, Dionisio Zavala, a miner from San Luis Potosí, and Carlos Grácidas, a typographer from Veracruz who formerly belonged to the COM. Among the Constitutional delegates there were also some revolutionaries who had been close to labor problems, and particularly to those of the Orizaba region, such as Heriberto Jara, Cándido Aguilar, and Victorio Góngora, who as head of the Veracruz Industrial Commission had sought the implementation of Aguilar's labor laws in Orizaba. Others, such as Cayetano Andrade, a physician and journalist from Michoacán, considered that their election as Constitutionalist deputies was based on labor support, and thus felt obliged to defend their interests. These deputies were crucial in how the Constitutionalist Congress transformed Carranza's original proposal, which sought only minor reforms to Article 5 of the 1857 Constitution dealing with the freedom to work.

Against those who considered that the Constitution should include only general principles, that the future labor laws should expand, Jara, Aguilar, and Góngora proposed that the Article should include more specific rights, such as the eight-hour workday, the right to equal pay for equal work, and payment for workers' diseases and accidents, supported by all the worker deputies and many others. If the Constitution included only broad and vague principles, deputy Victoria argued, "these public freedoms would pass as the stars over the head of the proletarians: far away." Moreover, "Who guarantees us that the new Congress will be integrated by revolutionaries?," the Pueblan journalist Froylán Manjarrez asked.[185] After several days of debates the deputies carried further Jara, Aguilar, and Góngora's proposal, voting in favor of including a whole chapter in the Constitution that explicitly stated all the workers' rights that they deemed necessary for improving laborers' working and living conditions.

In the following days, José Natividad Macías, one of the lawyers who had prepared Carranza's proposal for the Constitution, presented a project that would become the basis of Article 123. Macías had formerly written a project for a labor law, together with Luis Manuel Rojas, as a member of the Section of Social Legislation of Carranza's government in Veracruz.[186] The article was also nourished by the experiences of the recent labor legislation carried out in Veracruz and Yucatán.[187]

Traditional historiography has identified Article 123 of the 1917 Constitution as the major turning point in labor relations and working conditions for industrial workers. It was, in fact, one of the most progressive constitutional provisions of its time, granting the right to strike, legalizing unions, forbidding child labor, establishing maternity leave, reducing the daily shift to a maximum of eight hours, determining employers' responsibility for work-related accidents and occupational illnesses, and creating boards of conciliation and arbitration to settle disputes between capital and labor. Yet in the case of industrial workers in Veracruz, and perhaps also in varying degrees in other states such as Puebla, Tlaxcala, the state of Mexico, and Mexico City, this code only crystallized gains that had already been made during the previous decade. In those regions where the labor movement was strong, it basically only gave legal support to an already existing situation. In those regions where there was no strong labor movement to enforce Article 123, it remained an ideal that was very far from daily practice.

# CHAPTER 6

# Labor and the First
# Postrevolutionary Regimes

O N MAY 1, 1917, Venustiano Carranza took office as president of
Mexico, after having been elected by a majority. This was also
Mexico's first day under its new Constitution, which the *New York Times*
called "the most liberal and advanced ever attempted."[1] Thousands of
people acclaimed Carranza as he drove from the National Palace to the
Chamber of Deputies to take the oath to support the new Constitution.

Workers had high expectations for Article 123, but a long road had
to be traversed before it was put into practice, even in regions like the
Orizaba Valley where many of the rights it granted were already in place.
In the following months the Orizaba labor movement devoted its energies to adapting its organizations and practices to the new Constitution,
as well as to forcing the companies to comply with it. However, their
struggle also involved coping with ways the employers found to use the
new Constitution to set back some of the gains organized workers from
Orizaba had already achieved.

Only one day after the reestablishment of the constitutional order,
thousands of textile workers from Orizaba, Mexico City, and Michoacán
went on strike to demand an eight-hour shift and a wage raise that compensated the reduction in working hours, given that most workers were
paid by piece, as well as the hike in prices of the previous months.[2] In

the following weeks, textile workers from Querétaro, Puebla, Tlaxcala, and Jalisco went on strike for similar reasons.[3] Because the National Convention that the workers had planned never took place, separate conventions were carried out in Mexico City, Veracruz, and other states.

Orizaba workers were appeased with a resolution from the Veracruz Convention that gave them a wage raise substantially higher than that granted in any other region. Also implemented were the eight-hour shift and regulations requiring companies to provide coverage for accidents, sickness, and pensions contemplated in Article 123 of the new Constitution. Companies accepted such conditions because they were afraid that Carranza would seize any mill that did not attend their local conventions or accept their resolutions.[4]

On June 21, 1917, several unions from the Orizaba Valley signed a pact whereby they formed the Federación Sindicalista del Cantón de Orizaba, which replaced the Chamber of Labor of Orizaba, in order to adjust their organization to the 1917 Constitution. The Federation's pact established a procedure for nominating workers' representatives to the Arbitration Boards established by the Constitution. It also formalized the proceedings by which the Federation would support a strike organized by a factory union.[5]

The Federation's principles established that it would employ "the syndicalist struggle excluding all political action—meaning officially adhering to any group, party or person that seeks governmental power."[6] To guarantee the absolute independence of the Federation and the affiliated unions, any member who held a position on their committees would be immediately dismissed if he or she accepted an appointment or election to public office or a position in any association that organized a political campaign.

Affiliated unions should be exclusively resistance associations, which meant that they should be devoted to representing and defending workers' interests vis-à-vis those of employers. They could, however, carry out mutualist practices, as long as they did not interfere with syndicalism. In its principles, the Federation declared its interest in improving workers' education by establishing libraries and schools that followed the rationalist system of teaching, and supporting consumers' cooperatives. It would seek the enforcement of Article 123 of the Constitution, referred to as the "Labor Law" in Federation documents.[7] Recalling the experience of *La Revolución Social* and *Unión Obrera,* it founded the weekly *Pro-Paria* on February 6, 1917.[8] Orizaba's organized workers, like those of the nation in general, were at this moment caught between participating in politics and focusing on a purely syndicalist struggle. When the Federation determined its principles, it appears that the syndicalist strategy reigned; yet circumstances would soon draw the Federation into politics.

### The Veracruz Labor Law and the Boards of Conciliation and Arbitration

Article 123 of the Constitution gave jurisdiction over labor legislation to the states. Until 1931, when a federal labor code was adopted, state labor laws regulated capital–labor relations. Veracruz's labor law, published on January 14, 1918, was the first to appear, and was a model for several that followed. It codified several rights granted generally in Article 123, but also went beyond its precepts.

A major problem of Article 123 was that it did not explicitly articulate the concepts of labor organization or collective contract, and did not define the institution of conciliation and arbitration boards.[9] The Veracruz code sought to fill these vacuums by defining the individual and collective employment contracts, and establishing the requirements for the legal constitution of unions, which it understood as trade unions. Following the model of the labor regulations of Yucatán of 1915, the Veracruz statute set up Municipal Boards of Conciliation, and a Central Board of Conciliation and Arbitration.[10] These were defined as "administrative authorities dependent on the executive power with a tripartite membership of labor and business representatives, headed by a government official."[11] The central boards were given the responsibility to exercise jurisdiction over municipal boards and the special commissions on the minimum wage, to hear and resolve conflicts between labor and capital related to the labor contract, to approve factory rules, and to register or cancel the registration of labor organizations.

The law included many controversial articles. One of them mandated the payment of an extra 50% of the wage for the seven-hour night shift instead of the double pay that had been established by Aguilar's decree of October 1914.[12] Another article obliged employers to provide medical services and wages to their workers not only because of occupational accidents and disease, but also for nonoccupational illness, during which workers would draw half pay and receive free medical care and medicines from the companies. Finally, an article stipulated that the profit-sharing mandated in the Constitution take the form of an extra month's wages to every worker at the end of each year of service.[13] However, these articles were extremely difficult to enforce. The first was not complied with because the firms preferred to cancel the second shift rather than pay an over rate. The second was so ambiguous that it was easy for firms to avoid its full compliance. The third was completely futile; companies won the judicial fight that declared it unconstitutional.[14]

Implementing Article 123 and the Veracruz Labor Law became a difficult task because they did not fit well into the legal structure that the rest of the Constitution established. The Constitutionalists' decision to place labor rights in a new chapter, separate from Article 5, left open a contradiction between individual rights and social rights. If labor rights had been placed within the article on individual rights, they would have become expansive and self-executing. Locating them in the social and economic regulations gave them a lower legal status. Moreover, Article 123 provisions regarding the labor boards and minimum wage commissions were too vague to provide practical guidance for their establishment or to prevent them from being challenged in court. This opened up an arena of contention for the judiciary to resolve.[15]

According to mill owners, labor's strength in Orizaba during these years was the result not only of the strategic support government gave it, but also of government's inability to exert any effective repression or control over it. In May 1918 CIVSA's manager said that unions became more demanding every day "because of the weakness of the public authorities."[16] According to employers in Veracruz, government was so weak that it was unable to support companies against unions even if it was willing to. In June 1919, for example, CIVSA's manager spoke with Governor Armando Deschamps about the union's efforts to overrule the superintendents of the mill departments. CIVSA's manager said that the governor had offered his help to reduce the union's demands, but "unfortunately," the manager reported, "his authority is very slight, given the lack of troops in the region, and his fear that workers may join the mass of revolutionaries that are almost at the factories' doors."[17]

However, the employers were not powerless. From 1918 on, disputes between workers and employers were channeled to the Municipal Conciliation Boards. Here workers had strong support because in those years municipal presidents in the Orizaba mill towns were usually blue-collar workers. Thus, the CIVSA board complained in 1917 that "[because] in Santa Rosa he [the municipal president] is nothing but the puppet of labor unions, in consequence we will never win any case."[18] In 1918 the CIVSA board complained that municipal presidents, as part of the Municipal Conciliation Boards, always biased the board's decisions in favor of workers.[19]

However, if no accord was reached locally, which was usually the case, the disputes went to the Junta Central de Conciliación y Arbitraje (JCCA) in Córdoba, then the capital of the state, where government authorities were not as biased in favor of labor as the companies claimed. Eleven disputes between the unions and the textile companies of the Orizaba Valley were solved by the JCCA between 1918 and 1920. Six of them were settled in favor of the companies, three in favor of the unions, and two were middle-ground solutions.[20] However, in two of the three cases where the companies lost, and in one middle-ground solution, the companies filed writ of mandamus *(amparo)* petitions.[21] The companies won all the amparo lawsuits, two of which were decided by the Supreme Court. The only dispute that workers won was one in which the Federación Sindicalista del Cantón de Orizaba claimed that the companies disobeyed an award of the JCCA that obliged them to provide medical assistance to workers. Lack of compliance appears to have been yet another resource for the companies against labor regulations.[22] Thus the contention that during these years there was full transformation of the labor regime and that a workers' revolution had taken place needs to be qualified.[23]

These conflicts generated a long series of strikes that went from October 1918 through the following year, as well as several demonstrations against the Supreme Court rulings, which workers considered anticonstitutional.[24] The main reason behind the Supreme Court rulings was that until 1924 it did not recognize fully the legitimacy of the Boards of Conciliation and Arbitration, and considered that they could not impose mandatory orders.[25]

## The Birth of the CROM and Orizaba Labor

Between 1916 and 1918, many labor organizations in Mexico sought to create a national confederation of workers. However, deep divisions between the various labor groups, for both ideological and political reasons, made this a difficult task. The Federation of Trade Unions of the Federal District, under the leadership of Luis N. Morones, convened a labor congress in the port of Veracruz in March 1916, attended by representatives from all Orizaba mills.[26] The Labor Confederation of the Mexican Republic was created at this congress, but it never became functional. On one side stood the anarchists, represented most notably by Herón Proal, who was to become the leader of the radical tenants' movement in the state of Veracruz some years later. On the other side were the more pragmatic trade unionists, above all Morones himself, who regarded the romantic, anarchistic direction that the labor organizations had taken as a mistake. Given their irreconcilable positions, this Confederation's life ended with the closing of the congress that had created it.[27]

The second labor congress was organized by the Tampico unions that belonged to the branch of the city's COM. It was held in Tampico on October 13, 1917, and attended by delegates from twelve states.[28] Again the meeting dissolved into factional clashes between anarchists and syndicalists. Although a syndicalist program was adopted and a committee appointed to create a central federation, it never functioned either.[29]

The third, ultimately successful attempt at central organization was made under government auspices. Afraid of the influence that the COM and anarchist ideas still exerted over workers, Carranza's government sought to regain control over at least some of the organized workers.[30] The governor of Coahuila, Gustavo Espinosa Mireles, one of Carranza's trusted partisans, organized a labor convention in May 1918, out of which the CROM was born.[31] Eighteen states were represented by unions that embraced different tendencies. Its executive committee was composed of Jacinto Huitrón, an anarchist, Luis N. Morones, a trade unionist, Teodoro

Ramírez, a syndicalist, and Ricardo Treviño, an Industrial Workers of the World (IWW) affiliate.[32] The trade unionists represented by Luis N. Morones dominated the congress, and Morones became the CROM's first secretary general.[33]

Luis N. Morones, a former electrician, had proved to be a moderate and useful partner for Carranza. During the repression of the COM in Mexico City in 1916, instead of taking an active part in the strike, as manager of the Mexican Telephone Company, Morones aligned against the workers.[34] His view of "pursuing fewer ideals and more organization" shaped the nature of the CROM. The confederation's strategy was to forget about the concept of direct action and follow a policy of multiple actions instead, recognizing the weakness of labor organization in Mexico at a national level and acting to find governmental patronage that would give it political power.[35]

The base of the CROM was the union of workers of the same trade or same establishment. Local groups united into a local federation, local federations of each state joined into a state federation, and these in turn formed the national group. The central committee of the CROM was its managing board.[36] Final authority rested, theoretically, in the national convention, which met regularly from 1918 and 1928, and then not until 1932.[37] However, both the central committee and the national conventions followed very closely the dictates of a small and select inner circle known as the Grupo Acción, or Action Group. Its existence, in a practice inherited from European anarchism, provided the CROM with the necessary flexibility to forge deals with the government, something that brought the CROM to powerful positions in Obregón and Calles's governments. The concentration of power in this inner circle also made CROM authoritarian in its execution of decisions.

Only a year after its creation the CROM involved itself directly in electoral politics. In August 1919, the Grupo Acción signed a secret pact with Alvaro Obregón to support his presidential campaign against Carranza's protégé, Ignacio Bonillas. They promised to support him through a labor party they would create in return for a position of preference for the CROM should Obregón succeed in becoming president.[38] In June Obregón announced his candidacy for the presidency, and in December 1919 the Mexican Labor Party (Partido Laborista

Mexicano, or PLbM) was officially created as the political arm of the CROM.[39]

The Federación Sindicalista del Cantón de Orizaba joined the CROM in 1919. It was a logical step, given that the CROM's pragmatic ideology and strategy were not very different from those that Orizaba's textile unions had followed, at least since 1915. Despite the supposed rejection, in the Federation's principles, of any political involvement, Orizaba's textile unions found nothing unusual in forging alliances with the government, a practice that had given them fruitful rewards.

According to the CROM's regulations, unions and the local and state federations were autonomous as far as their own affairs were concerned. Because Orizaba's textile unions were considerably stronger and more cohesive than most other labor organizations in Mexico, they distinguished themselves among CROM's affiliates by their independence. Yet they were at the same time among the CROM's most loyal members.

In contrast with the CROM, the unions of the Orizaba Valley textile mills were ruled by democratic principles. Every six months their executive boards changed, allowing for a high turnover of union positions. The new boards were elected in a general assembly of union workers. In Santa Rosa, workers were given ballots to vote for a representative of their department and for the treasurer of the union. From those workers elected from the five departments of the mill, the assembly distributed the different union positions, including the secretary general, taking into account the workers' skills and capabilities, but also seeking to rotate the position of secretary general among the different departments. In San Lorenzo a similar process prevailed, although there were no written ballots. Instead in the General Assembly, workers proposed candidates for the different positions and then workers voted on them by raising their hands. Workers who wanted to hold a position campaigned before the election.[40]

The vote was not secret; when ballots were used, as in Santa Rosa, workers had to sign their names on their ballots. Yet this did not seem to have created problems at first, because there was not much power or money involved in holding a union position. Moreover, union representatives were not exempt, at first, from doing their regular jobs, so they had to carry out the union chores during their free time. However, prob-

Executive Committee of the Sindicato de Obreros y Artesanos Progresistas de Santa Rosa, 1926–1927. (Archivo General del Estado de Veracruz.)

lems arose as this changed and the union positions became more attractive, so, at least in Santa Rosa, the vote became secret.[41]

There were several political clubs in the Orizaba mill towns, such as the Club Político Mariano Escobedo, which belonged to the Partido Veracruzano del Trabajo, representative of the Partido Laborista Mexicano in the state.[42] To keep some distance, at least formally, between unions and politics, workers could not hold a position in a union's board and in the board of a political organization or in the government, at the same time. However, unions and politics were intricately related. Workers were chosen by the unions to occupy a political position or a job in the municipal government.[43] The workers chosen to occupy such positions were postulated as the candidates of the Partido Veracruzano del Trabajo, and in those days that was equivalent to winning the election.

## Conflict in the Workplace

In January 1916 the Orizaba unions, the company managers, and governor Cándido Aguilar had signed an agreement giving unionized workers preference in filling vacancies and management the power to fire workers who refused to join the union. This agreement was equivalent to establishing closed shops (or union shops) in the Orizaba mills, a major gain for the labor movement because it strengthened the unions in terms of both their membership and their control over the workplace.[44] However, as an American scholar wrote in 1918, "When he [the employer] is forced to grant such terms to the union he often considers the agreement merely a truce to be broken when opportunity offers."[45] The enactment of the Constitution of 1917, and of the Veracruz Labor Law, offered such opportunity to Orizaba employers, because it ended the legal validity of the 1916 agreement.[46] In fact, when Article 123 was being discussed, Congress refused to endorse an additional paragraph, proposed by Carlos Grácidas, to protect labor contracts in force that stipulated more extensive benefits than were being accorded in the constitutional articles. Grácidas reported that Veracruz employers were already canceling labor agreements in anticipation of the completion of the Constitution.[47]

Several of the labor conflicts that arose in 1918 in the Orizaba region were related to this problem. In Río Blanco, for example, the company filed a complaint against the Central Board of Conciliation and Arbitration because the union had expelled two workers who did not belong to the union, and because union workers had attacked some doorkeepers for the same reason. Its ruling stated that the company had the right to keep its doorkeepers and all the other workers in the positions that it deemed more convenient, and that the CIDOSA could make a labor contract with both union and non-union workers.[48]

Another clause that was now questioned was the 50% extra payment that night workers were supposed to receive according to the Veracruz law. This clause had made several mills cancel the night shift (4:30–11:30 p.m.) in several departments since 1915, leaving hundreds of workers without a job.[49] In August 1917 the CIVSA board decided not to reestablish the night shift in the spinning department. Unemployed night-shift workers did not belong to the union and were ready to work with only a 10% extra wage, but the unions were opposed to it.[50]

On October 22, 1919, a strike broke out in Cocolapan and expanded to all Orizaba mills. The mill was hiring non-unionized, or "free" workers as they were called, for the night shift and as substitutes, violating the

January 1916 agreement.[51] CIDOSA was hiring night-shift workers through individual contracts with a 10% additional wage and a stipulation that they could be fired with a fifteen-day notice, with a compensation decided by the company (instead of the three months of wage established by the Veracruz law).[52] Unions demanded that night workers should be hired under collective contract, and should thus be unionized workers.[53] All industries in the valley joined in the strike, including beer, tramway, and railway workers.[54]

According to CIVSA's manager, the strike had political motives, "being supported by the Obregónist party, which utilizes unions as a stairway to power."[55] Governor Cándido Aguilar, Carranza's son-in-law, also thought that the strike had political motives.[56] If their suspicions were right, then the Orizaba unions would have already been supporting Obregón even before the PLbM was born. The Chamber of Industrialists of Orizaba sought to profit from the political strife by trying to win Carranza's support against the strike, arguing that "the intellectual elements that lead the unions" were, at the same time, enemies of Carranza and the industrialists.[57] The minister of war, Francisco Luis Urquizo, promised the Chamber that it would expel the union leaders from the region as well as the state military commander, also considered to be an Obregonista. However, not everyone from Carranza's government agreed with the Ministry of War's taking the factories' side against workers.

The decision of the Federación Sindicalista del Cantón de Orizaba to join the CROM rendered immediate rewards, because the CROM announced that if the conflict was not solved promptly, it would organize a general strike.[58] This threat gave the conflict national dimensions, and forced the minister of industry, commerce and labor, Plutarco Elías Calles, to intervene. In November Calles held a meeting with the Chamber of Orizaba Industrialists at which he threatened them with government seizure of the mills if the strike did not end soon. Thus, after talking with Carranza, the companies agreed to end the strike, accepting the conditions that prevailed before October 1918, and wait for a resolution from the Central Conciliation and Arbitration Board.[59] On October 24, 1919, the Central Board decision stated that the January 13, 1916, agreement was legal and binding both for day and night shifts. The collective contract had apparently won the battle.[60] However, the companies filed an amparo against the Central Board's decision. After a long legal battle, in March 1922 a district judge ruled in favor of the companies.

The CROM played a prominent role in Obregón's campaign until April 1920. When it became clear that Carranza was not going to allow clean elections, the campaign turned into a revolt and several important generals, including Plutarco Elías Calles, joined Obregón against Carranza. The labor movement took Obregón's side and numerous strikes erupted throughout the country. A month later Carranza was deposed and assassinated, and Obregón had Adolfo de la Huerta appointed provisional president. In January 1920, after elections, Obregón became president of Mexico.[61]

During de la Huerta's and Obregón's presidencies the CROM enjoyed important governmental favors backed by the president. The CROM and the PLbM were given funds to carry out their work. Rafael Zubarán Capmany was appointed minister of industry, commerce and labor, with the approval of the CROM leaders.[62] Moreover, important positions were given to members of the Grupo Acción. Morones was made director of the Federal Military Factories, Celestino Gasca became governor of the Federal District, and Eduardo Moneda was made director of the new Department of Social Welfare.[63] The CROM and the Labor Party were allowed to collect funds from government employees through "spontaneous contributions," which were actually compulsory. This gave them all the money they needed for an ambitious program of propaganda and organization, and made the CROM careless about collecting its members' dues from the outset.[64] Yet the CROM and the PLbM had to compete for Obregón's favors against the National Cooperative Party and the National Agrarian Party (Partido Nacional Agrario, PNA), which Obregón set against each other in order to prevent either of them from gaining sufficient strength to become a menace.[65]

Although the CROM was Mexico's most important confederation of workers, it was not the only one. There were two important labor organizations independent from the CROM—the General Confederation of Workers (Confederación General de Trabajadores, CGT) and the Confederation of Railway Societies (Confederación de Sociedades Ferrocarrileras, CSF). The CGT was founded in 1921 by anarchists, communists, IWW members, and former members of the COM who distrusted the CROM.[66] However, only seven months later, ideological conflicts forced the communists to split from the confederation to form their own organizations. The CGT's greatest strength was among textile workers, particularly those of the Federal District, the state of Mexico, and Puebla. From its inception, the CGT, known then as "the Reds," entered into direct confrontation against the CROM.[67] The CSF, with sixteen affiliated railway unions, was the most powerful railway workers' organization in Mexico.[68]

The CROM's favored position led it to attempt to control other labor groups. If it failed through peaceful means, it tried again by force.[69] The first incident of the intense internecine rivalries that characterized the labor movement took place in February 1921, when the National Railways Company of Mexico refused to recognize the CSF, because of the opposition of the Unión de Conductores, Maquinistas, Garroteros y Fogoneros, affiliated to the CROM and supported by Obregón.[70] A strike started, joined by 80% of railway workers.[71] Orizaba unions' independence from the CROM became evident when they decided to strike in support of the CSF workers.[72] Obregón's government and the CROM also allied against the CGT. In 1922, for example, when the Union of Workers of the Federal District, affiliated to the CGT, went on strike, the Federal District police, under the orders of Governor Celestino Gasca, a member of the CROM, violently suppressed it, killing several workers.[73]

Although the Orizaba textile mills were not a CGT stronghold, several groups of workers supported it in the region. Of the forty-two founding groups of the CGT, three came from the Orizaba Valley: the Grupo Comunista de Orizaba, Río Blanco y Cocolapan, the Local Comunista Libertario de Orizaba, and the Sindicato de Obreros Progresistas de Santa Rosa, Orizaba, Veracruz.[74] The CGT was particularly important in Cocolapan, which was also the mill where more workers had joined the Red Battalions. Gonzalo San Juan Hernández was one of the leaders who organized Cocolapan workers in 1921 in favor of the CGT and was a member of its Centro Sindicalista Libertario.[75] He had been part of the Red Battalions and considered himself a libertarian communist. "As anarcho syndicalists," he recalled in an interview, "we did not agree with the behavior of Luis Morones and his group, because the centralization in only one organization had made the workers' leaders capricious, dishonest, and rude. . . . They had agreed to expel workers under any pretext, they took away the jobs, which was a treason. . . . It had become a movement of selfishness."[76]

By 1922, problems between unionized and "free" workers increased in the Orizaba Valley. In spite of the judiciary's rulings, in 1922 unions began to more forcefully demand unionization of all workers. In January Santa Rosa's union expelled a "free" worker and threatened several others. CIVSA's board decided that if this happened again, they would rather close the factory than accept "that others broke the contracts made by the firm."[77]

According to CIVSA's director, the struggle between the companies and the union was always the same—it was a battle over "diminishing our authority and increasing theirs."[78] In September 1923, when the second master of weaving passed away and a new one had to be hired, the union proposed one of its members for the position. The director considered this to be inadmissible, "in the first place because we could not accept that they had the right to intervene in the designation of the personnel, and in the second place because that person did not have our trust, neither in terms of his capacity, nor in terms of his morality." The company decided to hire another person, but when he arrived the weavers stopped the machinery and walked out. The firm demanded guarantees from the local authorities that they could hire the master weaver of their choice, threatening that otherwise they would shut down the mill.[79]

A month later, without having obtained the guarantees, CIVSA's board tried to install the master of weaving for a second time. His entrance provoked a tumult in the weaving hall and workers walked out again. The board decided to lock out workers on Friday, October 20. The director was called by the municipal president to negotiate with the workers, and thanks to his intervention the workers accepted, without reserve, what the company demanded and the mill started working again on Monday.[80]

In Puebla, conflicts between unionized and non-union workers were even more violent than in Orizaba, because CGT-affiliated unions were more powerful in that region. Textile companies in Atlixco refused to recognize the union and hired and supported "free" workers, to whom they even supplied arms.[81] All Puebla and Atlixco mills struck from June to July 1922 because textile companies did not recognize their unions, and violent battles between unionized and "free" workers followed suit.[82] In August, El León mill, also owned by CIVSA, stopped working because of the "arrival of a numerous communist delegation that impeded workers from going in to work, pretending again to unionize workers against the will of the majority."[83] In April 1923 another problem broke out at El León among workers of two different factions. A fight at the factory doors left several workers injured.[84]

The struggle over the control of hiring and firing was permanent, and it rose to the surface every now and then. In November 1923, CIVSA's manager complained that the union continued to demand that it be consulted before the company hired anyone. "It is they who in fact give or deny a job, given that any element who does not submit to them is expelled without the victim or anyone else being able to do anything against it."[85] His claim was not wholly true, because the companies were not totally impotent against the unions. However, it is true that the managers had to adjust to working with increasingly powerful unions, something they deeply resented.

In Veracruz, rivalry between the CROM and peasant organizations was exacerbated when the League of Agrarian Communities of Veracruz (Liga de Comunidades Agrarias del Estado de Veracruz) was created in 1923.[86] This organization, the most powerful and most radical peasant group in the nation, had very close ties with the Mexican Communist Party.[87] In Orizaba, in order to counteract its power, the Chamber of Labor waged a campaign to incorporate peasants into its ranks.[88] In accordance with this new objective, the Chamber of Labor of Orizaba changed its name to Syndicalist Confederation of Workers and Peasants of the Orizaba District (Confederación Sindicalista del Obreros y Campesinos del Distrito de Orizaba, CSOCO).[89]

## The Battles for Profit Sharing and for Disease Compensation

Between 1920 and 1924 and again from 1928 to 1932, Veracruz was governed by a radical revolutionary, Colonel Adalberto Tejeda. In 1921 he passed a law to make companies comply with the profit-sharing provisions of the Labor Law, which they had so far successfully ignored.

Instead of asking companies to pay an extra month's salary to each worker, Tejeda fixed the workers' share of profits as not less than 10% of the net income of the firms. It was nicknamed the "hunger law" by the companies and the newspapers, who claimed it would cause hunger by provoking the ruin of Veracruz business. Once again the firms won the legal battle, which reached the Supreme Court, arguing that the law was retroactive and put them at a disadvantage vis-à-vis their counterparts in other states.[90]

The article of Veracruz's Labor Law on companies' responsibilities to workers who suffered accidents or diseases was so ambiguous that it enabled employers to avoid payment of the compensation that workers were supposed to receive. The law did not define occupational illnesses, and thus caused debates and great delays before any payment was provided. Furthermore, given that company doctors were in charge of defining the nature of workers' diseases, they often claimed these were not occupational in order to allow companies to avoid paying compensation.

In June 1923, conflict over this issue reached a climax in a general strike.[91] It was called "the strike of the ten thousands" for the tens of thousands of workers who went on strike throughout the Orizaba Valley. The strike could have become even more widespread, because workers from Puebla wanted to join it on solidarity, but the CROM national leaders limited its geographical extension.[92] Workers demanded that sick workers receive half pay, medicines, and medical attention, whatever the type of disease (with the exception of venereal diseases and those caused by alcoholism). They also requested that tuberculosis, very common then in Orizaba, be classified as an occupational illness.

CIVSA's manager considered this the most dangerous strike of all that had taken place in the region. Workers stopped several tramway cars and forced the passengers to alight, then turned the cars upside down to shut down the tramway company. They also shut off the water supply to several mills, causing great losses for the companies, and compelled bakeries to shut down "to deprive the population of bread." CIVSA's manager feared "the most grave consequences, including the absolute loss of control of the mill, and even of its property."[93] In the state of Veracruz all commerce closed on June 30 by agreement of the Asociación Patronal, in support of Orizaba industrialists and against any reform of the Labor

Law.[94] Orizaba and Veracruz employers asked Obregón for the intervention of Guadalupe Sánchez, chief of military operations in the state and a leader of paramilitary troops *(guardias blancas)* that had recently crushed peasants from the agrarian movement supported by Tejeda. Although Obregón had previously supported Sánchez against Tejeda, he did not accept the industrialists' demand, because it would have generated a serious clash with the CROM.[95]

The strike ended on July 2, with Governor Tejeda's promise of a law concerning workers' health. He soon decreed the Law of Occupational and Non-Occupational Diseases (Ley de Enfermedades Profesionales y no Profesionales), causing business outrage.[96] The law imposed large penalties on firms that did not comply, and established that a doctor appointed by the government would decide on the nature of the illnesses.[97]

Firms once again fought judicially, but this time they did not win the amparo lawsuits at the first legal instance.[98] This was the result, according to CIVSA's manager, of political pressures on Veracruz's judge. "Municipal presidents had told the president about the threat of labor retaliation," the manager reported, "letting him realize that disorder would prevail if the judge awarded the amparo to the firms." CIDOSA had telegraphed Obregón, asking him to do justice, "but since this authority [Obregón] is prejudiced against us . . . he removed the attorney general from his post."[99] According to CIVSA's manager, Obregón was so annoyed with CIDOSA's telegram that he nearly expelled Levallois, the person who had signed it, from the country. CIDOSA "feared that they [Obregón's government] would expel all administrative personnel from the mills, so that the company would 'accidentally' be left under the command of the workers."[100] CIVSA's manager reported that the president was "some kind of a puppet for a political movement for which the general interest of the country was its least concern."[101] According to him, what was going on was a plot to ruin the companies, and the dispute over illnesses was only an incident; "if this was not there, there would be others."[102]

On July 17 the mill's director, Honnorat Signoret, was arrested for failure to pay indemnity to a worker who had suffered an occupational disease, "although the doctor had classified the sickness in a different way."[103] He was released the next day after paying a fine. Once again CIVSA brought its case to court and carried its legal demands up to the

Supreme Court.[104] On July 31, 1923, CIDOSA demanded an amparo for a similar reason, against the acts of the municipal president of Orizaba and the governor of Veracruz, who had imposed on it a fine of 1,222 pesos for not having supplied medicines, medical service, and full wages to two workers. On March 26, 1926, the Supreme Court ruled the amparo in favor of the company. The Court's resolution on CIVSA's amparo was not found in the archives, but the similarity with CIDOSA's case makes it likely that the Court also ruled in favor of the company and no indemnity was paid.[105]

In 1923 discussions about illnesses became very frequent because, according to CIVSA's board, union leaders wanted most illnesses to be considered occupational.[106] The level of conflict forced Dr. Escondria, Santa Rosa's doctor, to resign at the end of August. CIVSA's manager feared that other employees would follow his course, given that they were "totally demoralized." If this happened, "labor management would ensue automatically."[107]

According to CIVSA's manager, pseudodiseases had increased at a fantastic rate, occupying the mill's doctor from morning to night, "half of the time taken by discussions on the character or even the existence of an illness."[108] Every day, particularly on Mondays, many workers claimed to be sick, but "about 80% of them did not have anything," so the company doctor sent them to work. Then they went to the government's doctor, "who always finds something wrong with them and prescribes rest, then authorities try to make us pay for medicine and half their wages."[109]

After Dr. Escondria's resignation, CIVSA decided to follow CIDOSA's strategy and sign a contract with an insurance company to provide health services in the mill.[110] The companies contracted with Associate Employers Reciprocal, a branch of Sherman & Ellis Inc., an American insurance company, which complied with all the legal requirements.[111] However, the unions refused to deal with the insurance company, even when the local authorities approved of it.[112] In fact, their opposition to the provision of health insurance through this company had been one of the issues Orizaba workers had raised when they went on strike.[113] By November the insurance company raised CIVSA's premiums from 1.75% to 2.75%, because it could not cover the workers' demands on the original established basis.[114] In February 1924, CIVSA and

CIDOSA canceled their insurance contracts and once again provided the medical services directly. All injured and sick workers would be given full pay or half pay (depending on the nature of the disease) for six days of work. In the event of death, workers' families would receive an amount equivalent to the workers' full wages for four weeks.[115]

The Cámara de Industriales de Orizaba argued that the Veracruz law on workers' sickness and accidents put them at a serious disadvantage against their competitors. In their view the law generated large inefficiencies because it raised incentives for abusive behavior. According to their calculations, while in 1924 the health-insurance provider Sociedad Española de Beneficiencia de México spent 7.07 pesos per member in Mexico City, and 8.77 in Veracruz, to cover the costs of medical services and medicines, in contrast the companies in Orizaba spent 31.63 pesos per worker. This was partly the result of having an extremely high incidence of sick workers in Orizaba, which they considered proof that many diseases were faked. While the Sociedad Española statistics showed that during 1924, 33.23% of its members got sick in Veracruz, and 24.09% in Mexico City, this rate reached 162% in the Orizaba factories. Having tried and failed to hire private insurance for workers, the Cámara de Industriales decided that the only possible way out was for the government to establish a mandatory general insurance system for workers, paid for by taxes.[116] They would have to wait almost twenty years to see their proposal become a reality with the creation of the Instituto Mexicano del Seguro Social.

## The Delahuertista Revolt

In 1923, near the end of Obregón's presidential term, disagreements over succession once again led to armed revolt. In December, when it became clear that Plutarco Elías Calles was going to become Mexico's next president, Adolfo de la Huerta, backed by several generals, rebelled against Obregón. CROM workers were crucial in repressing the Delahuertista revolt. "Without the support of this labor group it is doubtful that Obregón and Calles would have triumphed—and it is certain that they would not have done so as rapidly and effectively as they did."[117] CROM's unions mobilized and sent a number of labor battalions into action. The

National Agrarian Party did likewise, raising troops among its peasant adherents.

The strategic importance of Orizaba workers showed its value on the battlefield. On December 14, Orizaba was taken by Delahuertista troops, who replaced all municipal authorities.[118] But industrial workers joined organized peasants *(agraristas)* in battalions that gave crucial support to Obregonista troops in the region, which became one of this rebellion's important battlefields. On the evening of December 27, when a battle was being fought at Esperanza, one railway stop up from Santa Rosa, an Obregonista battalion of industrial workers and peasants cut the railway and all communication between Santa Rosa and Esperanza. Then, on the mill's premises, it executed between twelve and fifteen Delahuertistas. Afterward it dispersed, "sacking all commerce that was not sympathetic to unions."[119] The following morning a group of Delahuertista rebels on their way out of the region entered the Santa Rosa mill by force, shot the mill's chemist in the arm, and took several mules and horses from the factory. In the evening government forces arrived in Santa Rosa by rail and occupied the city. The state government was temporarily removed to Orizaba.[120]

Not all workers were on Obregón's and Calles's side, however. Although the CGT and the CSF did not openly support de la Huerta, several affiliates joined the rebel forces.[121] This placed these organizations at a political disadvantage with respect to the CROM once de la Huerta was defeated. These events gave CIVSA and CIDOSA unions an excuse to purge the mills of non-union workers and employees by claiming they had supported de la Huerta.[122]

At a national level, the CROM found itself in a stronger position than before de la Huerta's defeat. "The part the Mexican Federation of Labor and the Mexican Labor Party played in that crisis made him [Calles] more indebted to that portion of organized labor than to any other group or party in the country."[123] Calles based his campaign almost wholly on his support for labor and his intention to enforce Article 123 of the Constitution. However, his support of labor was not general, but confined to the CROM and the Mexican Labor Party. The years from 1924 to 1928 became the "glorious" period of CROM's history.[124]

During this period CROM members benefited in many ways from CROM's political position—they had higher wages, better working conditions, liberal financial support, and increased and favorable labor inspection. However, the same was not true of independent unions or "free" or unorganized labor, which suffered an intensification of the autocratic and arbitrary practices that the CROM had undertaken since Obregón's regime.[125]

On taking office, President Calles appointed Luis N. Morones as minister of industry, commerce, and labor. From this position, Morones could bias government policy in favor of the CROM; because his ministry decided on the legality of strikes, he often used this power against independent unions.[126] Every strike that was non-CROM in its leadership was considered illegal, and doomed to failure. The extent to which the Ministry of Industry carried on this practice, and the problems it generated, led to the creation of the Federal Board of Conciliation and Arbitration in 1927, which took the power of ruling on major strikes away from it.[127]

Several of the corrupt practices that would later become a common feature of organized labor in Mexico started at this time. One was undertaking strikes for blackmail, as happened in the oil fields. To end strikes, oil companies paid large amounts of money to CROM leaders as strike pay for workers, who never received a centavo.[128]

## The Textile Convention of 1925–1927

The textile industry was the source of most labor disputes in the country. In 1922, for example, textile strikes were 71% of the total number of strikes. To find a solution, Morones and the Ministry of Industry, Commerce, and Labor summoned a 1925 textile convention to reform the 1912 textile agreement. The convention was attended by 117 employers and 110 workers of the 170 factories invited. The main purpose of this convention was to achieve agreements that would reduce the constant struggles between workers and employers in the textile industry that led to a great number of strikes and conflicts each year. Also, it was important to establish a uniform scale of wages that would be valid throughout the country, of the kind adopted in the 1912 Convention but gradually abandoned.

A uniform wage list was extremely difficult to achieve. Workers in high-wage regions would not accept a wage decrease, and employers in states where wages were lower would not agree to raise wages to equal those of Veracruz and Mexico City. In effect, this would have meant bankruptcy for several mills. Furthermore, convention regulations made this impossible. Every mill, regardless of its size, had an employer's vote and a workers' vote in the convention.[129] Through the established representation system, Puebla and Tlaxcala obtained the majority of votes, even though they represented the minority of the industry and the workers in it. They formed a block against the representatives of Veracruz, the Federal District, and the state of Mexico, which despite representing a larger share of the industry had fewer votes and also paid higher wages.

On May 12, 1926, the vice presidency of the Convention presented a proposal for wages that established that the textile industry would implement a two-tier wage system. The first group, paying higher rates, would include mills in the states of Sinaloa, Sonora, Veracruz, Hidalgo, Chihuahua, Nuevo León, Jalisco, and the Federal District. The second group, paying lower rates, would include factories in the states of Puebla, Querétaro, Oaxaca, Tlaxcala, Guanajuato, México, Coahuila, Chiapas, Guerrero, Colima, Michoacán, Durango, and Nayarit. Moreover, the industrialists from those regions where mills had a more-outdated technology, and less capacity to make new investments, made a coalition with the workers' representatives to oppose any flexibility in the wage schedule that could allow the introduction of modern technology.[130]

On May 21, the minister of industry, trade, and labor summoned the industrialists in the first group to a meeting to make them accept the proposal. The minister promised them to draw up in the short term (probably sixty days) a new classification of the textile industry to ensure that the same wage would be paid everywhere for the same type of cloth manufactured.[131] However, this new classification was never carried out. Most employers were against a new classification of factories, and in the final Convention General Assembly they refused to authorize the Ministry of Industry, Trade and Labor to modify the agreements of the Convention to the promised classification a posteriori.[132]

After this agreement was reached, it still took several months to establish the tariff basis for piecework. Workers claimed that employers were purposely delaying the establishment of the new wage list. On October 19 the CIVSA board reported that on the previous Monday a strike had been declared at all mills in Orizaba and Puebla in order to force the convention to complete its tasks on schedule.[133]

As a result of this pressure, on October 22, 1926, it was agreed that the new tariff would take effect on November 26, 1926, together with other issues that had already been accepted, concerning the collective contract and factory rules. However, employers established, as a condition for the implementation of the new wage list, that a tax increase, to be decreed before January 15, 1927, would be paid by mills that did not comply with the new wage list. Employers would pay the old wages until that date, promising to make up the difference that resulted from the actual payment they made and what resulted from the new wage list from November 26 to that date. The tax increase was decreed four days after the deadline established, giving employers a pretext for not paying the wage difference they had promised for the previous months. According to this decree, the sales tax for textile mills that followed the new wage list would be 5% and 13% for those that did not comply.[134] Other issues continued to be discussed until March 18, 1927, when the convention finally ended.

Besides wages, the Convention ratified several other important articles. It was decided that the textile industry would be subject to the federal jurisdiction rather than that of the states, which had prevailed until then. Mixed commissions, formed by representatives of workers and employers, were established to deal specifically with this industry. There should be a mixed commission per factory, one for each district, and a National Mixed Commission. When no accord was reached within this last commission, the Ministry of Industry, Commerce and Labor made a final resolution.[135] This decision was contested by the Supreme Court, which considered that the Central Conciliation and Arbitration Board could not be replaced as the final authority in capital–labor conflicts.[136]

Another very important result of the Convention was the inclusion of the exclusionary clause *(cláusula de exclusión)* in the cotton textile contract. It gave the unions the power to expel non-union workers.[137] This ended any further debate between the unions and the employers about the unions' right to be involved in the hiring and firing of workers in the mills. Where unions are weak, closed shops help limit the power of employers to expel union workers and destroy the unions. When unions are powerful, as they were by 1927, their major effect is to give union leaders excessive power and to distance them from their rank and file. This was the major consequence of the exclusionary clause at the time it was adopted, particularly because it added up to the rule that there should be only one union per firm. These decisions introduced in the textile industry the principles that the Federal Labor Law of 1931 would mandate for the whole economy a few years later.

### The Demise of the CROM and the Great Depression

Corruption and gangsterism defined Morones's term as minister of industry, commerce and labor. He and other CROM leaders became ostentatiously wealthy. Yet "it is too simple to regard Morones as a traitor to the working class, who sold himself to capitalist interests."[138] Morones enabled the labor movement to have greater influence than the number of industrial workers would suggest, making labor a decisive actor in the building of the Mexican state. Workers and artisans numbering less than 600,000 carried more weight than four million peasants. The CROM, with at most 100,000 members, became a respected political partner because through its Labor Party it had deputies and senators in Congress, and even gained control of several state governments.[139]

However, not everyone in the government favored the CROM. In 1925 Tejeda left the Veracruz governorship to become Calles's minister of the interior and was replaced by Heriberto Jara. The new governor was not a crony of the CROM. He gave his support to other labor federations, which began to challenge the CROM's power all over the state and even in Orizaba, where it was strongest.[140]

Inter-union struggle intensified in Orizaba by 1927. Opposition to the CROM came mainly from Cocolapan and Cerritos, where "red" workers were dominant. In 1927 they accused the CSOCO of trying to expel 150 workers. To impose its dominance over red unions, the CSOCO prohibited workers from reading the Communist weekly *El Machete* and expelled workers who distributed it.[141] In 1928 a battle between CROM and red workers reached violent levels at Cocolapan, where, in a confrontation between the two forces, the worker Reynaldo Pantoja was killed and the secretary general and secretary of the interior of the mill's union—an affiliate of the CSOCO—were injured.[142] The Cocolapan workers who had formed part of the Centro Sindicalista Libertario, led by Aureliano Medrano, were expelled from the factory and forced to retire from labor politics.[143]

Relations between Morones and Obregón had deteriorated since 1923–1924, in part as a result of Calles's strategy of playing one against the other to keep them under control. Since his days as president, Obregón had developed close ties with the PNA, and distanced himself from the CROM. Thus, the CROM disliked the idea of his reelection and at first opposed the changes in the Constitution required for it to take place. However, at the CROM's annual congress in September 1927, after difficult discussions, the CROM voted to support Obregón's campaign.[144]

In April 1928, when Obregón visited Orizaba as part of his presidential campaign, he suffered an attempt on his life. He had given a cold speech to CROM workers there, telling them he could not promise them anything. Thus the blame for the assassination attempt fell on the CROM.[145] Soon after Obregón's visit to Orizaba the Labor Party withdrew its support for his candidacy. The CROM believed that a red worker must have been behind the attempt on Obregón's life. The CSOCO therefore decided to purge its ranks of any member suspected of being red. This was particularly hard on workers at Cocolapan, where many were considered to be CROM's enemies.

Following the old Porfirian employers' practices, the CSOCO made a "black list" with the names of expelled workers so that no CROM union would hire them. To have greater control over its files, it gave workers new identification cards signed by the unions' executive committees. The CSOCO's Confederal Council distributed a circular stating that every member was obliged to inform the executive committee about any worker who handed out propaganda against the organization. Any worker who acted or talked disrespectfully toward the CROM would be expelled.[146] On the following May 1, the CSOCO suspended the traditional labor celebration, in which workers marched along the Calle Real (main street), suspecting that the reds would organize riots. Each union organized a soiree instead, where union leaders gave speeches against the reds and the "terrible situation they had created."

Unfortunately for the CROM, another assassination attempt on Obregón, on July 17, 1928, succeeded. Morones was suspected of having instigated the crime. Four days later, all Labor Party members in government positions—Luis N. Morones in the Ministry of Industry, Commerce and Labor, Celestino Gasca as the head of the federal military factories, and Eduardo Moneda as the director of the government printing shops—resigned their posts. The appointment of Emilio Portes Gil as interim president was a further blow to the CROM, since he was one of its most determined enemies.[147]

To cope with the crisis, in September 1929 President Calles declared that the era of *caudillos* had come to an end and a new era of an institutions had opened. Immediately the Partido Nacional Revolucionario (PNR) was founded. CROM leaders attacked both the government and the National Revolutionary Party, and refused to become part of it.[148] The break between the CROM and Calles came in December 1929 at the CROM's annual convention. Once referred to as "our friend" who "interprets our revolutionary feelings," Calles there became the "enemy of the leaders of the proletariat" and "anti-revolutionary."[149] It is difficult to understand Morones's rationale in forcing such a rupture with Calles. It meant cutting the CROM's last link with the government and joining the opposition.

Thereafter many of the methods the CROM used against other labor organizations were used against the CROM.[150] "The police and military forces so freely used by Morones in organizing for the CROM, were now used just as freely to destroy it; labor inspectors began to throw their influence against CROM organizations and to create opposing groups. In difficulties with employers, unions were given to understand that they would be entirely successful if, first, they separated from the CROM."[151] The rush to leave the CROM was as fast as it had been four or five years earlier to get into it. Disaffiliations from the CROM took place in all parts of the country.

The conflict between the CROM and the PNR was evident. In 1930, for example, the CSOCO asked its affiliates to be aware that the PNR was trying to destroy "the conquests of the Revolution," and to disregard its propaganda as well as the orders of the Ministry of Industry, Commerce, and Labor, because both "are united to destroy our organizations."[152] The loss of governmental subsidies, which it had grown accustomed to receiving, was a devastating blow to the CROM. In subsequent years the confederation suffered great financial difficulties. It managed to meet its obligations and survive thanks largely to the aid provided by Orizaba textile unions.[153] These unions not only kept paying their dues regularly, but also made important loans and donations to the CROM's central offices.[154]

Throughout the 1920s the CROM had developed state federations that were crucial for the confederal organization's survival once its headquarters lost governmental support. In 1927, in Orizaba, CROM unions in the state of Veracruz formed the Confederación Sindicalista de Obreros y Campesinos del Estado de Veracruz (CSOCEV).[155] This organization, in which the CSOCO played a major role, gave unions of the Orizaba district a broad sphere of influence and raised its leaders to more prominent levels within the CROM.

In 1929 the CROM was reorganized at the initiative of the CSOCO. A national council was created, consisting of representatives from each of its state, regional, and industrial federations. This national council was to perform many of the functions that the Grupo Acción had thitherto performed. It would have four meetings every year.[156] These reforms also sought to separate the CROM from politics by strictly complying with the forgotten article of the CROM's statutes stating that those members who held union office could not hold any political position. On April 18, 1929, the national council of the CROM was formally constituted.

Another important step taken by the CSOCO was the creation of the National Textile Federation in April 1930. This federation gave the CSOCO another position from which to influence the CROM at a national level. Its first secretary general, Viterbo Silva, was a worker at Santa Rosa who had previously been secretary of the interior on the CROM's central committee.[157]

After three years without an annual convention, the CROM convened in Orizaba in 1932.[158] There, Eucario León, a Santa Rosa worker and a distinguished member of its union, was elected secretary general of the CROM. His career star had risen rapidly, from a position in Santa

Rosa's union to the CSOCO to the CSOCEV to the CROM national headquarters.[159] He was the first secretary general of the CROM who did not belong to the Grupo Acción.[160] However, it was precisely when Eucario León was chosen as head of the CROM that Lombardo Toledano, who would become the most important labor leader in the following decades, separated from it and several important unions followed suit.

Martín Torres Padilla was another Orizaba prominent labor leader who contributed to maintaining the strength of region's labor organization. He was elected president of the Workers' Directive of the Textile Convention, and member (vocal) of its General Directive together with Lombardo Toledano, with whom he remained close. As the Convention's minutes tell, he was the most important workers' voice in its debates.[161] He was three times municipal president of Orizaba (1922–1923, 1932–1933, and 1938), twice federal deputy, and also twice local deputy. He served as secretary general of the CROM but in 1942 he separated from it to form the Confederación de Obreros y Campesinos.[162]

Thus the decline of the CROM nationally did not mean the weakening of Orizaba's labor organizations. In fact it might even have strengthened them, as they acquired a larger role in the confederation, which although less powerful was more independent. But together with the confederation's crisis came the economic crisis of the Great Depression.

Labor organization in the Orizaba district was remarkable, and very different from that elsewhere in Mexico. In 1934, after visiting the region, Marjory Clark wrote of it on the following terms:

> The textile unions of the Orizaba district will continue to control the situation. Their internal discipline is excellent and their unions have been singularly free from that personal ambition which has gone so far toward the weakening and even the destruction of other labor organizations. They have their own schools, in which thousands of children and a steadily increasing number of adults receive instruction each year; they have established a number of cooperative societies, including banks and savings and loan societies; when the CROM national convention met in Orizaba in September 1932, every factory in the district was closed for the week of the convention. This district has presented for years a picture of as complete worker control as exists anywhere in Mexico.[163]

Several circumstances combined in these years to make Orizaba's labor organizations unique. The Orizaba Valley held a large enough number of industrial workers to form a powerful organization able to become politically relevant. Workers in Orizaba were generally young, mostly male, single, and better educated than the rest of the population. These factors made workers there idealistic, combative, prepared to take risks, and capable of structuring protest and rebellion into organizations and concrete goals. The industrial firms in the valley were strong and profitable enough to meet the substantial workers' demands on their profits. This enabled unions to become relatively wealthy and independent, and capable of undertaking several important projects with their own resources. Moreover, Orizaba was in a strategic place, so that its organized workers were an important ally for the government or revolutionary forces. Finally, more than any other state in the country, Veracruz was ruled from 1914 on by radical governors, more willing (and also obliged) to take the side of labor than other generals in the revolutionary army.

# CHAPTER 7

# A Revolution in Work

## *Real Wages and Working Hours*

H OW DID THE MEXICAN REVOLUTION affect workers' real wages? We can begin to answer this question by looking at the evolution of CIVSA workers' nominal and real wages from 1900 to 1929. Two major changes took place during these years in terms of the variables that affect wages. The first was a radical change in the degree of organization of labor, passing from a situation in which there were no unions to one in which unions became powerful institutions. The second was a considerable deterioration of the Mexican economy between 1913 and 1917 as a consequence of the Revolutionary War. After 1917 the economy began to recover, and economic and political institutions began to be slowly rebuilt. However, CIVSA's performance during the 1920s suggests that the prosperity of the pre-revolutionary years was not recovered. Moreover, from 1926 on, the textile industry began to suffer the first symptoms of what was going to become the Great Depression.

The Mexican Revolution coincided with World War I and the radical changes it brought to the international environment, so it is difficult to isolate the impact of these two events. Therefore, whereas some of the changes in real wages were the consequence of the Revolution, others would have probably taken place even if there had been no Revolution.

Wages relate to highly specific characteristics of the workforce (skills needed per type of job, the relative scarcity of labor, and productivity levels). For this reason it is better to know about wages per type of job, industry, and city than to have a general wage index. This chapter will look at wages for a single factory: Santa Rosa. Santa Rosa's wage data was obtained from the mill's payrolls and other accounting books. Payrolls are weekly books that include payments per worker and the worker's name, position, and labor undertaken (the number of days worked for those paid by shift, or the amount and type of goods produced during the week for those paid by piecework). Cashier's books provide aggregate weekly payments per department. Wage series were calculated by dividing total payments per department reported in the cashier's books by the number of workers per department reported in the payroll for every week. Wages per type of labor, machinery used, or duration in the job were calculated from payroll samples.

The major obstacle to assessing the evolution of the purchasing power of wages during this period is the lack of a reliable price index. Two price indices have been developed for this purpose. Index I, which includes the prices of rent and electricity taken from Santa Rosa's payrolls, and Index II, which excludes these two items. Deflating wages with Index I provides a more accurate picture of how Santa Rosa's workers' wages fared, as well as those of the other Orizaba textile mills that charged workers similar fees for house rents and electricity. Deflating wages with Index II provides a more general view of how real wages might have changed during this period.[1] Although both real-wage calculations are presented in tables and figures, in text will refer to wages deflated with Index I.

Santa Rosa workers can be regarded as enjoying higher living standards than most industrial workers, both during the Porfiriato and afterward, for several reasons.[2] They worked in a factory that was more modern and productive than most other textile mills, and their union was at the forefront of the nation's labor movement. Veracruz was an important revolutionary arena, it was the seat of the revolutionary government of Carranza in 1914–1915, the governors of Veracruz were particularly radical and pro-labor, and many labor laws were applied in Veracruz before they were put into practice throughout the nation.[3] The findings regarding

Santa Rosa wages will be put in a broader perspective by comparing them to those for other factories and regions.

## The Evolution of Wages

Several historians have claimed that real wages of workers deteriorated during the Porfiriato. According to them, although there was a sharp increase in prices during this period, wages remained fixed at the same level, and thus real wages fell.[4] Santa Rosa data does not support this view. In the last decade of the Porfiriato, nominal wages in Santa Rosa increased by 41% and real wages grew by 3.7% (see Figure 7.1).[5] From 1900 to 1907 real wages increased by 17%.[6]

However, the evolution of Santa Rosa wages supports the view that worsening economic conditions might have contributed to the popular discontent that provoked the Revolution. From 1907 to 1911, there was a 14% reduction of real wages, most of which took place between 1909 and 1910, due mainly to an increase in prices during this period. Yet from 1907 to 1911, wages per hour decreased only by 6%, because daily working hours were reduced from twelve to eleven in August 1910.

The first years of the Revolution, coupled with the increasing strength of labor organization and a stable economic environment, brought about important gains to workers' standard of living. From 1911 to 1913 Santa Rosa real wages grew by 20%, redressing the previous loss in purchasing power. This resulted from significant nominal wage increases (22.9%) coupled with a low inflation rate of only 2.6%. In 1913 real wages were 2.1% above their highest point in 1907. This was a period with numerous strikes both in Santa Rosa and in the whole Orizaba region, as seen in Chapter 5.[7]

On December 13, 1911, Madero's government created the Department of Labor within the Ministry of Development.[8] Santa Rosa began the year of 1912 with a strike that lasted from January 1 to January 19 as part of a general strike in the textile industry. On January 20, to end the strike, the Department of Labor summoned several industrialists and workers' representatives to Mexico City. They agreed to a reduction of the daily working hours from eleven to ten, and a 10% wage increase. They also agreed to organize a general convention of industrialists and workers in

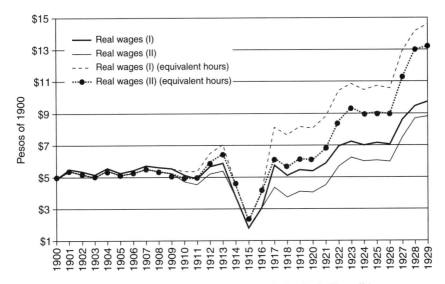

*Figure 7.1.* Average real wages. I: Consumer price index including all items.
II: Consumer price index without rent and electricity. *Notes:* From 1914 to 1915
the gold value of wages is used as a proxy for real wages. The figures for real
wages in equivalent hours assume a fixed 72-hour week. *Sources:* CIVSA payrolls.
See Aurora Gómez-Galvarriato, "The Impact of Revolution: Business and Labor
in the Mexican Textile Industry, Orizaba, Veracruz, 1900–1930" (PhD diss.,
Harvard University, 1999), appendix to chap. 5. Reprinted from Aurora
Gómez-Galvarriato, "The Political Economy of Protectionism: The Mexican
Textile Industry, 1900–1950," in *The Decline of Latin American Economies,*
ed. Sebastian Edwards, Gerardo Esquivel, and Graciela Márquez (Chicago:
University of Chicago Press, 2007), p. 386. © 2007 by the National Bureau of
Economic Research. All rights reserved.

the textile industry. In April the Workers Committee sent the Department of Labor its proposed set of factory regulations and wages.[9]

There was a significant wage increase as a result of the Textile Workers' and Industrialists' Convention organized by the Department of
Labor between July and August 1912. Wages at Santa Rosa grew less than
in most textile mills, since the wages set by the minimum tariff of 1912
were not as high as the wages already paid there.[10] Nonetheless, Santa
Rosa workers' standard of living increased significantly, recovering the
loss they had experienced between 1906 and 1911. From 1911 to 1912, Santa
Rosa workers' nominal wages increased by 13%, which can be attributed

to the new wage list. Hourly wages increased even further, because in January 1912 daily work hours were reduced from eleven to ten. Up to 1913 the Revolution brought wage increases, but no enormous inflation as of yet.

When Huerta came to power, he forced Mexico's major emission banks to give him credit to finance war against the Constitutionalist army, and to enable them to do so he lowered banks' reserve limits, allowing them to print more money. The credibility of paper money holders fell, and they rushed to the banks to change their banknotes into specie. On November 5, 1913, Huerta passed a law that ended the convertibility of paper money into metallic coins, and Mexico went out of the gold standard. At the same time, the revolutionary armies began to print their own paper money, also to finance war. Several types of paper money circulated in the country, depending on the timing and region of occupation of each revolutionary army. The large increase in the amount of money circulating in the economy escalated inflation rates.

During the spring of 1915, inflation reached new heights and companies began to set their prices in either U.S. dollars or gold pesos (in an equivalence of 1 gold peso to US$2). But wages continued to be paid in paper money, causing a dramatic fall in real wages, despite huge increases in nominal wages.

There were no strikes in 1915, but wages were increased severalfold, amounting to a 99.7% nominal increase for the year. In February Santa Rosa managers granted a 10% increase over the wages set by the minimum tariff of 1912, and in April wages increased by a further 23%.[11] This last increase in wages followed Carranza's decree to raise the wages of workers in the textile industry all over the country.[12] In August the maximum legal working hours were reduced from ten to nine and wages increased again by 11%.[13] On October 19, the managers at Santa Rosa wrote to the board of directors that they had given a 33% wage increase in accordance with Río Blanco, "given the high cost of the products of the most basic need."[14] From January 1914 to December 1915, nominal wages rose by approximately 153%. Yet CIVSA prices rose by 560% in the same period. Average real wages per week, deflated by the textile index, fell from 8 pesos in June and August 1914 to less than 2 pesos in July 1915 (see Figure 7.2).

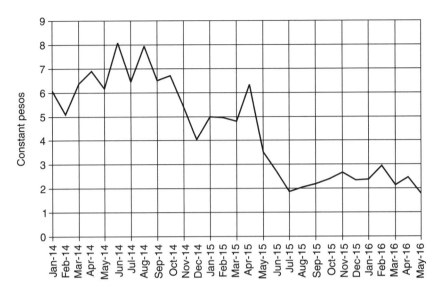

*Figure 7.2.* Average real weekly wages using the textile index: spinning, weaving, bleaching, and printing departments. January 1914 = 100. *Sources:* CIVSA payrolls. Textile index from Aurora Gómez-Galvarriato, "The Impact of Revolution: Business and Labor in the Mexican Textile Industry, Orizaba, Veracruz, 1900–1930" (PhD diss., Harvard University, 1999), appendix to chap. 4.

In January 1916, a 50% wage increase (300% over the "Uniform Wage Tariff" of July 1912) was granted to workers on condition that they promise not to strike.[15] However, any increase in wages was followed by a greater increase in prices, and wages in gold pesos kept falling, as can be seen from Figure 7.3.[16] This made workers aware that the only solution was to be paid in gold pesos. In February 1916 the executive committee of the Union of Free Workers of Spinning, Weaving and Printing of the factory sent a letter demanding that factory managers pay wages in gold pesos or their equivalent,

> given that daily wages are not enough to cover our living necessities, because merchants have raised their prices by 2,000% (since 1912) and given that we will never be able to get even with them by asking for an increase in wages, since we ask for a 300% increase and they raise prices by 2,000%, and to avoid abuses, we have agreed with all the unions of the state of Veracruz that from the 24th of this month,

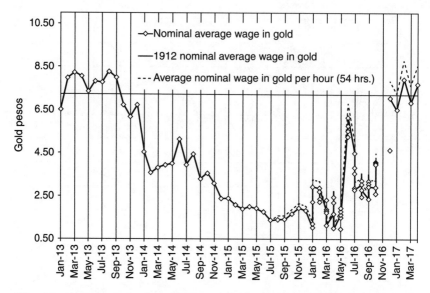

*Figure 7.3.* Average wages in gold pesos: spinning, weaving, bleaching, and printing departments, January 1913–March 1917. *Notes:* Before January 1916, wages were converted into gold using exchange rates. In August 1915, weekly working hours were reduced from 60 to 54. *Sources:* CIVSA payrolls. Exchange rates from Edwin W. Kemmerer, *Inflation and Revolution: Mexico's Experience of 1912–1917* (Princeton: Princeton University Press, 1940), tables 1 and 4.

> our wages should be paid in "national gold" or its equivalent in paper money calculated by the exchange rate at New York, in order to put ourselves on equal terms with the capital that charges in "American gold" for its merchandise.[17]

From the beginning of 1915 until May 1916, CIVSA workers were paid in "Veracruz" notes, the paper money issued by Carranza's provisional government while stationed in Veracruz. In May they began to be paid in the "infalsificable" notes that Carranza's government, by now stationed in Mexico City and in control of the country, issued to replace the myriad of revolutionary notes then circulating and in an attempt to stop the falsification of money. However, the government printed six times the paper money required to replace the previous emissions, so inflation escalated into hyperinflation.

In May 1916 Orizaba Valley workers joined a strike that went national.[18] To end this strike, companies and workers reached a compromise by which wages in "infalsificables" were set at the same nominal amount that they had in "Veracruz" paper money, despite the fact that an "infalsificable" was worth at least four times more than a "Veracruz" note.[19] This caused a 281% wage increase in terms of gold pesos (Figure 7.3).

The cost of living had risen so much that an aid program had to be organized. On June 20 the Chamber of Commerce of Orizaba asked each business in the region to provide funds to buy articles of "the first necessity" to be sold at cost price to the "needy classes." CIVSA gave US$2,000 on condition that the articles bought with this amount be sold in the municipality of Santa Rosa, the site of the factory.[20]

Although nominal wages were increased again in September and October, real wages kept deteriorating. Figure 7.3 shows that wages in gold pesos fell drastically in August 1916 but then regained some value in September when wages were increased by 500% (over the 1912 tariff). In October the Confederación Fabril agreed to give workers a further 80% increase (an increase of 900% over the 1912 tariff). These are the two jumps seen in Figure 7.3.[21]

Workers paid a high toll in their standard of living as a consequence of hyperinflation, in spite of their frequent strikes to raise wages. They wages had been reduced by 698% in terms of gold, comparing the average 1912 wage to that of May 1916, when wages bottomed out. Some goods might have lagged behind inflation in this period, making the loss in real purchasing power lower than 698%. Such goods included rent and electricity, which performed like real wages because their prices were set in paper money. Rent and electricity payments absorbed around 16% of workers' wages in 1915, so the fact that they did not grow with other prices helped workers survive the hyperinflationary period.

In November workers finally gained the right to be paid in gold pesos, after an important strike in all the Orizaba Valley mills that lasted more than two weeks.[22] They were the first workers in Mexico to obtain payment in metallic specie, an event that made newspaper headlines in Mexico City. At first workers were to be paid at least half their wages in coins, the other half in paper money according to the exchange rate that the Ministry of Finance set every ten days, but by the end of December the "infalsificables" stopped circulating and metallic specie—silver and gold coins—became the only means of payment in Mexico until 1931.[23]

As can be seen from Figure 7.3, by late 1916 and early 1917, labor regained the gold peso wages of the first semester of 1913 through this measure.

Conflicts over wage increases did not end in the Mexican industry when they were finally set in gold pesos at the end of November 1916. The tremendous decline in purchasing power that workers had faced in previous years finally ended. Nevertheless, given that prices continued to rise during 1917, even in terms of gold pesos, real wages would have continued to decline if workers had accepted stable nominal wages. Yet by this time workers no longer suffered from "money illusion"; they had built a strong labor movement to obtain raises, and they could count on the support of the government in previously unimagined ways.[24]

In April 1917 the government of Veracruz organized a series of conferences in Córdoba between workers and company representatives to discuss wage-related issues. Originally a national conference had been scheduled for Mexico City on May 1, but Carranza changed his mind, perhaps suspecting trouble, and ordered state governors to organize meetings separately in order to have conclusions ready by this date.

The CIVSA board of directors reported to its Comité Consultatif in Paris that although they knew that workers' demands were exaggerated, they surpassed their expectations. "Their demand is a minimum wage of 3.94 pesos for the day, that is the wage a janitor should receive, and the basis for the discussion of all other wages." This minimum wage should be compared to the minimum wage of 1.25 pesos set in the "Tarifa Mínima" of 1912, which meant a 252% increase over wages at that time. CIVSA managers reported that "given that that was inadmissible, since it would immediately imply the death of the industry, the Secretary of Government of Veracruz . . . provisionally interrupted the conference, and went to Mexico City to consult the federal government."[25]

On May 1, 1917, the work shift was officially reduced from nine to eight hours in compliance with the new Mexican Constitution signed in February. The Constitution also included legislation that required companies to provide coverage for accidents, sickness, pensions, and such. CIVSA managers reported that the supplementary expenditures included by the Constitution would increase the factory's labor costs by at least 15%.[26]

On May 15, in order to end a strike that started early that month, the government of Veracruz decided to give workers an increase of 80% over the 1912 minimum tariff for piecework and a 65% increase for work paid per shift.[27] Figure 7.3 shows this substantial wage rise between May and June 1917. This wage increase was higher for Veracruz mills than for those in the rest of the country. CIVSA managers claimed that this put them at a disadvantage vis-à-vis other mills because Puebla factories provided only a 20% increase for piecework and a 16% increase for shift work, while factories in Mexico City increased them by 55% and 20%, respectively.[28] This greater increase of wages in Veracruz might be the reason CIVSA wages in 1920 appear higher than the average wage of several other factories, which was not the case in 1912.

A commission of industrialists from Veracruz went to Mexico City to demand an audience with President Carranza to protest against this wage increase. However, even though they had an appointment with him, they waited for three days in the antechambers of the presidency without being received by Carranza.[29] The governor of Veracruz and the municipal president were of no more help. CIVSA managers complained that the governor of Veracruz had given workers a letter that the commission of industrialists had sent him asking to reduce their wages to the level of those paid in Mexico City.[30] The days when CIVSA could count on government support in repressing rebel workers were long gone.

In 1917 CIVSA decided to stop night work at the spinning department, unwilling to pay the increased night-shift wage. Without night spinning there was not enough thread to supply the rest of the departments, so management reduced work in the weaving and printing departments to only five days a week. Because wages shown in Figure 7.1 are average weekly wages, they conceal the fact that the factory was working fewer days a week and that days of work were fewer for several weeks due to the many strikes that took place during this period.[31] This is why CIVSA's manager complained that the "the few good workers that remain in the factory are leaving little by little because although wages are higher in Orizaba than elsewhere, the days of work per year are less, and therefore they prefer to work where they can do so more regularly."[32]

The huge nominal wage increase that took place between May and June 1917 was completely redressed in real terms by the enormous price increases of this period. From 1917 to 1918, nominal wages increased by 3% but real wages per week fell by 11% (Figure 7.1). This time the causality between prices and wages seems to have been different. Whereas in 1912, 1915, and 1916 inflation preceded wage increases, now wages moved before prices did.

There were no further significant wage increases recorded in company records until the end of 1920, except a 10% increase in August 1919 as a by-product of an important strike organized mainly to obtain a collective contract. Nevertheless, nominal wages continued rising as a result of the recovery in production figures. From 1917 to 1920, real wages fell by 6%, despite the large nominal wage increase of 16.3%. This shows how difficult it was for workers to sustain the purchasing power they had achieved by 1913.

There were several strikes between 1921 and 1929, yet only two of them were for an increase in wages. On January 23, 1923, workers asked for a wage increase for the doffers *(mudadores)* and helpers in the spinning departments. The strike soon ended when the companies agreed to increase these wages by 20% on January 30. In October 1924 workers at the spooling machine tenders *(cañoneros)* of the Orizaba region demanded a wage increase. In the whole Orizaba region an increase of around 44% to these workers was granted without a strike.[33]

In 1924, due to the Delahuertista revolt and the disruptions in communications it caused in Veracruz, work was reduced to four days a week from January to March, when in response to a petition by the state governor the company agreed to work five days a week.[34] Nominal wages in 1925 increased by 16%, not because of wage-rate increases that year, but due to the fact that 1925 was a prosperous year for the mill and workers were able to work six days a week. Because most wages were paid per piece, an increase in working days translated into an increase in wages. From 1920 to 1926, real wage increases surpassed considerably nominal wage increases because of a deflation of 13%.

During this period wage negotiations centered on the Convención Industrial Obrera del Ramo Textil that took place in Mexico City from October 1925 to March 1927. The disparities between wages paid in different regions for the same kind of job in the textile industry were enormous. Whereas weavers in Veracruz earned 3.04 pesos daily on average in 1923, weavers in Durango earned only 1.33 pesos. Spinners earned 2.30 pesos on average in Veracruz as opposed to only 90 cents in Chihuahua.[35] The wage gap between regions had increased together with the growing strength of the labor movement. Differences in wages paid in the textile industry were much greater in the 1920s than in Porfirian times. The variance of average wages in different states was 0.015 in 1893 and rose to 0.24 by 1925.[36] Economic theory suggests a close relationship between labor productivity and wages. In 1893–1896 the correlation between labor efficiency and average wage was 0.57, but in 1923–1925 it had declined to 0.21.[37] In contrast the correlation between the number of strikes in each state between 1920 and 1924 and the average wage was 0.61.

For CIVSA and factories in Veracruz and the Federal District, the question of achieving a standard wage rate was of the utmost importance.[38] However, as we have seen, this was impossible to accomplish. Veracruz and Federal District employers were disappointed at the convention's results, and those of Jalisco, Chihuahua, and Nuevo León even more so. While in 1923 they paid lower wages than their Puebla and Tlaxcala counterparts, they were placed in the group that had to pay higher wages (group 1). In Nuevo León, employers threatened to close the mills, and workers accepted wages as if they were in group 2. In Jalisco, employers were not only unwilling to pay group 1 wages, but even refused to pay group 2 level wages. In Michoacán, Hidalgo, Nayarit, Sonora, and San Luis Potosí, employers did not accept the results of the convention and convinced workers to agree to their partial implementation. This resulted in a set of different wages that varied considerably.[39]

After overcoming several obstacles to the establishment of the new wage list proposed by the Convention, the list was finally put into practice at the Santa Rosa mill in April 1927. The council reported that troubles arose with loom fixers *(correiteros)* because the new wage list was detrimental to them. The Convention wage list also established that the company should increase personnel in the loom fixers section. Finally an agreement was reached whereby the company would pay loom fixers on the previous basis, but not hire new workers.

CIVSA wages show a 17% increase in nominal wages from 1926 to 1927, which resulted from the application of the new wage list. Real wages increased even further as a result of deflation. From 1925 to 1929 real wages at Santa Rosa rose by 36%. This, combined with previous increases, produced a total increase in real wages of 70% from 1917 to 1929. Furthermore, as a result of the Convention, workers won the right to a week of

Table 7.1  Wages and employment in the cotton textile industry, 1925–1929

| State | 1925 | | 1929 | | Change in wages and employment, 1925–1929 | | | |
|---|---|---|---|---|---|---|---|---|
| | Nominal daily wage (pesos) | Wage index (Veracruz = 100) | Nominal daily wage (pesos) | Wage index, (Veracruz = 100) | Nominal wage | Real wage | No. of workers | Hours worked |
| *First group* | | | | | | | | |
| Veracruz | 3.04 | 164 | 3.91 | 170 | 28.7% | 51.1% | −8.8% | −22.4% |
| Jalisco | 2.59 | 140 | 2.41 | 105 | −6.7% | 9.5% | −10.6% | 1.8% |
| Federal District | 2.34 | 126 | 2.76 | 120 | 18.1% | 38.6% | −21.1% | 9.6% |
| Hidalgo | 2.22 | 120 | 3.27 | 142 | 47.3% | 72.8% | −26.0% | 9.7% |
| Sinaloa | 2.03 | 110 | 2.08 | 90 | 2.9% | 20.7% | −0.6% | −10.0% |
| Chihuahua | 1.91 | 103 | 2.44 | 106 | 27.9% | 50.1% | 46.2% | 87.7% |
| Nuevo León | 1.43 | 78 | 1.82 | 79 | 26.7% | 48.7% | 8.4% | −21.8% |
| Sonora | 1.48 | 80 | 2.83 | 123 | 90.7% | 123.9% | 36.0% | 6.2% |
| Average | 1.98 | | 2.69 | | 24.6% | 46.2% | 1.4% | 15.1% |
| *Second group* | | | | | | | | |
| Puebla | 2.16 | 117 | 2.56 | 111 | 18.6% | 39.2% | −14.8% | −4.7% |
| Michoacán | 2.03 | 110 | 1.98 | 86 | −2.6% | 14.4% | −5.5% | −37.1% |
| Coahuila | 2.00 | 108 | 2.24 | 97 | 12.3% | 31.8% | 5.6% | 17.7% |
| México | 1.91 | 103 | 2.20 | 96 | 15.4% | 35.4% | 2.3% | 4.4% |
| Tlaxcala | 1.80 | 98 | 2.68 | 116 | 48.5% | 74.3% | −7.7% | −9.6% |
| Guanajuato | 1.77 | 96 | 2.07 | 90 | 16.6% | 36.9% | 40.2% | −10.5% |
| Querétero | 1.41 | 76 | 1.52 | 66 | 7.7% | 26.4% | 16.7% | 89.3% |
| Nayarit | 1.35 | 73 | 2.05 | 89 | 52.4% | 78.9% | −13.0% | −30.3% |
| Durango | 1.34 | 72 | 1.58 | 69 | 18.5% | 39.1% | −62.9% | −35.4% |
| Oaxaca | 1.20 | 65 | 1.74 | 76 | 45.8% | 71.1% | 63.9% | −3.5% |
| Guerrero | 1.13 | 61 | 1.64 | 71 | 44.9% | 70.1% | 43.8% | −42.0% |
| Average | 1.82 | | 2.02 | | 16.3% | 36.5% | 8.6% | −9.0% |
| Average total | 1.85 | | 2.30 | | 24.7% | 46.3% | −9.9% | −3.4% |

*Source:* México, Secretaría de Hacienda y Crédito Público, Departamento de Impuestos Especiales, Sección de Hilados y Tejidos, Cuadro No.1, semestre del 1° de mayo al 31 de octubre de 1925 (mimeo).

paid vacation in the last week of the year, which began to be applied in December 1927.[40]

The Convention of 1925–1927 failed to achieve one of its main objectives, that of generating a uniform wage scale. It did not even narrow the wage gap between states. The variance of wages between states grew from 0.24 in 1925, to 0.37 in 1929.[41] Although the new wage list established that wages in Veracruz should be the same as in the Federal District, this did not in fact occur. In 1929 the average male wage for an eight-hour day in Veracruz was 4.12 pesos, whereas in the Federal District it was 2.93 pesos.[42] Table 7.1 shows that although wages in Veracruz were already higher than elsewhere in 1925, they increased more than the average wage. Wages at Santa Rosa increased even more than in Veracruz. On average, real wages increased through this period in the whole country. Conversely, employment diminished.

The wage list established by the Convention, if implemented strictly, would have placed several mills in a terrible situation. Its flexibility meant that significant wage gaps continued to exist. The varying strength of the labor movement in various regions, which had created the regional wage gap in the first place, continued opening it up, because it was in those states where labor was strong that the convention regulations were applied. This dynamic left Veracruz in a relatively poor situation for the development of its textile industry.

## An Overview: 1900–1929

From a three-decade perspective, real wages during the last decade of the Porfiriato appear relatively stable. They declined from 1907 to 1911 as a result of the rise in inflation during this period coupled with nominal wage stability. This decrease was 14% for workers who enjoyed relatively cheaper rents and electricity in company housing, but could have been as high as 18% if the rents and electricity workers paid elsewhere increased at the same rate as other products (see Figure 7.1). The fall in real wages during this period might have increased workers' discontent with Porfirio Díaz's regime. However, when we look at this fall from a broader perspective, it appears too small to have been a major cause of the Revolution.

The general trend of CIVSA real wages for the Porfiriato can safely be generalized for industrial workers, at least in the central region of Mexico during this period, because the evolution is not so much depicted by the changes in CIVSA's nominal wages as by the price index, which did not rise by much.

During the first years of the Revolution, before the fall of Francisco I. Madero, real wages at CIVSA increased. This was the result of the expansion of the labor movement and the support the new government gave it through the Department of Labor. This only raised real wages to nearly the same level they were at in 1907 in terms of weekly pay. However, wages per hour increased between 1907 and 1913 by 23% because the shift was reduced from twelve to ten hours. It is likely that real wages increased even more in most textile mills, as Santa Rosa wages were already high before the tariff was established. Factories that had lower wages prior to that year must have increased wages by a greater percentage.

After Huerta seized power and the war assumed greater proportions, political chaos gave way to monetary anarchy, which in turn led to hyperinflation. Inflation eroded nominal wage increases at CIVSA from 1914 to 1916, causing an impressive decline in workers' purchasing power, which fell to its lowest point in May 1916, down to only a seventh of what it had been in 1912 in terms of gold pesos. Given that Figure 7.1 shows annual averages of real wages, it underestimates their collapse during the worst months of 1914–1916. Yet the collapse appears enormous compared to any other fall in real wages during these three decades.

We can be fairly certain that workers' real wages in general experienced a tremendous decline during this period. One might think that real wages in general would have experienced an even greater decline than the deterioration of real wages at CIVSA. Inflation lowered real wages by a tremendous amount, which CIVSA workers were to a certain extent able to check with their numerous strikes. However, we know that CIVSA workers were not alone in their strikes and were instead part of a broader labor movement that organized and coordinated workers from several trades and industries in several regions of central Mexico. At the same time, it seems unlikely that workers who already earned subsistence wages previously to 1914 could have experienced such a dramatic fall in their wages, and those who received wages in specie, as agricultural workers normally did, were not hurt as much.

The high inflationary levels of 1915 and 1916 must have been an important factor in strengthening the labor movement. Workers were given an immediate and relevant reason to unite and to fight. In CIVSA most of the strikes organized in this period were highly effective, as we have seen, which would have given great prestige to the union among the mass of workers.

After the recovery of real wages in December 1916, when CIVSA workers finally won the fight to be paid in gold pesos, workers were able to regain the real wage they had earned in 1913 and lost during the inflationary period from 1914 to 1916. The purchasing power achieved from 1917 to 1920 was an improvement from the final years of the Porfiriato. Nevertheless, as can be seen in Figure 7.1, it was not much higher than the real wage earned in 1907. However, workers earned this wage in an eight-hour instead of a twelve-hour shift, a major gain.

Then, after a brief new fall in real wages during 1917 as a result of inflation, textile workers experienced a long period of growing real wages from 1918 to 1929. It was in the 1920s that workers saw a substantial improvement in the living standards over 1907 or 1913. Furthermore, the labor laws of Veracruz in 1914–1915 and the Constitution of 1917 had brought other nonpecuniary benefits to workers, such as sickness and accident compensation and retirement pensions.

From 1917 to 1929 CIVSA's real wage increased by 71% and real wage per hour by 81%. This wage rise cannot be generalized to other industries or regions; it was peculiar to the textile mills of Orizaba. Textile mills in other states increased their wages by a much lower rate. In fact the wage gap between regions grew in the 1920s relative to Porfirian times as a result of the varying regional strength of the labor movement. Nonetheless, wages in other regions also increased. From 1925 to 1929 the average national real wage increased by 38% to 48% (depending on the price index used), accompanied, though, by a fall in employment of nearly 10%.

Wages clearly evolved between 1900 and 1929. To understand how high or low they were, however, requires knowing what those wages could buy, and what the caloric and protein intake of workers and their families was. These figures are calculated for the average weekly wage of

1907, 6.74 pesos ($54.91 in 2010 U.S. dollars)—the highest during the Porfiriato, so it serves as a benchmark. A worker who lived in a CIVSA house would have paid 1.22 pesos weekly for rent and light (18.1% of the weekly wage). The rest of the weekly wage would have been spent as follows, according to the "distribution of expenses in a budget of the popular class" defined by the Mexican Ministry of Finance in 1910.[43] Workers would have spent 2.87 pesos (40.9% of wages) on the following items: beef (4.95 pounds), pork (1.36 pounds), lard (1.12 pounds), wheat (2.32 pounds), flour (1.46 pounds), corn (28.96 pounds), potato (3.73 pounds), beans (9.07 pounds), chile (15 ounces), salt (1.96 ounces), coffee (7.8 ounces) and sugar (13 ounces). They would have allocated 0.88 pesos (13.1% of the wage) on clothing, hats, and shoes. This amount would have allowed workers to buy 1.07 yards of denim, 1.45 yards of brown drill, and 1.45 yards of flannel at CIVSA sale prices. The remaining 1.77 pesos (26.2%) of wage would be allocated to fuel and other expenses. According to the Ministry of Finance, 62% of this amount would have been used to buy *pulque,* the fermented juice of the maguey plant.

The weekly food thus acquired contained 71,975 calories and 2,507 grams of protein.[44] But if we add *pulque* to this figure it would have contained 72,606 calories and 2,549 grams of protein.[45] Recent studies by the Mexican government consider that the minimum daily requirements for an adult male are 2,220 calories and 40 grams of protein to be considered above the nutrition poverty line.[46] Taking these figures into account, the food basket (excluding *pulque*) that could be acquired with CIVSA's average wage of 1907 would have been enough to feed 4.6 persons (four persons and a baby) with a daily intake each of 2,571 calories and 90 grams of protein.

## Working Hours

The improvement in real wages per hour from the Porfiriato to 1917 was a result more of the reduction of working hours than of an actual increase in weekly payments. In a single decade the workday fell by four hours and the workweek by twenty-four hours (Table 7.2). This reduction compares with a reduction of six hours in the workweek in the U.S. manufacturing industry between 1909 and 1919.[47]

*Table 7.2*  Workday changes at CIVSA and CIDOSA, 1907–1917

| Hours | | CIDOSA | CIVSA | Cause |
| From | To | | | |
| --- | --- | --- | --- | --- |
| 12 | 11 | June 17, 1907 | August 1910 | Strikes: CIDOSA, May 2–23, 1907, and May 30–June 7, 1907. CIVSA, August 10–16, 1910. |
| 11 | 10 | January 22, 1912 | September 1, 1912 | General strike, January 1–19, 1919. Agreement between workers, employers, and the Department of Labor in January 20, 1912. In CIVSA the implementation of the new working schedule came after a strike from July 3–22, 1912. |
| 10 | 9 | August 19, 1915 | August 24, 1915 | Decree No. 11 of governor of Veracruz, Cándido Aguilar. October 19, 1914. Put in practice a year later, after workers' demands. |
| 9 | 8 | May 1, 1917 | May 1, 1917 | Article 123 of the Constitution, February 5, 1915. Put in practice after negotiations between companies and unions. |

*Sources:* CIVSA and CIDOSA documents.

During the Porfiriato, work started early at Santa Rosa. A whistle blew twice, the first at 5:30 a.m. so workers got ready to walk to the factory in order to be there at 6:00 a.m. when work started. Workers were allowed ten minutes after the last whistle to be in their places. Until 1906 spinners, weavers, and all other workers who were paid by piecework worked until 8:00 p.m. They had a half-hour break between 8:00 and 8:30 a.m. to take breakfast. From 1:00 to 2:00 p.m. they had a lunch break outside of the factory, and the whistle blew again several times to get them back on time.[48] On Saturdays work ended at 5:30 p.m. and Sundays were free. Thus the weekly working hours were 72, or twelve hours and a half per day from Monday to Friday, and nine and a half hours on Saturday, twelve hours on average.[49]

Workers in the printing department worked only ten hours. Workers who were paid per day, such as mechanics, carpenters, and masons, worked from 6:00 a.m. to 6:00 p.m. If for some reason they had to work until 8:00 p.m., they were paid an additional one-fourth of their wage for the extra two hours. CIDOSA reported that at Cerritos and in some of the departments of Río Blanco and San Lorenzo there was a night shift that went from 8:00 p.m. to 6:00 a.m. (ten hours, but probably without breaks). The company reported that there was a weekly rotation of workers between day and night shifts.[50]

The workload in these factories seems to have been higher than in other textile mills of the state of Veracruz. At La Industria Xalapeña, work went from 6:00 a.m. to 7:30 p.m. with the same one and a half hours break as CIVSA and CIDOSA.[51] However, some mills must have worked longer hours. Graham Clark's report on textile mills for that period described a working schedule similar to that of CIVSA for most mills. But, he said that "a few mills worked even longer hours than this, starting at 5:30 in the morning and stopping at 9:00 at night. This is a 14-hour day, which is as long as is worked by the English mills in India." Clark explained that there was a federal law that established that mills should not work over twelve hours a day, including an hour for lunch, and that there was a law forbidding children under 10 years old to work, but, he said, "there is no attempt to enforce either law, and both are disregarded."[52]

On June 17, 1907, after a strike that lasted almost a month, Río Blanco workers managed to reduce the workday by one hour.[53] Henceforth, work ended at 7:00 p.m. In June 1907 *El Cosmopolita* reported under the headline "A Rainbow on the Industrial Sky" that CIDOSA had agreed to reduce the workday for one hour in its mills. Workers had asked for an hour and a half shift reduction, working on some holidays in exchange. In compensation, the company indicated that they would keep as holidays March 19 (Saint Joseph), June 29 (Saint Peter and Saint Paul), and August 15 (The Assumption), besides holidays already established, such as May 5, November 2, and September 16.[54] On its part, Santa Rosa's Council decided to let workers leave at 7:00 p.m. if they chose to, but to allow the rest to stay until 8:00 p.m. This new schedule was definitely adopted in August 1910 when, as a consequence of a strike, Santa Rosa's management conceded that the exit be at 7:00 p.m.[55]

In January 1912, as part of the negotiations with the Department of Labor to end a general strike, working hours were reduced to ten. Entrance was now at 7:00 a.m. and work ended at 6:00 p.m., with an hour lunch break at noon, but the former morning half-hour break was canceled. Because most work was paid per piece, every reduction in the working hours had to be accompanied with an increase on the price paid per piece, in order to leave workers with at least the same daily wage they previously received. Thus, in January 1912 there was a raise of 10% on wages paid per piece. In June the night shift was cut to nine hours. Similar working hours were established in CIVSA in September 1912.[56]

On October 19, 1914, Cándido Aguilar, governor and military commander of the state of Veracruz, issued a decree reducing the work shift to nine hours, day or night. Night work had to be paid twice the rate of day work. The decree established that violators would be punished by a fine of 50 to 500 pesos or jail time of 8 to 30 days.[57] Two weeks earlier he had issued a decree declaring Sundays as mandatory holidays.[58]

These decrees were not put into practice right away. In a letter sent by CIVSA's council to its managers in March 1915, they advised them not to mention the new nine-hour workday established by government's decree, as they were still working ten. The reduction of the work shift to nine hours was effective in CIDOSA and CIVSA from August 1915 on, after workers sent petitions to its directors demanding that Aguilar's decree be applied and that wages be increased to compensate for the workday reduction. Wages paid per day increased by 60% and for piecework by 50%. The intervention of the state government was also necessary. In September CIDOSA was fined 2,000 pesos and CIVSA 1,000 pesos for not implementing the decree of October 19, 1914, earlier.[59] Working hours from then on went from 7:00 a.m. to 5:00 p.m. with a one-hour break between noon and 1:00 p.m. from Monday to Saturday. The night shift was suspended in CIVSA and CIDOSA as a result of the 50% wage increase beginning in September 1915.[60]

In February 1917 the new Constitution established the eight-hour workday (seven hours for the night shift), to become effective in May. To ensure its implementation, the state governor convened a conference between workers and industrialists on April 14. The reduction in the working hours had to be compensated by a wage increase, which was obtained after a two-week strike in May. On this new schedule work went from 7:00 a.m. to 4:00 p.m. with an hour for lunch. Once the eight-hour shift was established, punctuality became important and doors were closed strictly on time. At first workers were not used to this and they complained to the government about this company practice. Río Blanco reported that on June 12 they had locked out sixty to seventy workers who had come late.[61]

After a strike in July 1919, CIVSA established a second shift in the spinning department that went from 4:30 p.m. to 11:30 p.m., paying the same wage as for the first shift for work paid per hour, and an additional 10% on wages for work paid per piece. CIVSA explained that this second shift was necessary in order to be able to work six days a week in the other departments. As a result of a strike, workers for the second shift were hired under a collective contract, and company managers were obliged to negotiate with the union on the hiring of workers, as was the case for the rest of the workers.[62]

In August 1924 the federal government decided that there would be three different time zones in the country—West, Central, and East—but the Veracruz legislature agreed to keep the old time schedule so work hours were moved ahead one hour. The first shift went from 8:00 a.m. to 1:00 p.m. and from 2:00 to 5:00 p.m.[63] Finally, on June 1927 the work schedule was rearranged in CIDOSA in order to have Saturday evening free. From Monday to Friday work hours went from 7:30 to 12:30 p.m. and from 2:00 to 5:30 p.m. On Saturdays they went from 7:30 a.m. to 1:00 p.m. This policy was followed by CIVSA a month later, and the "English week" was established.

The reduction in the work hours created a radical change in workers' lives. Now they had spare time they could use for other purposes. Some went to school; others formed music bands, a new cultural phenomenon of the period.[64] Many workers started playing sports, particularly baseball, which developed greatly in the region, gradually replacing the Aztec ball that was commonly played during the early years. Some workers participated as actors in plays that were organized by the unions, often based on historic events.[65] Others took second jobs, many times developing trades or small businesses on their own. Many participated more actively in union life, sometimes working as volunteers on union projects, such as the construction of schools.[66] Some, as company managers critically pointed out, simply spent relaxed evenings drinking *pulque* with their friends. In general the reduction of the working shift meant an extraordinary improvement in workers' lives that is difficult to quantify.

What were the forces behind this victory? In the United States most of the workday reduction in 1907–1919 resulted from the rapid expansion of the economy, which increased wages and drew new participants into the manufacturing sector, two factors that explain almost half the reduction in hours according to Whaples's empirical study. The fall in immigration explained another 20% of the workday reduction. In contrast, unionization explained only 14% of the fall in hours worked.[67] The logic behind this is that as the economy expands at a higher rate than the supply of labor, wages increase and working hours decrease as the workers begin to value having an extra free hour more than the wage they would receive from working that hour, given that their income per hour is also increasing.

Unfortunately there is no data available to do a similar analysis for Mexico. Nonetheless, from CIVSA's production and employment data it is possible to give some broad explanations. Part of the reduction in the workday that took place from 1907 to 1912, from twelve to ten hours, could have been the result of the expansion of the economy, because employment, production, and productivity levels increased during this period. However, none of the further reduction in the workday can be explained by the tightening of the supply of labor, because there was an important reduction in production and employment from 1913 to 1917.

The expansion of production could explain at most 25% of the fall in work hours in CIVSA between 1907 and 1917.[68] Therefore, most of the reduction of the workday in Mexico is explained by the growth in organized labor's strength coupled with federal and state legislation passed by the revolutionary governments. Unions were the major actors behind the workday reductions before 1912 that came about only after important strikes. After 1914, government legislation began to play a role. Yet laws were dead letters if unions did not press for their compliance. As late as 1925 there were still strikes in Puebla, Sinaloa, and Guerrero for the establishment of the eight-hour workday.[69]

In contrast with the commonly held view that the eight-hour day was obtained in one blow, as a result of the 1917 Constitution, the study of workday changes in Orizaba shows that it was a long battle.

# CHAPTER 8

# A Revolution in Daily Life

## Community and Living Conditions
## in the Mill Towns

WORKERS WHO ARRIVED in the Orizaba Valley at the end the nineteenth century to work in Río Blanco and Santa Rosa when the mills had just opened found that there was nothing else around except what the companies themselves had built and owned. During the early years, they were company towns in a strict sense of the term. The companies settled in a space that was not only physically, but also institutionally, empty. The presence of the state was feeble, and the settlements were too recent for a market for goods and services to have developed. Managers undertook most public works and controlled the municipal governments. The companies became responsible for the construction of urban infrastructure and other state duties, such as the keeping of public order, at its own expense. Additionally, they assumed responsibility for the provision of goods and services, which are normally provided by several private agents, such as housing, along with the commercialization of products of basic need.

A restricted number of actors combined with geographical isolation bring about a more acute level of confrontation than in differentiated and urban contexts. In cities the social actors are more diluted and get together only in the productive space, whereas in the company town or enclave, the productive space and the nonproductive space are inti- mately linked.[1] Thus, the arena of possible conflict is wider.[2] This was the situation in the Orizaba Valley mills, and particularly in Río Blanco and Santa Rosa, where the company was omnipresent not only during working time but in most aspects of the daily lives of workers and their families, generating greater strain in capital–labor relations.

During the decade or so following the establishment of the factories, the urban space gradually developed from mere settlements surrounding mills, into real towns. As the labor movement gained strength and unions were organized, their role in the mill towns increased and they took over many functions previously held by the companies. This process was re- inforced by the important change that took place in the municipal gov- ernments when workers, instead of company personnel, became the mu- nicipal presidents. After 1915 the unions gradually took over the role of companies outside the mills, and the villages evolved from being company towns into becoming union towns.[3]

The increasing role of the unions in ruling and managing the mill towns generated important improvements in the living conditions of the workers and their families. Housing infrastructure and educational fa- cilities improved, and consumer cooperatives enabled workers' families to buy goods at better prices. Moreover, through the unions' initiative new recreational facilities, such as cinemas and sport fields, were built. Until the end of the 1920s the state played only a small role in the trans- formation of these communities. Although the municipal governments undertook greater initiative, they acted more as a means to carry out unions' goals than as autonomous powers.

This transformation was carried out not solely by the workers but by the communities they formed together with their families. It changed workers' living conditions and community life, and these changes were expressed in the building of the towns. The role of the state, both na- tional and local, also changed dramatically throughout the period; at the turn of the century, the state was hardly a presence in the lives of the communities of the Orizaba Valley, and the Mexican Revolution had weakened it even further. Yet by the mid-1920s the state had become in- tegral to life in the workers' communities.

## Santa Rosa: The Town

Before the construction of the Santa Rosa mill, the narrow valley that the
town of Santa Rosa (now Ciudad Mendoza) was later to occupy was basically empty. It formed part of the municipality of Necoxtla, whose government (Cabecera) sat in the small Indian town of Necoxtla, up in the
hills that surrounded the Santa Rosa Valley. From its inception CIVSA
began negotiations with the state government to make a new municipality in the region where the factory was located, pledging to construct all
the necessary buildings. At first the government wanted to change the
municipal borderlines so that CIVSA would belong to the closer municipality of Nogales instead of Necoxtla. The CIVSA board disliked this
idea, knowing that the Nogales municipal government was controlled by
CIDOSA.[4] On April 25, 1898, the government of the municipality of
Necoxtla was moved from the old village of Necoxtla to the recently created town of Santa Rosa despite the Necoxtla Indians' protest.[5]

The factory was crucial to the urban development of the area, not
only because it attracted population to settle in the region, but also because of its direct involvement in providing the main public services in
the area. The municipal palace of Santa Rosa was built on CIVSA's budget and under its supervision, according to the indications of Governor
Teodoro Dehesa. The factory also financed the construction of the Catholic church, a project whose completion took many years, and gave 12
pesos weekly for the support of the priest.[6]

CIVSA was also important for improving communications between
Santa Rosa and the rest of the country. In 1897 it signed a contract with
the local tramway company to extend to Santa Rosa the tramway line
that previously ended in Nogales. In 1899 CIVSA made a deal with the
minister of communications to install a telegraph office in Santa Rosa.
The federal government installed the telegraph lines, but CIVSA built
its offices. CIVSA also pledged to pay the telegraphist and messenger
monthly salaries whenever the telegraph office incomes were not high
enough to cover them, and to give them housing.[7]

In 1897 CIVSA built a branch line of the railroad in Santa Rosa and
platforms for the loading and unloading of materials close to the so-
called Crucero de Santa Cruz. Then it gave the land and built the town

railroad station, in agreement with the Ferrocarril Mexicano, and paid the wages of the employees in charge of it.[8] The station was inaugurated on June 27, 1907. Many years later, in 1928, CIVSA gave 15,000 pesos for the construction of the Mexico–Veracruz highway, in agreement with CIDOSA and Cervecería Moctezuma, which donated a similar amount.[9]

In 1917, on the request of the municipality, CIVSA at its own expense built the pipelines to provide the municipality with drinking water.[10] At first these pipelines reached only a small part of the town, so in 1928 CIVSA gave the municipality 12,000 pesos to provide drinking water for the whole town as an advance payment of its taxes. After 1906 CIVSA provided street lighting for the town of Santa Rosa free of charge. It was not until 1929 that CIVSA signed a contract with the municipality to charge for the electricity it provided for street lighting.[11]

Santa Rosa's central plaza was also built with the aid of CIVSA. In July 1920 CIVSA donated 3,000 pesos and lent the municipality another 3,000 pesos to buy the plot for the plaza, and later to install the kiosk and benches. The construction of Santa Rosa's municipal market was also financed by CIVSA. In October 1929 the company lent the municipality 5,000 pesos to buy the plot where it was to be built and annually deducted its payment from municipal taxes.[12] In Río Blanco a similar situation prevailed. In 1922 CIDOSA reported that it owned the Catholic church as well as the market and that it rented the market to the municipality.[13]

In the 1920s CIVSA's union became more important than the company in providing public services for Santa Rosa. If CIVSA financed the construction of the town hall, church, and market, the union built the three other major public buildings, which still exist in Santa Rosa today: the school (1927), the playing field (1927), and the movie theater and public library (1949).[14]

Until 1930 the government played a marginal role in the construction of Santa Rosa's urban infrastructure compared with that played by CIVSA and its union. However, the role of the municipal government grew throughout this period as well. Whereas during the first decade of the century CIVSA provided the funding for and initiated and implemented the construction of urban projects, those projects subsequently were built under the municipal government's leadership and CIVSA only provided the funding, mostly only as credit.

The changing roles of the company and the union in the construction projects undertaken in the mill towns correspond to a similar shift in the political control of the municipal government. Whereas until 1916 all Santa Rosa's municipal presidents had been CIVSA white-collar employees supported by the company, after 1917 they were CIVSA blue-collar workers supported by the union.

## Housing

The lack of urban development in the sites where the factories were built obliged the companies to include dwellings for workers and higher-level employees in the mills' construction projects. The Santa Rosa factory construction plans included living quarters for workers from the outset. In June 1897 the CIVSA board decided to build eighteen rows of brick houses. In February 1898 they built twenty more houses, made of wood, in three rows.[15]

Housing conditions of CIDOSA workers appear to have been similar to those of CIVSA. In 1909 Graham Clark wrote: "At Río Blanco the operatives live in rows of long wooden barracks, which are kept neatly painted and are furnished with water and light by the mill." According to Clark these conditions were far better than those he found in other regions of the country. "Orizaba operatives' living surroundings are certainly better than those to be seen anywhere else in Mexico, as the mills in this section build neat wooden or adobe houses that are kept in good repair."[16] For their higher-level employees CIVSA and CIDOSA built enclosed neighborhoods that included sport and other amusement facilities, such as bars with billiards and bowling tables. The companies owned houses for employees who lived with their families, and dormitories and dining rooms for single employees.

Most CIVSA workers lived in Santa Rosa, but only a small percentage of them lived in company housing. In 1900 only 155 (11.4%) of the factory's workers appeared on the payrolls paying rents for company housing. Yet by 1911 almost one-fourth of CIVSA's workers lived on company premises, a share of workers that never increased significantly thereafter.[17] It was considered a privilege to get a room in the mills' housing, often possible only after working several years in the mill.

The majority of workers lived in lower-quality houses they built themselves, or in rented houses, often *patios de vecindad* (tenement houses) owned by private landlords.[18] Throughout the late nineteenth century and early twentieth century, *patios de vecindad*—usually each had a local name or descriptive term—were a common solution in Latin American cities to their great demographic urban expansion. They consisted of "a number of small rooms centered around a common courtyard where basic cooking and bathing facilities were located."[19] They often had wooden walls and soil floors. They were managed by a housekeeper *portera or casera,* whose pay, according to what was called the *ley del pacho,* was that the landlord allowed her (and her family) to live there without paying rent, plus the fines she could charge the tenants, which she kept. *Patios de vecindad* had strict regulations. The housekeepers closed their doors at 9:00 p.m.; anyone left outside had to pay the housekeeper 10 cents to be allowed in, but if it was very late, she could also refuse to let the tenant in. Most of the tenement houses were owned by few landlords, such as Mr. Cafarel, Mr. de la Llave, Mr. Soto, and the López brothers. An article from the *Pro-Paria* workers' newspaper from 1922 decried the deplorable state of rental housing in Orizaba, and pointed out that several tenement owners were charging high rents for rooms with deteriorating doors and roofs.[20]

Company housing improved substantially from 1900 to 1930. In 1906 CIVSA provided electricity from its electric plant to its workers houses; in 1908 it started to include charges for the electricity in the payrolls. Originally a water faucet and toilets (most probably latrines) were shared by each row of houses, but in 1910 CIVSA started installing a water faucet in every house. By 1911 this project was completed, and CIVSA installed toilets to be shared by a whole row of houses. There were no showers for workers until 1920, when, at the request of workers, the company installed public baths, which workers and their families could use for a small fee. Public showers for workers of Cocolapan and Cerritos were built in 1924.[21]

Article 123 of the Constitution of 1917 mandated big companies (those who employed more than 100 workers) to provide "comfortable and healthy" housing for their workers at a monthly cost of no more than 0.5% of their fiscal value.[22] The Labor Law of Veracruz passed in 1918 established similar duties. Nonetheless the availability of company housing did not increase much from 1917 onward.[23]

Although CIVSA did not build more houses for its workers, it undertook significant investments from 1921 to 1928 to improve them. New blocks of houses were built to replace the old wooden ones. In 1924 the CIVSA board reported that many wooden houses still survived but that they planned to replace all of them that year with brick houses that could be "judged by the most modern precepts of hygiene."[24]

Some blocks of houses still survive. From an on-site observation, it can be concluded that there were 324 homogeneous brick houses arranged in 22 rows. They had thick walls and high tile or sheet-metal roofs. The houses had a bedroom, a living room, a kitchen, and a small patio. They were 47 square meters (56 square yards) large, not counting the patio. Houses had no bathrooms, toilets continued to be shared by each row of houses, and showers were taken in the public bathing area. In 1947–1948, bathrooms were built in each house, using part of the patio area.[25]

The rent workers paid for company houses as a percentage of their wages was more than halved between the Porfiriato and the 1920s. Whereas from 1900 to 1914 those workers who lived in CIVSA's housing spent about 20% of their wages on rent and electricity bills, they only spent 7% to 9% of their wages on these items in the 1920s.

From 1914 onward, the percentage of wages spent on rent and electricity gradually fell as a consequence of inflation (see Figure 8.1). Because rents were set in current pesos, they suffered the same fate as wages, and diminished constantly between 1913 and November 1916. Moreover, rents fell even more than wages because nominal wages were raised more frequently than rents during this period as a result of strikes. This explains why the percentage of wages devoted to rents fell from 22.8% in 1914 to 0.6% in November 1916. The fall in rent and electricity costs during this period helps explain how workers managed to survive during this inflationary period despite the enormous drop in their real wages described in Chapter 7.

When hyperinflation ended and wages began to be paid on a gold peso basis, rents increased accordingly. Rents increased drastically from November 1916 to January 1917. Then in February, rents diminished as a result of the company's compliance with the law of payments (Ley de

Pagos) decreed by the federal government on December 14, 1916. This law stipulated that rent for houses that did not exceed 30 pesos should be reduced to 40% of their previous level.[26] In order to make landlords obey this law, tenants started organizing.

An article printed in *El Dictámen* shortly afterward proposed the formation of a tenants' organization, and on December 25, 1916, residents of the port of Veracruz formed a tenants' syndicate under the auspices of the Union of Workers of the Mexican Republic (Sindicato de Trabajadores de la República Mexicana).[27] Grassroots organizations emerged also in the Orizaba Valley. Tenants in Orizaba met on March 21, 1917, to form a tenant union "against landlord abuses." They contacted organizers in the port of Veracruz to work together on a common cause.[28]

The Revolution generated a housing problem in several cities of the state of Veracruz, and throughout the country, which became acute during the 1920s. Although the national population diminished from 1910 to 1921, it concentrated in urban areas and continued rising through out the 1920s. Thus, while Mexico's population grew only by 9.18% between 1910 and 1930, and rural towns such as Tepezintla, Veracruz, almost disappeared (population decreased 78%), population in Xalapa increased by 44%, in the city of Veracruz by 27%, in Orizaba by 17%, and in the mill towns of Santa Rosa, Río Blanco, and Nogales by 39%. This helps explain the strength of the tenant movement during this period.[29]

On December 1, 1917, Governor Cándido Aguilar passed a tenants' law, the Ley de Inquilinato, that attempted to keep the cost of popular housing under control. That same month, though, the federal government decreed a new law of payments that made contracts dating from 1916 onward effective, allowing landlords to charge full lease price.[30] In January 1918 and again a month later, CIVSA and CIDOSA tried to implement this law and restore rents to their December 1916 rate, but the governor of Veracruz forbade them to do so. There was a contradiction between the Labor Law of the state of Veracruz that established that rents should not exceed 0.5% of the assessed value of the premises, and the new law of payments that maintained that 1916 rents could be reestablished. In January 1918 CIDOSA was charging the full rent that prevailed in December 1916 for only 25% of its 1,174 houses, while the other 75% were paying only 40% of their previous rates.[31]

On March 22, 1918, an agreement was reached between representatives of landlords from Nogales and Santa Rosa and the unions, including the Tenants' Syndicate (Sindicato de Inquilinos), by which rents were to be paid at 75% of the value they had had in 1912, beginning on January 1, 1918. Landlords agreed to supply tenement houses with drinking water, toilets, and laundry sinks. The Nogales branch of the Tenant's Syndicate, however, did not agree to pay back rents, arguing that throughout 1917 landlords had been charging the full lease instead of the 40% that the December 1916 law of payments established. In 1922, 60% of CIDOSA's houses were still paying 40% of the rent.[32]

Tenants' organizations in the state of Veracruz acquired a new political dimension through the creation in February 1922 of the Revolutionary Syndicate of Tenants (Sindicato Revolucionario de Inquilinos) in the port of Veracruz, under the leadership of the anarchist Herón Proal. It soon gained national and even international attention because of the radical actions the union pursued. In March, tenants of several tenement houses (patios de vecindad) declared a rent strike. They demanded that rents be fixed at 2% of the cadastral value of the premises.[33] Tenants united to resist eviction, mostly peacefully, although force was also used. In July 5, 1922, the movement suffered a severe repression from the military that turned into a massacre. Its leaders, Herón Proal and Maria Luisa Marín, were arrested but the movement survived until 1926, when it gradually faded away.[34]

In the Orizaba Valley the tenant movement also grew stronger in 1922. Residents from Orizaba requested Herón Proal to help them found unions. Cocolapan worker Gonzalo San Juan recalled that Sebastián San Vicente (who changed his name to Luis Campos upon his arrival) was sent to help them organize. Shortly after they founded a tenants' newspaper, the *Periódico de Información Inquilinaria*. Aurelio Medrano, a worker from Cocolapan, was the head of the movement. Among its leading members there were several workers from Santa Rosa, Cocolapan, and Santa Gertrudis. Their family members, particularly their wives, were also very active in the movement.

Crowds gathered in front of the iron palace in downtown Orizaba where the movement's leaders gave radical speeches and everyone sang revolutionary songs. The syndicate organized meetings in every tenement, where they named representatives of the movement. Once the tenements joined the movement and its neighbors declared in strike, they grouped in committees and adopted a system of tokens devised by the Tenant's Syndicate to evenly spread the duties previously carried out by the housekeepers. Every token had written on its back a certain chore such as "please clean tomorrow," and they were distributed among the different committees. Every tenant had to pay 15 cents a week of which 10 cents went for the union and 5 cents remained for the committee's expenses. The syndicate had precise information on how many persons there were per committee, so no cheating or stealing was easily accomplished.[35]

As the French revolutionaries did in so many instances, the tenement neighbors changed the tenement names from saint or Porfirian names such as Patio San Juan de Dios, or Patio San Bartolo, or Patio Porfiro Díaz, to revolutionary names such as Patio Ricardo Flores Magón, Patio Francisco I. Madero, or Patios Fraternity, Equality or Brotherhood.[36] This tells a lot about the spirit of the movement, which was inspired by anarchist and libertarian communist ideas and was certainly much more than just about reducing rents or improving tenement conditions.

As a result of the rise of the tenant movement, Governor Adalberto Tejeda proposed a new Tenants' Law in June 1922. The State Congress passed the law (with some changes), and rents for popular dwellings had thereafter to be fixed either at the value they had in 1910 plus an increase of 10% or at an annual rate of 6% of the property's cadastral value.[37] As a result of landlords' opposition, the law was reformed in April 1923, raising rents to 9% of property value. By its very nature, this law was complicated to enforce because of the difficulty of defining the cadastral value of the premises. The problems between tenants and landlords thus continued with great tension.[38]

As can be seen in Figure 8.1, in CIVSA rents increased from 1922 to 1925. In this last year rents reached a level similar in real terms to those of the Porfiriato. If this trend reflected a more general trend, this would explain why the tenements movement gained increasing support during this period.

In September 1924 Río Blanco workers declared a rent strike. The following month Río Blanco reached an agreement with its union to end

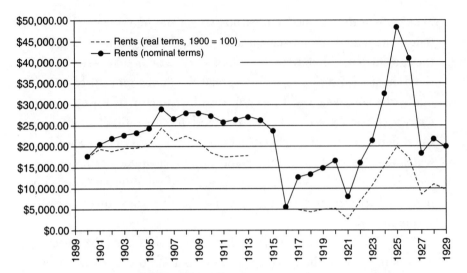

*Figure 8.1.* Rent charged for workers' housing, 1899–1929 (in pesos). *Sources:* CIVSA General Ledger, 1899–1900. The price index used to deflate was Index AB II. See Aurora Gómez-Galvarriato, "The Impact of Revolution: Business and Labor in the Mexican Textile Industry, Orizaba, Veracruz, 1900–1930" (PhD diss., Harvard University, 1999), chap. 4, table 8.

the strike. The company agreed to keep rents at 40% of the original (1916) value until the tenant changed, in which case 70% of the original amount could be charged. The rent for workers' houses where the full value was being paid would be reduced by 30%. The company also pledged to implement an additional 50% rent reduction whenever the company shortened the working week to three or fewer days, and to negotiate with the union on the percentage of rents to be paid whenever there was a strike. Moreover, the company promised to continue building new houses for workers.[39] This agreement enabled Río Blanco to recover some of its rental income, compared to previous years. By mid 1925, 41% of its tenants were paying 70% of the original rent, 55% were paying 40%, while 4% of the houses were leased at no cost to either the union or certain employees.[40]

The tenants strike was not confined to Río Blanco. It spread to the entire region of Orizaba and proved even more difficult for landlords different from the companies. In January 1925 the Orizaba Chamber of Landlords (Cámara de Propietarios de Orizaba) requested the support of the Cocolapan administrator, to no avail.[41] Figure 8.1 suggests that a similar process must have taken place at CIVSA, because from 1925 to 1930 rents declined, in both nominal and real terms. It seems that the tenants' movement was a crucial factor in this decline.

From 1917 to 1930, the share of wages allocated to rents fell from 9% to 7%. This was not the result of rents decreasing during this period; they increased more rapidly than food and textile prices. However, they grew at a lower rate than wages. This is why real wages deflated by the index that includes rents and electricity increased more than the index that excludes these items.

As a result, the companies' income from housing declined. In 1900 CIVSA made 17,540.29 pesos in rents from an investment in housing of 164,237.57 pesos, a 10.7% profit (without deducting management and maintenance costs).[42] However, the return on company housing declined consistently after 1912 to reach a minimum of 1.7% in 1916. Thereafter it gradually increased, reaching levels similar to those of the Porfiriato from 1924 to 1926. However, the decrease in rents from 1925 onward put a check on the returns on housing, which declined to levels between 4% and 5% for the rest of the decade. Whereas during the Porfiriato the average rate of return on company housing (net of depreciation) for the company was 11.58%, it was only 6.5% in the 1920s. A similar pattern prevailed in CIDOSA housing.[43]

During the 1920s, textile workers from the Orizaba Valley were no longer nomads. As workers gained stability in their jobs, they became more interested in settling in the region. Thus, establishment of workers' neighborhoods *(colonias)* became an important objective of the tenant's union.[44] Gradually neighborhoods of workers who owned their houses started appearing.

CIDOSA was a major landlord in the region and rented parts of it for agricultural purposes, which made it vulnerable to the agrarian reform that was taking place in the state of Veracruz. In early 1923 the Local Agrarian Commission started a legal battle with CIDOSA to have part of its land expropriated. The municipality distributed some of the company's land to peasants as *ejidos* (communal farms) under the Ley de Tierras Ociosas de la Federación (Federal Law of Vacant Land) of June 1920.[45] Moreover, the Veracruz Rent Law of April 8, 1923, passed by

Governor Adalberto Tejeda, made provisions for the expropriation of urban lands for the purpose of housing construction.[46] The Tenants' Syndicate of Orizaba asked Governor Tejeda to fraction the land from the companies to form colonias.[47] To avoid expropriation CIDOSA sold twenty lots to its workers at the so-called Barrio Motzorongo.[48] A similar process appears to have been taking place in Santa Rosa; in 1923 a neighbors' union, the Unión Central de Colonias de Obreros y Campesinos de Santa Rosa, was constituted, and by 1927 it had 500 affiliated neighbors.[49]

In 1924 the government invited owners of empty lots to cede them to the state so a corporation could built cheap wooden houses on them. CIDOSA managed to keep the lots it considered most valuable and sold the rest to the government at tax value plus 10%. In the following year CIDOSA sold several lots to 132 workers, which they paid for in 400 weekly installments.[50] Several workers' colonias were founded in those years, such as the Colonia de Inquilinarios, which later changed its name to Miguel Hidalgo, and the Colonia Benito Juárez.[51]

So many plots of land were sold to workers in Río Blanco that resident *(colono)* payments became a considerable share (56% in 1928) of the amount the company received for company housing rents. In 1928, at the workers' request, CIVSA devised a "colonization project" to sell plots of land to workers in the factory's surroundings. CIVSA's board considered that it was in the mill's interests to create a selected nucleus of stable inhabitants around the factory.[52]

By 1927 the CIVSA board considered company housing so unprofitable that it asked its manager to study the possibility of selling workers the houses they rented. They thought that, given that the houses that the company owned were a cause of conflict and administrative difficulties, and that they represented a cost rather than a profit for the company, it would be better to sell them to workers.[53] This idea was not implemented by CIVSA until the early 1970s, approximately five years after CIDOSA did so.[54]

## From Company Stores to Cooperative Stores and the Workers' Bank

During the Porfiriato, all textile mills in the Orizaba Valley had a company store. Their establishment did not seem to have been due solely to the greed of the employers. In 1897, when the Santa Rosa mill was still under construction, the CIVSA board decided that there was an urgent need to establish a provisional store because there were no commercial facilities in the surrounding area. The store was necessary, claimed the CIVSA board of directors, so that workers "do not lack what they need or waste time by having to go to find it as far away as Orizaba."[55] The region, which gradually urbanized and came to have several stores, seems to have had no store at all at that time.

By the end of the nineteenth century, it seems that other than the store at Nogales that served the San Lorenzo factory owned by CIDOSA, there were no stores except in Orizaba, eleven kilometers away from Santa Rosa. By 1898 Santa Rosa was connected to the tramway line that previously had gone only from Nogales to Orizaba.[56] Even then, it must have taken at least an hour to get there. Besides, it must have been expensive in terms of workers' budgets. By early January 1899, construction of the store was nearly completed and the CIVSA board of directors leased it to the Fuentes family, at a monthly rent of 150 pesos plus 5% commission on sales.[57]

Orizaba Valley company stores have been charged with maintaining a monopoly through issuing scrip *(vales)*, which only they could redeem, called a truck system. It has commonly been believed that workers were paid mostly in scrip. In fact, in the Orizaba Valley workers were paid most of their wages in silver coins, as we know from the weekly letters that came and went from Mexico City to the mills demanding large amounts of coins to pay weekly wages, or reporting on their remittance or arrival.[58]

Scrip was an advance on wages due the following payday. It was negotiable at the company store at its full value if it was traded for merchandise, or at 90% of its value if it was exchanged for money.[59] On the following Saturday, the amount advanced to workers in scrip during the week was deducted from their wages and paid to the company store, after deducting 5% commission.

At the turn of the century there were few alternatives to company stores. But as urbanization progressed in the region, the monopoly power of these stores diminished. By 1910 commercial facilities at Santa Rosa appeared very different from what they had been a decade earlier. In addition to the company store there were over twenty general stores in Santa Rosa, two stores that sold shawls *(rebocerías)*, two bakeries, and a drugstore. There was also a Singer sewing machine agency, which tells that Santa Rosa was a growing commercial district and that workers were able to afford sewing machines, with which women supplemented family incomes. There were also several traveling salesmen who came to Santa Rosa from Orizaba with boxes full of merchandise; these salesmen were known in the town as "the Italians" and "the Hungarians."[60]

Río Blanco's company store was leased to Victor Garcín, a Barcelonnette who had been in the region for some decades. In 1897 he was already an important landowner in the Orizaba Valley.[61] Eduardo Garcín, his brother, was CIDOSA's manager in 1903 and listed as a member of the CIDOSA board in the General Assembly minutes of 1905 and 1906. However, Garcín's store was not merely a company store but the largest store in the area.[62] It was a general store that sold all kinds of food, alcoholic beverages, clothes, and other dry goods. It also had a corn mill, a bakery, and a *pulquería,* a tavern where *pulque,* a fermented drink made from maguey juice, was sold. The store occupied a whole block and had a railway track at the back to facilitate the delivery of the merchandise.[63]

Garcín sold not only to workers but also to several stores in the region. Besides Río Blanco's company store, Garcín owned two other stores, El Centro Comercial at Nogales, and El Modelo at Santa Rosa, and nine *pulquerías.* Garcín was also a concessionaire of CIDOSA who bought cloth at wholesale prices to sell to several clients located in different and sometimes distant places throughout the country.[64]

If Víctor Garcín thought that other stores in the Río Blanco surroundings were taking customers away from him, he had enough power to close them down, as he apparently did with El Gallo Real and El Puerto de Veracruz, two small grocery stores in Río Blanco. Nonetheless, he did not hold complete monopoly power; in 1908 there were at least three other stores in the town: El Infierninto, El Chin-Chun-Chan, and Mi Tienda.[65] Although many of the stores established in the Orizaba Valley also sold on credit, company stores had an advantage over them because the factory guaranteed their credits.

Data from CIVSA payrolls furnish some interesting insights on the relationship between workers and the company store. The percentage of workers indebted to the company store was on average 15.6% of all workers, and the percentage discounted from their weekly income to pay debts was on average 26% of wages. The fact that both figures were far below 100% indicates that, even in 1900, workers purchased supplies at alternative locations (see Table 8.1).

Around 14% of CIVSA workers earned less than 3 pesos per week, 44% of CIVSA workers earned 3 to 6 pesos, and 42% earned more than 6 pesos. The percentage of lower-income workers indebted to the company store (8%) was almost half of those with higher wages (17%).[66] However, the share of wages deducted from them (44%) was much higher than the shares deducted from those with higher incomes (30% for those who earned 3 to 6 pesos, and 23% for those who earned over 6 pesos). This was the case because their income was lower, not because they owed more to the store. One could say that company stores were very important for

*Table 8.1*   CIVSA workers' expenditures at the company store

| Year | Income | | | Total |
| | Below 3 pesos | Between 3 and 6 pesos | Over 6 pesos | |
|---|---|---|---|---|
| *Percentage of workers who used the company store, by wage level* | | | | |
| 1900 | 7.40% | 23.20% | 18.00% | 16.83% |
| 1901 | 6.80% | 15.50% | 16.70% | 14.18% |
| 1902 | 6.08% | 13.73% | 13.60% | 12.12% |
| 1903 | 12.50% | 21.40% | 18.30% | 18.41% |
| 1904 | 8.90% | 19.50% | 15.40% | 15.57% |
| 1905 | 9.80% | 14.30% | 20.80% | 16.42% |
| 1906 | 6.80% | 16.20% | 17.70% | 15.53% |
| 1907 | 9.62% | 11.36% | 8.82% | 10.08% |
| 1908 | 3.32% | 24.17% | 22.72% | 20.10% |
| Avg. 1900–1906 | 8.33% | 17.69% | 17.21% | 15.58% |
| *Percentage of wages deducted to pay debts to company store, by wage level* | | | | |
| 1900 | 38.30% | 21.80% | 13.90% | 18.65% |
| 1901 | 38.00% | 27.10% | 18.80% | 22.38% |
| 1902 | 39.02% | 30.75% | 16.59% | 22.02% |
| 1903 | 39.80% | 34.00% | 23.90% | 28.39% |
| 1904 | 51.90% | 34.74% | 29.60% | 33.50% |
| 1905 | 57.30% | 26.80% | 28.20% | 28.59% |
| 1906 | 47.30% | 33.00% | 27.40% | 29.55% |
| 1907 | 47.33% | 22.91% | 9.64% | 29.33% |
| 1908 | 41.98% | 20.36% | 10.05% | 11.42% |
| Avg. 1900–1906 | 44.52% | 29.74% | 22.63% | 26.15% |

*Source:* CIVSA Payrolls, Week 6, 1900–1908.

*Note:* The wages reported here are weekly wages.

low-income workers; for example, at CIVSA in February 1905, those who purchased at the company store spent on average 57% of their income with them. However, only 9.8% of low-income workers had debts to the store.

The analysis of the payroll of February 1905 shows that 45% of workers with debts to the store were deducted less than 20% of their weekly income for store purchases, more than 70% were deducted less than 40% of their wages, and only 10% were deducted more than 80% of their income. The company did not allow workers to carry debts beyond the week. The most credit workers could get with the store was their total weekly wage minus all the other expenditures (rent, light, and doctor's fees). During the first week of February 1905, twelve workers (0.54% of CIVSA workers) had credits with the company store that accounted for more than 90% of their wage and received no monetary payment. All of them belonged to the factory's workshop department and were mostly construction workers, smiths, and carpenters. In the case of eight of these employees the reason for such large indebtedness was that they were absent at least half the week. Thus, it seems to have been an exceptional situation due to sickness or other problems. Only two of these twelve employees remained with the company during the first week of December 1906. One of them had no debt with the store on that occasion; the other, a horse keeper named Magdaleno Beristain, once again had a large debt with the store and received no monetary wage.[67]

Although it was impossible to carry out a similar analysis for CIDOSA due to lack of access to the company's payrolls, the following evidence shows that workers' indebtedness to the Río Blanco company store must have resembled that of CIVSA workers. In 1905 and 1906 at least once a week a check was paid by CIDOSA to Garcín of around 870 pesos.[68] This could have been the money the company was deducting from the payrolls for debt to the store (redeeming the scrip) and giving to Garcín. If this is true, then around 30% of the payroll was paid in the form of *vales* to Garcín.[69]

In January 1907 workers from the textile mills of the Orizaba Valley set fire to and sacked several stores in the region, in what has been known as the "Río Blanco strike." As attention focused on the company stores, on January 12 the CIVSA board instructed the factory manager to dissolve any obligation the company had with the store and to stop charging the 5% commission on workers' expenses. Accounting books were to be doctored so that the company would not have to hide anything from government authorities, whom they feared could visit the factory. CIVSA's manager was also instructed to advance some money to needy workers but "by no means they should be charged any percentage for it."[70]

In June 1908, CIVSA stopped deducting workers' debts to the store from the payroll. Thereafter its company store had no special advantage over the other stores established in the area. The rent the company charged Fuentes for the store was reduced in August 1910 to 120 pesos per month instead of the previous 150. As time went by, the rent continued to diminish.[71]

After the riots, Víctor Garcín sold his property to his former partner, the Spaniard Manuel Diez, and left the region. Diez, who also owned a store called El Fenix, reopened the store in Río Blanco in June 1908. El Fenix is still a chain of small supermarkets in the region today. An account written by a worker on the reopening asked workers to be alert, because although the store was not going to be a company store *(tienda de raya),* the previous experience had cost them dearly.[72]

Company stores were explicitly prohibited by almost all the labor legislation passed by the revolutionary governments. Their prohibition was first included in the factory regulations resulting from the Textile Workers' and Industrialists' Convention of July 1912. Subsequently Article 14 of Governor Cándido Aguilar's decree No. 11 of October 19, 1914, forbade any business—industrial or agricultural—from establishing *tiendas de raya,* demanding freedom of trade.[73] Article 123 of the 1917 Constitution established that wages ought to be paid in current money and not in script *(vales),* coupons *(fichas),* or merchandise. Finally, the Veracruz Labor Law contained several articles related to company stores.[74]

Workers soon realized that the end of the *tiendas de raya* was not enough to improve their conditions of consumption and credit, since they continued to be charged very high interest rates. In April 1908, workers wrote to *El Paladín* that a small store called Mi Tienda owned by Delfino Espíndola, a Río Blanco employee nicknamed "El Torero," was yielding good profits through its "excellent and legal credit operations, charging 12% weekly interest rates or the loss of the article pawned."[75] This rate does not seem lower than what company stores used to charge, nor does it seem to have been exceptional. Another letter to *El Paladín* stated that La Bella Concha in Santa Rosa charged 20% weekly interest rates in mid-1907 against articles pawned. In mid-1908 workers protested to *El Paladín* that money lenders in Santa Rosa charged a 12% weekly interest rate.[76]

Moreover, the end of company stores did not end abuses. A letter to *El Paladín* said that the Río Blanco employee "El Torero" favored workers who did business with him and discriminated against those who did not. He was trying to open a pawnshop "not content with the big profits he obtains from Mi Tienda and from the speculation he undertakes within the factory premises."[77] It concluded, "The factory, workers, and the neighboring stores are seriously damaged by this employee who infringes at his will the regulations that cost more than a little blood on January 7 of the previous year."[78] It referred to one of the articles of the factory's regulations that forbade employees from carrying out business inside the factory and from receiving money in exchange for protection.

Purchasing and credit conditions worsened as a consequence of the scarcity and high inflation rates that the revolutionary conflict produced after 1913. Early on, workers decided to organize consumer cooperatives, which they considered a way to get goods at better prices. In 1915 Cocolapan mill workers sent a letter to the governor and military commander of the state of Veracruz, Agustín Millán, to inform him that on December 4 they had established a cooperative association "to free ourselves from the merchants who have extorted us so much with the pretext of the revolution, considering that the revolution is not to blame for merchants swindling the proletarian people, and to avoid it, or at least to defend us against it."[79]

In Santa Rosa a cooperative store was also established using one of the factory houses as its premise "so the families could buy at cheaper prices and with more convenience." The workers who promoted this enterprise formed part of the Club Político Liberal Esteban Zúñiga, the first political club established in Santa Rosa. The club was named in honor of one the Santa Rosa workers who were killed together with Camerino Mendoza on March 8, 1913. One of its main advocates, Lorenzo Castañeda, was one of the Santa Rosa workers who had joined the Red Battalions. Its first president was the worker Angel López.[80]

The next available sources regarding the organization of consumer cooperatives in the region date from 1920. In November 1920, the Federation of Unions of the Orizaba District (FSCO) and employers of the Orizaba Valley held a series of meetings in Orizaba that resulted in the creation of consumers' cooperatives aimed at "lowering the price of basic products."[81] Firms agreed to provide funds for the creation of consumers' cooperatives, instead of granting the 100% wage increase that workers demanded. They agreed to donate 50,000 pesos, which would be divided between the different companies. The companies also agreed to provide the premises for the establishment of such cooperative stores at no cost and to support the stores in the transportation of merchandise and to provide them with cheap cloth. Unions wanted to have absolute control of these cooperatives, but the companies asked the state government to supervise them, which was apparently accepted.[82]

Cooperative stores opened in the surroundings of almost every factory in the region: Santa Rosa, Río Blanco, Mirafuentes, San Lorenzo, and Santa Gertrudis.[83] Following the example of the Federation of Cooperative Stores of France, with whose secretary general, Comrade Poisson, workers of the region had an interview in 1922, the cooperative stores of the region formed a federation, the Sociedad Cooperativa de Consumo Obreros Federados. In June 1924 the administrative board of the Sociedad Cooperativa de Consumo announced that they just opened a head office store in downtown Orizaba. The building that housed the store was donated by the Tenants' Union.

The Society of Consumer Cooperative had a large membership. The report stated that they had undertaken a successful campaign among the workers' unions of the region to affiliate as many members as possible. Workers from the Cervercería Moctezuma, la Constancia, Cocolapan, Cigarreros, Cerritos, Santa Gertrudis, Santa Rosa, Mirafuentes, San Lorenzo, Río Blanco, and Cervecería Orizaba became members. The Santa Rosa union decided that all its members automatically became shareholders.[84]

Cooperative stores sold groceries, crockery, clothes, and footwear. Some of them also sold milk, bread, and meat.[85] It was common practice to sell goods on credit to workers. Many debts were not paid for months or even years. Cooperative stores spread from Orizaba to other parts of the country. By 1927 they had become so important in the unions' lives that at the eighth convention of the Confederación Regional Obrera Mexicana (CROM), its Central Committee established a Department of Cooperatives to take charge of consumption and production for cooperatives on a national level.[86]

Cooperative stores were not without troubles. In 1928 the Sociedad Cooperativa de Consumo had 32% of its assets in credits to workers and another 23% in credits to affiliated cooperative stores. This compares with only 8% of total assets held in merchandise. The same year, a project to reorganize the cooperative stores was submitted by a commission of the confederate board of the workers' chamber (Consejo Confederal de la Cámara del Trabajo). They proposed that workers be obliged to spend at least one peso per week at the cooperative stores. Affiliated unions would supervise this obligation by requiring workers to present receipts of their purchases every week. Repayment of credits on groceries had to be made within two weeks. Failure of payment would promptly be notified by the credit committee to the unions, which would proceed "as they judged fit," in order to secure reimbursement of the debt.[87] This indicates that cooperative stores faced serious problems as regards repayment of their credits and in attracting workers as clients.

Nonetheless, it seems that stores were able, at least for some years, to achieve their objective of providing cheaper goods for workers. In 1929 the *Pro-Paria* journal reported that whereas private merchants had raised the prices of basic goods, the cooperative store of Río Blanco had been able to keep them stable at lower prices. It argued that as a result of the cooperative store's competition, private merchants were forced to lower their prices very soon afterward. It concluded that "cooperative stores, when managed, as they are now, by *compañeros* aware of the needs of working people, fulfill a high mission that benefits all."[88]

Another attempt to overcome the credit problem workers faced was made by the Santa Rosa Union in 1927, through the creation of a workers' bank, the Banco Cooperativo Obrero. The union provided three-quarters of the initial capital of the bank (25,000 pesos) and the rest was given by CIVSA as a loan. The CIVSA board thought it best to support the bank because its existence would relieve the company from the cumbersome task of having to provide credit for its workers, "allowing us to reject in the future, the multitude of small advance payments and loans on account of wages that workers frequently request and which we do not always find it easy to refuse."[89]

The bank was located on the main street of Santa Rosa opposite the mill's main entrance. It was inaugurated on April 20, 1928, by the former president of Mexico, Alvaro Obregón, and the secretary general of the Confederation of Unions of Workers and Peasants (COSCO) of the state of Veracruz, Manuel Sánchez Martínez.[90] A council elected by the General Assembly of the union controlled the operation of the bank. Its members were obliged to provide a weekly report of the bank's situation to the General Assembly of the Union.

The Banco Obrero operated more as a rotating savings cooperative association than as an actual bank. It gave a 1% annual interest rate on savings and charged 2% interest rates on loans. These rates were lower than regional usurers' 10% per month. The bank's regulations set workers' monthly wages as a maximum amount for loans in order to prevent workers from incurring debts that went beyond their means. Payments were due weekly.[91] In the event a worker did not pay his debt, the union could intervene with the company so that the amount the worker owed would be deducted from his wages. Budget constraints subsequently made the bank limit its credits even further, only providing credit for sickness, death, or educational expenses. The bank generated annual profits that were used to support union projects, such as the América school, the Juárez movie theater, and a sports field built by the union. The bank operated until 1957.[92]

## Education

A real revolution in education took place in the Orizaba Valley between 1912 and 1930. Although by 1895 the city of Orizaba had ten schools attended by 411 girls and 435 boys, mill towns in the Orizaba Valley had only one or two municipal schools each.[93] These schools taught at most up to third grade of elementary school and had no more than forty students in a single classroom. In contrast, by 1930 there were several elementary schools in every mill town of the region with one teacher per grade that went up to sixth grade. The schools were attended by hundreds of students. Furthermore, several night and vocational schools for workers opened where students learned basic reading and writing skills as well as textile and clerical trades. Crowds of workers attended these schools.

Most of what has been written on the historical evolution of education in Mexico has focused on government policies.[94] Indeed, these studies assume that any improvement in education must have been the product of governmental action. However, this is not what the study of education in the Orizaba Valley between 1900 and 1930 shows. In fact, the promotion of education that took place in this region during the second and third decades of the century resulted from the mobilization of workers organized in unions and from the action of civil society in general.

During the Porfiriato, the federal government, through the Ministry of Education and Fine Arts (Secretaría de Instrucción Pública y Bellas Artes) created in 1905, was in charge of education only in the Federal District and the territories; state governments had complete freedom as regards educational policies.[95] In Veracruz, unlike most states in Mexico during the Porfiriato, schools were administered by municipal governments rather than by the state government.[96]

The 1917 Constitution made elementary education compulsory (Article 3), yet it said very little about how the government would provide or regulate education. It did not make clear what entity—federal, state, or municipal government—should control public education. It abolished the Secretaría de Instrucción Pública and thus "divested the central state of the little power it had in this area."[97] In February 1921 the Constitution was revised to permit more federal intervention in education policy throughout the nation, and the Secretaría de Educación Pública (SEP) was formally created in October 1921. Its first minister was José Vasconcelos, a man deeply committed to improving education in Mexico. The SEP gradually expanded its control over education at a national level.[98]

The federal budget for education expanded in the 1920s after the sharp reduction it experienced during the Revolution. In 1922 it was 78% higher than the 1910 education budget (in real terms).[99] However, during the Porfiriato these resources were used exclusively in the Federal District and the territories but after 1921 they had to be distributed throughout the country. Thus, the SEP faced a stringent budget constraint that limited the scope of its influence over the nation's educational development.

Veracruz state resources allocated to education grew even more than federal resources. In 1922 they were 225% greater than those of 1910 in real terms, even though the total state budget had only expanded by 90% over the same period. However, municipal resources devoted to education must either have diminished or grown at a much smaller rate, because the relative budget of the municipalities decreased vis-à-vis that of the state government.[100]

Analysis of government expenditure on education would suggest the federal and state governments must have had a pivotal influence on educational development in the Orizaba region. However, they played a very limited role in the educational spurt that the region experienced during these years. The spurt was the result of the interaction between unions and municipal governments, which after 1917 were mostly under the leadership of textile workers. The job in fact was done by the dozens of commissions, committees, and boards to support public education that appeared in the municipal governments, in the unions, and among the inhabitants of the villages.

Access to education, both for workers and for their children, was an important demand of the Orizaba labor movement from its origins. As we have seen, the GCOL set the establishment of a school and a library in each factory as one of its major goals. In letters to *El Paladín* workers demanded that the government establish schools for children, who from the age of 8 were already working in the mills. They asked Governor Dehesa to order that schools in the village be properly attended and that the law of compulsory education be complied with.[101]

The first night school in the region was founded during the early 1900s by the Liberal Mutualist Circle of Orizaba. In January 1907, as part of the repression of the labor movement that followed the "Río Blanco strike," the Orizaba municipal government began to harass the Circle and evicted the school and library from their premises, under the pretext that they were slightly behind in their payments.[102] However, the Circle was able to keep the school working by moving it to a smaller site. Rafael Mendoza, a Cocolapan worker, was a student there. He recalled that Enrique Lobato taught the elementary school courses and Gabriel Gavira taught lineal drawing, and that Heriberto Jara was also one of its teachers. What he learned in the night school helped him to later become an engraver at the mill.[103]

This school closed after the demise of the GCOL in January 1907, but workers did not remain passive. In July 1907 Santa Rosa workers sent a petition to the factory manager, requesting that a night school be established for the instruction of workers, as the president of the Republic had promised in his *laudo*.[104] Workers kept struggling to pursue this objective and, as a result of their initiative, between 1912 and 1916 a night school opened in almost every textile mill in the region.

In 1912 a night school was created at the San Lorenzo mill in Nogales and installed in the Miguel Hidalgo elementary day school.[105] The municipality wrote to CIDOSA that attendance was greater than expected: seventy-five students were attending the classes, and they thought many more would come. By 1916 night schools had also been opened also in Río Blanco and Santa Rosa. In May 1916 the Río Blanco union (Sindicato de Obreros y Similares de Río Blanco) decided to establish the night school in houses that had been previously rented by CIDOSA to pulque shops, because this had an important symbolism.[106] In 1916 CIVSA estimated that there were 200 illiterate workers at the mill and that 150 of them attended night school. CIVSA paid part of the teachers' wages, provided a house to accommodate them, and free electricity for the night school.[107] Santa Rosa's union took a strong stand on workers' education: illiterate workers did a disservice to the union and their education should therefore be made compulsory. The pro-school committee fined workers who did not attend school daily and punished them with days of suspension from work.[108]

By 1931 there were six union schools in the Orizaba Valley with 1,528 students. The Escuela Suplementaria para Obreros in Santa Rosa had 120 students, the Escuela Suplementaria para Obreros y Campesinos in Nogales had 121 students, and the Escuela Suplementaria para Obreros y Campesinos in Cerritos had 131 students; all of these schools went up to the fourth grade. The Escuela Nocturna para Obreros en Mirafuentes that went to third grade had 70 students. The Centro Educativo Obrero in Orizaba had 732 students. In Río Blanco the Escuela Pro-Paria taught first and second grade, and the Escuela Suplementaria Municipal para

Obreros y Campesinos went from third to sixth grade; together the two schools had 354 students.[109]

The schools' program included language, arithmetic, geometry, music, physical education, an artisan trade *(oficios)* such as carpentry or blacksmith skills, and a series of conferences workers had to attend "to rectify their orientation and behavior in the class struggle." In 1932, students attended conferences on topics such as "January 7," "The Economic Situation of the Porfiriato," "The Mexican Revolution from a Social Perspective," "The Proletarian Revolution," or "The History of Socialism in France, Germany, England, North America, and Mexico."[110] In Río Blanco a Textile School was opened in 1925 that offered courses for workers who had already studied in elementary school; these included "Theory of Weaving." Employees from the mills were often the teachers.[111]

Former workers interviewed in the 1970s indicate that several of them attended the night school, and that what they learned there was important for their future careers. Gonzalo San Juan, a Cocolapan spinner, studied as a child until the second grade of elementary school. In 1928, when he was 31 years old, he decided to join the night school. He finished elementary school and then he studied three years of commercial studies, where he learned typing, shorthand writing, math, English, and accounting principles. To be able to study, he hired a helper for his spinning job, whom he paid from his wages. He sat on a box in the near the work area and studied most of the day while overseeing the helper from time to time. His studies were very useful for his career, because he got a better job as an electrician and became secretary general of the Cocolapan union some years later. As he explained, "In 1935 [when he finished school] I began to feel empowered with a strong authority to talk, since now I had an education."[112]

Delfino Huerta, a Río Blanco weaver, studied as child until third grade. He believed it was good fortune that his teachers held a liberal ideology and supported the Revolution. When he was 22 years old he started attending night school but that lasted for only a few years because he found the schedule exhausting. He had to work from 6:00 a.m. to 5:00 p.m. (with an hour for lunch). When he left work, he went home, cleaned up, and then attended school from 6:00 p.m. to 8:30 p.m. Only five years later, in 1926, he became secretary general of the Río Blanco union, and then again in 1930, and 1954. He also held other union positions on several occasions.[113]

Valentín Cueto did not know how to read and write at the age of 17 when he worked as a doffer in the Santa Gertrudis jute mill. He had attended a Catholic school as a child, but he said that there he only was taught to pray. One day when he was walking home with several friends, as they passed in front of the school Professor Miguel Velázquez invited them to come in. They went back the next day, and he gave them pencils and notebooks for free. The six of them finished elementary school. Later Professor Velázquez convinced Professor Francisco Rico, who taught in the private Universidad Libre Veracruzana, to allow them in his class to learn lineal drawing, "and that is what saved my situation," recalled Valentín Cueto, who later became an engraver. However, he believed that the other five students in the group took even greater advantage of their education because they were good at math. One of them, a Río Blanco worker nicknamed *"guarache sabio"* (wise sandal) because he was too poor to buy shoes and extremely bright, was one of the authors of the wage tariff of the 1925–1927 Convention. Later he became municipal president of Río Blanco.[114]

Gonzalo García Ortíz had studied until second grade before starting to work in Santa Rosa as a child. When he was around 20 years old and already a three-looms weaver, he started night school. There he was able to finish elementary school. He recalled that there were five to seven students in his class and that Professor José Santos González, who had a passion for teaching, worked with them for as long as was necessary for them to learn the lessons at hand. Because they were so eager to learn, they always chose to stay several hours more than the regular schedule. Thanks to his studies Gonzalo later became a loom fixer.[115]

Workers also struggled to put in place better educational facilities for their children. By 1906 there were two schools in Santa Rosa, the Josefa Ortiz de Domínguez school for girls and the Enrique C. Rébsamen school for boys, maintained by the municipal government. They were small schools, each with only one teacher. Obviously these schools were not enough to provide basic education for the children of Santa Rosa, considering that there were 512 children from 6 to 10 years old and 309 from 11 to 15 years old living in the municipality by 1900.[116]

Children of the Municipal School of Santa Rosa with Professor Ricaño, 1907.
(Unidentified photographer, Museo de Historia de Mendoza.)

In 1908 workers complained about the way schools were run in letters
to *El Paladín*. They explained that the boys' school teacher, Mr. Ricaño,
was a former priest who only taught children Catholic doctrine and how
to sweep the floor. Workers wrote that "between nothing and Ricaño,
nothing was always better."[117] He left by mid-1906 and was replaced by a
"lyrical teacher"—that is, one with no preparation as such. In February
1908 the school had no teacher. Workers considered this particularly unfair because from 1906 to 1908 "personal" taxes had increased from 0.32
to 1.08 pesos and the tax for public instruction from 0.13 to 0.39 pesos.[118]

Citizens of Santa Rosa soon began to organize to improve their schools.
In 1909 Camerino Z. Mendoza, an owner of a local store who later became a revolutionary leader, formed a Patriotic Board (Junta Patriótica)
to raise resources to construct the first buildings of these two schools. In
that year these schools taught first through third grades of elementary
school.[119] Although the government had no resources to support schools,
factories did, and the communities organized to pressure factories to

donate funds for education. By March 1913 a local board of elementary education (Junta de Instrucción Primaria) had been created and sent a letter to CIVSA asking for a monthly donation to support the Santa Rosa schools. CIVSA complied.[120]

A similar drive to promote education emerged in other towns in the region. In 1914 the Escuela Mixta de Cerritos was created at the CI-DOSA Cerritos mill. The Cerritos mill had donated the premises where the school was established to the municipal government and paid 50 pesos monthly to its teacher, Natalia Rivera. She also charged parents 10 cents weekly per child to complement her wage. When the school was opened, it only went up to second grade of elementary school, but in 1915 third grade was added. In that year, 48 children were registered in the school, a low figure if we consider that there were around 430 workers in the Cerritos mill.[121]

The other CIDOSA mills did not have elementary schools installed by the company, but the companies assisted the municipal schools in their surroundings. In Río Blanco, CIDOSA donated the land to the municipality and helped construct an ad-hoc building for the school for boys and girls. Once the school was built, CIDOSA made the necessary repairs as well to the other municipal schools, at no cost to the municipality. In addition it made periodic donations of school materials to the municipality and to private schools.[122]

There were several private schools in the region, and they also asked for the companies' support. In 1916 Elena Jouan asked CIDOSA to rent her a house in order to establish a small elementary school. "Given that there was no suitable school" to send their children to, employees organized to create this school and supported it with their own fees. In 1921 several residents of Santa Rosa asked CIVSA to help them remodel the Catholic school building. CIVSA agreed because its board considered the "moralizing action" of this school important.[123]

The spirit of Article 3 of the Constitution was that the authority and responsibility for national education lay with the government. However, Article 123 required owners of businesses employing over 100 workers to found schools at their own expense where there were no schools in the region. This legislation had very little effect in the Orizaba Valley because by 1914 there were already municipal schools in all the mill towns.

Nevertheless, the laws that required factories to install schools had a positive collateral effect in making companies believe they had some obligation to support education. In 1917, when the inspector of elementary schools asked CIVSA to cooperate in repairing the town schools, the company agreed because "those repairs did not cost much and . . . paragraph XII of the article 123 of the Constitution mandated it."[124]

The union played an increasing role in the education effort. A "pro-education" committee, the Sindicato de Obreros y Artesanos Progresistas de Santa Rosa, was created within the Santa Rosa union. Its members, elected every six months, were responsible for ensuring that the municipal schools functioned properly. To this end they commissioned a worker to be in the schools all morning or afternoon. They checked teachers' punctuality and attendance, and saw that teachers were paid, that there was no lack of school material, and that schools were clean.[125]

After 1916, when the municipal presidency passed into the hands of workers, it became an active promoter of education. The municipality appointed the teachers of municipal schools after formal searches, and most of the teachers it hired were qualified primary school teachers *(maestros normalistas)*. It also inspected schools and examined the reports school directors had to submit to the municipality. The municipal governments of Santa Rosa spent at least 30% of their income on education. The Enrique Rébsamen and Josefa Ortiz de Domínguez municipal schools, which had had only one teacher each during the Porfiriato, hired thirteen teachers by 1920, and nineteen by 1928. In this last year these schools taught 394 boys and 294 girls.[126] In 1919 the Santa Rosa union opened a town library and paid the librarian's wages. In 1923 the union inaugurated a new building for the library.[127]

In spite of the progress achieved by the municipal schools, the Santa Rosa union desired to go even further, and build a new, larger, and better school. In August 1922 it asked for CIVSA's support to undertake this project, but the board refused to give a donation, arguing that their assistance had to be channeled through government institutions. Nonetheless, CIVSA's workers continued with their project and in 1923 a new school was opened in Santa Rosa, the Centro Obrero Primario Federal "Acción," which taught the six elementary grades.[128] At first the school did not have a building of its own and was established in houses belonging to the Hernández family. The enthusiasm of Professor Manuela Contreras de Carballo was crucial to the union's pro-school committee in materializing the project. She came to the region as a member of the cultural missions that the federal government promoted as part of José Vasconcelos's educational campaign and became the school director. At the school's inception there were nine teachers besides her. Funds for the school came from the union and from the federal government.[129]

In 1926 Professor Contreras and Santa Rosa's union pro-school committee, under the active leadership of the weaver Acisclo Pérez, started a campaign to build a new building for the Centro Obrero Primario Federal "Acción." They bought a large plot of land measuring over 17.6 square miles (28,452 square meters). Funding for the school construction came primarily from Santa Rosa workers through a deduction of 0.5% from their weekly wages. The money collected by this means made up 73.3% of the school's total costs. Federal and state governments provided only 9.4% of total expenses. Local merchants contributed 7.4% of total costs, while donations from other individuals amounted to 4.3%. Charity fairs, bullfights, baseball games, and musical and literary evenings organized by the pro-school committee provided another 3.1% of funds. The rest came from other sources, including fines imposed by the union on workers who did not attend night school.[130] To speed up construction, the union organized groups of volunteers, who helped build the school with their own hands.[131]

The school was a two-story building, a more spacious and handsome structure than any of the public schools built in Mexico today. It is still the building of the school of Santa Rosa, although some remodeling was undertaken in 1954–1956. In 1930 the Centro Primario Obrero Federal moved there under a new name, Escuela América. New workshops were established for blacksmithing, tinwork, mechanics, carpentry, ceramics, tailoring, and dressmaking. All these workshops were fully equipped, and their production was of an exceptional quality, as can be seen from the photographs taken of their yearly exhibitions. In 1934 the school became a state school rather than a federal institution. That year, a middle school (seventh through ninth grade) opened on the same land. Its schedule was specially designed to allow factory workers to attend. Though it served children during the day, it was a school for workers in the evening.[132]

The School América, later renamed Esfuerzo Obrero, 1948. (José Mayorga, photographer, Museo de Historia de Mendoza.)

Preschool education also advanced in the 1920s in Santa Rosa. While in 1923 the Alborada municipal kindergarten was already functioning in the town, Santa Rosa's union inaugurated another, the Jardín Miguel Hidalgo, which was supported by union funds. The number of children who attended this kindergarten went from 37 in 1924 to 193 in 1928.[133] The real dimension of the development of preschool education in Santa Rosa can be assessed only by considering that in 1925 there were only thirty-one federal kindergartens in the whole country. Xalapa, the capital of Veracruz, had only one kindergarten, even though it was the state capital with the highest number of schools in the country.[134]

In other districts in the Orizaba Valley, elementary education prospered in a similar way to that of Santa Rosa. In 1928, school No. 35 of Río Blanco had thirty-six classrooms in which 600 students were taught during the day and 700 in the evening. The Río Blanco school provided instruction up to fifth grade. Two-year courses on dressmaking and hand and machine embroidery were given for girls, and courses on tailoring were provided for boys.[135]

Educational improvements rendered substantial fruits for the sons and daughters of the generation of workers born in the first decades of the twentieth century. Most of them finished elementary school, and many continued their education further. Mostly they took jobs outside the mills. Macario Ventura Ochoa's son, for example, became a veterinarian, his two daughters studied until junior high school and then got married. Gabriel and Salvador, the two sons of Rafael Mendoza, became first-grade teachers and then English teachers. Both moved to Mexico City, and one became a professor at the Instituto Politécnico Nacional. His daughters only finished elementary school. Gonzalo San Juan's daughter and son, Victoria and Tomás, studied typing and shorthand. She became first a teacher and then the director of the Commercial Academy Aragón. Tomás worked as a white-collar employee. Delfino Huerta had ten sons, only the oldest one became a textile worker, the rest attended college at the Instituto Politécnico Nacional. Four of them became chemical-industrial engineers, one a systems engineer, another a textile engineer, and one became a textile technician.[136]

The lives of workers and their families improved substantially between the Porfiriato and 1930. The textile towns in the Orizaba Valley became a better place to live in. Urban and housing infrastructure improved, educational facilities increased, consumer cooperatives and union banks allowed families to get goods and credit at better prices and interest rates. These improvements began to take place during the Porfiriato but ameliorated substantially as a consequence of the workers' and their communities' empowerment.

# CHAPTER 9

# The Impact of the Mexican Revolution on CIVSA's Performance

THE CHANGES IN CIVSA's PROFITABILITY, productivity levels, and international competitiveness from 1900 to 1930 can provide a better understanding of the factors that affected its performance throughout this period, as well as the longer-term consequences. And a look at the still-broader picture can indicate how the Mexican Revolution affected the textile industry.

When the Santa Rosa mill started operating in 1899, several of its departments were still unfinished, and construction of the mill was to continue for several years. From 1902 to 1913, production of cloth and sales fluctuated around twenty million meters annually (see Figure 9.1). Production increased at the same pace as investment, and sales kept pace with production. Demand for CIVSA products was so high, however, that in most of the years before 1907 CIVSA was unable to supply many customers' orders. In 1906 the board explained that sales would have been even higher if they had had more merchandise to sell. Thus, optimistic about the future, they proposed a plan of machinery expansions and improvements.[1] CIVSA doubled its looms from 1899 to 1906 (see Figure 9.2). To supply the power necessary for all the new machinery, the company installed a hydroelectric power plant at Zoquitlán in 1904 and enlarged it in 1908–1909.

However, the U.S. financial panic and crash of 1907 and the intense depression it unleashed in 1908 hit the Mexican economy severely.[2] As Figure 9.3 shows, sales in real U.S. dollars diminished in 1907 and failed to recover their 1904–1906 values for the rest of the decade.[3] Many workers were dismissed, going from 2,139 in 1907, the decades' highest number, to 1,850 in 1910, a 14% decline (see Figure 9.2).

The Mexican Revolution had a strong negative impact on CIVSA's performance, but not until 1913. In 1911 CIVSA's president happily reported at the shareholders' annual meeting that "the disturbances the country experienced in 1911 have not been felt in our factory and . . . in spite of the abnormal situation and the lack of communications we suffered for several months, our sales have been growing."[4] Again in 1912 he reported that "in spite of the country's political situation, business has been normal and the returns obtained satisfactory."[5] As Figures 9.1 and 9.3 show, meters of cloth sold and sales in real U.S. dollars increased in 1911 and 1912, reaching a peak in the latter year. However, investment in CIVSA diminished considerably after 1911, reflecting first caution and then despair over the events that were taking place in the nation (see Figure 9.4). Moreover, it became increasingly difficult to obtain new funds.

After Madero's government fell in 1913, the possibility of financing through banks ended, because banks stopped lending.[6] The problems banks encountered also put at risk the firms' assets that were deposited in banks, and complicated its daily transactions with clients and suppliers. Until 1913 CIVSA kept its deposits in the Banco Central Mexicano, a private bank that acted as a clearinghouse for other banks, and the Compañía Bancaria de París y México, the two banks where CIVSA's major shareholders held influential positions.[7] In December 1913 the situation of the Banco Central became very difficult because it was besieged by holders of notes from the several states' banks, seeking to exchange them for notes from the two national banks: the Banco Nacional de México (Banamex) and the Banco de Londres y México.[8] When the Central Bank announced that it would exchange notes at only 25% of their face value, CIVSA moved all its deposit to Banamex. Yet this bank's situation also became vulnerable in 1914, and CIVSA shifted its deposits to banks in New York.[9] This was a shrewd maneuver, because in late December the government issued a decree authorizing banks not

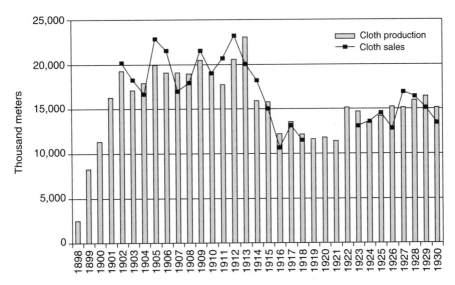

*Figure 9.1.* Production and cloth sales at Santa Rosa. *Source:* Archive of the
Compañía Industrial Veracruzana S.A., Estados del Movimiento General and
Actas del Consejo de Administración, 1898–1928.

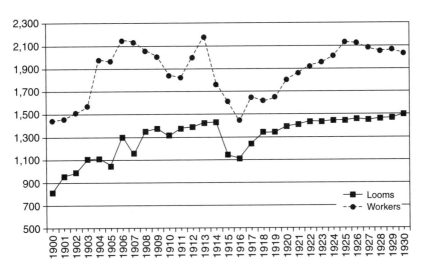

*Figure 9.2.* Looms and workers at Santa Rosa. *Sources:* CIVSA payrolls and
Archive of the Compañía Industrial Veracruzana S.A., Manifestaciones para el
Timbre, 1900–1930.

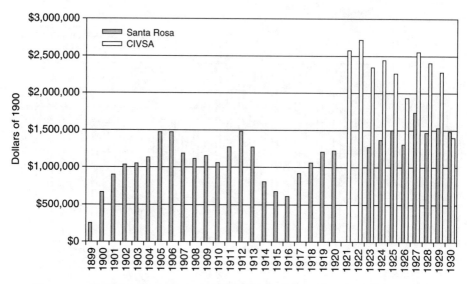

*Figure 9.3.* Net sales, Santa Rosa and CIVSA, 1899–1930. *Sources:* Archive of the Compañía Industrial Veracruzana S.A., Ventas de la Compañía Industrial Veracruzana S.A., Libros de Ventas, 1919–1921; Movimientos de Mercancía, 1900–1930; Actas de la Asamblea General, 1923–1926; and Income Tax Reports, 1926–1930.

to redeem bank notes in gold and decreed a bank holiday until January 2, 1914.[10]

CIVSA's president informed the annual shareholders meeting that the political situation in the country had generated serious difficulties for business in general, particularly the textile industry, because the war had diminished the supply of raw cotton. Nonetheless he considered CIVSA's situation to be normal.[11] Production continued to grow in 1913, although sales diminished.

Through 1914 banks were forced to make substantial loans to the government and were compelled to issue more notes than the General Banking Act of 1897 allowed. This began an inflationary process that put banks in an even more difficult situation. In mid-January 1914, CIVSA's president informed the board that all banks had stopped granting credit and were demanding immediate payment of all outstanding credits. The Compañía Bancaria de París México S.A. canceled its credit and told CIVSA that it was going to take payment from the company's deposits in the bank. CIVSA desperately tried to obtain funds to make the cotton purchases necessary to keep the mill running. In October the Banco Nacional granted CIVSA a 200,000 peso loan, but this was the last loan CIVSA received from Mexican banks until at least 1930.[12]

Problems accumulated and business deteriorated in 1914. CIVSA's production and sales diminished because frequent interruptions in the railway system stopped the supply of raw materials and the distribution of manufactures. Workers at Santa Rosa as well as the number of looms operating diminished during this year, starting a declining trend that reached its nadir in 1916 (see Figure 9.2). However, CIVSA was still able to make some profit.[13]

The economic situation worsened further in 1915. CIVSA's president reported that the troubles of the previous year had become more serious, affecting all industrial and commercial business in Mexico. Production and sales decreased, and the deterioration and instability in the value of money caused additional problems. To deal with this last problem, the company decided to adopt the gold peso as the standard for all transactions, except wages, as well as in all the corporate accounts.[14]

In September 1915 Carranza issued a decree that the government would liquidate all banks that had issued more banknotes than allowed under the law. Only nine of the twenty-seven banks of issue operating remained open after this decree.[15] A year later Carranza's government assumed control of the banks, appointing seizure boards (Juntas de Incautación) to supervise their daily operations, and they were officially closed to the public.[16] When banks in Mexico ceased to provide CIVSA with the services it required, the company had to resort to banks abroad. CIVSA's daily transactions were then carried out through banks in New York, even when they involved customers or suppliers in Mexico. From 1915 to 1918, CIVSA immediately changed the payments it received into U.S. dollars and sent the funds to New York through its agent D. Lousteau & Co., in Veracruz, or through drafts in U.S. dollars sent by its customers to New York. CIVSA also made its payments with drafts on New York, for which D. Lousteau & Co.'s intermediary services were often used.[17] This practice obviously entailed high transaction costs.[18]

From 1916 to 1919, CIVSA continued to experience problems with the railway lines, which were interrupted frequently, causing an increase in the cost of raw materials and difficulties in obtaining them.[19] This was further complicated by the reduction in tariffs that the government decreed in mid-1917 that forced the company to reduce its prices. In 1917 CIVSA's president judged that Mexico was going through a "chronic crisis." He considered one of the major problems that year to have been "the general conflicts between capital and labor, a consequence of the state of transformation in which we live."[20] In 1918 he reported that conflicts with labor became more frequent and complicated every day "because of the state of agitation that dominated the labor movement as well as a result of the labor law that had been adopted in the state of Veracruz."[21] The firm experienced several strikes.

Nonetheless, after 1916 net sales, employment, and the number of looms working began to increase (see Figures 9.2 and 9.3). By 1919 CIVSA's board became more confident about the future and decided to expand production by renting the Covadonga mill in Puebla, "considering that there is great demand for the products we manufacture and that this situation will prevail for some time."[22] Covadonga had 432 looms, which CIVSA was going to increase to 500, as well as bleaching, printing, and finishing machines. Because Covadonga did not produce enough cloth to fill the capacity of the printing machines, CIVSA also subcontracted for the production of coarse cloth at two other Puebla mills, Amatlán and La Claudina.

Other mills faced an even more difficult financial situation, facilitating CIVSA's acquisition of El León mill in Atlixco, Puebla, in December 1920. When CIVSA purchased El Léon for US$700,000, it held El León in debt for US$303,500.[23] As Figure 9.4 shows, the acquisition of El León as well some reforms carried on in that mill meant a considerable investment in 1921. Throughout the rest of the decade most of CIVSA's investment went to the Puebla mills.

After 1920 CIVSA's production and sales were no longer only those of Santa Rosa but also those of Covadonga and, from 1921 on, also those of El León.[24] After El León began producing, it supplied Covadonga with all the coarse cloth it could process, so it was no longer necessary to subcontract it.[25] CIVSA's production and sales almost doubled in 1920 as a result of the lease of Covadonga and the acquisition of El León. Yet difficulties continued; two railroad strikes, one from April to May and an-

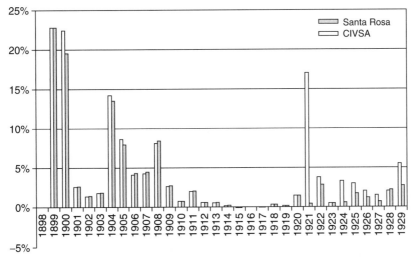

*Figure 9.4.* Investments in real estate, machinery, and equipment at CIVSA as a percentage of the firm's total fixed assets. *Source:* CIVSA and Santa Rosa General Balances, 1900–1929. Reprinted from Aurora Gómez-Galvarriato, "The Political Economy of Protectionism: The Mexican Textile Industry, 1900–1950," in *The Decline of Latin American Economies,* ed. Sebastian Edwards, Gerardo Esquivel, and Graciela Márquez (Chicago: University of Chicago Press, 2007), p. 388. © 2007 by the National Bureau of Economic Research. All rights reserved.

other in July, paralyzed traffic and left Santa Rosa without fuel and cotton for several weeks, so the mill had to stop production for some weeks.[26]

CIVSA's expansion between 1919 and 1921 was possible because, in spite of all the troubles the company faced as a consequence of the Revolution, it was able to cope with them better than several of its counterparts. Moving part of CIVSA's production to Puebla was also an attempt to escape from Veracruz's highly organized and combative labor movement. Yet CIVSA also encountered difficulties with labor in Puebla. In 1921 CIVSA's president complained about a strike at El León in October and November 1921 that delayed the reforms implemented at that mill.[27]

Production increased substantially between 1920 and 1923, averaging 25 to 30 million meters of cloth per year for the rest of the decade. This level of production was considerably higher than the annual 20 million meters around which Santa Rosa's production fluctuated during the Porfiriato (see Figures 9.1 and 9.3). However, Santa Rosa continued to produce approximately 15 million meters through the 1920s, never recovering its Porfirian production levels. This means that Covadonga and El León should be understood not only as an expansion of CIVSA, but also as a move of part of CIVSA's production away from the Orizaba Valley into Puebla.

After 1918 CIVSA placed some of its deposits in the Banco Francés de México and the Compañía Bancaria de París y México, allowing the company to carry out daily transactions with greater ease.[28] However, they also faced difficulties because the banking system was still very weak. In December 1920, rumors generated a run on the Compañía Bancaria de París y México, forcing it into bankruptcy. CIVSA had trouble recovering its deposits in that bank and moved them to the Banco Francés and New York.[29] However, in November 1922 the Banco Francés de México also failed. CIVSA tried to recover the US$9,000 it held in that bank through "extrajudicial" means.[30]

Keeping money in Mexican banks was risky. Nonetheless, as CIVSA's board explained in July 1922, the company had to retain certain funds in banks in Mexico in order to carry out current operations. "Naturally," they said "we take all necessary precautions, and try to keep those deposits as low as possible . . . and we try to spread them between several banks."[31] However, the company was also worried about its deposits in the United States. In June 1922, as CIVSA's directors watched Mexico's relations with the United States deteriorate, they thought that their access to the company's funds in the United States could be blocked. The company therefore sent letters to its bankers in the United States asking if, in this event, they could move CIVSA's funds to a bank in Canada.[32] Although no information is available on the allocation of CIVSA's deposits after 1925, we know that the company kept them abroad until at least 1928.[33]

By 1922 several of the problems the company had experienced since 1913 appeared to be ending, but in 1923 they arose again. In that year Santa Rosa suffered two important strikes. Moreover, general economic conditions in Mexico deteriorated once again, and the company was forced to lower its prices below the cost of raw materials. Finally, the company was seriously affected by the revolt of Adolfo de la Huerta in December of that year. The interruption of communications, which again curtailed the supply of raw materials and the distribution of manufactured goods, forced the suspension of production in the three mills. For all these reasons, sales declined in 1923, even though production kept rising.[34] The Delahuertista rebellion had a more negative effect in 1924, severely affecting production and sales for the first three months of the year.[35] A strike at Santa Rosa and another at El León further curtailed production. CIVSA's president also complained that year about a Veracruz decree compelling companies to provide medical assistance, medicine, and sick pay for workers. While all these factors increased costs, the firm had to reduce its prices to "deplorable levels" to meet competition; thus income diminished through the year despite the increase in sales.[36]

The next year, 1925, was a good year for CIVSA: no major strike took place at any of its mills, new machinery was installed at El León, and production recovered. However, in 1926 a downturn in the business cycle suffered globally by the textile industry began to affect CIVSA. International cotton prices faced a tremendous decline, which reduced the value of the company's stock of cotton and its manufactured products. In spite of the reduction in prices, sales declined considerably during the second semester of that year, and the inventory of manufactured products began to grow. In an attempt to solve the problem, CIVSA sent a sales agent to Central America, but found that cloth prices in that region were below their cost of production at CIVSA. The decline in the value of the silver peso with respect to the gold peso further damaged the company's financial situation. Finally, a three-month strike at El León increased production costs.[37] All these conditions generated a financial loss in that year, the second the company had experienced.

The economic situation failed to improve in 1927. The resolutions of the Workers' and Industrialists' Convention that had been held from 1925 to that year implied a wage increase. Although sales increased over the previous year, they were not enough to allow CIVSA's production to run at full capacity. Thus labor was dismissed, reducing production in all three mills and eliminating night shifts at the Puebla mills.[38] However, the company fared better that year than in the previous one because in 1927 its input costs had diminished.

In 1928 CIVSA's president believed that although the entire country was experiencing a general crisis, affecting all businesses, the textile industry was being hardest hit. He spoke of a trend toward overproduction in the industry that generated sharp competition among all textile manufacturers. Prices had to be reduced in order to keep sales at the levels of the previous years. It was better, he said, to make these sacrifices than to lose the company's market share "to competitors in a more favorable situation because they pay lower wages, and because they are located in a region where the charges that ballast the industry are less heavy." Moreover, reducing production levels would increase production costs even further. Thus, production levels were kept at 1927 levels and sale prices were reduced to allow only a minimum profit. The financial result for 1928 was therefore not very good, but was considered satisfactory, given the terrible situation in which the company had to operate.[39]

Lack of demand and deflation worsened throughout 1929. CIVSA was once again forced to reduce its prices to limit the accumulation of stock. This strategy enabled CIVSA to maintain sales at the level of the previous years and to allow a modest financial profit, of which CIVSA's president was proud, considering the economic environment.[40] Nonetheless, the stock of manufactured products kept rising. In October 1929 CIVSA was trying to get a loan from the Equitable Trust Co. of New York to purchase cotton.[41] The New York stock market crashed a few weeks later, and CIVSA could not obtain these funds.

The economic depression worsened in 1930 and stock kept accumulating, so CIVSA decided to reduce its working days per week. This reduction was not easy; labor opposed it and employers disagreed about it. However, in November 1930 an agreement was reached through the mediation of the minister of Industry, Commerce, and Labor, by which weekly working days were reduced to four for a period of four months. The effect of such a measure was positive, because although the accumulated inventory of manufactured products did not diminish, at least it stopped rising. The decline in the price of cotton and silver further damaged the company financially in 1930. The drop in cotton prices forced the company to lower the value of cloth in their inventory, which was the main cause of the financial loss the company reported that year. CIVSA decided to accept silver pesos instead of gold pesos or U.S. dollars in its transactions from January 1931 onward, in spite of the exchange-rate risk this implied. Throughout 1930, CIVSA lobbied together with several other companies for a revision and reform of the agreements of the 1925–1927 Convention, as well as for an increase in cotton cloth tariffs in order to cope with the difficult economic situation.[42] They did not achieve the former, but they were successful in convincing the government to raise tariffs, and this allowed the company to survive.

## Profitability

CIVSA was a very profitable investment for those who bought its stock early or at the right time. It was more profitable than buying government or bank bonds, and certainly better than buying U.S. corporate bonds. CIVSA was also more profitable than most other Mexican manufacturing companies and also more profitable than CIDOSA.[43] CIVSA was certainly a great investment for its major shareholders, who were able to acquire substantial additional profits through transfer pricing even in the worst years the company experienced.

The company's profitability can be assessed by looking at its returns on assets and its returns on equity. The first gives a sense of how efficiently the firm used its assets to produce income, and the second indicates how the stockholders fared during the year.[44] As Figure 9.5 shows, once the factory started producing regularly in 1900, the firm's profit levels were good. Between 1902 and 1905, they were extremely high, but in the following years, profitability declined, reaching its lowest level for the decade in 1908, recovering in 1909, but decreasing once again in 1910 because sales diminished.

For a better assessment of CIVSA shareholders' true earnings, their stock value on the market and the dividends paid per share have to be analyzed. The dividend yield reveals how much of a return was gained by investors who purchased stock in that year.[45] From 1900 to 1910, on average, CIVSA stock paid higher dividend yields than did either government bonds or bank stock. The average yield of government bonds between 1900 and 1910 was 4.9% and on bank stock 6%, whereas CIVSA's was 6.4%.[46] CIVSA dividend yields were higher than those for CIDOSA, which was a larger firm and the market leader. Between 1901 and 1910, the average dividend yield was 6.4% for CIVSA and 6% for CIDOSA.

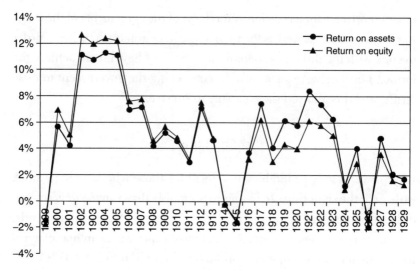

*Figure 9.5.* CIVSA's returns on assets and equity. *Source:* Archive of the Compañía Industrial Veracruzana S.A., Balances Generales y Estados de Resultados, 1898–1910.

Dividends are not the only means by which shareholders gain or lose money on their shares, because as share prices fluctuate they generate substantial capital gains or losses for shareholders. The annual rate of return on a stock shows the stock's profitability from year to year.[47] However, shareholders usually keep their shares for several years, so a better measurement of shares' profitability is provided by the net present value (NPV) of investing in a stock and its internal rate of return (IRT).[48] Table 9.1 shows the NPV and IRT of CIVSA stock bought in 1896 and sold in the year indicated in the table. Accordingly, investing in CIVSA became profitable as soon as the company started producing in 1899. Shareholders who sold their stock at any year between 1899 and 1913, except 1902 or 1903, would have made a greater profit than by investing in Mexican government bonds or in American corporate bonds (which gave an annual interest rate of 3.3%), as the net present value figures show.[49] The highest yield would have been obtained by selling CIVSA's stock in 1906; afterward it declined as a result of reductions in the dividends paid. These figures were also calculated assuming stock was bought in 1901 in order to make them comparable with CIDOSA's, because information for this company is not available for the previous years. The figures indicate that it would have been more profitable to buy CIVSA stock than CIDOSA's.

CIVSA's main shareholders made even greater profits than those described in the previous tables through discounts on their purchases. Because CIVSA's most important customers sat on its board, they got the lion's share of the discounts provided. Table 9.2 shows that CIVSA's most important stockholders obtained through discounts several times the revenue they got through dividends. This means, for example, that A. Reynaud & Co. received a dividend yield that was not the 6.1% obtained by an anonymous shareholder, but 15.3%.

As with production and sales, profits at CIVSA were not negatively affected by the Revolution until 1913. In fact, in 1912 the company was able to reverse the declining trend in its returns on assets and on equity that had begun in 1906 to achieve levels similar to those of 1907 (see Figure 9.5).[50] However, after 1912 CIVSA's returns on assets and on equity began a drastic decline, bottoming out in 1915, when the firm experienced its first loss. After that year, recovery was swift and, in 1917 the company's returns on assets reached their 1912 level, although returns on equity remained lower. These variables declined again in 1918, and then increased slowly from 1919 to 1921. On average, returns on equity and assets throughout the revolutionary decade were about half the returns achieved by the company between 1899 and 1910. Only in 1912 were these returns similar to those obtained in 1906 and 1907, and they never matched those the company enjoyed between 1902 and 1905. In 1919 and 1920, returns on assets and equity were similar to those obtained from 1908 to 1910.

The stock market valuation of CIVSA's shares paralleled the trend of returns on assets and equity. Share prices rose until 1912, thereafter falling drastically until 1915 (see Figure 9.6). Recovery of share prices was not as fast as the company's returns but was more consistent, prices in 1920 reaching the same level in terms of U.S. dollars they had had in 1912. When the stock's value is considered in terms of real U.S. dollars, however, share prices never recovered to their Porfirian levels.

Nonetheless, dividend yields were higher than those commonly obtained during the Porfirian years (see Table 9.1). This was so because the company did not reduce its dividend payments by much in terms of real U.S. dollars, with respect to those paid during the Porfiriato, except from

*Table 9.1*  CIVSA profitability, 1896–1930 (1900 U.S. dollars)

| Year | CIVSA Stock prices | Dividends | Dividend yield | Annual rate of return | Stock purchased in 1901 NPV | IRT | CIDOSA Stock prices | Dividends | Dividend yield | Annual rate of return | Stock purchased in 1901 NPV | IRT |
|---|---|---|---|---|---|---|---|---|---|---|---|---|
| 1896 | $63.3 | $0.0 | 0.0% |  |  |  |  |  |  |  |  |  |
| 1897 | $56.6 | $0.0 | 0.0% | −10.6% |  |  |  |  |  |  |  |  |
| 1898 | $53.1 | $0.0 | 0.0% | −6.1% |  |  |  |  |  |  |  |  |
| 1899 | $76.8 | $2.0 | 2.7% | 48.4% |  |  |  |  |  |  |  |  |
| 1900 | $72.8 | $7.3 | 10.0% | 4.3% |  |  |  | $7.8 |  |  |  |  |
| 1901 | $71.2 | $4.3 | 6.0% | 3.7% |  |  | $88.1 | $4.3 | 4.8% |  |  |  |
| 1902 | $58.3 | $4.7 | 8.1% | −11.5% | −$9.85 | −11.5% | $56.3 | $4.7 | 8.4% | −30.7% | −$28.09 | −30.7% |
| 1903 | $59.1 | $4.8 | 8.1% | 9.5% | −$6.56 | −1.9% | $62.4 | $4.8 | 7.6% | 19.3% | −$19.91 | −10.0% |
| 1904 | $67.0 | $5.2 | 7.8% | 22.2% | $3.27 | 5.0% | $76.9 | $5.2 | 6.8% | 31.6% | −$4.39 | 1.4% |
| 1905 | $91.2 | $5.5 | 6.1% | 44.5% | $26.72 | 12.9% | $97.7 | $5.5 | 5.7% | 34.3% | $15.88 | 8.1% |
| 1906 | $110.4 | $5.0 | 5.4% | 27.5% | $44.90 | 15.4% | $118.0 | $6.4 | 5.4% | 27.3% | $25.19 | 11.4% |
| 1907 | $102.9 | $5.6 | 5.4% | −1.8% | $40.46 | 12.7% | $110.5 | $6.0 | 5.4% | −1.3% | $20.86 | 9.4% |
| 1908 | $88.7 | $5.3 | 6.0% | −8.6% | $30.99 | 10.0% | $103.2 | $5.7 | 5.6% | −1.5% | $26.80 | 8.1% |
| 1909 | $80.1 | $4.7 | 5.9% | −4.4% | $25.92 | 8.5% | $94.1 | $5.1 | 5.4% | −3.8% | $21.35 | 6.8% |
| 1910 | $79.3 | $4.6 | 5.8% | 4.6% | $26.69 | 8.1% | $96.4 | $5.0 | 5.2% | 7.7% | $24.36 | 6.9% |
| 1911 | $78.8 | $4.7 | 6.0% | 5.4% | $27.81 | 7.9% | $96.2 | $5.5 | 5.7% | 11.8% | $25.83 | 6.8% |

| Year | | | | | | | | | | | | |
|---|---|---|---|---|---|---|---|---|---|---|---|---|
| 1912 | $78.3 | 6.5% | $5.1 | 5.8% | $29.16 | 7.8% | $87.2 | $5.5 | 6.3% | −3.6% | $21.30 | 6.0% |
| 1913 | $83.3 | 5.7% | $4.7 | 12.5% | $33.85 | 8.1% | $82.4 | $5.3 | 6.4% | 0.5% | $19.71 | 5.7% |
| 1914 | $28.1 | 2.3% | $0.7 | −65.5% | −$2.53 | 2.8% | $53.2 | $1.5 | 2.9% | −33.5% | $0.45 | 3.4% |
| 1915 | $13.0 | 0.0% | $0.0 | −50.1% | −$11.74 | 0.8% | $28.4 | $0.0 | 0.0% | −46.7% | −$15.88 | 0.8% |
| 1916 | $11.9 | 19.9% | $2.4 | 21% | −$11.84 | 0.8% | $25.0 | $1.7 | 7.0% | −5.8% | −$17.42 | 0.6% |
| 1917 | $24.3 | 10.6% | $2.6 | 125.2% | −$3.45 | 2.7% | $27.3 | $2.5 | 9.2% | 19.4% | −$15.10 | 1.1% |
| 1918 | $26.9 | 11.4% | $3.1 | 23.4% | −$0.73 | 3.2% | $30.6 | $3.0 | 9.8% | 23.1% | −$12.09 | 1.7% |
| 1919 | $40.4 | 10.8% | $4.4 | 66.4% | $8.44 | 4.5% | $38.4 | $5.3 | 13.9% | 43.1% | −$5.52 | 2.6% |
| 1920 | $37.0 | 10.6% | $3.9 | 1.2% | $7.99 | 4.4% | $52.1 | $4.8 | 9.2% | 48.1% | $3.48 | 3.7% |
| 1921 | $48.8 | 14.3% | $7.0 | 50.8% | $16.88 | 5.3% | $77.9 | $7.6 | 9.7% | 63.8% | $19.45 | 5.0% |
| 1922 | $52.2 | 13.5% | $7.0 | 21.4% | $21.19 | 5.6% | $78.7 | $7.0 | 9.0% | 10.2% | $22.07 | 5.1% |
| 1923 | $55.2 | 10.9% | $6.0 | 17.4% | $24.68 | 5.9% | $67.1 | $5.9 | 8.8% | −7.3% | $18.10 | 4.8% |
| 1924 | $49.4 | 4.7% | $2.3 | −6.4% | $22.22 | 5.6% | $60.6 | $3.0 | 5.0% | −5.2% | $15.50 | 4.6% |
| 1925 | $45.6 | 6.4% | $2.9 | −1.7% | $21.12 | 5.5% | $52.7 | $2.9 | 5.4% | −8.3% | $12.39 | 4.4% |
| 1926 | $46.8 | 0.0% | $0.0 | 2.6% | $20.98 | 5.5% | $45.0 | $0.0 | 0.0% | −14.7% | $8.30 | 4.0% |
| 1927 | $37.3 | 8.0% | $3.0 | −13.8% | $17.66 | 5.2% | $26.1 | $0.0 | 0.0% | −19.8% | $3.99 | 3.7% |
| 1928 | $40.5 | 6.5% | $2.6 | 15.5% | $19.49 | 5.3% | $35.0 | $0.0 | 0.0% | −3.0% | $3.07 | 3.6% |
| 1929 | $37.8 | 6.1% | $2.3 | −0.9% | $18.82 | 5.2% | $29.2 | $0.0 | 0.0% | −16.7% | $0.35 | 3.3% |
| 1930 | $31.1 | 0.0% | $0.0 | −17.6% | $15.83 | 5.0% | $23.9 | $0.0 | 0.0% | −18.0% | −$2.00 | 3.1% |

*Sources*: Archive of the Compañía Industrial Veracruzana S.A., Balance Sheets, 1900–1910; *Estado del Movimiento General, 1900–1910*; Share prices taken from *El Economista Mexicano*, 1900–1915; *El Demócrata*, 1916; and *Boletín Financiero y Minero*, 1918–1930. U.S. price index taken from U.S. Department of Commerce, Bureau of the Census, *Historical Statistics of the United States, Colonial Times to 1970* (Washington, D.C.: U.S. Government Printing Office, 1975), 200. Shaded areas indicate difficult years for the company.

*Table 9.2*  Discounts over purchases in 1905 and 1926

| Customers and shareholders | Shares | Share value | Total purchase | Discounts (% of purchase) | Discount value | Dividend yield | Discount yield | Dividend + discount yield |
|---|---|---|---|---|---|---|---|---|
| *1905* | | | | | | | | |
| A. Reynaud & Co. | 8,205 | $800,152 | $777,185 | 9.5% | $73,833 | 6.1% | 9.2% | 15.3% |
| S. Robert & Co. | 3,981 | $388,207 | $502,692 | 9.5% | $47,756 | 6.1% | 12.3% | 18.4% |
| P. and J. Jacques & Co. | 604 | $58,934 | $145,797 | 8.8% | $12,757 | 6.1% | 21.6% | 27.7% |
| Auddifred Hnos. & Co. | 1,376 | $134,165 | $29,339 | 5.0% | $1,467 | 6.1% | 1.1% | 7.2% |
| F. Manuel & Co. | 1,376 | $134,165 | $28,563 | 5.0% | $1,428 | 6.1% | 1.1% | 7.2% |
| J. Desdier & Co. | 551 | $53,707 | $26,777 | 5.0% | $1,339 | 6.1% | 2.5% | 8.6% |
| Bellón Agorreca & Co. | 687 | $66,980 | $26,475 | 5.0% | $1,324 | 6.1% | 2.0% | 8.1% |
| M. Bellón & Co. Sucs. | 500 | $48,762 | $25,377 | 5.0% | $1,269 | 6.1% | 2.6% | 8.7% |
| P. Richaud & Co. | 825 | $80,458 | $21,314 | 4.5% | $959 | 6.1% | 1.2% | 7.3% |
| *1926* | | | | | | | | |
| A. Reynaud & Co. | 37,599 | $3,156,582 | $800,589 | 20.75% | $166,122 | 2.4% | 5.3% | 7.6% |
| S. Robert & Co. | 8,003 | $671,883 | $412,596 | 19.25% | $79,425 | 2.4% | 11.8% | 14.2% |

*Sources*: Archive of the Compañía Industrial Veracruzana S.A., Actas del Consejo de Administración, Libro de Ventas, 1905, 1926; Archive of the Compañía Industrial Veracruzana S.A, Actas de la Asamblea General, 1905, 1922, 1926, 1930.

*Note*: Figures in current U.S. dollars.

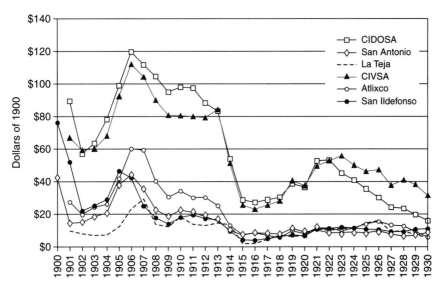

*Figure 9.6.* Share prices of textile manufactures, 1900–1930. *Sources: El Economista Mexicano,* 1900–1915; *El Demócrata,* 1916; and *Boletín Financiero y Minero* 1918–1930; George F. Warren and Frank A. Pearson, *Prices* (New York: John Wiley & Sons, 1933), 13.

1914 to 1916. Additionally, the sharp reduction in stock prices after 1912 was so important that from 1916 onward dividend yields became very large. As during the Porfirian era, CIVSA dividend yields were generally higher than those of CIDOSA in the revolutionary decade. The dividend yields of both companies show a similar trend, although CIVSA's dividend yields after 1915 recovered more strongly and consistently than those of CIDOSA. Investors who bought CIVSA stock in 1896 and later sold it in any year of the Revolution except 1914 and 1915 made higher profits through those investments than if they had acquired U.S. corporate bonds. Yet they would have preferred to have sold it before the Revolution started.

It is evident that CIVSA's profit levels deteriorated after 1913 as a consequence of the Mexican Revolution. However, the company experienced a vigorous recovery after 1916. In spite of all the problems the firm faced throughout this period, it coped with the crisis well enough to provide its shareholders with competitive profit rates throughout most of the decade. Moreover, because CIVSA's discount policy from 1911 to 1920 was not any different from that followed during Porfirian times, its major shareholders must have obtained substantially higher profits from their investment than the profit rates calculated above indicate.

Returns on equity and assets between 1921 and 1923 were similar, in general terms, to those obtained between 1906 and 1912 (see Figure 9.5). However, levels fell sharply after 1924. They were lower on average from 1921 to 1930 than in the revolutionary decade. Although during the Revolution CIVSA faced two years of serious difficulties, 1914 and 1915, after which the situation improved, in the 1920s the company had four terrible years, 1924, 1926, 1928, and 1929. If 1930 had been included in this table, the decade would appear even worse, because in that year the company suffered a financial loss once again.

Dividend yields tell a similar story, being on average lower for both CIVSA and CIDOSA in the 1920s than in the revolutionary decade (see Table 9.1). After 1923 the company could no longer keep dividend payments above 20 gold pesos, which it had managed to do from 1919 until then, and it paid no dividends in 1926 and 1930. However, it fared better than CIDOSA, which paid no dividends after 1926 for the rest of the decade. Investors who purchased CIVSA stock in 1896 saw their internal rate of return steadily improve from 1920 to 1923, after which it began to decrease.

Gains through discounts on sales continued to be substantial in the 1920s. In 1926, for instance, although CIVSA paid a small dividend (on the 1925 profits), its main shareholders received significant discounts, as Table 9.2 shows. If discounts were considered equivalent to yields paid per share, then A. Reynaud would have received 7.6% and S. Robert 14.2%.

The 1920s were a difficult decade for CIVSA, trapped between a Revolution that had not completely ended, a labor movement that had grown strong, in part because of the Revolution itself, and the beginning of a worldwide depression in the textile industry. Nonetheless, the company managed to cope with the problems it faced better than many of its counterparts, including CIDOSA.

## CIVSA's Productivity and International Competitiveness

During the Mexican Revolution, a major transformation in the relative power of workers and employers took place in the Orizaba textile mills. It would become an important factor to explain changes in productivity and competitiveness from then on. Although international competitiveness and comparative productivity levels attained in 1911 by CIVSA were modest, as time went by they deteriorated. A similar situation probably prevailed across the Mexican textile industry as a whole. Thus, at least until the late 1980s when the Mexican economy opened up to international trade, it was during the Porfiriato that the textile industry reached its peak in terms of international competitiveness.[51]

Profitability declined from the Porfiriato to the 1920s, because it witnessed a substantial increase of its production costs as a percentage of net sales. Whereas production costs were an average of 62% of net sales during the Porfiriato, they rose to 78% during the revolutionary decade, and to 94% in the 1920s (see Figure 9.7). This was partly a result of the increase in wages relative to sales. Although real net sales increased on average by 9%, between these two periods wages increased by 75%. This is not the whole story, though, because there was an even greater increase of other costs (besides wages and cotton) of 177%.

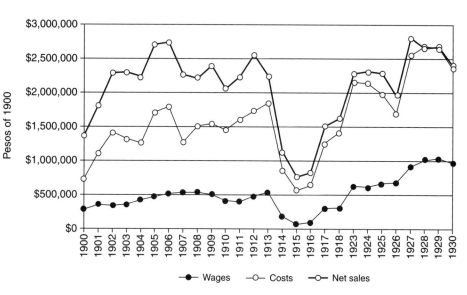

*Figure 9.7.* Net sales and production costs at Santa Rosa, 1900–1930. *Notes:* Production costs do not include general expenses. Data deflated with Index II AB gold. The years from 1919 to 1922 have been omitted for lack of data. *Source:* Archive of the Compañía Industrial Veracruzana S.A., Estados del Movimiento General, 1900–1930.

Productivity levels at Santa Rosa, measured in terms of the number of machines per worker and production per worker, remained virtually unchanged from 1900 to 1950. The number of looms per worker remained constant through the period, while the number of meters of cloth a worker produced in a week diminished slightly from the first decade of the century to the 1920s and a little more during the Revolution. However, because working hours diminished and production per worker did not, productivity per hour worked increased (see Table 9.3). Whereas real wages increased substantially after 1917, productivity did not, and therefore real wages per meter of output rose notably after that date.

After 1930 the number of looms tended per weaver gradually increased to reach almost four. Yet this represents a minor increase in productivity when compared to what was attainable by introducing automatic looms. In the spinning department there was no parallel productivity improvement after 1930. On the contrary, data even shows a reduction in productivity after 1940.

Given the radical change experienced on the shop floor from control by managers to a situation where the union had great influence, it might seem surprising that productivity levels did not fall as a result of the Revolution. The fact that they did not means that the Santa Rosa union was effective at guaranteeing workers' discipline and effort. Moreover, workers were able to produce more per hour as the shift was reduced, despite the fact that they were performing their tasks with basically the same machinery with which they had worked during the Porfiriato. The intensity of labor was higher during the shorter working day.[52]

However, this was not all that was required to keep the industry's international competitiveness at the levels it had maintained during the Porfiriato, let alone improve them. As Adam Przeworski explains, "No one drew the blueprint and yet the [capitalist] system is designed in such a way that if profits are not sufficient, then eventually either wages must fall, or employment, or both. . . . Decisions by capitalists to save and choose techniques of production constitute the parameters which constrain the possibility of improvement of material conditions of anyone."[53] There was a substantial reduction in CIVSA's investment rates after the Porfiriato that was partly a consequence of the decline in profit rates (see Figure 9.5).[54] Yet there were other forces behind the reduction of invest-

Table 9.3   Weavers and spinners, productivity, 1900–1950

**Weavers**

| Years | Meters per worker (weekly) | Meters per worker (hourly) | Meters per loom (weekly) | Looms per worker | Real wage per meter | Real wage per week | Meters per loom per hour |
|---|---|---|---|---|---|---|---|
| 1900–1910 | 625 | 8.7 | 263 | 2.39 | $0.009 | $4.36 | 3.6 |
| 1911–1920 | 588 | 10.3 | 222 | 2.64 | $0.010 | $7.03 | 4.5 |
| 1921–1929 | 591 | 11.6 | 244 | 2.42 | $0.016 | $13.42 | 4.7 |
| 1931–1940 | 714 | 15.9 | 210 | 3.40 | $0.018 | $12.67 | 4.7 |
| 1941–1950 | 752 | 15.8 | 199 | 3.77 | $0.018 | $13.86 | 4.2 |

| | Spinners (warp no. 29) | | | | Spinners (weft no. 30) | | |
|---|---|---|---|---|---|---|---|
| Years | Real wage per kilo | Kilos per worker (weekly) | Kilos per worker (hourly) | | Real wage per kilo | Kilos per worker (weekly) | Kilos per worker (hourly) |
| 1900–1910 | $0.028 | 233 | 3.24 | | $0.035 | 234 | 3.15 |
| 1911–1920 | $0.027 | 197 | 3.99 | | $0.030 | 216 | 4.25 |
| 1921–1929 | $0.044 | 216 | 4.53 | | $0.047 | 229 | 4.90 |
| 1931–1940 | $0.054 | 184 | 4.06 | | $0.056 | 284 | 5.01 |
| 1941–1950 | $0.051 | 110 | 3.93 | | $0.057 | 168 | 4.72 |

*Source:* A sample was taken from Archive of the Compañía Industrial Veracruzana S.A., Payrolls, June and November, 1900–1930. For further detail, see Aurora Gómez-Galvarriato, "The Impact of Revolution: Business and Labor in the Mexican Textile Industry, Orizaba, Veracruz, 1900–1930" (PhD diss., Harvard University, 1999), chap. 8, tables 8 and 9.

*Notes:* Wages in pesos of 1910. The year 1930 has been omitted for lack of data.

ment rates, namely labor regulation restrictions on the adoption of new technology and the tariff policy pursued in the late 1920s.

New technology adopted by the textile industry worldwide was not introduced in Mexican mills. One of the most notable improvements in textile production was the introduction of automatic looms.[55] Other important technological innovations that became widespread in the 1920s were the double-length loom; the one-process picker *(batiente de un solo proceso),* which reduced bale-breaking, lapping, and picking to only one step; high-speed warping *(altos estirajes),* which reduced the number of times yarn was passed through the fly frames *(veloces);* and the use of artificial silk (rayon) to mix with cotton.[56]

Automatic looms were not introduced by CIVSA in the 1900s because they demanded higher investment and more technical assistance than power looms. This technology was not very widespread at the time, so it was not as crucial for the Mexican textile industry to adopt it then as it would become in later years, when, after being tested and improved, it became standard through the world. In the 1920s certain Mexican textile companies tried to acquire automatic looms, but unions opposed this "labor-saving" machinery. In the early 1920s CIVSA had attempted to install 100 Northrop automatic looms, but its union did not permit them and the company was forced to sell them at a discount to several other companies in small sets. Atoyac Textil, one of the mills of the Rivero Quijano family, bought some of them, but it also was unable to put them into operation because of problems like those at Santa Rosa. Moreover, according to one of Atoyac Textil's owners, Jesús Rivero Quijano, it was necessary to have at least 100 automatic looms running for a company to reap the benefits of this new technology; even if they had been adopted at Atoyac, there would not have been enough of them to show what "automation" could do.[57]

In 1923 Atoyac Textil decided to give automatic looms another chance and bought twenty-four Stafford looms. However, "in order to introduce them it was necessary that the president of Stafford Looms travel to Mexico to have an interview with General Calles and General Obregón, to deal later with Luis N. Morones about the installation and operation of these machines."[58] The government accepted the installation of these automatic looms on condition that they were considered an "exhibition."

Once they were mounted, however, unions blocked their operation. The worker who ran the looms was stabbed to death. His successor soon started receiving death treats and promptly resigned. No one else dared to tend the looms, and they were abandoned until some technicians transformed them into ordinary power looms.[59]

Later on, as a result of the Convention of Workers and Industrialists of 1925–1927, a legal restriction was imposed on the adoption of new technologies such as automatic looms, one-process pickers, and high-speed warping. The wage list fixed the maximum number of machines per worker and established specific wages per piece. Under these conditions, industrialists had no incentive to introduce better machinery because it would not enable them to reduce labor costs, since wages per piece and the number of workers per machine had to remain invariable.[60]

In spite of the important technological changes the textile industry had undergone since 1912, the same technical principles adopted to build the "1912 Tariff" (based on the English Blackburn wage list of 1905) were used for the wage list of 1927.[61] In spinning, the concept of "one worker per machine" prevailed, forcing Mexican mills to either adopt spinning machines that were larger than recommended by their builders, or to join two spinning machines, which created several technical problems.[62] As in England, by lowering the piece rates on larger and faster spinning frames, wage lists encouraged capitalists to try to maximize spindles per workers.[63] In contrast, in weaving, by setting piece rates irrespective of the number of speed looms tended, wage schedules encouraged employers to try to minimize the number of looms per weaver.

In carding, the wage list of 1927 established that one worker should operate eight carding machines. However, by introducing simple modifications to machinery and organization, it was possible for one worker to tend forty carding machines with no additional effort. The wage list created no incentive for Mexican mills to introduce these changes; if they were allowed to implement them, mills would have to pay five times more to the card tender that remained working and give severance pay to the four who would have to be dismissed. These costs, together with the investment required to modernize the carding machines, were greater than the benefits the mills would obtain through cost reductions.[64]

The decision to establish fixed wage schedules per piece and limits on machines per worker was not made unknowingly. In 1926 the Saco-Lowell Shops of Massachusetts, fearing that the agreements of the Convention would affect demand for their machinery in Mexico, sent a letter to the president of the Convention, explaining how detrimental the new regulations were to the adoption of new technology. The letter described the advantages of automatic looms and of machinery specifically designed for the processing of scrap cotton. It explained why these innovations would not be adopted with the new wage list and regulations proposed by the Convention.[65] However, the majority of votes in the Convention were in favor of the rigid wage schedule. Workers regarded modern machines as a threat to employment, industrialists as a threat to the survival of their decrepit mills, while government perceived the threat of social discontent. It was easier to raise tariffs and let the industry survive as it was. The overrepresentation of smaller, more old-fashioned mills in the Convention may also have contributed to this result.

CIVSA documents show the effects of the Convention regulations on the company's investment decisions. In 1927, for example, double-length looms, not considered in the Convention's wage list, were installed in Santa Rosa.[66] However, a year later the CIVSA board of directors decided to remove them because the wages demanded by the Santa Rosa union for their operators made production too costly. In May 1929 CIVSA's main engineer presented a cost-benefit analysis explaining the advisability of installing new high-speed-warping machines that would generate substantial savings. CIVSA's board of directors decided to postpone purchasing them until they were able to get a "fair" wage rate for operating these new machines. Together with CIDOSA, CIVSA started negotiations with the Ministry of Industry on this matter, but at least until the end of 1930 these proved fruitless.[67]

Although the effects of rigid regulations on technological innovation must have been worse in those states, such as Veracruz, where the labor movement was strongest, contemporary studies on the textile industry indicate that they prevailed throughout the entire country.[68] Aggregate data for Mexico's textile industry show little investment in new technology for most of the twentieth century. The change in the number of spindles provides a good estimate of investment because spindles were the most important capital input for the production of cotton textile goods.[69] The annual rate of growth of the number of spindles decreased considerably between 1912 and 1930 in comparison to earlier Porfirian growth rates. Whereas from 1879 to 1912 the number of spindles increased yearly by 3.4%, from 1912 to 1925 this figure was only 0.7%, and from 1925 to 1930 it grew by just 0.1% (see Table 1.2). Although some new factories were built in the 1920s, most of them were small establishments devoted to the production of knitwear *(bonetería)*, mainly of artificial silk. This is why, although the number of factories increased by 2.3% yearly from 1921 to 1930, the number of active spindles and looms increased yearly only by 1% and 0.8%, respectively.

Labor efficiency, measured by loom equivalents per worker, increased during the Porfiriato from an average of 0.89 for the period 1879–1900 to 0.99 for the period 1901–1912 (see Table 1.2). During the revolutionary years this figure increased because production, the number of workers hired, and the length of the workday declined. Yet the increase in production in the 1920s was not accompanied by productivity growth; this figure decreased to 0.97 during the period 1920–1930. Cotton consumed per worker and real sales per worker (proxies of production per worker) also decreased between the Porfiriato and the 1920s.

During the first half of the 1920s the industry grew but productivity deteriorated. In contrast, between 1926 and 1930, while the industry stagnated, labor productivity increased, as loom equivalents per shift and sales and production per worker show. This was the result of the reduction of employment and hours worked per mill as a consequence of the depression. According to contemporary observers, "This increase was by no means the result of an improvement in machinery in the mills."[70]

Increased protection levels were necessary to keep Mexican mills running. As Figure 9.8 shows, there was a substantial increase in ad valorem tariffs after 1927, which came together with the conclusion of the Workers' and Industrialists' Convention. Before that year governments had been actually less protectionists than the Porfirian government. After 1916 Carranza's government began to pursue a liberalization of tariff policy that drastically diminished tariffs on basic commodities, seeking to reduce consumer prices.[71] However, there was also a theoretical reason behind the liberalization policy. At the First National Congress of

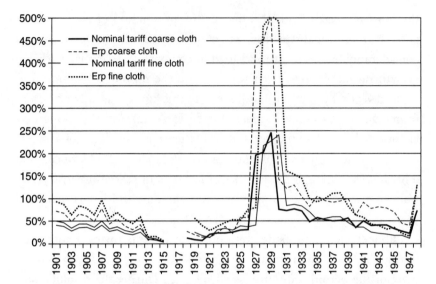

*Figure 9.8.* Tariffs for coarse and fine cloth. *Source:* Aurora Gómez-Galvarriato, "The Political Economy of Protectionism: The Mexican Textile Industry, 1900–1950," in *The Decline of Latin American Economies,* ed. Sebastian Edwards, Gerardo Esquivel, and Graciela Márquez (Chicago: University of Chicago Press, 2007), tables 10.4 and 10.5. © 2007 by the National Bureau of Economic Research. All rights reserved.

Industrialists held in Mexico City in September 1917, Alberto J. Pani, minister of industry and commerce, made it clear that "free national and international competition" was one of the main principles behind the revolutionary industrial policy.[72] Once Obregón came to power, the free-trade spirit waned and duties were gradually increased. However, although specific tariffs for cloth were higher between 1921 and 1926 than during the Porfiriato, ad valorem tariffs were not, because prices had also increased.[73] Moreover, the effective rate of protection for cloth fell, because between the two periods, ad valorem tariffs for raw cotton rose more than those for cloth.[74]

In the Workers' and Industrialists' Convention of 1925–1927, the three major actors in the political economy of the textile industry—businessmen, labor, and the government—chose an institutional arrangement that offered no incentives for technological transformation and therefore required high tariffs. Moreover, the depression that affected the textile industry from 1926 onward also created incentives worldwide for increased protectionism. This explains the substantial increases in the tariffs on cloth from 1927 to 1933, which made them several times higher than those that prevailed during both the Porfiriato and the early 1920s. This enabled most mills to survive, jobs to continue, and social order to endure. However, the lack of technological innovation in an industry sheltered by high rates of protection condemned Mexico's textile industry to become increasingly more outdated and unable to compete in world markets.

The rise in protectionism was long-lasting. From 1933 to 1947, ad valorem tariffs decreased as a result of the rise in cloth prices. The depreciation of the peso from 2.6 pesos per U.S. dollar in 1931 (when Mexico left the gold standard) to 5.5 in 1940, though, provided the industry with a further margin of protection. World War II generated an exceptional situation, when the Mexican textile industry was capable of exporting vast quantities of cloth. When the war ended, the situation reversed and the industry demanded a new increase in tariffs. This came about at the end of 1947, when the new tariff schedule was changed to include both an ad valorem and a specific duty. This was accompanied by a depreciation of the peso. Moreover, after 1947 the import of specific items in the tariff schedule was forbidden for some years.

The agreements crafted during the Convention of 1925–1927 may be understandable under the circumstances of worldwide depression in the textile industry. Nevertheless, the precepts adopted there were ratified over and over again. In spite of the efforts made by industrialists in 1932 and 1935 to introduce a more flexible wage schedule, the Textile Workers' and Industrialists' Convention of 1937–1939 kept it unchanged.[75] As late as 1943, a memorandum from the Ministry of Labor to the president of Mexico explained that the adoption of "Toyada" automatic looms in Japan had generated misery among Japanese textile workers. Furthermore, if some mills adopted the new technology, others would go bankrupt, resulting in increased levels of unemployment. It explained that England had taken wise measures to protect its industry both from the adoption of automatic looms and from Japanese competition. It concluded that Mexico should do likewise because workers should not be sacrificed to gain competition in world markets.[76]

After World War II, when the old equipment was worn out and needed to be replaced, industrialists made another attempt to change the restrictions imposed on the implementation of new technology. In 1945 CIVSA's president explained that it was urgent for Santa Rosa, as well as for Mexican textile industry as a whole, to fully modernize its equipment in order to be able to produce efficiently in "conditions of intense competition." "It is a matter of life and death for the national industry," he argued, "but full modernization generates problems of personnel, wage lists, etc., that need to be solved uniformly and evenly."[77] According to him, CIVSA and other companies were only waiting for a favorable agreement by the Convention of Workers and Industrialists of the Textile Industry to be held on that year, to carry out the project. However, despite their efforts, they had no success.[78] Only new plants established after the war were exempt from restrictions imposed by the industry-wide labor contract, and thus only a handful of modern mills were established.[79] Old mills had to replace their worn-out equipment with used equipment. In 1956, for example, a considerable share of the machinery imported (29.07% of the looms, 38.28% of the spinning frames, and 52.98% of the carding machines) was used equipment.[80]

In 1950 CIVSA's president explained that after several months of negotiations, restrictions on the modernization of the industry had not been lifted. That same year a National Union for the Modernization of the Textile Industry (Unión Nacional de Industriales para la Modernización Textil), to which CIVSA belonged, was created to make the legal restrictions on the use of new technology more flexible. However, a minority of industrialists favored continuing to work with outdated machinery; together with the unions they were able to prevent any modification of the labor laws and wage lists.[81]

Early in 1951 employers and workers finally agreed on the general rules to be followed in the modernization of equipment, rationalization of working methods and wage scales, and specialization within the industry. Yet this agreement was only "a preliminary outline of principles that needed to be followed by other agreements to implement specific programs." According to the International Bank of Reconstruction and Development, although the agreement was an important initial step, it was "not expected to have significant consequences for the time being."[82]

From 1951 onward, the "General Rules for the Modernization of the Textile Industry" were included as an addendum to the wage list.[83]

These rules allowed more flexibility in the operation of modern machinery, and they set rules for the dismissal of excess workers. However, the minority of firms that had already begun the modernization process, which included CIVSA and CIDOSA, were opposed to them, in the belief that the specific criteria established by the new regulations, in terms of wages, severance fees, and workloads, imposed severe restrictions on the modernization of the industry. The National Union for the Modernization of the Textile Industry considered it unacceptable that these rules were voted for by the whole industry rather than by only those mills that had begun modernizing their machinery since 1946. They argued that modernization was against the interest of firms operating with old machinery, which "only seek their indefinite subsistence." Because outdated firms had the majority of the votes in the Workers' and Industrialists' Convention, no set of regulations that would effectively promote modernization could come out from a process that included the whole industry on a basis of one vote per mill. Moreover, outdated firms had allied with labor in their hostility to modernization. Workers, traditional opponents of modernization, were particularly against it because most of them worked in antiquated mills.[84] Although these new laws permitted the creation of some modern mills and the modernization of certain departments of old mills, the restrictions imposed on the process, together with high rates of protection, effectively blocked modernization of the industry.

The result was that the textile industry became increasingly more outdated. Whereas in Mexico there had been no major changes in the industry's methods of production since 1912, in the United States the introduction of new technologies had already generated a significant reduction in labor requirements. Between 1910 and 1936, the labor required to produce the same quantity of coarse cloth was reduced by 50% in yarn preparation, by 27% in spinning, by 36% in spooling and drawing, by 53% in weaving, and by 14% in cloth reception.[85]

At the 1945 Textile Convention, CIDOSA presented a detailed comparative analysis of productivity levels in the Mexican, American, and English industries.[86] Its results showed the disastrous state of the Mexican industry. According to CIDOSA, the structure of the collective labor contract for the industry was one of the main reasons. In addition to the rigid wage list, it forced the industry to keep the same number of workers hired; any worker who left the mill for any reason had to be replaced. Moreover, because it established a promotion system based on seniority, it prevented firms from choosing and promoting personnel on the basis of aptitude and effort.[87]

England's productivity levels had also lagged behind those of the United States as a result of a "fixed" collective labor contract that determined the wages to be paid per unit of production and type of work, the number of workers per machine, and their duties. Nevertheless, in England fixed labor was gradually phased out, allowing the industry to implement certain technological changes (such as installing the warp stop-motion system in plain looms).[88]

A study commissioned by the United Nations on the productivity of the Latin American textile industry, published in 1951, indicated that as many as 85% of the spindles and 95% of the looms working in Mexico were out of date, that is, built during the first quarter of the century or earlier.[89] Likewise, a Mexican public financial study (Nafinsa) reported that in 1957, 34.4% of the spindles, 46% of the carding machines, and 33% of the looms operating that year had been built before 1910. Technological backwardness was worst in states such as Veracruz, where labor regulations were more strictly implemented because of their stronger labor movements, and where the mills were older.[90] In that state, 67% of the spindles, 72% of the carding machines, and 73% of the looms working in 1957 had been manufactured before 1910. The industry gradually moved away from those states where the labor movement was strongest, wages highest, and labor regulations most effective. In 1923, 20.8% of spindles and 22.37% of looms in Mexico were in Veracruz, but by 1950 these figures had declined to 14.81% and 17.81%, respectively.[91] In the end, the strength of Veracruz's labor movement was the cause of its own demise.[92]

According to the United Nations study, the number of man hours per kilogram of production was 269% higher in the Mexican cotton textile industry than in a standard modern industry. Modernization of equipment could increase productivity by 260% in spinning and 281% in weaving. Yet this would have caused the displacement of more than 15,000 workers and would have required an investment of over $100 million in 1950 U.S. dollars.[93] According to a Nafinsa study, the modernization of the industry in 1958 was feasible because it would have required 103,394,800 pesos (US$8,271,584), which represented only 0.67% of the annual aggregate investment made in Mexico in 1957. If the process had taken place over ten years, it would have generated an annual displacement of 896 workers, who could have been relocated to other sectors.[94]

The consistent opposition of textile trade unions to the introduction of labor-saving methods and machinery was mirrored by the wage list imposed by the labor law *(contrato colectivo)*, which rigidly limited the possibilities of modernizing and rationalizing the industry.[95] Yet it is difficult to assess whether the unions' policy of keeping the wage schedule unchanged responded to the wishes of their rank and file. Lack of investment in the textile industry generated a decline in the real wages of cotton textile workers larger than that experienced by workers in other manufacturing sectors. Whereas between 1939 and 1954, real wages in the Mexican manufacturing industry as a whole declined by 11%, wages in the cotton textile industry fell by 38%.[96] Moreover, wages paid by old mills were far lower than those established by law for modern ones. The wage list of 1955 (Contratos Ley) established, for example, a daily wage of 12.70 pesos for a card tender working in an old mill, but 26.02 for one working in a plant with modern equipment.[97]

Government's protectionist policy placed the incentives to maintain the status quo indefinitely. "Since the high protective tariff has made it possible to operate profitably in spite of technical inefficiency, management and labor have become complacent about the prevailing state of affairs in the industry."[98] However, modernization of the industry could not be postponed forever, and as time went by and the industry became more outdated, the problem became increasingly difficult to solve.

Mexico was not alone in this difficult quandary. In Rio de Janeiro, Brazil, and Ecuador, the textile industries in 1951 were in a similar or worse situation, facing restrictions on the adoption of new technology caused by a rigid organization of labor comparable to those in Mexico.[99] Given the similarity between these three countries on this issue, and because nothing like the Mexican Revolution had happened in the other two countries, it is not clear that the growth of labor organization in Mexico and its consequences for industrial development can be attributed to the Revolution.

The analysis of productivity levels in Mexican textile mills indicates that the relative power of workers to control the relationship between effort and pay is a crucial factor in determining the technology employed and therefore levels of competitiveness and productivity, as William Lazonick has pointed out.[100] In accordance with the findings of Susan Wolcott and Gregory Clark for the case of India, it is clear that in Mexico the poor performance of the textile industry, particularly after the Revolution, was a problem of "the low labor input per mill worker."[101] Yet it is also evident that this did not result from a "low taste for effort on the job," or from managerial incompetence, but from a more complex situation, caused in part by the power exercised by workers in the labor market to block reductions in the number of workers for fear of unemployment. However, it was also determined by the power exerted by the owners of smaller mills, who were either unwilling or unable to make new investments and were fearful of going bankrupt. The power of these two actors would probably have not been enough to shape the evolution of the industry, though, without the support of a government that valued social and political stability above economic development and therefore pursued the tariff and labor policies that would maintain the status quo.

## The Impact of the Mexican Revolution in the Cotton Textile Industry

The idea that the Mexican Revolution destroyed the industrial capital formed during the Porfiriato was dismissed long ago. John Womack, in his now-classic article on the Mexican economy during the Revolution, explains that industrial enterprises suffered little physical damage.[102] Stephen Haber's findings on the economic performance of several firms during the Revolution go in the same direction. Most of the country's industrial plant remained intact, and the monopolistic and oligopolistic structure of the Mexican industry, far from being destroyed, was reinforced by the Revolution.[103] In fact, an econometric analysis of the mills that survived the Revolution in comparison to those that closed shows that larger mills found it easier to survive than smaller ones, and that the more modern mills had greater chances of surviving than more outdated ones.[104]

While difficulties in transportation generated a recession in the textile industry from 1913 to 1915, by 1916, the main industrial centers were again producing continuously, reaching levels of production similar to those of 1910 by the end of the decade.[105] This pattern corresponds to the evolution of the main variables of the textile industry shown in Table 1.2 and Figure 9.9.

By 1920, active spindles and employment in the textile industry were 18.7% and 7.3% above their pre-revolutionary levels, but cotton consumption and sales in real terms remained slightly below their 1910 performance (see Table 1.2). By 1925 all variables except sales in real terms and the number of workers adjusted by working hours were above pre-revolutionary figures. These figures suggest the modest impact that the Revolution had on the industry in terms of overall production; but it was not negligible, as most indicators did not fully recover for ten years.[106]

Revolutionary warfare had a relatively limited short-term effect on the textile industry, but the Revolution did have a profound impact on its subsequent development. Although the Revolution did not change productive capacity or the production levels of the textile industry, it did make a difference in terms of investment and productivity growth. The Revolution was a watershed for textile firms in terms of capital–labor relations and the ways government and industry related. Before the Revolution the industry operated under a laissez-faire regime, where workers were unorganized and wages were determined by the laws of supply and demand. After the Revolution the industry had to deal with a well-organized labor force, often supported by the government. These changes were not exclusive to Mexico, but took place to different degrees throughout the world in industrialized and certain nonindustrialized nations. Thus, it would be inaccurate to say that unionization would not have taken place if the Revolution had not occurred. Yet in Mexico the Revolution led to an important change in labor relations, and this had significant consequences.

It is difficult to disentangle the effects of the Mexican Revolution from those of World War I or the global financial crisis. It is thus necessary to make some international comparisons for this purpose, for which Brazil provides useful data (see Figure 1.2). Mexican machinery imports started declining in 1907 and then recovered slowly from 1910 to 1912. In Brazil

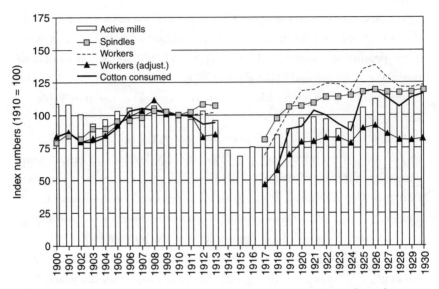

*Figure 9.9.* Evolution of the textile industry, 1900–1930. Workers adjusted per shift of twelve hours for 1900–1911, ten hours for 1912–1916, and eight hours for 1917–1930. *Sources:* México, Secretaría de Hacienda [Emiliano Busto], *Estadística de la República Mexicana* (Mexico City, 1880); México, Dirección General de Estadística, *Anuario Estadístico de la República Mexicana* (Mexico City, 1894); 1895–1911: México, Secretaría de Hacienda y Crédito Público, *Boletín de Estadística Fiscal,* several issues; México, *Mexican Year Book 1908;* Archivo General de la Nación, Departamento del Trabajo, 5/4/4, "Manifestaciónes presentadas por los fabricantes de hilados y tejidos de algodón durante enero a junio de 1912"; 1913: Archivo General de la Nación, Departamento del Trabajo, 31/2/4, "Estadística semestral de las fábricas de hilados y tejidos de algodón de la República Mexicana correspondiente al semestre de 1913"; México, Secretaría de Hacienda y Crédito Público, *Boletín de Estadística Fiscal,* several issues; México, *The Mexican Year Book 1908:* 523–531; *Boletín de Estadística,* January 1924, 52–55; *Estadística Nacional,* September 30, 1925, 5–17; México, Secretaría de Hacienda y Crédito Público, Departamento de Impuestos Especiales, Sección de Hilados y Tejidos, "Estadísticas del Ramo de Hilados y Tejidos de Algodón y de Lana," typewritten reports. Prices have been deflated using the textile (gold) index in Aurora Gómez-Galvarriato, "The Impact of Revolution: Business and Labor in the Mexican Textile Industry, Orizaba, Veracruz, 1900–1930" (PhD diss., Harvard University, 1999).

the 1907 financial crisis only briefly interrupted the high rates of growth in machinery imports the country had been experiencing since 1901, and growth continued at a fast pace from 1909 to 1912. In both countries machinery imports decreased substantially from 1913 to 1915, which suggests that even without a Revolution they would have decreased substantially in Mexico during those years as a consequence of World War I. Surprisingly, in spite of the Revolution, from 1915 to 1921 Mexican machinery imports grew faster, and reached higher levels, than those of Brazil. This must have been partly a result of the great increase in oil production in Mexico in those years and a greater need for spare parts and machinery replacements after such a long period with few machinery imports. The differences in investment rates in both countries widened the gap between the Brazilian and Mexican cotton textile industries. Though the number of spindles operating in Mexico in 1905 was very similar to those working in Brazil (91%), by 1913 there were only half as many active spindles in Mexico compared to Brazil in 1915.[107]

Machinery imports show that, after 1921, Mexico lagged behind Brazil in terms of investment. Through the 1920s the Mexican textile industry continued to fall behind the Brazilian industry; by 1927 the number of working spindles in Mexico was 31% of the total working in Brazil. This suggests that the different evolution of the industries from 1900 to 1930 was not solely the result of disparate financial markets at the turn of the century. Differences in the evolution of the macroeconomic and institutional environment, such as changes in real exchange rates, the distinct impact of the financial crisis of 1907, and the long-term consequences of the Mexican Revolution also played substantial roles.[108]

The evolution of CIVSA's profitability from 1900 to 1930 indicates that the world financial crisis of 1907 and the preambles of the Great Depression were strongly felt by the company. This was true for CIVSA from 1907 to 1911 and from 1926 to 1932. Yet Mexican companies such as CIVSA also suffered through this period from additional negative cycles caused by the Revolution. Political instability that translated into war, financial instability, and the disruption of communications caused severe problems for the company.

During the Porfiriato, CIVSA's production costs were not too far off those of industrial nations. However, its international standing deteriorated from then on because wages increased and because the new political arrangement foreclosed the adoption of new labor-saving technology that industrial nations were generally adopting during the 1920s. This was the result of a deal between the unions, the owners of smaller and less modern mills, and the government that enforced it and made it possible through high tariffs. CIVSA, along with CIDOSA and the other large modern mills, opposed it for several decades, but every three years when the Convention met, a similar arrangement was reached.

What took place was a complex interaction in which unions, industrialists, and government found themselves better off in the short run by maintaining the technology employed in the industry unchanged. Unemployment, widespread bankruptcies, and social unrest were the alternatives. Yet every time the decision to change the textile labor contract and begin to process of modernization was postponed, the problem for the future worsened. If at a given moment the status quo was maintained for fear of unemployment and of mills' bankruptcies, as the gap between the technology used by the Mexican industry and that in the industry's leaders elsewhere in the world widened, the danger of widespread unemployment and bankruptcies in the industry only increased. In the late 1980s, when the economic crisis forced the government to open up the economy, the industry was hit hard.[109]

# Conclusion

THIS HAS BEEN THE STORY of workers who made a revolution without taking up arms. Because they wanted to keep working in the mills, although not under the same conditions, they did not leave their jobs but fought and won important battles on the shop floor and in the mill towns. They organized in unions and obtained substantial improvements to their living and working conditions. Moreover, their organizations became strong enough to promote important institutional changes in the way capital and labor related, not only in their hometowns but also throughout the whole nation.

Because Mexican industrial workers were of negligible importance in the revolutionary armies of 1910–1920, the Mexican Revolution has generally been treated as mainly an agrarian phenomenon. Yet the Constitution of 1917 included as many changes for industrial workers (Article 123) as it did for peasants (Article 27).

Organized industrial workers were more important in shaping the Mexican Revolution than has generally been assumed. Despite their relatively small number compared with peasants and agricultural workers, and despite their scant participation in Revolutionary battles, they were able to pose a substantial enough threat and influence to emerging governments to make themselves heard. Moreover, they had well-defined aims in terms of working conditions, the way labor and capital should relate in production, and the basic improvements they wished for their lives, such as education. These helped shape what would become the Revolution's ideals and goals.

The significant role that industrial workers played during the Revolution was in great part a result of the strategic importance of the region where they lived. The corridor that runs along the railroad line between the port of Veracruz and Mexico City became vitally important for the Constitutional army to control during the latter part of the Revolution. It was there that some of the largest industrial centers of the country were located. It was also there that some of the most powerful workers' organizations in Mexico had already evolved from 1906 onward.

Some industrial workers, such as those who joined the Red Battalions in support of Carranza, did take up arms. Because of their participation in the Revolution as soldiers, the historiography on the role of workers in the Revolution has centered on them. However, joining revolutionary armies was not the main course of action that industrial workers took to join the Revolution. A more significant strategy, at least in Orizaba—but also in Puebla and Mexico City—was to change working and living conditions in their factories and communities. This began to take place in the Orizaba Valley several years before Díaz was deposed, but acquired a greater scope and speed once the Revolution began.

Organized workers, appropriating spaces that a weaker and less structured government left open, and posing a big enough threat to force those seeking to achieve or remain in power to deal with them, were able to obtain considerable improvements in their lives. They strengthened their organizations, took control of municipal governments, reduced their working hours, fought against the deterioration in the purchasing power of their wages, and even opened and ran schools for their children and for themselves. Through a pragmatic strategy and a realistic perspective (which the massacre of January 1907 probably helped to shape) Orizaba workers consciously used, and let themselves be used by, the revolutionary armies, the governments, and, later, larger workers' organizations on good terms with the government, when these external actors could offer them an advantageous deal. From our comfortable couches in warm, well-lit homes, and with our stomachs full, it is easy to find fault with their manipulations of power, but it is evident that their strategy worked.

The Orizaba workers did not aim for the proletarian, Bolshevik-style revolution some historians have struggled to find and some contemporaneous industrialists had nightmares about. Nor was it a revolution that brought changes because a new and idealistic government came to power and implemented them from above. It was indeed a revolution, however, and a triumphant one at that, for in the mills and in the mill towns workers' lives improved dramatically. For this period of time, every aspect of living conditions analyzed, from real wages to housing and education, substantially improved. But these improvements were largely the result of workers' actions, and not government concessions. Clever governments, of course, often supported these actions, tried to make them appear to be a result of their policies, and gained prestige from them. Yet the improvements would not have come about without the effort of organized labor and civil society.

The legal changes achieved as a result of the Revolution, including the Constitution itself, did not come out of nowhere or spontaneously out of the minds of well-intentioned citizens. Instead, somewhere in Mexico, workers made real demands or established their own alternatives to prevailing practices, and the threat that organized groups in those regions posed to stability was large enough to matter. Legal changes would become effective only in those regions where there already were substantial popular organizations strong enough to enforce them, or to ensure that they were enforced.

The cotton textile industry, which was established in Mexico relatively early compared to elsewhere in Latin America and other underdeveloped economies, did not develop and prosper during the nineteenth century at the same pace as in industrialized nations. Mexico's institutional frailty and the resulting slow growth of its economy as a whole were obstacles too large for the industry to surmount. The industry did manage to continue growing and evolving technologically throughout that century, although at a slow pace and in a geographically dispersed way. When political stability was finally achieved in the 1880s and railroads were built, banks created, and laws reformed, the textile industry experienced a revolution in distribution and production, Chandlerian in type but Mexican in style. Cloth distribution shifted from small family run stores *(cajones de ropa)* to huge department stores such as El Palacio de Hierro or Las Fábricas Universales, which controlled a substantial part of the wholesale cloth business. Its entrepreneurs combined the capital accumulated in these commercial enterprises to build new textile manufacturing joint-stock companies. New textile mills were built, and old mills were modernized, incorporating what was then state-of-the-art technology, including hydroelectric power. The Compañía Industrial Veracruzana S.A. (CIVSA) and the Compañía Industrial de Orizaba S.A. (CIDOSA) are good examples of this process.

The introduction of new technologies in communication, transportation, and production radically transformed the landscape and lives in regions such as the Orizaba Valley in a short period of time. It brought together vast numbers of people from different parts of Mexico, and from throughout the world, to live together in a rapidly changing and seething environment that posed new challenges to its inhabitants.

In spite of the considerable institutional transformation that Porfirian Mexico experienced, these changes were not large enough, broad enough, or fast enough to guarantee individual rights to all citizens, certainty in legal contracts, or to create financial institutions that could provide investment capital to promising, well-backed projects, irrespective of the name of the entrepreneur. The government remained too weak to enforce law throughout the country and to permit a general diffusion of education and other public services across all levels of society. In this context, it is easy to understand why living and labor conditions were so harsh in the Porfirian textile company towns. It also explains why certain ethnic groups, with capital, education, and strict moral codes, such as the Barcelonnettes, became so prominent in the Mexican economy and played such an important role in the revolution of distribution and production that took place in the textile industry.

The new textile firms created during the Porfiriato were in very good shape, as far as technology and productivity were concerned. Contrary to all expectations, CIVSA's products appear to have been fairly competitive when compared with English cloth, from which Mexico obtained most of its imports. While the Porfirian regime followed a protectionist strategy to promote industry, the tariffs it granted cotton cloth were not higher than those the U.S. government established for the American textile industry during the same period.

These firms also appear to have been highly profitable. Studying CIVSA's corporate accounts and CIVSA and CIDOSA stock-market reports, it is clear that these firms achieved high rates of profit during the Porfiriato. Although they were able to survive the Revolution and even make good profits in some of the years when the armed revolution took place, levels of profitability decreased and remained low in the 1920s.

Here is where the two stories come together. Of all the changes that the Revolution brought about, the most enduring and pervasive one for the textile industry was the change in relations between labor and capital that developed in the course of the 1910s and 1920s. Although workers' movements and protests had ignited before the Revolution, the Revolution provided plenty of fuel for the fire. In the course of the revolutionary decade in the Orizaba Valley, unions and confederations of unions were created and became powerful counterparts in dealing with employers. By the end of the decade, most workers in Orizaba textile mills had been unionized and hired through collective contracts and the union's mediation.

Labor productivity did not decline in CIVSA as a consequence of the Revolution. In fact, labor productivity per hour increased when working hours diminished, maintaining daily production per worker at the same levels as before. Yet labor productivity did not increase further to keep pace with the changes experienced in exporting nations. This was partly the result of a reduction in investment generated by lower profit levels. It was also the product of an institutional arrangement created during these years that had long-lasting consequences for the development of the industry. In 1912 a general wage schedule meant to govern over the whole country was adopted by industrialists, workers, and the government at a Convention organized to stop frequent strikes. This wage schedule, which rigidly set wages in terms of each particular input and machine, was shaped according to the prevailing wage lists that governed capital and labor relations in the English textile industry of the time. Without any modifications of its technical specifications, the basic form of this wage schedule was adopted again at the Workers' and Industrialists' Convention of 1925–1927, and so on until 1951. Then it was gradually reformed, allowing for some modernization of the industry, but still maintaining substantial obstacles to the adoption of new technology until shortly before 1994, when it was abolished.

These wage schedules placed severe limits on the Mexican mills' capacity for modernization. That the wage schedule was approved, again and again, without changes, was the result of a situation in which workers, industrialists, and the government gained in the short run by making such decisions, but they left an increasingly severe problem for the future to solve. Unions did not want unemployment, industrialists— particularly those with little capital to invest—did not want to go bankrupt, and the government did not want social unrest. In 1927, when the structure of the wage schedule adopted in 1912 was first approved without any changes, the decision was marked by the first waves of the Great Depression that were beginning to wash over the textile industry. This made the appeal of such a conservative arrangement even greater. After that, path dependency set in. It was always too difficult to choose another course, particularly because the government generously increased tariff protection as needed, keeping tariffs high for several decades to come.

Although Orizaba workers' living standards gradually deteriorated, this type of arrangement was beneficial for those who worked there from the Revolution to the 1970s. It gave them better living conditions than those of their Porfirian counterparts, than other Mexican workers with similar skills in non-unionized sectors, and than those they would probably have obtained if the labor contract had changed and tariff protection had been reduced. Of course, this was achieved at the expense of higher costs and lower-quality cloth for most Mexicans, but that is another story.

The basic structure of the arrangement agreed on by industrialists, workers, and government in 1927 remained with few changes until in the late 1980s, when in the midst of economic devastation, tariffs were reduced and the industry was forced to compete internationally. This was followed by the North American Free Trade Agreement signed in 1993. Most of the old textile industry went bankrupt and was forced to close. But new mills, mostly in the north of the country, became able to export vast quantities of cloth, specializing in denims. Old industrial towns like Orizaba have yet to see a better future. Their present, plagued by unemployment and decay, remains very distant from their glorious past.

The history of the textile industry from 1890 to 1930, from a period when no unions existed to a time when they became powerful institutions, offers important insights into the role of unions and their impact on industrial development and workers' well-being. It shows how positive and constructive unions were in securing improvements in workers' living and working conditions. It also demonstrates how they can become barriers to industrial development when set in nondemocratic institutional arrangements designed for the preservation of a political regime. The history of this period also illustrates the ever-present dilemma that exists between providing better living conditions for workers and building an industry capable of competing internationally, when productivity growth is left out of the equation. Because substantial improvements to workers' living conditions may be obtained in the short to medium run by disregarding international competition, it becomes assumed that it is rational and politically profitable to support this course of action. This strategy creates a long-lasting equilibrium with embedded self-perpetuating forces. Unfortunately, taking this path generates lower national economic growth and therefore lowers standards of living for the population in general. Moreover, this strategy is destined to fail in the long run, with terrible consequences for those workers who have the misfortune to see it collapse.

The Mexican Revolution cannot be fully understood without exploring the impact of the forces triggered by the Industrial Revolution. At the same time, the consequences of the Mexican Revolution helped determine how these forces would take shape in the nation. In the long run, the transformations unleashed by the Industrial Revolution had a more enduring impact than the Mexican Revolution itself.

Historians believe in the importance of disentangling how social, economic, and political processes take place in order to shed some light on the broader questions of why they occur. The story of the social and economic changes that took place in the Orizaba Valley between 1890 and 1930 provides some insights into the nature of Mexico's early industrialization and the Mexican Revolution, revealing the accomplishments but also the limitations of both processes. This story also furnishes some missing pieces of the complex and unfinished puzzle of Mexico's development.

# Abbreviations

| | |
|---|---|
| AAG | Actas de la Asamblea General (Minutes of the General Assembly) |
| AC | Actas del Consejo (Minutes of the Board of Directors) |
| AFL | American Federation of Labor |
| AGEV | Archivo General del Estado de Veracruz |
| AGN | Archivo General de la Nación, Mexico |
| AHN | Archivo Histórico de Notarías |
| ASSR | Archivo del Sindicato de Santa Rosa |
| Banamex | Archivo Histórico del Banco Nacional de México |
| CCP | Comité Consultatif de Paris |
| CD | Archivo de la Compañía Industrial de Orizaba S.A. |
| CGT | Confederación General de Trabajadores |
| CIASA | Compañía Industrial de Atlixco S.A. |
| CIDOSA | Compañía Industrial de Orizaba S.A. |
| CIM | Centro Industrial Mexicano |
| CIVSA | Compañía Industrial Veracruzana S.A. |
| COM | Casa del Obrero Mundial |
| COSCO | Confederation of Unions of Workers and Peasants of the State of Veracruz |
| CR | Correspondence (Copiadores de Cartas) |
| CROM | Confederación Regional Obrera Mexicana |

| | |
|---|---|
| CSF | Confederación de Sociedades Ferrocarrileras |
| CSOCEV | Confederación Sindicalista de Obreros y Campesinos del Estado de Veracruz |
| CSOCO | Confederación Sindicalista de Obreros y Campesinos del Distrito de Orizaba |
| CV | Archivo de la Compañía Industrial Veracruzana S.A. |
| DT | Departamento del Trabajo |
| FSCO | Federation of Unions of the Orizaba District |
| FSODF | Federation of Workers' Unions of the Federal District |
| GCOL | Gran Círculo de Obreros Libres |
| GPDC | General Porfirio Díaz Correspondence |
| IWW | Industrial Workers of the World |
| JCCA | Junta Central de Conciliación y Arbitraje |
| MX | Mexico City |
| OHMW | Oral Histories of Mexican Workers |
| PLbM | Partido Laborista Mexicano |
| PLM | Partido Liberal Mexicano |
| PNA | Partido Nacional Agrario |
| PNR | Partido Nacional Revolucionario |
| RB | Río Blanco |
| SEP | Secretaría de Educación Pública |
| SME | Mexican Electricians Union |
| SR | Santa Rosa |
| UIA | Archivo Histórico Universidad Iberoamericana |
| VHDB | Veracruz, Historical Data Bank |

# Notes

*Note*: All translations of foreign-language sources are mine unless indicated otherwise.

## Introduction

1. After the 1917 Bolshevik revolution, they took on a different character, as socialist ideas and the effects of this revolution itself changed their nature and understanding.
2. On the historiography of the Mexican Revolution and its comparison to other revolutions, see Alan Knight, "Revisionism and Revolution: Mexico Compared to England and France," *Past & Present* 134 (1992): 159–199; Friedrich Katz, "El papel de la violencia y el terror en las revoluciones mexicana y rusa," in *Nuevos ensayos mexicanos* (Mexico City: Era), 257–274; Gustavo Leyva, "Sobre la idea de la Revolución: Pasado, presente y futuro," in Gustavo Leyva, Brian Connaughton, Rodrigo Díaz, Nestor García Canclini, and Carlos Illades, eds., *Independencia y Revolución: Pasado, presente y futuro* (Mexico City: Universidad Autónoma Metropolitana and Fondo de Cultura Económica, 2010), 664–699.

## 1. The Mexican Textile Industry

1. Carmen Ramos Escandón, *Industrialización, género y trabajo femenino en el sector textil Mexicano: El obraje, la fábrica y la compañía industrial* (Mexico City: Publicaciones de la Casa Chata, 2004), 39–41; Carmen Viqueira and José Ignacio Urquiola, *Los obrajes en la Nueva España: 1530–1630* (Mexico City: Conaculta, 1990); Aurora Gómez-Galvarriato, "Premodern Manufacturing," in Victor Bulmer-Thomas, John H. Coatsworth, and Roberto Cortés Conde, eds., *The Cambridge Economic History of Latin America* (New York: Cambridge University Press, 2006),

376–377; Manuel Miño Grijalva, *La protoindustria colonial hispanoamericana* (Mexico City: El Colegio de México, 1993), 185–193; Richard J. Salvucci, *Textiles and Capitalism in Mexico: An Economic History of the Obrajes* (Princeton: Princeton University Press, 1987).

2. In the putting-out system, middlemen residing in a commercial center coordinate various stages of production, from the purchase of raw materials to the sale of final products—supplying, or "putting out," raw materials to artisans who manufacture the products in their households. See Guy Thomson, "The Cotton Textile Industry in Puebla during the Eighteenth and Early Nineteenth Centuries," in Nils Jacobsen and Hans Jurgen Puhle, eds., *The Economies of Mexico and Peru during the Late Colonial Period, 1760–1810* (Berlin: Colloquium Verlag, 1986), 169; Manuel Miño Grijalva, *Obrajes y tejedores de Nueva España, 1700–1810: La industria urbana y rural de una economía colonial* (Mexico City: El Colegio de México, 1998); Guy Thomson, "Continuity and Change in Mexican Manufacturing, 1800–1870," in Jean Batou, ed., *Between Development and Underdevelopment: The Precocious Attempts at Industrialization of the Periphery, 1800–1870* (Geneva: Libr. Droz, 1991), 259.

3. Robert A. Potash, *Mexican Government and Industrial Development in the Early Republic: The Banco de Avio* (Amherst: University of Massachusetts Press, 1983).

4. Miño Grijalva, *Obrajes y tejedores*, 266–267; Thomson, "Continuity and Change," 260; Guy Thomson, *Puebla de los Angeles: Industria y sociedad de una ciudad Mexicana, 1700–1850* (Mexico City: Benemérita Universidad de Puebla, 2002), 84–85; Richard J. Salvucci, *Textiles y capitalismo en México: Una historia económica de los obrajes, 1539–1840* (Mexico City: Alianza, 1992), 238; Thomson, *Puebla de los Angeles,* 244–245.

5. Carlos Marichal, "Paradojas fiscales y financieras de la Temprana República Mexicana, 1825–1855" (paper presented at the Seminario de Historia Económica, Fundación Ramos Areces Obstáculos al Crecimiento Económico en Iberoamérica y España 1790–1850, Madrid, Spain, May 18–19, 2007); Inés Herrera Canales, *El comercio exterior de México, 1821–1875* (Mexico City: El Colegio de México, 1977).

6. Salvucci, *Textiles and Capitalism,* 156.

7. Rafael Dobado, Aurora Gómez-Galvarriato, and Jeffrey Williamson, "Mexican Exceptionalism: Globalization and De-Industrialization 1750–1877," *Journal of Economic History* 68, no. 3 (2008): 758–811.

8. Potash, *Mexican Government and Industrial Development,* 32.

9. Aurora Gómez-Galvarriato, "Fragilidad institucional y subdesarrollo: La industria textil Mexicana en el siglo XIX," in Aurora Gómez-Galvarriato, coord., *La industria textil en México* (Mexico City: Instituto Mora, El Colegio de Michoacán, El Colegio de México, and IHH-UNAM, 1999), 142–182.

10. Egypt had 400,000 spindles by 1834. Jean Batou, "Muhammad Ali's Egypt, 1805–1848: A Command Economy in the 19th Century?," in Batou, *Between Development and Underdevelopment,* 181–218.

11. Stanley J. Stein, *The Brazilian Cotton Manufacture* (Cambridge, Mass.: Harvard University Press, 1957), 191; Mexico, Dirección de Agricultura e Industria [Lucas Alamán], *Memoria sobre el estado de la agricultura e industria de la República en el año de 1843* (Mexico City: Imprenta de J. Lara, 1843), table 5.

12. Alamán was also an entrepreneur and owned textile factories in Orizaba and Celaya.

13. Potash, *Mexican Government and Industrial Development,* 40–42.

14. Ibid.

15. Ibid., 55, 124; Mexico, Dirección General de Estadística [Antonio Peñafiel], *Anuario estadístico de 1893* (Mexico City, 1894).

16. Walter Bernecker, *De agiotistas y empresarios* (Mexico City: Universidad Iberoamericana, 1992), 254.

17. Stephen Haber, *Industry and Underdevelopment: The Industrialization of Mexico, 1890–1940* (Stanford: Stanford University Press, 1989), 21.

18. See Aurora Gómez-Galvarriato, "Fragilidad institucional subdesarrollo," 152.

19. Potash, *Mexican Government and Industrial Development,* 129.

20. Mexico, *Memoria sobre,* 22–23.

21. Letter from Estevan de Antuñano to Antonio López de Santa Anna, Puebla, January 22, 1843, in de Antuñano, *Economía Política: Documentos clásicos para la historia de la industria moderna* (Mexico City, n.d.), 6–7, quoted in Carlos Illades, "La empresa industrial de Estevan de Antuñano (1831–1847)," *Secuencia* 15 (1989): 12.

22. Decree of April 12, 1843, *El Observador judicial y de legislación,* 3, 366–367; *Memoria que el secretario de hacienda presentó,* 1844, 15, both quoted by Potash, *Mexican Government and Industrial Development,* 142; Bernecker, *De agiotistas y empresarios,* 226, 265.

23. David W. Walker, *Parentesco, negocios y política: La familia Martínez del Río en México, 1823–1867* (Mexico City: Alianza, 1991), 200; Bernecker, *De agiotistas y empresarios,* 200, 215, 221.

24. Mario Trujillo, "La Fábrica Magdalena Contreras (1836–1910)," in Carlos Marichal and Mario Cerutti, eds., *Historia de las grandes empresas en México, 1850–1930* (Mexico City: Fondo de Cultura Económica, 1997), 245–274; Illades, "La empresa industrial."

25. See Bernecker, *De agiotistas y empresarios,* 183–190.

26. Robert Brooke Zevin, "The Growth of Cotton Textile Production after 1825," in Robert W. Fogel and Stanley L. Engerman, eds., *The Reinterpretation of American Economic History* (New York: Harper and Row, 1971), 122–144.

27. John H. Coatsworth, *Los orígenes del atraso* (Mexico City: Alianza Editorial, 1990), 83.

28. Jan Bazant, *Estudio sobre la productividad en la industria Algodonera Mexicana en 1843–1845* (México City: Sobretiro de Volúmen VII de la colección para la Historia del Comerio Exterior, 1964), 55–56.

29. Thomas J. Farnham, *Mexico: Its Geography, Its People, and Its Institutions* (New York: H. Long and Brother, 1846), 29.

30. Ibid.

31. Bazant, *Estudio sobre la productividad,* 64–72. A cloth piece *(pieza de manta)* was unbleached cloth one *vara* wide and between 30 and 36 varas long (a vara equals 0.8359 meters). A piece of manta was about 2.3 feet wide and 68.8 to 82.5 feet long. Interests rates in the period were between 10% and 12%.

32. Walker, *Parentesco, Negocios y política,* 183–219.

33. Robert L. Sheina, *Latin America's Wars: The Age of the Caudillo, 1791–1899* (Dulles, Va.: Brassey's, 2003), vol. 1.

34. Ernest Sánchez Santiró, "El desempeño de la economía Mexicana tras la independencia, 1821–1870: Nuevas evidencias e interpretaciones" (paper presented at the Seminario de Historia Económica, Fundación Ramón Areces, Obstáculos al Crecimiento Económico en Iberoamérica y España 1790–1850, Madrid, Spain, May 18–19, 2007); Carlos Alejandro Ponzio, "Essays on the History of Economic Growth in Mexico" (PhD diss., Harvard University, 2004), 144.

35. The series was calculated by taking an average of Robert Potash's estimate of the capital invested during this period (11 million pesos). Machinery and millwork were considered to account for 50% of the total investment. Potash, *Mexican Government and Industrial Development,* 151. All figures were transformed into real pounds using the price index in Brian R. Mitchell, *European Historical Statistics, 1750–1975* (New York: Macmillan, 1980), 773–774.

36. Dawn Keremitsis, *La industria textil Mexicana en el siglo XIX* (Mexico City: SEP-Setentas, 1973), 55.

37. Although in 1843 the average mill in terms of spindles per mill was roughly of the same size as the average mill in the United States in 1831, by 1878 it was only 20% of the average 1880 American mill.

38. Mexico, *Memoria sobre;* Mexico, Secretaría de Hacienda [Emiliano Busto], *Estadísticas de la República Mexicana,* 3 vols. (Mexico City: Imprenta de Ignacio Cumplido, 1880), vol. 1.

39. Labor productivity is output produced per worker; total factor productivity is output produced per units of several inputs, weighted by their shares in the production process. Armando Razo and Stephen Haber, "The Rate of Productivity in Mexico, 1850–1933: Evidence from the Cotton Textile Industry," *Journal of Latin American Studies* 30, no. 3 (1998): 496–497.

40. Haber, *Industry and Underdevelopment,* 21–22.

41. Keremitsis, *La industria textil Mexicana,* 41–42; Daniel Cosío Villegas, *La cuestión arancelaria en México,* vol. 3, *Historia de la política aduanal* (Mexico City: Ediciones del Centro de Estudios Económicos, 1932), 13, 43, 92.

42. Dobado, Gómez-Galvarriato, and Williamson, "Mexican Exceptionalism."

43. Ronnie C. Tyler, *Santiago Vidaurri and the Southern Confederacy* (Fort Worth: Texas State Historical Association, 1973), 121; Mario Cerutti, *Burguesía, capitales e industria en el norte de México* (Mexico City: Alianza, 1992), 74–87.

44. Charles Lempriere, *Notes in Mexico in 1861 and 1862: Politically and Socially Considered* (London: Longman, Green and Longman, Roberts and Green, 1862), 133, quoted by Tyler, *Santiago Vidaurri,* 110.

45. Coatsworth, *Los orígenes del atraso,* 83.

46. Mexico, *Memoria sobre;* Mexico, Dirección de Agricultura e Industria [Lucas Alamán], *Memoria sobre el estado de la agricultura e industria de la República en el año de 1845* (Imprenta de J. Lara, 1846); Mexico [Busto], *Estadísticas de la República Mexicana,* vol. 1: José María Pérez Hernández, *Estadísticas de la República Mexicana* (Guadalajara: Tipografía del Gobierno a cargo de Antonio de P. González, 1862).

47. John H. Coatsworth, *Growth against Development: The Economic Impact of Railroads in 19th Century Mexico* (DeKalb: Northern Illinois University Press, 1981).

48. Mexico [Busto], *Estadísticas de la República Mexicana*, 2:319.

49. The use of water and wood as sources of power could also explain a dispersed pattern of location. However, if this had been the major source of the dispersion, the industry would have located where water power and wood were cheaper, which was not always the case in Mexico.

50. See Kevin M. Murphy, Andrei Shleifer, and Robert W. Vishny, "Industrialization and the Big Push," *Journal of Political Economy* 97, no. 5 (1989): 1003–1026.

51. Dobado, Gómez-Galvarriato, and Williamson, "Mexican Exceptionalism."

52. Potash, *Mexican Government and Industrial Development*, 163; Thomson, *Puebla de los Angeles*, 373; Walker, *Parentesco, negocios y política;* Keremitsis, *La industria textil Mexicana*, 71.

53. Friedrich Katz, "The Liberal Republic and the Porfiriato, 1821–1867," in Leslie Bethell, ed., *Mexico since Independence* (Cambridge: Cambridge University Press, 1991), 49–74.

54. Nicolás D'Owler, "Las inversiones extranjeras," in Daniel Cosío Villegas, ed., *Historia moderna de México* (Mexico City: Hermés, 1964), 1006–1010; Jan Bazant, *Historia de la deuda externa de México, 1823–1946* (Mexico City: El Colegio de México, 1995), 134–137; Jaime Enrique Zabludowsky, "Money, Foreign Indebtedness and Export Performance in Porfirist Mexico" (PhD diss., Yale University, 1984), 123.

55. Mexico, Instituto Nacional de Estadística, Geografía e Informática, *Estadísticas históricas de México* (Mexico City: INEGI, 1986), 2:569–570.

56. Marcello Carmagnani, *Estado y mercado: La economía pública del liberalismo Mexicano, 1850–1911* (Mexico City: El Colegio de México and Fondo de Cultura Económica, 1994), 191–234.

57. Edward Beatty, "Commercial Policy in Porfirian Mexico: The Structure of Protection," in Jeffrey L. Borzt and Stephen Haber, eds., *The Mexican Economy, 1870–1930* (Stanford: Stanford University Press, 2002), 225–226.

58. Marichal, "Obstacles to the Development of Capital Markets in Nineteenth-Century Mexico," in Stephen Haber, ed., *How Latin America Fell Behind* (Stanford: Stanford University Press, 1997), 127–132.

59. Beatty, "Commercial Policy in Porfirian Mexico," 206.

60. Ibid., 220–221.

61. Aurora Gómez-Galvarriato and Jeffrey Williamson, "Was It Prices, Productivity or Policy? Latin American Industrialization after 1870," *Journal of Latin American Studies* 41 (2009): 663–694.

62. Ibid.; and Edward Beatty, "The Impact of Foreign Trade on the Mexican Economy: Terms of Trade and the Rise of Industry, 1880–1923," *Journal of Latin American Studies* 32 (2000): 399–433.

63. Loom equivalents is an index of the number of spindles and looms per worker. The index is constructed by giving looms a weight of 1 and ring spindles a rate of 0.011. This rate corresponds to the relative numbers of workers needed to work weaving sheds and ring spindle rings in Britain in 1910. The index should be adjusted to a

per-shift basis when the number of hours worked varies. See Gregory Clark, "Why Isn't the Whole World Developed? Lessons from the Cotton Mills," *Journal of Economic History* 47, no. 1 (1987): 149. The length of the workday was considered to be twelve hours from 1900 to 1911, ten hours from 1912 to 1916, nine hours in 1917, and eight hours from 1917 to 1930.

64. Beatty, "Commercial Policy in Porfirian Mexico," 232.

65. Gómez-Galvarriato and Williamson, "Was It Prices, Productivity or Policy?"

66. This was particularly the case in the capital- and technology-intensive sectors, where throughput efficiencies and economies of speed, standarization, and mass markets could be achieved. The textile industry was not one of those sectors. Alfred Chandler Jr., *Scale and Scope: The Dynamics of Industrial Capitalism* (Cambridge, Mass.: Harvard University Press, 1990), 1–2, 235–294, 322–334. However, the emergence of large-scale manufacture in the New England textile industry, carried out by limited-liability corporations, has been considered part of the same process. William Lazonick, *Competitive Advantage on the Shopfloor* (Cambridge, Mass.: Harvard University Press, 1990).

67. Mary B. Rose, *Firms, Networks, and Business Values: The British and American Cotton Industries since 1750* (Cambridge: Cambridge University Press, 2000). This was also the case also in the United States for some specific textile sectors. See Phillip Scranton, *Proprietary Capitalism: The Textile Manufacture at Philadelphia, 1800–1885* (Cambridge: Cambridge University Press, 1983).

68. Noel Maurer and Tridib Sharma, "Enforcing Property Rights through Reputation: Groups in Mexico's Early Industrialization, 1878–1913," *Journal of Economic History* 61, no. 4 (2001): 925–955; Noel Maurer and Stephen Haber, "Institutional Change and Economic Growth: Banks, Financial Markets, and Mexican Industrialization, 1878–1913," in Borzt and Haber, *The Mexican Economy*, 23–49; Aurora Gómez-Galvarriato, "Networks and Entrepreneurship: The Modernization of the Textile Business in Porfirian Mexico," *Business History Review* 82, no. 3 (2008): 475–502.

69. Carles Sudriá, "Los orígenes de la empresa industrial: Algunas reflexiones," in Francisco Comín and Pablo Martín Aceña, eds., *La empresa en la historia de España* (Madrid: Editorial Civitas, 1996), 65.

70. Chandler, *Scale and Scope*, 332–334.

71. Patrice Gouy, *Péregrinations des "Barcelonnettes" au Mexique* (Grenoble: Presses Universitaires de Grenoble, 1980), 21–42; Jean Meyer, "Les Français au Mexique au XIXe siècle," *Cahiers des Ameriques Latines* 9–10 (1974): 57.

72. Meyer, "Les Français au Mexique," 62; Maurice Proal and Martin Charpenel, *L'empire Barcelonnette au Mexique* (Marseille: Éditions Jean Laffitte, 1986), 9–16.

73. United Kingdom, British Parliament, Diplomatic and Consular Reports, "Report of the Year 1906 on the Trade and Commerce of Mexico" (August 1907), 57.

74. From 320 francs to 20 francs, for 100 kilograms of merchandise. Meyer, "Les Français au Mexique," 63. This is a greater savings than the railroads achieved in land transport.

75. Ibid., 63.

76. Gouy, *Péregrinations*, 60.

77. Proal and Charpenel, *L'empire Barcelonnette au Mexique,* 104–121; Meyer, "Les Français au Mexique," 58–59.

78. Quoted by Meyer, "Les Français au Mexique," 59.

79. Gouy, *Péregrinations,* 60.

80. Oliver Williamson, "The Governance of Contractual Relations," in Louis Putterman and Randall S. Kroszner, eds., *The Economic Nature of the Firm* (Cambridge: Cambridge University Press, 1996), 125–135.

81. Cerutti, *Burguesía, capitales e industria,* 64.

82. Alfred Chandler Jr., *The Visible Hand: The Managerial Revolution in American Business* (Cambridge, Mass.: Belknap Press of Harvard University Press, 1977), 224–239.

83. United States, Department of State, "Commercial Relations of the U.S. Cotton Goods Trade to the World: The Cotton Goods Trade in Mexico" (October 1885).

84. François Arnaud, "Description des Magasins," quoted by Proal and Charpenel, *L'empire Barcelonnette au Mexique,* 104.

85. "Le premier grand magasin construit à Mexico," *Le Mexique,* 1904, quoted by Gouy, *Péregrinations,* 60–62.

86. Ibid.

87. Mexico [Busto], *Estadísticas Históricas de México,* 1, 24; Proal and Charpenel, *L'empire Barcelonnette au Mexique,* 34–60.

88. *El Economista Mexicano,* July 6, 1904, 401.

89. "Le premier grand magasin," 60–63.

90. Ibid.

91. Proal and Charpenel, *L'empire Barcelonnette au Mexique,* 34.

92. "La France au Travail," *Boletín Financiero y Minero de México,* July 14, 1928.

93. *Le Courier Français,* September 3, 1888.

94. See Stephen Haber, "Financial Markets and Industrial Development: A Comparative Study of Governmental Regulation, Financial Innovation, and Industrial Structure in Brazil and Mexico, 1840–1930," in Haber, *How Latin America Fell Behind,* 148.

95. Proal and Charpenel, *L'empire Barcelonnette au Mexique,* 64–65; *The Mexican Year Book, 1914* (London: McCorquodale and Co., 1915), 38–41; Maurer and Haber, "Institutional Change," 39–40.

96. Economies of scale exist when increasing all the inputs of production (labor, capital, raw materials) by the same factor causes production to increase by an amount greater than that factor.

97. Meyer, "Les Français au Mexique," 64; D'Owler, "Las inversiones extranjeras," 1116; Luis Evaraert, *Centenario 1889–1989* (Mexico City: Compañía Industrial de Orizaba S.A., 1989), 60.

98. Evaraert, *Centenario 1889–1989,* 64–67.

99. Nora E. Pérez-Rayón, *Entre la tradición señorial y la modernidad: La familia Escandón Barrón y Escandón Arango* (Mexico City: Universidad Autónoma Metropolitana, Unidad Azcapotzalco, 1995), 140–141.

100. Archivo de la Compañía Industrial Veracruzana, Ciudad Mendoza, Veracruz, price list, 1907. It includes seventy-four different items.

101. In 1912, mills operated by limited-liability companies had, on average, 12,592 spindles each; in contrast, other mills had only 4,224 spindles. Archivo General de la

Nación (hereafter AGN), Fondo del Departamento del Departamento del Trabajo (hereafter DT), 5/4/4, "Manifestaciones presentadas por los fabricantes de hilados y tejidos de algodón durante enero a junio de 1912."

102. See Alex M. Saragoza, *The Monterrey Elite and the Mexican State, 1880–1940* (Austin: University of Texas Press, 1988); Cerutti, *Burguesía, capitales e industria,* 231–232.

103. Leticia Gamboa, "De las sociedades de personas a las sociedades de capitales: Los Quijano Rivero en la industria textil de Puebla, 1864–1921," in Leticia Gamboa and Rosalinda Estrada, eds., *Empresas y empresarios textiles de Puebla* (Puebla: Universidad Autónoma de Puebla, 1986), 11–12, 34–38.

104. In 1912, mills in Puebla and Tlaxcala had only 2.2% of old spindles and 4.1% of old looms operating, in contrast to a national average of 5.5% and 9.2%, respectively. AGN, DT, 5/4/4, "Manifestaciónes." More detailed information can be found in Gómez-Galvarriato, "The Impact of Revolution: Business and Labor in the Mexican Textile Industry, Orizaba, Veracruz, 1900–1930" (PhD diss., Harvard University, 2000), 82.

105. Razo's and Haber's panel regressions for the period from 1850 to 1913 show that transportation and communication changes in the 1880s increased the minimum efficient scale of production. Razo and Haber, "Rate of Productivity," 499.

106. In New Hampshire, Maine, and Massachusetts, the average number of spindles per mill in 1880 was 25,004. U.S. House of Representatives, *Cotton Manufactures: Report of the Tariff Board on Schedule I of the Tariff Law* (Washington, D.C.: Government Printing Office, 1912), 1:169.

107. Razo and Haber, "Rate of Productivity," 507. Their estimates show positive and significant economies of scale for 1893 on the order of 33%, but not for the following years for which data are available. This could mean that those firms that did not increase size went out of business and no longer appeared in the censuses.

108. The data available tells whether the machinery was new or old, but unfortunately it does not indicate what precisely was meant by those terms. Mexico [Busto], *Estadísticas de la República Mexicana;* Mexico, *Anuario estadístico de 1893,* vol. 1; Mexico, Secretaría de Hacienda y Crédito Público, *Boletín de Estadística Fiscal,* various issues; *Mexican Year Book,* 1908; AGN, DT, 5/4/4, "Manifestaciónes"; AGN, DT, 31/2/4, "Estadística semestral de las fábricas de hilados y tejidos de algodón de la República Mexicana correspondiente al semestre de 1913."

109. Keremitsis, *La industria textil Mexicana,* 102; Ernesto Galarza, *La industria eléctrica en México* (Mexico City: Fondo de Cultura Económica, 1941) 12–14; Trujillo, "La Fábrica Magdalena Contreras," 265–270.

110. Fernando Rozenzweig, *El desarrollo económico en México, 1800–1910* (Mexico City: El Colegio Mexiquence and ITAM, 1989), 425.

111. The eight largest textile conglomerates were the companies listed in Table 1.4 plus La Hormiga S.A., with the exception of La Compañía Industrial de San Ildefonso, which produced woolens. AGN, DT, 5/4/4, "Manifestaciónes."

112. Gouy, *Péregrinations,* 64.

113. The Herfindahl index was 0.0209, rose to 0.0637 in 1902, and then declined to 0.0343 in 1912. Haber, "Financial Markets and Industrial Development," 163.

114. In terms of the distribution of the spindles relative to the distribution of the population. See Gómez-Galvarriato, "The Impact of Revolution," chap. 1, figs. 2 and 3.

115. Manuel Plana, *El reino del algodón en México* (Monterrey: Universidad Autónoma de Nuevo León, Unversidad Iberoamericana, Plantel Laguna, Centro de Estudios Sociales y Humanísticos de Saltillo, 1996), 123–128; Graham W. A. Clark, *Cotton Goods in Latin America,* part 1: *Cuba, Mexico, and Central America* (Washington D.C.: Government Printing Office, 1909), 27.

116. Gómez-Galvarriato and Williamson, "Prices, Productivity or Policy?"

117. Figure 1.2 includes machinery imports by Brazil from the United States, the United Kingdom, Germany, and France, as calculated by Wilson Suzigan. Machinery imported by Mexico includes machinery imported from the United Kingdom and the United States, following Wilson Suzigan's methodology. Whenever the data were disaggregated enough to allow it, agricultural, construction, transportation, mining, and electric generation machinery are excluded. Wilson Suzigan, *Indústria Brasileira:. Origem e desenvolvimento* (São Paulo: Editora da Unicamp, Editora Hucitec, 2000), 384–395.

118. Stephen Haber, "The Political Economy of Industrialization," in Bulmer-Thomas, Coatsworth, and Cortés Conde, *Cambridge Economic History of Latin America,* 2:542.

## 2. CIVSA

1. Archivo de la Compañía Industrial Veracruzana S.A. (hereafter CV), Actas de la Asamblea General (Minutes of the General Assembly) (hereafter AAG), Asamblea Constitutiva (organization meeting), November 24, 1896, art. 1.

2. CV, AAG, Asamblea Constitutiva, art. 9. November 24, 1896. In 1897 the peso-dollar exchange rate was 1.91. The figure for 2007 U.S. dollars was calculated with the GDP deflator using Samuel H. Williamson, "Six Ways to Compute the Relative Value of a U.S. Dollar Amount, 1790 to Present," http://www.measuringworth .com; CV, AAG, Asamblea General Ordinaria (stockholders ordinary meeting), July 31, 1897.

3. CV, AAG, Asamblea General Extraordinaria (stockholders extraordinary meeting), July 29, 1899; CV, AAG, AO, March 15, 1900.

4. CV, Diario No. 1 Acciones.

5. CV, AAG, 1930.

6. CV, Correspondence (Copiadores de Cartas) (hereafter CR), CIVSA–Comité Consultatif de Paris (hereafter CCP), February 17, 1920; CV, Actas del Consejo (Minutes of the Board of Directors) (hereafter AC), July 17, 1899; CV, AC, October 4, 1897.

7. CV, AC, January 9, 1899; February 6, 1899; and May 22, 1899.

8. CV, Balances Generales, 1901–1917.

9. CV, AC, April 23, 1899; CV, AC, May 1, 1899; "El señor gobernador del estado y la inauguración de la fábrica Santa Rosa," *El Cosmopolita,* May 21, 1899, 1–2; "Estreno de la fábrica de Santa Rosa," *El Cosmopolita,* April 23, 1899, 1.

10. Mexico, Secretaría de Hacienda, *The Mexican Year Book, 1911* (London: Mexican Year Book Publishing Co., 1911), 287.

11. CV, CR, CIVSA–CCP, November 25, 1919; Patrice Gouy, *Péregrinations des "Barcelonnettes" au Mexique* (Grenoble: Presses Universitaires de Grenoble, 1980), 116; George Duby, *Histoire de la France* (Paris: Larousse, 1970), 538–550.

12. AGN, DT, 5/4/4, "Manifestaciones presentadas por los fabricantes de hilados y tejidos de algodón durante enero a junio de 1912."

13. Extracts from Francisco Trentini, *La prosperité du Mexique* (Mexico City: J. Ballesca, 1908), reprinted in Maurice Proal and Martin Charpenel, *L'empire Barcelonnette au Mexique* (Marseille: Éditions Jean Laffitte, 1986), 67.

14. *The Mexican Year Book, 1911*, 127–144.

15. Aurora Gómez-Galvarriato, "Networks and Entrepreneurship: The Modernization of the Textile Business in Porfirian Mexico," *Business History Review* 82, no. 3 (2008): 475–502; Jean-Louise D'Anglade, *Un grand patron Barcelonnette au Mexique: Joseph Ollivier et sa famille* (Barcelonnette, Abzac: Sabença de la Valéia, 2006), 115, 160.

16. Archivo Histórico de Notarías (hereafter AHN), Fondo Antiguo, Notary 725 José Villela, vol. 4988, Escritura 2, Fojas 2–7.

17. AHN, Fondo Contemporáneo, Notary 5 Bernardo Cornejo, vol. 8, Escritura 223, Fojas 226–229; Erika Galán Amaro, *Estrategias y redes de los empresarios textiles de la Compañía Industrial de Orizaba S.A., 189–1930* (PhD diss., Universidad Veracruzana, 2010).

18. Trentini, *La prosperité du Mexique;* Mexico, Secretaría de Hacienda, *The Mexican Year Book, 1908* (London: Mexican Year Book Publishing Co., 1908), 524; *The Mexican Year Book, 1911*, 289; Antonio Peñafiel, *Noticias del movimiento de las Sociedades Mineras y Mercantiles, 1886–1910* (Mexico City: Secretaría de Fomento, 1911), 204–205, 256–257, 266–267; Stephen Haber, *Industry and Underdevelopment: The Industrialization of Mexico, 1890–1940* (Stanford: Stranford University Press, 1989), 72.

19. Archivo Histórico de Banco Nacional de México (hereafter Banamex), R. G. Dunn & Co., Private Reports from August 28, 1899, to January 11, 1904, 241–242.

20. Ibid., 242.

21. Ibid., 158.

22. Ibid.

23. Ibid., 338.

24. Ibid., 340.

25. Cámara Nacional de Comercio de la Ciudad de México, *Anales de economía, finanzas, industria y comercio* (Mexico City: Author, n.d.), 262.

26. Ibid.

27. Peñafiel, *Noticias del movimiento.*

28. Raúl Mille y Alberto Leduc, dirs., *Almanaque Bouret, 1897* (Mexico City: n.d.), 312.

29. Alfred Chandler Jr., *The Visible Hand: The Managerial Revolution in American Business* (Cambridge, Mass.: Belknap Press of Harvard University Press, 1977), 9–10.

30. This happened, for example, in December 1917. The members' votes were split in regards to the discounts to be set, so the president's "vote of quality" set the dispute in favor of his proposal. CV, AC, December 4, 1917.

31. CV, AAG, Asamblea Constitutiva, November 24, 1896, art. 35.

32. CV, AC, January 10, 1911; April 25, 1911; and April 25, 1925.

33. This was the case, for example, for José Signoret, president of the CIVSA board in 1897 and 1906–1907. He was head of A. Reynaud & Co. in Mexico and manager of Las Fábricas Universales.

34. CV, AC, September 3, 1900.

35. CV, AC, January 10, 1911. The general manager's and assistant manager's duties were defined in great detail by the board of directors. CV, AC, April 25, 1911.

36. Entrepreneurial decisions and actions refer to those that affect the allocation or reallocation of resources for the enterprise as a whole, and operating decisions and actions refer to those that are carried out by using the resources already allocated. Alfred Chandler Jr., *Strategy and Structure: Chapters in the History of the American Industrial Enterprise* (Cambridge, Mass.: MIT Press, 1962), 11.

37. There were 21 clerical and staff employees working in Mexico City offices, 88 in Santa Rosa, 36 in Covadonga, and 20 in El León. There were 1,730 workers in Santa Rosa, 989 in Covadonga, and 548 in El León. CV, Anexos a la declaración del Income-Tax, Resumen de Profesionistas, Empleados y Obreros con los emolumentos que percibieron en el año de 1926.

38. CV, AC, January 19, 1897.

39. A set of CIDOSA's price lists was found in the file that contained CIVSA's price lists.

40. CV, AC, April 28, 1898.

41. CV, AC, December 1, 1914; December 8, 1914; July 27, 1915.

42. CV, AC, March 28, 1911. Article 3 of the statutes was modified to allow the company to have special offices in foreign countries, run by consultant advisors *(consejeros consultivos)* or their managers.

43. CV, AC, June 13, 1911, and December 5, 1911; CV, AC, June 25, 1911.

44. For example, in 1917 CIVSA's general manager wrote to the Advisory Committee in Paris to ask for approval of a US$2.50 dividend proposed by the board. CV, AC, April 12, 1917.

45. For example, in 1902, plans to increase the production of hydroelectric power required the approval of A. Reynaud & Co. in Paris. CV, AC, September 28, 1903; December 14, 1903.

46. CV, CR, CIVSA–CCP, August 14 and October 4, 1919; July 10, August 21, and September 19, 1920.

47. CV, CR, CIVSA–CCP, October 24, 1919.

48. CV, Libro de Ventas, 1905, 1925.

49. Imports of coarse, white, and colored cloth in relation to total domestic consumption (domestic sales plus imports) were 11% in 1895, 12% in 1907, 12% in 1923 and 1924, and 4% in 1932. *Boletín de Estadística Fiscal,* 1894–1895, 1906–1907, and *Revista de Estadística,* 1925.

50. In 1912 CIDOSA accounted for 13.5% of the industry's total sales, and CIVSA 6.3%.

51. CV, Estados de Movimiento, 1918–1926. Data for other years do not include this kind of information.

52. AGN, DT, 5/4/4, "Manifestaciones."

53. CV, AC, August 4, 1902.

54. CV, AC, April 9, 1918.

55. CV, AC, February 19, 1900; CV, AC, January 21, 1913; CV, AC, August 26, 1913.

56. The lists of discounts for the various years appeared in CV, AC, May 29, 1899; December 31, 1900; January 4, 1903; November 16, 1903; December 16, 1905; December 29, 1905; November 21, 1906; November 19, 1907; December 24, 1908; January 4, 1910; January 10, 1911; December 19, 1911; January 6, 1913; December 23, 1913; January 26, 1915; December 28, 1915; December 29, 1916; December 4, 1917; January 7, 1919; December 23, 1919; December 28, 1920; December 28, 1921; December 26, 1922; January 11, 1926. Discounts were given only to customers with contracts with the company.

57. In 1907, for instance, there was a debate between two proposals. CV, AC, November 19, 1907. There was a harsh discussion in the board when setting discounts for 1918; when votes were split, the president by his "vote of quality" decided in favor of his proposal. CV, AC, December 4, 1917.

58. CV, AC, January 10, 1927.

59. CV, AC, May 29, 1899.

60. Lourdes Macluf and Martha Díaz de Kuri, *Del Líbano a México: Crónica de un pueblo emigrante* (Mexico City: Gráfica, Creatividad y Diseño, 1995); Theresa Alfaro-Velcamp, "Immigrant Positioning in Twentieth-Century Mexico: Middle Easterners, Foreign Citizens and Multiculturalism," *Hispanic American Historical Review* 86, no. 1 (2006): 70.

61. CV, AC, June 18, 1918; CV, CR, J. Maurel to Santa Rosa, March 4, 1919; CV, CR, C. Maure to Santa Rosa, February 14, 1923.

62. CV, CR, J. Maurel to Santa Rosa, March 4, 1919; CV, CR, C. Maure to Santa Rosa, February 14, 1923. CV, CR, Camille Maure to Santa Rosa, January 16, 1919.

63. CV, AC, May 29, 1899.

64. A study of the kind I have undertaken for CIVSA would be required for CIDOSA and the other major textile firms in order to test my hypothesis fully. Hopefully these studies will be undertaken sometime in the future.

65. Leticia Gamboa, *Los empresarios de Ayer: El grupo dominante en la industria textil de Puebla, 1906–1929* (Puebla: Benemérita Universidad Autónoma de Puebla, 1985), 117–148.

66. See Gómez-Galvarriato, "Networks and Entrepreneurship."

67. Stephen Haber, "Financial Markets and Industrial Development: A Comparative Study of Governmental Regulation, Financial Innovation, and Industrial Structure in Brazil and Mexico, 1840–1930," in Stephen Haber, ed., *How Latin America Fell Behind* (Stanford: Stanford University Press, 1997), 161–169.

68. Carlos Díaz Dufoo, "Industrial Evolution," in Justo Sierra, ed., *Mexico: Its Social Evolution* (Mexico City: J. Ballescá and Co., 1902), 2:156.

69. CV, AC, November 22, 1896; February 5, 1897; June 6, 1898. De Quevedo, for example, modified certain features of the English plans regarding the turbine system, in order to run the turbines on dirty water. CV, AC, January 8, 1897.

70. CV, AC, November 29, 1897.

71. CV, AC, December 27, 1897; CV, AC, November 15, 1897.

72. CV, invoice from Jauffred & Gariel, Manchester to CIVSA, June 1, 1898, from Mather & Platt Limited; Manchester to Jauffred & Gariel (for CIVSA), February 13, 1900, from John Hetherington and Sons; Limited to Jauffred & Gariel, April 20, 1898, from John Musgrave & Sons. Ltd.; Manchester to Jauffred & Gariel, June 2, 1902, from Devoge & Co.; Manhester to Jauffred & Gariel, June 3, 1902, from John Musgrave & Sons Ltd.; Bolton, Lancashire to Jauffred & Gariel, January 23, 1903.

73. From France: CV, AC, September 13, 1897, and from *L'Union,* from Paris in 1902. CV, invoice from L. Union, Paris to CIVSA, May 31, 1902; CV, invoice from Grosselin Père & Fils to CIVSA, August 4, 1908. From Germany: CV, invoices, from Fr. Gebauer Machinenfabrik, Berlin N.W. to CIVSA, August 19, 1906, and February 25, 1911. From the United States: CV, invoice from John W. Barlow, Lawrence, Mass., to CIVSA, September 12, 1900, and from Westinghouse Electric & Manufacturing Company, Pittsburgh Penn., to G.& O. Braniff & Co for CIVSA, May 4, 1904.

74. See Table 1.2.

75. The contrary is said in Stephen Haber, Armando Razo, and Noel Maurer, *The Politics of Property Rights: Political Instability, Credible Commitments and Economic Growth in Mexico, 1876–1929* (New York: Cambridge University Press, 2003), 126.

76. United States, House of Representatives, 62nd Congress, Second Session, *Cotton Manufactures: Report of the Tariff Board on Schedule I of the Tariff Law* (Washington, D.C.: Government Printing Office, 1912), 2:350–351.

77. See William Lazonick, "Factor Costs and the Diffusion of Ring Spinning in Britain Prior to World War I," *Quarterly Journal of Economics* 96, no. 1 (1981): 90–109.

78. Susan Wolcott and Gregory Clark, "Why Nations Fail: Managerial Decisons and Performance in Indian Cotton Textiles, 1890–1938," *Journal of Economic History* 59, no. 2 (1999): 418; CV, invoices from Dobson & Barlow Ltd. to Santa Rosa, 1899–1908; and CV, CR, Santa Rosa (hereafter SR)–Mexico City (hereafter MX), June 1, 1899.

79. Geo. Draper & Sons., *Facts and Figures for Textile Manufactures: Concerning the Proper Methods of Equipping and Running Mills* (Hopedale, Mass.: Cook & Sons., 1896), 163. Geo. Draper & Sons was the sole agent of Northrop Loom Co.

80. Anna P. Benson, *Textile Machines* (Lowell, Mass.: Shire, 1983), 27.

81. Geo. Draper & Sons, *Facts and Figures,* 174.

82. Ibid., 163–173.

83. Benson, *Textile Machines,* 27.

84. Geo. Draper & Sons., *Facts and Figures,* 173.

85. CV, AC, December 11, 1896, and December 28, 1896. Unfortunately the letter where A. Reynaud explained why he found these looms inconvenient for CIVSA was not in the archive.

86. CV, AC, July 18, 1898. CV, AC, December 24, 1896; April 17, 1899. CV, CR, SR–MX, April 16, 1899. There were 400 looms that ran at 220 revolutions, 144 at 180, 54 at 140, 8 Northrop looms, and 2 in need of repair.

87. The interest rate for the United States is the commercial paper annual average rate, 1890–1899, from Homer Sidney and Richard Sylla, *A History of Interest Rates* (New Brunswick, N.J.: Rutgers University Press, 1996), 9, 320. The Mexican interest rate is the rate CIVSA paid for the bank credits it negotiated. CV, AC, August 15, 1898.

88. Geo. Draper & Sons., *Facts and Figures,* 174.

89. CV, CR, SR–MX, April 20, 1899.

90. Whereas in 1911 less than 1% of the looms working in England were automatic, more than 30% of the American looms were automatic. United States, *Cotton Manufactures,* 1:11, 169.

91. Tariff schedule paragraphs considered were 458–461 from 1903 to 1905 and 333–336 from 1906–1908. Sources: México, Secretaría de Hacienda y Crédito Público, *Boletín de Estadística Fiscal,* various years. Mexican textile imports came mostly from England.

92. Jeffrey G. Williamson, "Explaining World Tariffs, 1870–1938: Stolper-Samuelson, Strategic Tariffs and State Revenues," in R. Findlay et al., *Eli F. Heckscher, International Trade, and Economic History* (Cambridge, Mass: MIT Press, 2006).

93. United States, *Cotton Manufactures,* 1:69.

94. The effective rate of protection (EPR) is the percentage excess of the domestic price of the value-added unit over its world market price. Bela Balassa and Associates, *The Structure of Protection in Developing Countries* (Baltimore: Johns Hopkins Press, 1971), 5–6, 315–318.

95. Raw cotton prices reported for the United States were spot prices of "Upland Middling" at New York, from U.S. Department of Commerce, Bureau of the Census, *Historical Statistics of the United States* (Washington, D.C.: Government Printing Office, 1975), 208. Prices for CIVSA come from company documents, including inventories, purchase invoices, and the cost of cotton reported in its books for *Movimientos Generales.*

96. United States, *Cotton Manufactures,* 1:410.

97. CV, invoices, from Jauffred & Gariel to CIVSA and from the above-mentioned companies to Jauffred & Gariel.

98. United States, *Cotton Manufactures,* 1:467.

99. This disagrees with Gregory Clark's conclusions that "real labor costs turn out to be as high as those in Britain in most countries except for the very low-wage competitors of Asia." In weaving, however, findings for CIVSA are in accordance with Clark's argument. Gregory Clark, "Why Isn't the Whole World Developed? Lessons from the Cotton Mills," *Journal of Economic History* 47, no. 1 (1987): 151.

100. Output per spindle in Lancashire was considerably higher for ring spindles than for mule spindles. Timothy Leunig, "The Myth of the Corporate Economy" (PhD diss., Oxford Unversity, 1996), 174.

101. In 1910, New England textile towns had an advantage of about $0.0015 per pound over Lancashire mills using American cotton. Clark, "Why Isn't the Whole World Developed?," 144.

102. William Lazonick, *Competitive Advantage on the Shopfloor.* (Cambridge, Mass.: Harvard University Press, 1990),163.

103. Benson, *Textile Machines,* 27; Geo. Draper & Sons., *Facts and Figures,* 174.

104. CV, payrolls, 1911 (Week 6); United States, *Cotton Manufactures,* 1:11.

105. United States, *Cotton Manufactures,* 1:11.

106. Such as bringing the weft from the storeroom, sweeping, oiling, cleaning, examining the roll of cloth, and repairing imperfections, trimming the edges, picking off threads, and carrying cloth to cloth room. Ibid., 480.

107. See Haber, *Industry and Underdevelopment,* 194.

## 3. The Nature of the Labor Force

1. Aristotle, *Politics,* bk. 1, chap. 4, quoted in John Womack Jr., "The Historiograpy of Mexican Labor," in Elsa C. Frost, Michael C. Mayer, and Josefina Zoraida Vázquez, *El trabajo y los trabajadores en la historia de México* (Mexico City: El Colegio de México and University of Arizona Press, 1979), 751.

2. "Es muy urgente que se modifique el sistema de tiendas de raya," *El Diario,* January 15, 1907, 1.

3. Andrés Molina Enriquez, *Los grandes problemas nacionales* (Mexico City: Era, 1978), 171.

4. "Las tiendas de raya," *La Semana Mercantil,* 2nd ser., 22, no. 4, January 28, 1907, 1–2.

5. Pablo Piccato, "El Paso de Venus por el disco del sol: Criminality and Alcoholism in the Late Porfiriato," *Mexican Studies/Estudios Mexicanos* 11, no. 2 (1995): 211.

6. *La Cagarruta,* December 20, 1906, 4, quoted in María Elena Díaz, "The Satiric Penny Press for Workers in Mexico, 1900–1910: A Case Study in the Politicisation of Popular Culture," *Journal of Latin American Studies* 22, no. 3 (1990): 507.

7. Ibid., 508.

8. He was imprisoned as a result of the January 7, 1907, violent events that will be fully described in Chapter 4.

9. "Entran a trabajar los obreros de Río Blanco," *El Diario,* June 1, 1907, 1.

10. Ibid.

11. Piccato, "El Paso de Venus," 230.

12. John Womack Jr., "Prólogo," in Bernardo García, ed., *La huelga del Río Blanco* (Mexico: Gobierno del Estado de Veracruz, Universidad Veracruzana), 15.

13. See Alan Knight, "The Working Class and the Mexican Revolution, c. 1900–1920," *Journal of Latin American Studies* 16, no. 1 (1984): 51–79.

14. CV, AC, December 20, 1897.

15. CV, Actas de la Asamblea General, July 29, 1899.

16. CV, payrolls, 1900–1930; Mexico, D. G. d. E. (1894), Anuario Estadístico 1893, A. Peñafiel, Mexico City; AGN, DT, 68/8, "Lista de las fábricas con especificación de sus propietarios que conforme al decreto del 14 de diciembre de 1912 y reglamento de 2 de enero de 1913 pueden disfrutar del 50% sobre el impuesto del 8% que causa la hilaza y tejidos de algodón de producción nacional si cumplen con la tarifa aprobada por el departamento del trabajo para el pago de salarios."

17. CV, AC, January 3, 1898; February 14, 1898; May 30, 1898; April 2, 1900.

18. CV, AC, January 3, 1898.

19. CV, AC, February 5, 1897.

20. CV, AC, December 4, 1899.

21. Archivo de la Compañía Industrial de Orizaba S.A. (hereafter CD), Río Blanco, Veracruz, CR, Cuestionario Sobre el Trabajo, July 12, 1920.

22. They represented 30% of total workers at Santa Rosa in that year. The year of entry for these workers varies from 1895 to 1907.

23. CV, list of workers, weaving department, 1907.

24. Oral Histories of Mexican Workers (hereafter OHMW), Veracruz, interview with Ernesto Palacios Garcés by Ana Laura Delgado Rannauro, Nogales Veracruz,

August 25, 1975; OHMW, Veracruz, interview with Mr. Gonzalo San Juan Hernández by Bety and Pepe, Orizaba, July 20, 1975.

25. OHMW, Veracruz, interview with Mr. Delfino Huerta by Ana Laura Delgado Rannauro, Nogales, August 26, 1975.

26. OHMW, Veracruz, interview with Mr. Gonzalo San Juan Hernández, by Bety and Pepe, Orizaba, July 20, 1975.

27. CV, list of workers, weaving department, 1907. If we grant that workers whose origins are reported only as Puebla, México, and Querétaro were from the cities so named, where there were several old textile mills, the figure would rise to 52.33%.

28. OHMW, Veracruz, interview with Mr. Gonzalo García Ortíz by Bernardo García Díaz, Ciudad Mendoza, July 9, 1975.

29. OHMW, Veracruz, interview with Mr. Ernesto Palacios Garcés by Ana Laura Delgado Rannauro, Nogales, August 25, 1975; OHMW, Veracruz, interview with Mr. Gonzalo San Juan Hernández, by Bety and Pepe, Orizaba, July 20, 1975; OHMW, Veracruz, interview with Mr. Delfino Huerta by Ana Laura Delgado Rannauro, Nogales, August 26, 1975; OHMW, Veracruz, interview with Mr. Gonzalo García Ortíz by Bernardo García Díaz, Ciudad Mendoza, July 9, 1975.

30. Because Orizaba was already a consolidated city, its population increased by 11.5% in this period, an increase very close to the national population growth. Mexico, Dirección General de Estadística [Antonio Peñafiel], *Censo general de la República Mexicana verificado el 28 de octubre de 1900* (Mexico City: Oficina tip. de la Secretaría de Fomento, 1901); Mexico, Secretaría de Agricultura y Fomento, Dirección de Estadística, *Tercer censo de población de los Estados Unidos Mexicanos: Verificado el 27 de octubre de 1910* (Mexico City: Dirección de Estadística, 1918).

31. Womack, "Prólogo."

32. Bernardo García Díaz, *Textiles del Valle de Orizaba (1880–1925)* (Xalapa: Universidad Veracruzana, Centro de Investigaciones Históricas, 1990), 54–55.

33. Leticia Gamboa Ojeda, "La Comunidad Obrera de El León, 1899–1909," in Seminario Sobre Movimiento Obrero y Revolución Mexicana, *Comunidad, cutura y vida social: Ensayos sobre la formación de la clase obrera* (Mexico City: INAH, 1991), 93–171; García Díaz, *Textiles del Valle de Orizaba*, 44–55.

34. CV, CR, CIVSA–Comité Consultatif de Paris (hereafter CCP), September 3, 1921.

35. CV, CR, CIVSA–CCP, May 20, 1924.

36. CV, list of workers, weaving department, 1907.

37. Whereas the lowest age for children in Mexico was 6, in the U.S. it appears to have been 10.

38. Leticia Gamboa Ojeda, *La urdimbre y la trama: Historia social de los obreros textiles de Atlixco, 1899–1924* (Mexico City: Fondo de Cultura Económica and Benemérita Universidad Autónoma de Puebla, 2001), 105.

39. CV, list of workers in the weaving department, 1907; and Gavin Wright, *Old South, New South: Revolutions in the Southern Economy since the Civil War* (New York: Basic Books, 1986), 139.

40. Mexico, *Tercer censo de población de los Estados Unidos Mexicanos.*

41. Illiteracy in Necoxtla was higher because the municipality included an Indian village.

42. Mexico, Instituto Nacional de Geografía Estadística, *Estadísticas Históricas de México* (Mexico City: INEGI, 1986), 90, 102; Mexico, Dirección General de Estadística [Antonio Peñafiel], *Anuario Estadístico 1893* (Mexico City: Oficina tip. de la Secretaría de Fomento, 1894); Mexico, Dirección General de Estadística [Antonio Peñafiel], *Censo y división territorial del Estado de Veracruz en 1900* (Mexico City: Oficina tip. de la Secretaría de Fomento, 1901); Mexico, Dirección General de Estadística, *Quinto censo de población 1930* (Mexico City: Talleres Gráficos de la Nación, 1934), 191–221.

43. Díaz, "Satiric Penny Press," 497–526.

44. OHMW, interview with Mr. Rafael Mendoza by Rosario Domínguez, Orizaba, July 27, 1975.

45. OHMW, interview with Mr. Gonzalo San Juan by Bety and Pepe, Orizaba, July 20, 1975.

46. CD, CR, Cuestionario sobre trabajo, San Lorenzo; Cuestionario sobre trabajo, Río Blanco; Cuestionario sobre trabajo, Cocolapan; Cuestionario sobre trabajo, Cerritos, July 12, 1920.

47. CV, payrolls, week 6, 1900–1930.

48. For further detail, see Carmen Ramos Escandón, *Industrialización, género y trabajo femenino en el sector textil Mexicano: El obraje, la fábrica y la Compañía Industrial* (Mexico City: CIESAS, Publicaciones de la Casa Chata, 2004), 217–222.

49. In this study, the Center includes Distrito Federal, Estado de México, Puebla, Veracruz, Guanajuato, Hidalgo, and Querétaro; the North includes Durango, Coahuila, Chihuahua, and Nuevo León; and the West includes Sonora, Sinaloa, Jalisco, Nayarit, and Michoacán. Gabriela Cordourier and Aurora Gómez Galvarriato, "La evolución de la participación laboral de las mujeres en la industria: Una visión de largo plazo," *Economía Mexicana* 13, no. 1 (2004): 63–104.

50. Susie S. Porter, *Working Women in Mexico City: Public Discourses and Material Conditions, 1879–1931* (Tucson: University of Arizona Press, 2003), 11, 12.

51. Dawn Keremitsis, "Latin American Women Workers in Transition: Sexual Division of the Labor Force in Mexico and Colombia in the Textile Industry," *The Americas* 40, no. 4 (1984): 495, 502.

52. Ann Farnsworth-Alvear, *Dulcinea in the Factory: Myths, Morals, Men, and Women in Colombia's Industrial Experiment, 1905–1960* (Durham, N.C.: Duke University Press, 2000), 235.

53. CV, payrolls, week 6, 1905 and 1908. See Aurora Gómez-Galvarriato, "The Impact of Revolution: Business and Labor in the Mexican Textile Industry, Orizaba, Veracruz, 1900–1930" (PhD diss., Harvard University, 1999), table 11 in chapter 3.

54. OHMW, interview with Mr. Gonzalo García Ortíz by Bernardo García Díaz, Ciudad Mendoza, Veracruz, July 9, 1975.

55. Porter, *Working Women in Mexico City,* 3.

56. Ibid., 109–117.

57. "Alrededores de Orizaba," *El Paladín,* March 4, 1906, 2.

58. "Orizaba al vuelo y sus alrededores: Nogales, Capataces verdugos," *El Paladín,* August 15, 1907, 1–2.
59. "Río Blanco, alrededores de Orizaba," *El Paladín,* March 15, 1908, 4.
60. Ibid.
61. CD, letter from Juan B. Lastra to Pedro Durán, April 7, 1916.
62. Ibid.
63. "Orizaba al vuelo y sus alrededores: Santa Rosa, Caifás, Heródes y Pilatos," *El Paladín,* July 2, 1908, 1.
64. Veracruz, Historical Data Bank (hereafter VHDB), Civil Registries, 1880–1940.
65. Ibid.
66. OHMW, interview with Mr. Valentín Cueto, n.d.; OHMW, interview with Mrs. Concepción Andrade Sarmiento, Río Blanco, n.d.; OHMW, interview with Mr. Delfino Huerta Muñoz by Ana Laura Delgado Rannauro, Nogales, August 28, 1975.
67. VHDB, Civil Registries, 1880–1940.
68. OHMW, interview with Mr. Gonzalo San Juan Hernández by Bety and Pepe, Orizaba, July 20, 1975.
69. Mexico, *Tercer censo de población de los Estados Unidos Mexicanos.*
70. OHMW, interview with Mr. Gonzalo García Ortíz by Bernardo García Díaz, Ciudad Mendoza, Veracruz, July 9, 1975.
71. CV payrolls, week 7, 1910; Mexico, *Tercer censo de población de los Estados Unidos Mexicanos,* 396.
72. OHMW, interview with Mrs. Concepción Andrade de Sarmiento and Mrs. Gudelia Cebada by Olivia Domínguez Téllez, Río Blanco, Veracruz, August 1975.
73. Archivo General del Estado de Veracruz (hereafter AGEV), Ayuntamiento de Orizaba, Departamento del Trabajo. Junta Municipal Permanente de Conciliación, "Ensayo de Monografía con Referencia a los Trabajos llevados a cabo por la Junta Municipal Permanente de Conciliación de la Ciudad de Orizaba de noviembre de 1931 a octubre de 1932," September 1932, 13–14; Jeffrey Bortz, *Revolution within Revolution. Cotton Textile Workers and the Mexican Labor Regime, 1910–1923* (Stanford: Stanford University Press, 2007), 60 and 162.
74. OHMW, interview with Mrs. Concepción Andrade de Sarmiento and Mrs. Gudelia Cebada by Olivia Domínguez Téllez, Río Blanco, Veracruz, August 1975.
75. OHMW, interview with Mr. Gonzalo San Juan Hernández by Bety and Pepe, Orizaba, July 20, 1975.
76. AGEV, Ayuntamiento de Orizaba, DT, Junta Municipal Permanente de Conciliación, "Ensayo de Monografía con Referencia a los Trabajos," 13–14; Heather Fowler-Salamini, "Gender, Work, and Working-Class Women's Culture in Veracruz Coffee Export Industry, 1920–1945," *International Labor and Working-Class History,* 63 (2003): 105.
77. A regional dish made of fried tortillas filled with beans or meat, served with a sauce.
78. OHMW, interview with Mr. Gonzalo San Juan by Bety and Pepe, Orizba, July 20, 1975; OHMW, interview with Mrs. Concepción Andrade Sarmiento by Olivia Domínguez, Río Blanco, Veracruz, 1975; OHMW, interview with Mr. Gonzalo García Ortiz by Bernardo García Díaz, Cuidad Mendoza, July 9, 1975.

79. OHMW, interview with Mr. Delfino Huerta made by Ana Laura Delgado Rannauro, Nogales, August 26, 1975; OHMW, interview with Mr. Macario Ventura Ochoa by Ana Laura Delgado Rannauro, Santa Rosa, n.d.
80. VHDB, Civil Registries, 1880–1940.
81. CV, payrolls, week 6, 1900–1930.
82. Gómez-Galvarriato, "The Impact of Revolution," appendix A.3.2.
83. CV, payrolls, week 6, 1905 and 1928.
84. The standard deviation of wages in 1905 was 4.5, while in 1925 (in 1905 pesos) it was 6.49. CIVSA payroll, week 6, 1905; CIVSA payroll, week 6, 1925. Prices deflated using Annual Price Index AB.
85. OHMW, interview with Mr. Ernesto Palacios Garcés by Ana Laura Delgado Rannauro, Nogales, Veracruz, August 25, 1975.
86. OHMW, interview with Mr. Gonzalo San Juan by Bety and Pepe, Orizaba, Veracruz, July 20, 1975.
87. OHMW, interview with Mr. Macario Ventura Ochoa by Ana Laura Rannuro, Santa Rosa, n.d.
88. OHMW, interveiw with Mr. Valentín Cueto, Orizaba, n.d.
89. OHMW, interview with Mr. Luis Garcés Velázquez by Ana Laura Delgado Rannauro, Santa Rosa, July 26, 1975.
90. These results come from an econometric analysis developed in Gómez-Galvarriato, "The Impact of Revolution," appendix A3.3.
91. See, for example, E. A. H. Tays, "Present Labor Conditions in Mexico," *Engineering and Mining Journal* 84, no.14 (October 5, 1907): 620–624.
92. CIVSA workers list, 1907. In the sample there were 46 female workers and 511 male workers. Notes in the margin were recorded between the last months of 1906 and the first months of 1916.
93. CV, list of workers, weaving department, 1907.

## 4. Labor Organization during the Porfiriato

1. Moisés González Navarro, "Porfiriato: Vida social," in Daniel Cosío Villegas, ed., *Historia moderna de México* (Mexico City: Hermes, 1985), 303, 306; Bernardo García Díaz, "Migraciones internas a Orizaba y formación e la clase obrera en el Porfiriato," in Bernardo García Díaz, ed., *Textiles del Valle de Orizaba (1880–1925)* (Xalapa: Universidad Veracruzana1, 1990), 56; and CV, CR, SR-MX, February 8, 1899.
2. Jean-Pierre Bastian, "Metodistas y Magonistas," in Bernardo García Díaz ed., *La Huelga del Río Blanco* (Mexico: Universidad Veracruzana and Gobierno del Estado de Veracruz, 2007), 123.
3. González Navarro, "Porfiriato," 303.
4. "El señor gobernador del estado y la inauguración de la fábrica de Santa Rosa," *El Cosmopolita*, May 21, 1899, 1–2.
5. James D. Cockroft, *Precursores intelectuales de la Revolución Mexicana (1900–1910)* (Mexico City: SEP and Siglo XXI, 1985), 127–138.
6. Ibid., 130.

7. Rodney D. Anderson, *Outcasts in Their Own Land: Mexican Industrial Workers, 1906–1911* (DeKalb: Northern Illinois University Press, 1976).

8. Gabriel Gavira, *General de Brigada Gabriel Gavira: Su actuación político militar revolucionaria* (Mexico City: A. del Bosque, 1933), 7.

9. The name of this column was "Orizaba al vuelo y sus alrededores." It appeared regularly from January 1906 to December 1908.

10. "Veracruz al Vuelo," *El Paladín*, April 8, 1906, 4; and "Notas veracruzanas: La policía de Orizaba," *El Paladín*, May 17, 1906, 4.

11. Ibid. Political chiefs *(jefes políticos)* were officers appointed by the government to rule over a cluster of counties *(municipios)* called *cantones*. Cockroft, *Precursores intelectuales*, 93.

12. Ibid., 87–96.

13. "Valiente carta de unos obreros de Santa Rosa (Veracruz)," *El Paladín*, January 11, 1906, 3.

14. Bastian, "Metodistas y Magonistas," 127, 130–131; François-Xavier Guerra, *México: Del Antiguo Régimen a la Revolución*, 2 vols. (Mexico: Fondo de Cultura Económica, 1988), 2:63.

15. No copies remain of these charters. The only source that gives details of the secret program is Germán List Arzubide and Armando List Arzubide, *La Huelga de Río Blanco* (Mexico City: Publicaciones del Departamento de Bibliotecas de la Secretaría de Educación Pública, 1935), 12–16. The public program is described in "Ante el Sr. Presidente, expone un obrero aspiraciones de progreso," *El Diario*, May 31, 1907, 1; and "Los empleados intermedios de las fábricas, calumnian a los obreros," *El Diario*, June 1, 1907, 1; Anderson, *Outcasts*, 104.

16. "Los empleados intermedios," 1.

17. Manuel Avila showed the program of the PLM to the textile workers, and José Neira was a personal friend of Camilo Arriaga, keeping close contact with him and the PLM. Cockroft, *Precursores intelectuales*, 130.

18. Ibid., 100.

19. "Orizaba al vuelo y sus alrededores: Tragedia en Río Blanco," *El Paladín*, May 27, 1906, 2; "Prisión y huelga en Santa Rosa," *El Paladín*, June 7, 1906, 4; "La Cananea grande y la Cananea pequeña," *El Paladín*, June 10, 1906, 4.

20. Bernardo García Díaz, *Un pueblo fabril de Porfiriato: Santa Rosa, Veracruz* (Mexico City: Fondo de Cultura Económica, 1981), 101–102.

21. Anderson, *Outcasts*, 105.

22. "Obreros quejosos en Río Blanco," *El Paladín*, June 21, 1906, 4.

23. "Orizaba al vuelo y sus alrededores," *El Paladín*, June 14, 1906, 3; García Díaz, *Un pueblo fabril*, 103; "Declara Neira que los obreros de Orizaba Tenían Razón," *El Diario*, June 2, 1907, 4; "Carta del obrero Neira al Sr. Presidente de la República," *El Diario*, June 2, 1907, 8.

24. Archivo Histórico Universidad Iberoamericana (hereafter UIA), General Porfirio Díaz Correspondence (hereafter GPDC), letter from Teodoro Dehesa to Porfirio Díaz, Xalapa, July 13, 1906; "Las clases obreras," *El Diario*, June 2, 1907, 4; "Carta del obrero Neira," *El Diario*, June 2, 1907, 8; Anderson, *Outcasts*, 106.

25. UIA, GPDC, letters from Teodoro Dehesa to Porfirio Díaz, Xalapa, July 4, 1906, and July 13, 1906; "Orizaba al vuelo y sus alrededores," *El Paladín*, June 28, 1906, 3.

26. "Las Cananeas," *El Paladín*, June 24, 1906, 2.

27. UIA, GPDC, letters from Teodoro Dehesa to Porfirio Díaz, Xalapa, July 4, 1906, and July 13, 1906; "Periodistas encarcelados," *El Diario del Hogar*, July 12, 1906, 2.

28. "Las Cananeas," 2.

29. "Santa Rosa, Río Blanco y Nogales en estado de sitio," *El Paladín*, June 28, 1906, 3.

30. Ibid.

31. Anderson, *Outcasts*, 110–111.

32. Guerra, *México*, 55.

33. "La Cananea grande y la Cananea pequeña," *El Paladín*, June 10, 1906, 4.

34. "Ecos de Orizaba," *El Paladín*, July 8, 1906, 2.

35. UIA, GPDC, letter from Porfirio Díaz to Teodoro Dehesa, June 22, 1906; GPDC, letter from Teodoro Dehesa to Carlos Herrera, Xalapa, June 25, 1906; letter from Carlos Herrera to Teodoro Dehesa, Orizaba, July 8, 1906; letter from G. A. Harrington (CIDOSA) to Carlos Herrera, Río Blanco, June 30, 1906; letter from A. Vargas (CIVSA) to Carlos Herrera, Santa Rosa, July 5, 1906; letter from Teodoro Dehesa to Porfirio Díaz, Xalapa, July 2, 1906; letter from Fernando Todd (Lucas Martín) to Teodoro Dehesa, Lucas Martín, June 26, 1906; letter from Rafael Neve (La Probidad) to Teodoro Dehesa, Xalapa, June 27, 1906; letter from Gabriel J. Montes (Fábrica Industrial Xalapeña) to Teodoro Dehesa, Xalapa, June 29, 1906; and letter from M. Mijares (San Bruno) to Teodoro Dehesa, June 30, 1906.

36. UIA, GPDC, letter from Teodoro Dehesa to Porfirio Díaz, July 13, 1906.

37. Guerra, *México*, 57.

38. "Nuestos ideales: No queremos huega," *El Paladín*, July 18, 1906, 1–2.

39. "Orizaba al vuelo y sus alrededores," *El Paladín*, July 29, 1906, 4.

40. "El Alcalde no debe ser empleado de la compañía," *El Paladín*, January 18, 1906, 2; "Las Cananeas," 2; "Nuestos ideales," 1–2.

41. "El Médico Alcalde de Santa Rosa: Toque de queda," *El Paladín*, August 9, 1906; CV, AC, August 6, 1906.

42. "Carta abierta al C. Gobernador del Estado de Veracruz," *El Paladín*, August 2, 1906, 1–2; "Firmas para sorpresa de la Secretaría de Guerra (Sobre Río Blanco)," *El Paladín*, August 12, 1906, 1.

43. "Los obreros de Río Blanco en acción," *El Paladín*, August 19, 1906, 4.

44. Anderson, *Outcasts*, 133.

45. Guerra, *México*, 58–62.

46. García Díaz, *Un pueblo fabril*, 107–108.

47. "Los obreros de Río Blanco en acción," *El Paladín*, August 19, 1906, 4.

48. Ibid.

49. "La revolución," *El Paladín*, August 23, 1906, 3.

50. "Quejas de unos obreros: Siguen las multas (Santa Rosa)," *El Paladín*, August 26, 1906, 3.

51. This change is clear in *El Paladín* from 1903 to 1906 as well as in CIVSA's board meeting minutes.

52. CV, AC, December 4, 1899, and August 5, 1901.

53. CV, AC, August 6, 1906; November 26, 1906; November 30, 1906; January 14, 1907; May 21, 1907; May 28, 1907; June 4, 1907; June 11, 1907; and August 6, 1907.

54. *El Paladín,* various issues, 1903–1908.

55. The GCOL operated both as a confederation and a union. Where labor organizations already existed, such as the Liga de Obreros Estevan de Antuñano, they became affiliated to the GCOL, and where they did not exist the GCOL created them. On August 26, 1906, its Río Blanco branch announced its official establishment. "Quejas de unos obreros: Siguen las multas (Santa Rosa)," *El Paladín,* August 26, 1906, 3.

56. García Díaz, *Un pueblo fabril,* 109.

57. Marjory R. Clark, *Organized Labor in Mexico* (Durham, N.C.: Duke University Press, 1934), 12–13; and Anderson, *Outcasts,* 128–150.

58. García Díaz, *Un pueblo fabril,* 109.

59. UIA, GPDC, letter from Dehesa to Porfirio Díaz, January 11, 1907; and letter from Ramón Rocha to Gral. Rosalino Martínez, January 9, 1907.

60. *La Lucha Obrera* 1, no. 11 (Puebla, December 16, 1906). In AGN, Ramo de Gobernación, file 817, quoted in García Díaz, *Un pueblo fabril,* 109.

61. Ibid., 112–113.

62. Anderson, *Outcasts,* 132.

63. "A los obreros de la república y al público en general," flyer from the Gran Círculo de Obreros Libres, Río Blanco, dated November 6, 1906. AGN, Ramo de Gobernación, file 817.

64. AGN, Ramos de Gobernación, file 817, "Informe sobre la huelga ocurrida en la fábrica de Santa Rosa el 27 de octubre de 1906," quoted in García Díaz, *Un pueblo fabril,* 114.

65. CV, AC, May 6, 1907; and García Díaz, *Un pueblo fabril,* 115.

66. Anderson, *Outcasts,* 134.

67. UIA, GPDC, letter from Samuel Ramírez to Porfirio Díaz, November 23, 1906.

68. Anderson, *Outcasts,* 134.

69. CV, AC, November 26 and November 30, 1906.

70. "Reglamento aprobado por la clase obrera de Puebla," *El Diario,* December 11, 1906. El Reglamento del Centro Industrial Mexicano was found in AGN, DT, box 21, file 12/478.

71. CV, AC, November 30, 1906.

72. "A ultima hora," *La Lucha Obrera,* December 16, 1906.

73. Anderson, *Outcasts,* 143–144.

74. Daniel Cosío Villegas, *Historia moderna de México: El Porfiriato, La vida política interior, parte segunda* (Mexico: Hermes, 1972), 10:727.

75. Porfirio Díaz, *Laudo,* in Fernando Rodarte, *7 de enero de 1907* (Mexico City: A. del Bosque, 1940), 20–23.

76. *El Imparcial,* January 10, 1906.

77. Gabriel García Márquez, *Vivir para contarla* (Mexico City: Diana, 2002), 79–80.

78. This has been pointed out in Anderson, *Outcasts,* 154.

79. Workers said the store employees themselves started the fire; other versions are that the workers started it. Anderson, *Outcasts,* 157–169; García Díaz, *Un pueblo fabril,*

138–156; UIA, GPDC 31, 101, letter from "Mejicanos que sufren" to Porfirio Díaz and Executive Palace, January 10, 1907; Jacinto Huitrón, *Orígenes e historia del movimiento obrero en México* (Mexico City: Editores Mexicanos Unidos, 1978), chap. 10.

80. According to CIVSA's list of workers, the weavers Justo González (age 20) and Mariano Vallejo (age 27) were killed by the 13th Battalion, CV, list of workers, 1907.

81. Archivo Municipal de Ciudad Mendoza, legajo suelto, "Memorándum de los acontecimientos habidos en la cabecera de la municipalidad de Santa Rosa," cited in García Díaz, *Un pueblo fabril,* 145.

82. Gen. Rosalino Martínez seems to have been Porfirio Díaz's expert in popular repression. He had been in charge of crushing the Papantla Indian rebellions of 1879 and 1896 and had ruthlessly fought the Maya in Yucatán. Emilio Kouri, "The Business of the Land" (PhD diss., Harvard University, 1996), 355.

83. Anderson, *Outcasts;* John Kenneth Turner, *México bárbaro* (Mexico City: Editorial Epoca, 1998), 174; Francisco Bulnes, *El verdadero Díaz y la Revolución* (Mexico City: Eusebio Gómez de la Puente, 1920), 61; Jacinto Huitrón, *Orígenes e historia,* 59; "Declara Neira que los obreros de Orizaba tenían razón," *El Diario,* June 2, 1907, 4–8.

84. The CIVSA list of workers tells, for example, that the weavers Enrique Manzano (age 29), Mauro Manzano (age 16), and José Ríos (age 20) were taken to Quintana Roo. CV, list of workers, 1907.

85. Anderson, *Outcasts,* 157–169; and UIA, GPDC 32, 101, letter from "Mejicanos que sufren" to Porfirio Díaz and Executive Palace, January 10, 1907. CIVSA's list of workers shows that weavers Enrique Manzano (age 29), Mauro Manzano (age 16), and José Ríos (age 20) were taken to Quintana Roo. CV, list of workers, 1907.

86. El Correo Español, "En la casa amiga de la obrera," January 12, 1909, 2.

87. Archivo Municipal de Ciudad Mendoza, legajo suelto, "Memorándum de los acontecimientos habidos en la cabecera de la municipalidad de Santa Rosa," cited in García Díaz, *Un pueblo fabril,* 145.

88. "Los sucesos de Río Blanco," *El Imparcial,* January 9, 1907, 1.

89. García Díaz, *Un pueblo fabril,* 149.

90. Anderson, *Outcasts,* 156–158.

91. CV, Caja Santa Rosa, 1900–1918.

92. CD, Río Blanco, Veracruz, AAG, March 22, 1907, *Ejercicio* of 1906.

93. CD, CR, letter from A. Reynaud to Río Blanco, January 14, 1907.

94. Guerra, *México,* 64

95. "El éxodo obrero," *El Cosmopolita,* December 30, 1906, 2.

96. Ibid.

97. CV CR, SR–MX, January 4, 1907.

98. AGN, Fondo de Gobernación, 817/8, "Señores Comerciantes, Propietarios y Compatriotas en General." A merchant, Ramón Villagómez, was the commissioner in charge of collecting the donations from the merchants of Orizaba. Donations were also received in the printing offices of *La Unión Obrera,* a workers' journal.

99. "Nuevos detalles sobre los acontecimientos en Río Blanco y Nogales: Entevista con el Sr. José Morales, testigo ocular de los sucesos," *El Diario,* January 11, 1907, 1.

100. Rex Lucas, *Minetown, Milltown, Railtown* (Toronto: University of Toronto Press, 1971), 232.

101. El Imparcial was heavily subsidized by the government. Carlo Fornaro, *México tal cual es* (New York: International, 1909), 107–121.

102. "Los Huelguistas se convierten en criminales," *El Imparcial,* January 8, 1907, 1.

103. "Propaganda peligrosa: Quiénes son los falsos amigos de los obreros," *El Imparcial,* January 10, 1907, 1.

104. Ibid.

105. "Los sucesos de Río Blanco"; "Propaganda peligrosa."

106. "Obreros amotinados," *El Tiempo,* January 9, 1907, 1.

107. "El por qué del motín de Río Blanco: Sobran las inculpaciones gratuitas," *El Diario,* January 9, 1907, 1. Carlo de Fonaro, a journalist for the newspaper, reported that Garcín offered 5,000 pesos to *El Diario* to rehabilitate his image. Fornaro, *México tal cual es,* 54–56.

108. "El por qué del motín en Río Blanco," *El Diario,* January 10, 1907, 1.

109. "Más datos de lo ocurrido en los motines de obreros en Orizaba," *El Diario,* January 10, 1907, 1.

110. "Nuevos detalles."

111. "Los Obreros de Río Blanco se amotinan," *El Imparcial,* January 8, 1907, 1.

112. "Los sucesos de Río Blanco."

113. "Los sucesos de Río Blanco II," *La Semana Mercantil,* January 21, 1907, 1–2.

114. Letter from Francisco I. Madero to Don Francisco Sentíes, January 19, 1907, in Archivo de Don Francisco I. Madero, *Epistolario (1900–1909),* 2nd ed., vol. 1, Biblioteca de Obras Fundamentales de la Independencia y la Revolución (Secretaría de Hacienda y Crédito Público, 1985). Francisco de P. Sentíes was a collaborator of *El Diario del Hogar* and *La Patria,* the editor of the newspaper *Mexico Nuevo,* and one of the founders of the Partido Democrático.

115. Letter from Francisco I. Madero to Don Francisco Sentíes, January 30, 1907, in ibid., 181–182.

116. Ibid.

117. Letter from Francisco I. Madero to Don Fernando Iglesias Calderón, January 30, 1907; and letter from Francisco I. Madero to Lic. Rafael L. Hernández, January 30, 1907, in *Epistolario,* 180–182.

118. Letter from Francisco I. Madero to Don Fernando Iglesias Calderón, January 30, 1907, in *Epistolario,* 180–181.

119. News from this event reached the international press. "Thirty Strikers Killed," *New York Times,* January 9, 1907.

120. "Muere el círculo de obreros," *El Imparcial,* January 11, 1907, 1.

121. CV, AAG, 1907, March 3, 1908.

122. UIA, GPDC, 66:133, letter from Díaz to Dehesa, January 7, 1907.

123. Roque Estrada, *La Revolución y Francisco I. Madero* (Guadalajara: 1912; reprint, 1985), 228.

124. Anderson, *Outcasts,* 206.

125. CV, CR, Board of Directors to Santa Rosa manager, January 12, 1907; and CV, payrolls, 1907, 1908; CV, payrolls, weeks 6 and 7, February 1907; and CV, CR, Santa Rosa to Board of Directors, February 7, 1907.

126. "Nuevos conflictos entre obreros y patrones," *El Imparcial,* May 2, 1907, 2; "Nueva huelga en Orizaba," *El Imparcial,* May 8, 1907, 1.

127. "Del público: La huega y los patrones," *El Imparcial,* May 10, 1907, 2; "Nuevos vonflictos"; "Sigue la huelga en Río Blanco," *El Diario,* May 7, 1907, 1.

128. "Se temen serios encuentros entre los obreros de Río Blanco y los 1,500 que van a sustituirlos: La fábrica de Santa Rosa custodia por tropas," *El Diario,* May 30, 1907, 1.

129. "Origen de la ultimas huelgas en Orizaba," *El Imparcial,* June 8, 1907, 3; "Se Temen Serios Encuentros," *El Diario,* May 30, 1907, 1; "Los obreros sustituidos en Río Blanco falta que entren al trabajo, porque 'ahí hay hombres.' Se teme que la huelga tome un sesco muy grave," *El Diario,* May 31, 1907, 1.

130. "Se Temen Serios Encuentros"; "Se agrava la situación en Orizaba," *El Imparcial,* May 31, 1907, 1.

131. "Los obreros sustituidos en Río Blanco," *El Diario,* May 31, 1907, 1; "Se agrava la situación."

132. "Río Blanco invadido de pronto por las aguas: Un juez arrebatado y muerto por la corriente: La ciudad y las casas de los obreros inundadas," *El Diario,* June 1, 1907, 1; "Ya no hay agua en las calles de Río Blanco," *El Diario,* June 2, 1907, 2; "Los obreros de Río Blanco han sido engañados," *El Diario del Hogar,* June 8, 1907, 1.

133. Anderson, *Outcasts,* 207–208.

134. "Más de Santa Rosa," *El Paladín,* August 13, 1908, 4.

5. Textile Workers and the Mexican Revolution

1. Francisco I. Madero, *La sucesión presidencial* (Mexico City: Secretaría de Gobernación, 1999 [1909]), 199–206.

2. Rodney D. Anderson, *Outcasts in Their Own Land: Mexican Industrial Workers, 1906–1911* (DeKalb: Northern Illinois University Press, 1976), 214, 228.

3. Gabriel Gavira, *General de Brigada Gabriel Gavira: Su actuación político militar revolucionaria* (Mexico City: A. del Bosque, 1933), 7, 9–12.

4. Ibid.; Roque Estrada, *La Revolución y Francisco I. Madero* (Guadalajara, 1912; reprint, 1985), 229.

5. Anderson, *Outcasts,* 256–258, 349.

6. Gavira, *General de Brigada Gabriel Gavira,* 14–15.

7. Anderson, *Outcasts,* 256, 265–266.

8. Ibid., 232–233; John Lear, *Workers, Neighbors and Citizens* (Lincoln: University of Nebraska Press, 2001), 124.

9. Lear, *Workers, Neighbors and Citizens,* 135.

10. Anderson, *Outcasts,* 230, 231, 235.

11. Gavira, *General de Brigada Gabriel Gavira,* 15–17.

12. Letter from Francisco I. Madero to Gustavo A. Madero, May 24, 191. Archivo de Don Francisco I. Madero, *Epistolario (1900–1909),* 2nd ed., vol. 1, *Biblioteca de obras fundamentales de la independencia y la revolución* (Mexico City: Secretaría de Hacienda y Crédito Público, 1985), 158–159.

13. Estrada, *La Revolución,* 228.

14. Alfonso Taracena, *La verdadera Revolución Mexicana: Primera etapa (1901–1911)* (Mexico City: Editorial Jus, 1960), 274–275.

15. Jesús Silva Herzog, *Breve historia de la Revolución Mexicana,* 2nd. ed., 2 vols. (Mexico City: Fondo de Cultura Económica, 1995), 1:144–145.

16. Anderson, *Outcasts,* 277, 285.

17. UIA, GPDC, letter from Miguel Gómez to Porfirio Díaz, December 12, 1910, 35:20446–20447.

18. "Se Han Levantado Ayer en armas los obreros de Orizaba," *El Diario,* November 21, 1910, 1; "En Río Blanco, cerca de Orizaba ocurrieron algunos deórdenes," *El Imparcial,* November 21, 1910, 1.

19. UIA, GPDC 35:16958–16959, letter from Vicente F. Sánchez, November 15, 1910; Anderson, *Outcasts,* 284.

20. "En Río Blanco, cerca de Orizaba," 1, 7.

21. Gavira, *General de Brigada Gabriel Gavira,* 24, 28.

22. "En Orizaba reina la calma," *El Imparcial,* November 19, 1910, 6; "Ha operado más detenciones la policía de la capital," *El Diario,* November 20, 1910, 1, 5.

23. Telegram from Gonzalo Luque to Díaz, November 22, 1910, UIA, GPDC 69:4826–4827; letter from Gómez to Díaz, November 22, 1910, UIA, GPDC 35:17210–17211.

24. Leticia Gamboa Ojeda, *Camerino Z. Mendoza: Un revolucionario olvidado,* vol. 2, *Cuadernos el Museo Comunitario de Ciudad Mendoza Veracruz* (Ciudad Mendoza: FOMECA, PACMYC, 1999), 14.

25. Gavira, *General de Brigada Gabriel Gavira,* 29–30.

26. "La obra de los agitadores en Río Blanco y Gómez Palacio," *El Imparcial,* November 22, 1910, 4; "En Orizaba ha reinado la tranquilidad y parece sofocado el motín," *El Diario,* November 22, 1910, 1, 6.

27. "Orizaba poseída por el pánico, se alista para la defensa," *El Diario,* November 21, 1910, 1; "Todo está en paz en Orizaba," *El Imparcial,* November 23, 1910, 6.

28. Jean Meyer, *La Revolución Mexicana* (Mexico City: Jus, 1991), 36.

29. UIA, GPDC 69:5613, telegram fom Gómez to Díaz, December 2, 1910.

30. "Todos niegan participación en el asunto," *El Imparcial,* November 30, 1910, 1.

31. UIA, GPDC 69:5613, telegram fom Gómez to Díaz, December 2, 1910.

32. UIA, GPDC 35:14434, letter from Gómez to Díaz, September 19, 1910; UIA, GPDC 69:5612–5613, telegram from Gómez to Díaz, December 2, 1910; UIA, GPDC 35:20446–20447, letter from Gómez to Díaz, December 12, 1910.

33. Gavira, *General de Brigada Gabriel Gavira,* 33–41.

34. UIA, GPDC 36:6340, letter from Gómez to Díaz, April 28, 1911.

35. OHMW, interview with Mr. Rafael Mendoza by Rosario Domínguez, July 7, 1975.

36. David G. La France, *Madero y la revolución en Puebla* (Puebla: Universidad Autónoma de Puebla, 1987), 76, 94, 104; Gamboa Ojeda, *Camerino Z. Mendoza,* 22.

37. Anderson, *Outcasts,* 292–293.

38. Ibid., 292.

39. The argument that industrial workers were not crucial actors in the Mexican Revolution is developed in Alan Knight, "The Working Class and the Mexican Revolution, c. 1900–1920," *Journal of Latin American Studies* 16, no. 1 (May 1984).

40. La France, *Madero y la revolución,* 96.

41. Ibid., 104–105, 130–131.

42. Gavira, *General de Brigada Gabriel Gavira,* 50–59.

43. Andrea and Jorge Fernández Martínez, "Ensayo, asambleísmo, 'espontaneidad,' huelga y maderismo; Una ojeada y muchas preguntas sobre las movilizaciones de 1911 en el sector textil," *Historia Obrera, 2a época* 5, no. 20 (September 1980): 33–34; AGEV, Fondo Departamento del Trabajo, Sección Fomento, 35-C, 1915, "Exención de impuestos concedida a una pequeña fábrica establecida por la Sociedad 'Unión y Progreso' de Orizaba."

44. "Mil docientos obreros huelgan en Río Blanco," *El Imparcial,* June 6, 1911, 1; CV, Ciudad Mendoza, Veracruz, CR, June 5, 6, 7, 10, and 12, 1911.

45. "Más de cinco mil obreros se dirigieron a la Ciudad de Orizaba," *El Imparcial,* June 10, 1911, 1.

46. "Terminó la huelga de Río Blanco," *El Imparcial,* September 15, 1911, 1.

47. "Los obreros de Santa Rosa se declaran en huelga," *El Demócrata,* October 2, 1911, 1; CV, AC, September 28 and 29, and October 4, 5, 7, 8, 9, 10, 12, 13, 14, and 16, 1911.

48. "Emiliano Zapata en Río Blanco," *El Demócrata,* October 21, 1911, 1.

49. Bernardo García Díaz, *La Escuela Esfuerzo Obrero: Cuadernos del Museo Comunitario de Ciudad Mendoza Veracruz* (Ciudad Mendoza: Fomeca, 1998), 12.

50. "Decreto por el que se Establece el Departamento del Trabajo," Diario Oficial de la Federación, December 18, 1911; and Departamento del Trabajo, *Boletín Mensual del Departamento del Trabajo* 1, no. 1 (July 1913): 3.

51. Ramón Eduardo Ruiz, *La Revolución Mexicana y el movimiento obrero,* 4th ed. (Mexico City: Era, 1987), 46, 49.

52. "Siete mil obreros piden aumento de sueldo," *El Demócrata,* January 4, 1912, 1; "5000 obreros huelguistas recorrieron ayer las calles de la capital," *El Imparcial,* January 4, 1912, 1; Lear, *Workers, Neighbors and Citizens,* 146; Jeffrey Bortz, *Revolution within Revolution: Cotton Textile Workers and the Mexican Labor Regime, 1910–1923* (Stanford: Stanford University Press, 2007), 190.

53. CV, CR, SR-MX, January 1 and 19, 1912; "No se soluciona la huelga en Puebla," *El Imparcial,* January 6, 1912, 1.

54. "Los obreros Orizabeños ante un ministro," *El Demócrata,* January 8, 1912, 1.

55. "El obrero trabajará sólo diez horas," *El Demócrata,* January 21, 1912, 1.

56. "Oficina de la Convención Nacional de Obreros," *El Demócrata,* January 9, 1917, 1.

57. Ruiz, *La Revolución Mexicana,* 43.

58. "Otro telegrama al Departamento del Trabajo," *El Imparcial,* February 8, 1912; "El Cierre de Fábricas," *El Imparcial,* February 10, 1912; Bernardo García Díaz, *Textiles del Valle de Orizaba (1880–1925)* (Xalapa: Universidad Veracruzana, Centro de Investigaciones Históricas, 1990), 89; "15,000 obreros sin trabajo en Orizaba," *El Imparcial,* February 10, 1912, 1; "El movimiento huelguista en Orizaba," *El Imparcial,* February 11, 1912, 1.

59. "Los obreros están dispuestos a ir al trabajo," *El Imparcial,* February 13, 1912, 1; "Terminó la huelga en Orizaba," *El Imparcial,* February 14, 1912, 1; "Solución definitiva de la huelga en Orizaba," *El Imparcial,* February 21, 1912, 1.

60. Ruiz, *La Revolución Mexicana,* 54.

61. Marjory R. Clark, *Organized Labor in Mexico* (Durham: University of North Carolina Press, 1934), 20.
62. AGN, "Las primeras tarifas (salarios) mínimas en la industria textil (1912)," *Boletín del Archivo General de la Nación,* 3rd ser., 8, nos. 3–4 (July–December 1984); DT, *Boletín Mensual,* 34–38; AGN, DT, 979/3/13, "Resolución que el Departamento da a la Comisión nombrada por el Centro Industrial Mexicano, para hacerle las aclaraciones a la Tarifa Mínima Uniforme."
63. Clark, *Organized Labor in Mexico,* 21.
64. Ibid.
65. Ibid., 20.
66. "Sangrienta lucha entre obreros y voluntarios," *El Imparcial,* July 3, 1912, 1, 5.
67. "Cómo ocurrió la espantosa matanza de Río Blanco," *El Imparcial,* July 4, 1912, 1, 5.
68. "Sangrienta lucha," 1.
69. "La Cía: Industrial de Orizaba hace una rectificación," *El Imparcial,* July 5, 1912, 1.
70. "Los obreros de Orizaba presentan un ocurso," *El Imparcial,* July 5, 1912, 5.
71. "Los sucesos de Río Blanco según el Sr. Procurador," *El Imparcial,* July 10, 1912, 1.
72. "El conflicto entre voluntarios y obreros," *El Imparcial,* July 12, 1912, 1, 8.
73. "Los sangrientos sucesos registrados en Orizaba," *El Imparcial,* July 14, 1912, 1.
74. Ibid., 10.
75. "Fueron aprehendidos los Sres Reynaud y Ollivier," *El Imparcial,* July 16, 1912, 1, 5.
76. "Los sucesos de Río Blanco," *El Imparcial,* July 17, 1912, 4; "Los voluntarios se quejan de que no se les pagó," *El Imparcial,* July 21, 1912, 1, 5.
77. Ibid., 5.
78. CV, CR, F. Vinatier to CCP, August 20, 1912; CV, CR, SR–MX, August 5, 1912.
79. "El conflicto obrero en Río Blanco," *El Imparcial,* July 26, 1912, 1, 8.
80. "Dejarán lanzadera y peinazo por el arado," *El Imparcial,* July 28, 1912, 1, 9.
81. Ibid., 9. Flores Magón proposed that they work in the cotton harvest and at the National Arsenal in Mexico City. "Estalló en Puebla una huelga general de obreros," *El Imparcial,* August 6, 1912, 1, 2.
82. "Ayer llegaron a la capital 87 obreros expulsados," *El Imparcial,* August 12, 1912, 1, 8; "Una Comisión de Obreros," *El Imparcial,* August 14, 1912, 4.
83. Departamento del Trabajo, *Boletín del Departamento del Trabajo* 1, no. 3 (September 1913): 214.
84. AGN, DT, 68/5.
85. "Ayer clausuró la convención de los industriales," *El Imparcial,* August 2, 1912, 1 and 7.
86. CV, CR, SR–MX, August 5, 1912.
87. "Estalló en Puebla una huelga general de obreros," *El Imparcial,* August 6 1912, 1 and 2; "Decrecen las energías de los huelguistas en Puebla y Orizaba," *El Imparcial,* August 8, 1912, 1 and 4; "Termina la huelga en Río Blanco," *El Imparcial,* August 10, 1912, 5; "Dos mil obreros en tormentosa asamblea lanzan mueras a los industriales," *El Imparcial,* August 5, 1912, 1 and 8; "Estalló en Puebla una huelga general de obreros," *El Imparcial,* August 6, 1912, 1 and 2.
88. Labor organization was not exclusive to Mexico City. In Tampico, the Gremio Unido de Alijadores was founded in June 1911. In 1912 the Society of Mine Workers

was founded at La Rosita Coahuila, and the association Miners of Cananea in Sonora. In Torreón the Labor Confederation (Confederación del Trabajo) and in Veracruz a Confederation of Trade Unions of the Mexican Republic (Confederación de Sindicatos Obreros de la República) were created. Clark, *Organized Labor in Mexico,* 19.

89. Ruiz, *La Revolución Mexicana,* 45; Rosendo Salazar, *Antecedentes del movimiento obrero revolucionario en México* (Mexico City: Instituto Nacional de Estudios Históros de la Revolución Mexicana), 1973), 56–57.

90. Lear, *Workers, Neighbors and Citizens,* 167–170.

91. Ruiz, *La Revolución Mexicana,* 45; Clark, *Organized Labor in Mexico,* 19; Rosendo Salazar and José G. Escobedo, *Las Pugnas de la Gleba,* 2 vols. (Mexico City: Editorial Avante, 1923), 1:37.

92. Five foreigners active in the organizations were expelled from the country. Clark, *Organized Labor in Mexico,* 17.

93. Charles Curtis Cumberland, *La Revolución Mexicana, los años constitucionalistas* (Mexico City: Fondo de Cultura Económica, 1975), 233; Ruiz, *La Revolución Mexicana,* 45, 72.

94. Lear, *Workers, Neighbors and Citizens,* 171.

95. Clark, *Organized Labor in Mexico,* 22; Ruiz, *La Revolución Mexicana,* 45.

96. Clark, *Organized Labor in Mexico,* 23.

97. Salazar and Escobedo, *Las pugnas de la gleba,* 1:41.

98. Cumberland, *La Revolución Mexicana,* 235.

99. Salazar and Escobedo, *Las pugnas de la gleba,* 1:39, 40–44.

100. The "Constitutionalist" national movement was formally founded in April 1913 when the governor of Coahuila Venustiano Carranza published his Plan de Guadalupe to oust Huerta and arrange legitimate succession to Madero. John Womack Jr., *Zapata and the Mexican Revolution* (New York: Vintage, 1970), 164.

101. Ruiz, *La Revolución Mexicana,* 61–63.

102. Ibid., 63.

103. "Camerio Mendoza intentó sublevarse en Orizaba," *El Imparcial,* March 9, 1913, 1, 6; "Una grave acusación presentada contra las fuerzas del General Llave," *El Independiente,* March 11, 1912, 1–2.

104. *Nueva Era,* November 16, 1912, quoted in García Díaz, *Textiles del Valle de Orizaba,* 91; Gamboa Ojeda, *Camerino Z. Mendoza,* 48–49.

105. On May 1, 1912, the Socialist Party had commemorated that date with a soirée and the publication in its journal *El Socialista* of articles that referred to the 1886 events, but no important workers' demonstration took place on that date. Salazar and Escobedo, *Las pugnas de la gleba,* 1:61–63; Lear, *Workers, Neighbors and Citizens,* 234–235.

106. Clark, *Organized Labor in Mexico,* 23–25. A year earlier, on May 1, 1912, was the first time the date was commemorated in Mexico. Ruiz, *La Revolución Mexicana,* 45; Salazar and Escobedo, *Las pugnas de la gleba,* 1:65–72.

107. Salazar and Escobedo, *Las pugnas de la gleba,* 1:74–80.

108. Cumberland, *La Revolución Mexicana,* 233; Salazar and Escobedo, *Las pugnas de la gleba,* 1:80.

109. John Womack Jr., *Posición estratégica y fuerza obrera: Hacia una nueva historia de los movimientos obreros* (Mexico City: El Colegio de México and Fondo de Cultura Económica, 2007), 50–52.

110. John Womack, "The Mexican Revolution 1910–1920," in Leslie Bethel, ed., *Mexico since Independence* (Cambridge: Cambridge University Press, 1991), 140–166.

111. Ley Sobre Descanso Dominical en el Estado de Veracruz, Decreto No.7, *Gaceta Oficial del Estado de Veracruz*, October 4, 1914; Ley de Cándido Aguilar, *Gaceta Oficial del Estado de Veracruz*, Decreto No. 11, October 29, 1914; AGN, DT, 88/21.

112. "Adiciones al Plan de Guadalupe: Codificación de los Decretos del C. Venustiano Carranza," 136, quoted in Clark, *Organized Labor in Mexico*, 27.

113. It was reinaugurated on September 14, 1915.

114. Rosendo Salazar, *Antecedentes del movimiento obrero revolucionario en México* (Mexico City: Biblioteca de Estudios Históricos de la Revolución Mexicana, 1973), 134.

115. See ibid., 135, and Ruiz, *La Revolución Mexicana*, 73, 75–76.

116. Salazar, *Antecedentes*, 132, 134–135.

117. Clark, *Organized Labor in Mexico*, 29; Pacto Celebrado Entre la Revolución Constitucionalista y la Casa del Obrero Mundial, in Salazar, *Antecedentes*, 138–141.

118. Clark, *Organized Labor in Mexico*, 29. The COM made an effective effort to unionize workers throughout the Carranza-controlled territory. By the end of 1915 it had thirty-six branches all over Mexico, and represented about 800,000 workers, 52,000 of whom belonged to the Mexico City COM's headquarters. Jean Meyer, "Los obreros en la Revolución Mexicana: Los Batallones Rojos," *Historia Mexicana* 21, no. 1 (July–September 1971), 19.

119. Clark, *Organized Labor in Mexico*, 30; Meyer, "Los obreros en la Revolución Mexicana," 10.

120. Meyer, "Los obreros en la Revolución Mexicana," 1.

121. Salazar, *Antecedentes*, 147–152; Salazar and Escobedo, *Las pugnas de la gleba*, 1:137–138.

122. García Díaz, *Textiles del Valle de Orizaba*, 65–71.

123. Ibid., 81.

124. Ibid., 82; AGN, DT, letter from Marcos López Jiménez to Adolfo de la Huerta, November 15, 1915, 95/10, and "Gastos de supresión de la agencia local del Departamento del Trabajo en Orizaba," 95/3.

125. CD, CR, Marcos López Jiménez to Cerritos, Río Blanco, San Lorenzo and Cocolapan, January 25, 1915.

126. García Díaz, *Textiles del Valle de Orizaba*, 86–87; AGN, DT, 104/7, letter from Chief of the Department of Labot to Manuel Sánchez Martínez, February 1915; and AGN, DT, 104/20, "Acta de la sesión celebrada en Río Blanco," February 1915.

127. AGEV, Fondo Departamento del Trabajo, Secretaría de Gobierno, Sección Fomento, 8-N, "Acta de la sesión celebrada en Nogales," sent to General Cándido Aguilar, Governor of the State of Veracruz, from Enrique H. Hinojosa and Hilario Huerta Moreno, President and Secretary of the Resistance Association of the San Lorenzo Mill, January 26, 1915.

128. García Díaz, *Textiles del Valle de Orizaba*, 94–95.

129. Marcos López Jiménez to Cerritos Manager, February 4, 1915.
130. AGEV, Fondo Departamento del Trabajo, Secretaría de Gobierno, Sección Fomento, 55-F, letter from the Members of the Board of the Resistance Society of the Santa Gertrudis Mill to Governor Cándido Aguilar, July 31, 1915.
131. AGN, DT, 98/22, letter from Enrique H. Hinojosa to Macario Reyes, March 12, 1915.
132. García Díaz, *Textiles del Valle de Orizaba*, 95–98; AGN, DT, 98/22, letter from Enrique H. Hinojosa to Macario Reyes, Veracruz, Ver., March 12, 1915; AGN, DT, 7/16, letter from Enrique H. Hinojosa and others to the Director of the Drepartment of Labor, Veracruz, Ver., March 15, 1915.
133. CD, CR, CIDOSA to Chief of Labor Department, March 26, 1915.
134. AGN, DT, 97/30, letter from Macario Reyes to Manuel R. Díaz, March 13, 1915.
135. In April, CIDOSA asked for the immediate evacuation of houses occupied by the families of workers who had joined the COM. CD, CR, Felipe Sánchez Martínez, Srio. Gral. del Comité Revolucionario de la Casa del Obrero Mundial to Manager of Río Blanco, April 7, 1915.
136. Berta Ulloa, *La encrucijada de 1915* (Mexico City: El Colegio de México, 1979), 30.
137. Decreto de aumento de jornales a los obreros de la industria textil, Venustiano Carranza, March 22, 1915, Veracruz; CD, CR, Marcos López Jiménez to CIDOSA, April 2, 1915; CV, CR, MX-SR, April 7, 1915.
138. AGN, DT, 104/6, letter from Macario Reyes to Daniel Galindo, March 28, 1915; AGN, DT, 104/6, letter from Enrique H. Hinojosa to Daniel Galindo, March 28, 1915.
139. García Díaz, *Textiles del Valle de Orizaba*, 106.
140. OHMW 7, interview with Mr. Gonzalo San Juan Hernández, Orizaba, July 20, 1975.
141. OHMW 7, interview with Mr. Gonzalo García Ortíz by Bernardo García Díaz, Cd. Mendoza, Veracruz, July 9, 1975.
142. This is what Carranza told them, according to Rosendo Salazar, a member of the COM commission. Salazar, *Antecedentes*, 137.
143. Ruiz, *La Revolución Mexicana*, 27.
144. García Díaz, *Textiles del Valle de Orizaba*, 107–108.
145. Ibid., 110–111.
146. CV, CR, SR–MX, October 5, 1915.
147. In 1916, when it decided that workers' diseases or deaths deserved compensation, CIDOSA gave 10 pesos to sick workers and 25 to 40 pesos to the relatives of dead workers. CD, CR, letters from Secretary General Herrera to CIDOSA's management, January 8, 1916, and April 6, 1916; letters from Celso Ramírez to CIDOSA's management, January 11, 12, and 13, 1916; letter from Secretary General Sosa to Spitalier, June 9, 1916.
148. CD, CR, letter from Comisión de Sanidad, Celso Rarmírez, Juan Romero and Sindicato de Obreros Libres de Río Blanco to CIDOSA's manager, January 24, 1916; CD, CR, letter from Comisión de Sanidad, Lucio Victoria and Juan Romero to CIDOSA, February 29, 1916; CD, CR, letter from E. Ropiot to Río Blanco's management, July 12, 1916.

149. CD, CR, letter from Góngora to CIDOSA, September 29, 1915; CD, CR, letter from CIDOSA to Góngora, September 30, 1915.

150. Fines went from 500 to 1,000 pesos for infringing Aguilar's decree. CV, CR, SR–MX, September 4, 1915; CD, CR, letter from Río Blanco to Governor of the State, September 11, 1915; CD, CR, letter from President of the Junta de Acción, Federico Hernández, to Río Blanco, October 1, 1915, and letter from President of the Junta de Acción, Federico Hernández, to San Lorenzo, October 2, 1915.

151. CD, CR, letter from CIDOSA to Department of Labor, Veracruz, August 10, 1915, and CIDOSA to Río Blanco, Cocolapan, Cerritos, and San Lorenzo, August 20, 1915; CV, CR, SR–MX, September 4, 1915.

152. CD, CR, letter from M. García Jurado to CIDOSA, September 22, 1915.

153. CV, CR, SR–MX, September 11, 1915.

154. This was not a mere change of name, as Jeffrey Bortz suggests, but also a change in the complexity, role, and legal status of the workers' organizations. See Bortz, *Revolution within Revolution,* 150–168.

155. García Díaz, *Textiles del Valle de Orizaba,* 109–110.

156. AGEV, Fondo del Departamento del Trabajo, Seretaría de Gobierno, Sección Fomento, 8-N, letter to Governor Cándido Aguilar from Arnulfo A. Salazar, Secretary General, David Fobon, Secretary, Emigdio González, Treasurer, and Petrolino Velazquez, member of the council, May 27, 1915.

157. Archivo del Sindicato de Santa Rosa (hereafter ASSR), file 010, September 21, 1915; Incorporation Articles of the Sindicato de Obreros y Artesanos Progresistas de Santa Rosa, quoted by Ana Laura Delgado Rannauro, "El sindicato de Santa Rosa y el movimiento obrero de Orizaba Veracruz" (BA thesis, Universidad Veracruzana, 1977), 25.

158. CD, CR, letter from the Sindicato de Obreros Libres de Río Blanco to CIDOSA, March 14, 1916; CD, CR, letter from the Sindicato de Obreros Libres de Hilados y Tejidos de la Fábrica de Cocolapan to Cocolapan Manager, April 11, 1916.

159. CD, CR, letter from Sindicato de Obreros Progresistas de San Lorenzo to San Lorenzo's manager, March 14, 1916. It would be interesting to know what progress meant for them.

160. García Díaz, *Textiles del Valle de Orizaba,* 113–115.

161. *Gaceta Oficial,* T.2, 144, October 31, 1915.

162. Ley de Asociaciones Profesionales de Agustín Millán, Decreto No. 45, in *Gaceta Oficial del Edo. de Veracruz,* December 14, 1915.

163. Ley de Asociaciones Profesionales de Cándido Aguilar, Decreto No. 15, in *Gaceta Oficial del Edo. de Veracruz,* February 8, 1916.

164. CV and CD, correspondence.

165. AGEV, Fondo del Departamento del Trabajo, Seretaría de Gobierno, Sección Fomento, 8-N, letter from Junta de Administración Civil de Nogales to Obreros de la Fábrica de San Lorenzo, June 21, 1915.

166. CV, CR, Santa Rosa manager to the Board of Directors in Mexico City, January 18, 1916; CV, CR, Board of Directors, MX to CCP, Paris, June 10, 1916.

167. Clark, *Organized Labor in Mexico,* 36.

168. Ibid., 37.

169. Ruiz, *La Revolución Mexicana*, 80.

170. "La huelga de los ferrocarrileros asume mayores proporciones," *El Nacional,* May 18, 1916, 1; "El tráfico ferroviario quedó reestablecido en todo el norte de la Repúbica," *El Nacional,* May 20, 1916, 1.

171. "El tráfico ferroviario," 1; "No abandonaron el trabajo todos los ferrocarrileros" *El Nacional,* May 20, 1916, 2

172. Ruiz, *La Revolución Mexicana*, 81.

173. Clark, *Organized Labor in Mexico,* 35.

174. Salazar and Escobedo, *Las pugnas de la gleba,* 1:203–208; García Díaz, *Textiles del Valle de Orizaba,* 144; Clark, *Organized Labor in Mexico,* 42; and Ruiz, *La Revolución Mexicana,* 81.

175. García Díaz, *Textiles del Valle de Orizaba,* 143.

176. Ibid., 117–201.

177. Ibid., 142.

178. Ibid., 153, 157, 162–163.

179. Ibid.

180. Ibid.

181. CV, CR, CIVSA–CCP, March 19 and April 30, 1917.

182. "Orizaba al vuelo y sus alrededores," *El Paladín,* January 18 and February 6, 1906.

183. CV, CR, CIVSA–CCP, December 5, 1916.

184. Pastor Rouaix, *Génesis de los artículos 27 y 123 de la Constitución Política de 1917* (Mexico City: Partido Revolucionario Institucional, 1984), 48–49.

185. Ignacio Marván Laborde, *Nueva edición del diario de debates del Congreso Constituyente de 1916–1917,* 3 vols. (Suprema Corte de Justicia de la Nación, 2006), 1:375–377, 397, 409.

186. Ibid., 1:465–480.

187. Mario de la Cueva, *Derecho Mexicano del trabajo* (Mexico City: Librería de Porrúa Hnos. y Cia., 1938), 117. For a splendid analysis of the creation of Article 123, see William J. Suarez-Potts, "The Making of Labor Law" (PhD diss., Harvard University, 2005), 145–176.

## 6. Labor and the First Postrevolutionary Regimes

1. "Carranza Becomes Mexico's President," *New York Times,* May 2, 1917, 13.

2. "35,000 obreros se han declarado en huelga en varios centros fabriles de la República," *El Demócrata,* May 8, 1917, 1; "Ni industriales, ni obreros de Veracruz han cedido," *El Demócrata,* May 11, 1917, 1; "Los industriales tendrán, hoy, una junta con los obreros, ante el c. gobernador," *El Demócrata,* May 11, 1917, 3.

3. Alvaro Matute, *Historia de la Revolución Mexicana, 1917–1924: Las dificultades del nuevo estado* (Mexico City: El Colegio de México, 1995), 236–237.

4. CV, CR, CIVSA–CCP, May 15, 1917; CV, CR, telegram SR–MX, May 3, 1917; CV, CR, SR–MX, May 15, 1917; CV, CR, CIVSA–CCP, April 30, 1917.

5. Pacto de Solidaridad entre las Agrupaciones que Forman la Federación de Sindicatos Obreros del Cantón de Orizaba, Veracruz, Orizaba, June 21, 1917, ASSR 610/02,

included in Ana Laura Delgado Rannauro, "El sindicato de Santa Rosa y el movimiento obrero de Orizaba Veracruz" (BA thesis, Universidad Veracruzana, 1977), appendix 1, 217–219.

6. Ibid.

7. De lo Dicho en el "Pacto" surge la Declaración de Principios, Orizaba, June 21, 1917, ASSR 620/02, included in Rannuro, "El sindicato," appendix 2, 220–221.

8. The newspaper indicates that it was registered as second-class mail at the local mail office on February 6, 1917. *Pro-Paria,* December 19, 1964, 1.

9. William J. Suarez-Potts, "The Making of Labor Law" (PhD diss., Harvard University, 2005), 175, 189.

10. Mario De la Cueva, *Derecho Mexicano del trabajo* (Mexico City: Librería de Porrúa Hnos. y Cia, 1938).

11. Suarez-Potts, "Making of Labor Law," 178.

12. *Excelsior,* November 11, 1918, 3.

13. Marjory R. Clark, *Organized Labor in Mexico* (Durham: University of North Carolina Press, 1934), 53–54.

14. CV, CR, CIVSA–CCP, November 19, 1918.

15. Suarez-Potts, "Making of Labor Law,"166, 188, 190.

16. CV, CR, CIVSA-Comité Consultatif de Paris (CCP), May 17, 1918.

17. CV, CR, Board of Directors to CCP, June 25, 1919.

18. CV, CR, CIVSA–CCP, July 28, 1917.

19. CV, CR, Santa Rosa manager to the Board of Directors in Mexico City, September 12, 1918.

20. Archivo General del Estado de Veracruz (AGEV), Secretaría de Gobierno (SGG), Junta Central de Conciliación y Arbitraje (JCCA), 1918, box 1, exp. 3, CIDOSA-Obreros; 1918, box 1, exp. 5, CIDOSA, CIVSA y Cía. de Luz y Fuerza-JCCA; 1918, box 3, exp. 32 bis, Sindicato de Obreros Libres de Río Blanco—CIDOSA; 1918, box 5, exp. 56, Sindicato de Obreros-CIVSA; 1918, box 5, exp. s/n, complaint of the Federación Sindicalista del Cantón de Orizaba; 1918, box 5, exp. s/n, Federación Sindicalista de Orizaba-Industriales; 1919, box 7, exp. 3, Crescencio Ramírez–CIDOSA; 1919, box 7, exp. 8, CIVSA-JCCA; 1919, box 8, exp. 20, Cámara del Trabajo de Orizaba–CIDOSA; 1920, box 12, exp. 39, Miguel Cid to Administrador Mario Giraud; AGEV, SGG, Fomento, Asuntos Laborales, Sindicatos, Santa Rosa; 1918, box 97, exp. 50, Separación de los Señores Horacio Cruz y Andrés Anglarill.

21. A federal lawsuit available in Mexico to challenge resolutions by authorities that affect individual rights protected by the Constitution. It is similar to the writ of mandamus, a court order to overturn an illegal act by the executive branch, seldom used any longer in the United States or the United Kingdom.

22. AGEV, SGG, JCCA, 1918, s/n, Federación Sinciallista de Orizaba-Industriales.

23. This argument is developed in Jeffrey Bortz, *Revolution within Revolution: Cotton Textile Workers and the Mexican Labor Regime, 1910–1923* (Stanford: Stanford University Press, 2007).

24. "Se negó el amparo a dos de las principales compañías petroleras," *Excelsior,* November 14, 1918, 1, 2, 3; "Esta semana será la audiencia para varios amparos petroleros," *Excelsior,* November 18, 1918, 1, 5; "Algunos petroleros se desistirán de los

amparos presentados," *Excelsior,* November 25, 1918, 1, 2; Matute, *Historia de la Revolución Mexicana,* 243.

25. Suprema Corte de Justicia de la Nación, *La Suprema Corte de Justicia Durante el Gobierno del Presidente Plutarco Elías Calles (1924–1928),* ed. Lucio Cabrera Acevedo (Mexico City: Suprema Corte de Justicia de la Nación, 1997); Suarez-Potts, "Making of Labor Law," 191–239.

26. Delgado Rannauro, "El sindicato de Santa Rosa," 16; Rosendo Salazar and José G. Escobedo, *Las pugnas de la gleba: Primera parte* (Mexico City: Editorial Avante, 1923), 170–180.

27. Clark, *Organized Labor in Mexico,* 57–58.

28. Salazar and Escobedo, *Las pugnas de la gleba,* 243–247.

29. Clark, *Organized Labor in Mexico,* 58–59.

30. Ibid., 59.

31. Salazar and Escobedo, *Las pugnas de la gleba,* 8–12. The CROM was known in the United States as the Mexican Federation of Labor.

32. The Industrial Workers of the World (IWW) is an international union that was founded in Chicago in June 1905 at a convention of socialists, anarchists, and radical trade unionists from all over the United States who were opposed to the policies of the American Federation of Labor (AFL). The IWW promoted industrial unionism instead of the craft unionism of the AFL. It emphasized rank-and-file organization, as opposed to empowering leaders who would bargain with employers on behalf of workers.

33. Clark, *Organized Labor in Mexico,* 59–60.

34. Ibid., 43; Luis N. Morones, "Orientaciones," in *Luz,* July 28, 1917, quoted in Barry Carr, *El movimiento obrero y la política en México, 1910–1929* (Mexico City: Era, 1981), 87.

35. Luis Morones in *El Demócrata,* August, 19, 1918, quoted in Carr, *El movimiento obrero,* 87, 92.

36. Confederación Regional Obrera Mexicana (hereafter CROM), *Memoria,* 1934, 37, 5.

37. Clark, *Organized Labor in Mexico,* 61–62.

38. Ibid., 71–73.

39. Salazar and Escobedo, *Las pugnas de la gleba,* 68–71.

40. OHMW 7, interview with Mr. Ernesto Palacio Garcés by Ana Laura Delgado Rannauro, Nogales, Veracruz, August 25, 1975.

41. OHMW 7, interview with Mr. Gonzalo García Ortíz by Bernardo García Díaz, Ciudad Mendoza, Veracruz, July 9, 1975; interview with Mr. Delfino Huerta by Ana Laura Delgado Rannauro, Nogales, Veracruz, August 26, 1975.

42. Rocío Guadarrama, *Los sindicatos y la política en México: La CROM, 1918–1928* (Mexico City: Era, 1981), 226–232.

43. OHMW 7, interview with Mr. Delfino Huerta by Ana Laura Delgado Rannauro, Nogales, Veracruz, August 26, 1975.

44. A closed shop is an arrangement whereby an employer agrees to hire—and retain in employment—only persons who are members in good standing of the trade union. Encyclopaedia Britannica Online, 2009, http://www. Britannica.com/EBchecked /topic/122178/closed-shop.

45. H. E. Hoagland, "Closed Shop versus Open Shop," *American Economic Review* 8, no. 4 (1918): 760–761.

46. "Los obreros libres de Orizaba se niegan a secundar a los sindicalizados: No accedieron a declararse en huelga," *El Universal,* October 24, 1919, 1, 11; "Los obreros libres no secundan la huelga porque juzgan que es injusta y perjudicial," *El Universal,* October 27, 1919, 1, 5.

47. Suarez-Potts, "Making of Labor Law," 169.

48. AGEV, SGG, JCCA, 1918, box 1, exp. 3, CIDOSA-Obreros.

49. AGEV, SGG, Fomento, Asuntos Laborales, Sindicatos, Cerritos, 1915, box 96, exp. 41, Carta del Administrador de Rentas de Orizaba al Gobernador y Comandante Militar del Estado; SGG, Fomento, Asuntos Laborales, Sindicatos, 1917, box 96, exp. 30, "Pases que expidió el gobierno a obreros que quedaron sin trabajo en las Fábricas de Cerritos, Río Blanco, y Mirafuentes"; SGG, Fomento, Asuntos Laborales, Sindicatos, Orizaba, 1919, box,97, exp. 63, "Sindicato de Obreros sin Trabajo."

50. CV, CR, CIVSA–CCP, August 22, 1917, and June 25, 1919.

51. Matute, *Historia de la Revolución Mexicana,* 244.

52. Salazar and Escobedo, *Las pugnas de la gleba,* 56–58.

53. CV, CR, CIVSA–CCP, October 24, 1919.

54. Bernardo García Díaz, *Textiles del Valle de Orizaba (1880–1925)* (Xalapa: Universidad Veracruzana, 1990), 210.

55. CV, CR, CIVSA–CCP, October 24, 1919.

56. *El Monitor Republicano,* November 26, 1919, quoted in Carr, *El Movimiento Obrero,* 114.

57. CV, CR, CIVSA–CCP, October 24, 1919.

58. Matute, *Historia de la Revolución Mexicana,* 245.

59. CV, AC, November 28, 1919; CV, CR, Board of Directors, MX to CCP, Paris, October 23, 1919; CV, CR, CIVSA–CCP, November 29, 1919; Salazar and Escobedo, *Las pugnas de la gleba,* 58–59.

60. Matute, *Historia de la Revolución Mexicana,* 246–247.

61. Carr, *El movimiento obrero,* 115–121.

62. Clark, *Organized Labor in Mexico,* 97–98.

63. Ibid., 76; Ramón Eduardo Ruiz, *La Revolución Mexicana y el movimiento obrero* (Mexico City: Era, 1987), 133.

64. Clark, *Organized Labor in Mexico,* 105.

65. Ibid., 77, 132.

66. Ruiz, *La Revolución Mexicana,* 134; Salazar and Escobedo, *Las pugnas de la gleba,* 116–118; Guillermina Baena Paz, "La Confederación General de Trabajadores (1921–1931): Obreros rojos," in Alejandra Moreno Toscano, ed., *75 años de sindicalismo Mexicano* (Mexico City: Instituto de Estudios Históricos de la Revolución Mexicana, 1986), 366–367.

67. Clark, *Organized Labor in Mexico,* 81–86.

68. Ruiz, *La Revolución Mexicana,* 117.

69. Several examples of repression promoted by the CROM against independent unions are given in Clark, *Organized Labor in Mexico,* 98–101.

70. Salazar and Escobedo, *Las pugnas de la gleba,* 118–119.
71. Ruiz, *La Revolución Mexicana,* 117–118.
72. CV, CR, CIVSA–CCP, April 22, 1921, the letter reports that the strike lasted from March 15 to March 29, 1921; García Díaz, *Textiles del Valle de Orizaba,* 244; Ruiz, *La Revolución Mexicana,* 119.
73. Ruiz, *La Revolución Mexicana,* 135.
74. Paco Ignacio Taibo II and Rogelio Vizcaino, *Memoria roja: Luchas sindicales de los años 20* (Mexico City: LEEGA/JUCAR, 1984), 106–107; Guillermina Baena Paz, "La Confederación General de Trabajadores (1921–1931)," *Revista Mexicana de Ciencia Política* 83 (1976): 130–132.
75. A propaganda and ideology center of the CGT meant to educate union leaders. Baena Paz, "La Confederación General de Trabajadores (1921–1931)," *Revista,* 140–141.
76. OHMW, interview with Mr. Gonzalo San Juan Hernández, Orizaba, July 20, 1975.
77. CV, AC, January 17, 1922.
78. CV, CR, CIVSA–CCP, October 24, 1919.
79. CV, CR, CIVSA–CCP, September 23, 1922.
80. CV, CR, CIVSA–CCP, October 26, 1922.
81. Ruiz, *La Revolución Mexicana,* 111–117.
82. CV, AC, July 18, 1922; Ruiz, *La Revolución Mexicana,* 112–115.
83. CV, AC, August 8, 1922.
84. CV, AC, April 9, 1923.
85. CV, CR, CIVSA–CCP, November 12, 1923.
86. Clark, *Organized Labor in Mexico,* 154.
87. This was true until 1929, when the Liga broke off relations with the party and instead established close links with Governor Adalberto Tejeda. Heather Fowler Salamini, *Movilización campesina en Veracruz (1920–1938)* (Mexico City: Siglo XXI, 1979), 73–102.
88. They succeeded in incorporating at least one peasants' union, Obreros y Campesinos de San Antonio y Jalapilla, in which a cooperative store was installed. "Sociedad Cooperativa de Consumo de Responsabilidad Limitada," *Pro-Paria,* special edition, January 7, 1928, 2.
89. Delgado Rannauro, "El sindicato de Santa Rosa," 26–27.
90. CV, CR, CIVSA–CCP, July 20, 1921; August 8, 1921; August 23, 1921; September 3, 1921; September 23, 1921; February 5, 1922. On September 3, CIVSA won the amparo against the 1921 regulations in the state court, but then the case went to the Supreme Court, which did not rule on the case until February 1922. In the end CIVSA as well as other companies won the amparos. García Díaz, *Textiles del Valle de Orizaba,* 207; and CV, AC, April 17, 1923.
91. CV, AC, June 19, 1923, June 26, 1923; CV, CR, CIVSA–CCP, June 18, 1923.
92. Enrique Rajchenberg, "Orizaba, junio de 1923: La huelga olvidada," in Ma. Eugenia Romero Sotelo et al., eds., *México entre dos revolucines* (Mexico City: UNAM, Facultad de Economía, 1993), 109, 118.
93. CV, AC, May 1, 1923; May 15, 1923; June 5, 1923.
94. "A las 10 a.m. cerró su s puertas el comercio de Veracruz," *Excelsior,* July 1, 1923, 1.
95. Rajchenberg, "Orizaba, junio de 1923," 115.

96. Ibid., 207; CV, AC, July 3, 1923; CV, CR, CIVSA-CPP, July 6, 1923; García Díaz, *Textiles del Valle de Orizaba,* 207.
97. "La ley que fue aprobada," *Excelsior,* July 1, 1923, 1.
98. CV, CR, CIVSA-CPP, July 19, 1923.
99. CV, CR, CIVSA-CPP, August 2, 1923.
100. Ibid. In 1921, based on Article 33 of the Constitution, which allowed the government to expel pernicious foreigners from the country, Obregón expelled from Mexico several Spanish managers of Atlixco mills, and in 1922 he threatened that he would expel the owners of the Carolina mill in Atlixco if the company continued disavowing union rights. Ruiz, *La Revolución Mexicana,* 111–112.
101. Ibid.
102. Ibid.
103. CV, AC, July 17, 1923.
104. CV, AC, July 30, 1923; CV, CR, CIVSA–CCP, July 19, 1923, and August 2, 1923; Cámara de Industriales de Orizaba, *La legislación Veracruzana sobre responsabilidad patronal en las enfermedades de los trabajadores* (Orizaba: Cámara de Industriales de Orizaba, 1925), 35.
105. Central Archive of the Suprema Corte de Justicia de la Nación, 1a. Secc. auxiliar, 1923–3848, "Pral. Toca al amparo a revisión promovido por Cía Industrial de Orizaba S.A. contra actos de Gobierno del Estado y otros ante el Juez de Distrito de Veracruz, fallado."
106. CV, AC, August 6, 1923.
107. CV, CR, CIVSA–CCP, August 2, 1923.
108. CV, CR, CIVSA–CCP, September 6, 1923.
109. CV, CR, CIVSA–CCP, September 10, 1923.
110. CV, AC, August 21, 1923.
111. Cámara de Industriales de Orizaba, *La legislación Veracruzana,* 43.
112. CV, AC, October 9, 1923.
113. Rajchenberg, "Orizaba, junio de 1923," 119.
114. CV, CR, CIVSA–CCP, October 12, 1923; CV, AC, November 13, 1923.
115. CD, Circular 104, February 21, 1924; CV, AC, February 26, 1924.
116. Cámara de Industriales de Orizaba, *La legislación Veracruzana,* 53, 57–60.
117. Clark, *Organized Labor in Mexico,* 101; Ruiz, *La Revolución Mexicana,* 136.
118. CV, CR, CIVSA–CCP, December 13, 1923.
119. CV, CR, CIVSA–CCP, February 5, 1924.
120. Ibid.
121. Ruiz, *La Revolución Mexicana,* 102.
122. CV, AC, February 12, 1924; CV, CR, CIVSA–CCP, February 5, 1924, February 23, 1924, and April 12, 1924; CD, CR, Río Blanco to Río Blanco Municipal President, March 15, 1924.
123. Clark, *Organized Labor in Mexico,* 106.
124. Ibid., 104, 106.
125. Ibid., 110–111.
126. This took place, for example, against a strike in the Isthmus Railway that Morones declared illegal and for which the CROM provided strikebreakers. Ibid., 114.

127. Ibid., 119–120.
128. Ibid., 118–119.
129. México, Secretaría de la Economía Nacional Mexico [Moisés T. de la Peña], *La industria textil en México: El problema obrero y los problemas económicos* (Mexico City: Talleres Gráficos de la Nación), 49.
130. Ibid., 48.
131. CV, AC, June 1, 1926.
132. México, *La industria textil en México,* 69; CV, AC, March 13, 1928.
133. CV, AC, October 19, 1926.
134. México, Secretaría de Industria, Comercio y Trabajo, *La industria, el comercio y el trabajo en México durante la gestión administrativa del Sr. Gral. Plutarco Elías Calles* (Mexico City: Tip. Galas, 1928), 3:250–255.
135. Ibid., 227–249.
136. Suarez-Potts, "Making of Labor Law," 272–276.
137. Jeffrey Bortz, "The Genesis of the Mexican Labor Relations System: Federal Labor Policy and the Textile Industry, 1925–1940," *The Americas* 52, no. 1 (1995): 48–50.
138. Jean Meyer, "Revolution and Reconstruction in the 1920s," in Leslie Bethel, ed., *Mexico since Independence* (Cambridge: Cambridge University Press, 1991), 229.
139. Ibid.
140. Carr, *El movimiento obrero,* 171, 205.
141. It was the expulsion of Mauro Tobón, who was caught distributing *El Machete,* that started the conflict that ended in Reynaldo Pantoja's death. "Nueva fase de las dificultades habidas en la fábrica de hilados de Cocolápam originadas por elementos nocivos al conglomerado obrero de la C.R.O.M.," *Pro-Paria,* April 21, 1928, 1–8.
142. Delgado Rannauro, "El sindicato de Santa Rosa," 135–136.
143. OHMW, interview with Mr. Gonzalo San Juan Hernández, Orizaba, July 20, 1975.
144. Carr, *El movimiento obrero,* 234–237, 240.
145. Delgado Rannauro, "El sindicato de Santa Rosa," 138.
146. According to *Pro-Paria,* a meeting of the *Partido Regional Veracruzano* hatched the assasination of several CROM workers, among whom was Reynaldo Pantoja. The article stated that red workers were influenced by *El Machete.* "Fue asesinado de la manera más vil y cobarde nuestro camarada Reynaldo C. Pantoja," *Pro-Paria,* April 14, 1928, 1–8.
147. Clark, *Organized Labor in Mexico,* 134; Kevin J. Middlebrook, *The Paradox of Revolution: Labor, State, and Authoritarianism in Mexico* (Baltimore: John Hopkins University Press, 1995), 81.
148. Clark, *Organized Labor in Mexico,* 141, 215.
149. Delgado Rannauro, "El sindicato de Santa Rosa," 148–149.
150. Middlebrook, *The Paradox of Revolution,* 81.
151. Clark, *Organized Labor in Mexico,* 134.
152. ASSR, Folio 611.03, September 3, 1930, circular # 91 de la CSOCO a las agrupaciones confederadas de la region quoted by Delgado Rannauro, "El sindicato de Santa Rosa," 158.
153. Clark, *Organized Labor in Mexico,* 143.
154. Delgado Rannauro, "El sindicato de Santa Rosa," 155.

155. Ibid., 143.
156. Ibid., 154.
157. Ibid., 158.
158. Ibid., 145.
159. Ibid., 239–241. Eucario Leon's house in Mendoza, Veracruz, suggests that he became a wealthy man.
160. Clark, *Organized Labor in Mexico*, 65.
161. México, *La industria, el comercio y el trabajo*, 171–208.
162. Dante Octavio Hernández Guzmán, *Gran diccionario enciclopédico de la región de Orizaba* (Orizaba: Ayuntamiento de Orizaba, 2008). Martín Torres was the worker leader best remembered by those workers who were interviewed in the 1970s, and there are many unions, schools, and union locals with his name.
163. Clark, *Organized Labor in Mexico*, 193.

7. A Revolution in Work

1. A detailed methodological explanation of how the price indices and wages series were calculated can be found in Aurora Gómez-Galvarriato, "The Impact of Revolution: Business and Labor in the Mexican Textile Industry, Orizaba, Veracruz, 1900–1930" (PhD diss., Harvard University, 1999), appendixes to chaps. 4 and 5.
2. In 1912 the average wage of workers in the Veracruz textile industry was the highest in the country, reaching 3.19 pesos. In 1921 the national average daily wage in the textile industry was 2.63 pesos, while CIVSA's average daily wage was 5.08 pesos. *Boletín Estadística Fiscal; Anuario del año fiscal 1912–13;* and *Fábricas de Hilados y Tejidos en la República en el año 1921,* AGN, DT, file 399, box 1.
3. Mario de la Cueva, *Derecho Mexicano del trabajo* (Mexico City: Librería de Porrúa Hnos. y Cia., 1938), 98–104.
4. See Fernando Rozenzweig, *El desarrollo económico en México, 1800–1910* (Mexico City: El Colegio Mexiquence and ITAM, 1989), 247; Clark W. Reynolds, *The Mexican Economy: Twentieth-Century Structure and Growth* (New Haven, Conn.: Yale University Press, 1970), 43–44; Friedrich Katz, *The Secret War in Mexico: Europe, the United States, and the Mexican Revolution* (Chicago: University of Chicago Press, 1981), 3–49; Marjory R. Clark, *Organized Labor in Mexico* (Durham: University of North Carolina Press, 1934), 9; Alan Knight, *The Mexican Revolution,* 2 vols. (Lincoln: University of Nebraska Press, 1990), 1:127–130; Hans Werner Tobler, *La Revolución Mexicana: Transformación social y cambio político, 1876–1940* (Mexico City: Alianza, 1994), 137–139; Luis Cerda, "¿Causas Económicas de la Revolución Mexicana?," *Revista Mexicana de Sociología* 53, no. 11 (1991): 307–347; Seminario de Historia Moderna de México, *Estadísticas económicas del Porfiriato* (Mexico City: El Colegio de México, 1960), 2:17.
5. The series of average weekly nominal wages used here includes wages of all workers in the spinning, weaving, bleaching, and printing departments of Santa Rosa. It represents 83% of the total labor force at the mill. Because most of the workers at the factory were paid for piecework, wages varied depending on the number of hours and days per week actually worked.

6. CV, CR, SR–MX, February 6, 1907.

7. CV, CR, June 5, 6, 7, 10, and 12, 1911; CV, CR, September 28 and 29, and October 4, 5, 7, 8, 9, 10, 12, 13, 14, and 16, 1911.

8. DT, *Boletín mensual del Departamento del Trabajo,* year 1, no. 1, July 1913, 3.

9. CV, CR, SR–MX, January 1 and 19, 1912; CV, CR, SR–MX, April 26, 1912.

10. CV, CR, SR–MX, July 16, 1912.

11. CV, CR, SR–MX, February 20, 1915, and April 7, 1915; CD, CR, telegram from Marcos López Jiménez to CIDOSA, April 2, 1915.

12. CD, CR, telegram from Marcos López Jiménez to CIDOSA, April 2, 1915.

13. CV, CR, SR–MX, August 23, 1915; CD, CR, letter from Río Blanco to the Department of Labor of Veracruz, August 10, 1915.

14. CV, CR, SR–MX, October 19, 1915.

15. CV, CR, SR–MX, January 18, 1916.

16. See Gómez-Galvarriato, "The Impact of Revolution," table A5.4.

17. CV, CR, SR–MX, February 21, 1916.

18. CV, CR, SR–MX, May 16, 1916. Newspapers reported that bakers, electricians, and tramway, telephone, and potable water workers in Mexico City were also part of this strike. *El Nacional,* May 23, 1916.

19. There is a problem in defining the equivalence between "Veracruz" notes and "infalsificables." A government decree dated May 19, 1916, sets its equivalence as 4 to 1. However CIVSA documents set the equivalence as 5 to 1 during the first week of June, as 8 to 1 during the second week, and as 10 to 1 thereafter.

20. CV, CR, SR–MX, June 20, 1916.

21. CV, CR, SR–MX, September 12, 1916, and October 24, 1916.

22. CD, CR, MX–Río Blanco (hereafter RB), October 27 and 30, November 1 and 17, 1916.

23. *El Nacional,* October 31, November 1, November 7, November 14, and November 21, 1916.

24. Bernardo García Díaz, *Textiles del Valle de Orizaba (1880–1925)* (Xalapa: Universidad Veraruzana, 1990), 203–247.

25. CV, CR, letter from J. Michel to CCP, April 30, 1917.

26. Ibid.

27. CV, CR, telegram SR–MX, May 3, 1917; *El Pueblo,* May 9, 1917, front page; CV, CR, SR–MX, May 15, 1917.

28. CV, CR, letter from J. Michel to CCP, May 15, 1917.

29. Ibid.

30. CV, CR, letter from J. Michel to CCP, July 28, 1917.

31. CV, CR, letter from J. Michel to CCP, August 22, 1917.

32. CV, CR, letter from J. Michel to CCP, June 19, 1917.

33. CV, AC, January 23 and 30, 1923, and October 28, 1924.

34. CV, AC, January 2 and March 4 and 25, 1924.

35. México, Secretaría de la Economía Nacional [Moisés T. de la Peña], *La industria textil en México: El problema obrero y los problemas económicos* (Mexico City: Talleres Gráficos de la Nación, 1934), 22.

36. For these correlations, data per state were taken from: Mexico, Dirección General de Estadística [Antonio Peñafiel], *Anuario Estadístico de 1893* (Mexico City, 1894);

México, Secretaría de Hacienda y Crédito Público, Departamento de Impuestos Especiales, Sección de Hilados y Tejidos, Cuadro No. 1, semestre del 1° de mayo al 31 de octubre de 1925 (mimeo).

37. Labor efficiency refers to the number of machines each worker tended. The index is adjusted to a per-shift basis, considering a 12-hour shift for 1893, an 8-hour shift for 1925, and a 55-hour week as a common basis for comparison. These calculations replicate the technique followed in Gregory Clark, "Why Isn't the Whole World Developed? Lessons from the Cotton Mills," *Journal of Economic History* 47, no. 1 (1987). Data for looms, spindles, and workers per state were taken from: México, *Anuario Estadístico de 1893,* and México, Secretaría de Hacienda y Crédito Público, Departamento de Impuestos Especiales, Sección de Hilados y Tejidos, Cuadro No. 1, semestre del 1° de mayo al 31 de octubre de 1925. Data for wages taken from United States, Special Consular Reports, *Money and Prices in Foreign Countries* (Washington, D.C.: Government Printing Office, 1896); and México, *La industria textil en México.*

38. CV, AC, February 16, 1926.

39. México, *La industria textil en México,* 65–66.

40. CV, AC, April 26, 1927, and December 13, 1927.

41. Variance of wages reported in Mexico, Secretaría de Hacienda y Crédito Público, Departamento de Impuestos Especiales, Sección de Hilados y Tejidos, cuadro no.1, semestre del 1° de mayo al 31 de octubre de 1925 and semestre del 1° de mayo al 31 de octubre de 1929.

42. México, Secretaría de Hacienda y Crédito Público, Departamento de Impuestos Especiales, Sección de Hilados y Tejidos, cuadro no.1, semestre del 1° de mayo al 31 de octubre de 1929.

43. Memoria de Hacienda, 1909–1910, document no. 225, "Cuadros de precios de artículos de primera necesidad formados por el Departamento de Crédio y Comercio." We used the average prices of the year reported in that source and in the *Semana Mercantil.*

44. Caloric and protein contents were calculated using the tables provided by USDA National Nutrient Database, 2008, www.nal.usda.gov.

45. A liter of pulque with 48 hours of fermentation has 1 gram of protein and 4.75 grams of sugars plus several minerals and vitamins. It is 10.35% alcohol. Mario Cervantes-Contreras and Aura Marina Pedroza-Rodríguez, "El pulque: características microbiológicas y contenido alcohólico mediante espectroscopia Raman," *Nova: Publicación Científica en Ciencias Biomédicas* 5, no. 8 (2007): 135.

46. Comité Técnico para la Medición de la Pobreza, "Medición de la pobreza: Variantes metodológicas y estimación prelliminar," in Miguel Székely, ed., *Números que mueven al mundo: La medición de la pobreza en México* (Mexico City: SEDESOL, CIDE, ANUIES, Porrúa, 2005).

47. The figure for the United States is for the whole manufacturing industry. According to the Census of Manufactures, the average "normal" workweek fell from 57.31 hours in 1909 to 51.26 hours in 1919. Robert Whaples, "Winning the Eight-Hour Day, 1909–1919," *Journal of Economic History* 50, no. 2 (1990): 394.

48. UIA, GPDC, 31:8691, letter from A. Vargas to Carlos Herrera, Jefe Político del Cantón de Orizaba, July 5, 1906. This coincides with what CIDOSA reports as their working hours for weavers and other workers that were paid by piecework.

49. CIDOSA, 72/6, reported that the working day was twelve hours on average. UIA, GPDC, 31:8690, letter from G. A. Hartington to Carlos Herrera, Jefe Político del Cantón de Orizaba, June 30, 1906.

50. UIA, GPDC, 31:8690, letter from G. A. Hartington to Carlos Herrera, Jefe Político del Cantón de Orizaba, June 30, 1906.

51. At "San Bruno," working hours went from 6:00 a.m. to 6:00 p.m. At "Lucas Martín" work paid by the day went until 6:00 p.m., and when they worked longer, extra wage was assigned. "La Probidad" reported that the work shift was twelve hours. UIA, GPDC, 31:8661, letter from Fdo Todd to Teodoro A. Dehesa, June 26, 1906; 8662, letter from Rafael Neve to Teodoro A. Dehesa, June 27, 1906; 8663, letter from Gabriel J. Montes to Teodoro A. Dehesa, June 29, 1906; 8664, letter from Mijares to Teodoro Dehesa, June 30, 1906.

52. Graham W. A. Clark, *Cotton Goods in Latin America, Part I,* ed. U.S. Bureau of Foreign and Domestic Commerce, vol. 31, Special Agent Series (Washington D.C.: Government Printing Office, 1909), 24.

53. "Carta abierta de los obreros del Cantón de Orizaba al Jefe Político," *El Paladín,* May 12, 1907, 2; "Orizaba al vuelo y sus alrederes," *El Paladín,* May 19, 1907, 2; "Las huelgas: ¿Quiénes son los verdaderos culpables?," *El Paladín,* May 23, 1907, 2; "Orizaba al vuelo y sus alredores," *El Paladín,* May 30, 1907, 2; "Orizaba al vuelo y sus alredores," *El Paladín,* June 6, 1907, 2.

54. "Un arco iris en el cielo industrial: Los obreros de Río Blanco mejoran: Los polos se comunican," *El Cosmopolita,* June 16, 1907, 1.

55. CV, CR, MX–SR, June 17 and 18, 1907; CV, AC, August 2, 1910.

56. CV, AC, January 22, 1912, and August 20, 1912; CD, CR, RB to Cerritos and Coco-lapan, January 22, 1912; CV, CR, MX–SR, June 18 and July 4, 1912.

57. "Decreto No. 11. Cándido Aguilar. Gobernador y Comandante Militar del Estado Libre y Soberano de Veracruz-Llave, a sus habitantes, sabed," art. 2, AGN, DT, 88/21/2–3.

58. "Decreto 7. Ley sobre Descanso Dominical en el Estado de Veracruz," Gaceta Oficial del Estado de Veracruz 4-X-1914.

59. CV, AC, March 30, 1915; CD, CR, CIDOSA, RB to Department of Labor, Veracruz, August 10, 1915; CV, AC, August 17 and 24, 1915; CD, CR, RB to Governor of the State of Veracruz, September 11, 1915; CV, AC, September 7, 1915.

60. CD, CR, RB-MX, December 14, 1916; CD, CR, RB-MX, Cocolapan, Cerritos, and San Lorenzo, September 17, 1915; CV, AC, September 21, 1915.

61. CV, AC, April 17, 24, and 30, 1917; CD, CR, RB to Governor at Córdoba, June 13, 1917.

62. CV, AC, July 22 and 29, 1919.

63. CD, CR, RB, Circular 115, August 18, 1924.

64. CV, AC, November 26, 1919. On this date CIVSA donated uniforms to thirty members of the factory's music band.

65. OHMW, interview with Mr. Gonzalo García Ortíz by Bernardo García Díaz, Ciudad Mendoza, Veracruz, July 9, 1975; interview with Mr. Delfino Huerta by Ana Laura Delgado Rannauro, Nogales, Veracruz, August 26, 1975; interview with Mr. Rafael Mendoza by Rosario Domínguez, Orizaba, Veracruz, July 27, 1975.

66. Ana Laura Delgado Rannauro, "El sindicato de Santa Rosa y el movimiento obrero de Orizaba Veracruz" (BA thesis, Universidad Veracruzana, 1977).

67. Whaples, "Winning the Eight-Hour Day," 399.

68. Given that half of the workday reduction took place between 1907 and 1913, and that 50% of the workday reduction was explained by economic growth in the United States. This would be an upper-bound estimate, because the Mexican economy did not expand as much as the U.S. economy did during this period.

69. México, *La industria textil en México,* 34.

## 8. A Revolution in Daily Life

1. Francisco Zapata, *Enclaves y polos de desarrollo en México: Notas para discusión* (Mexico City: El Colegio de México, 1985), 33; Francisco Zapata, "Enclaves y sistemas de relaciones industriales en América Latina," *Revista Mexicana de Sociología* 2:723–726.

2. John Dunlop, *Industrial Relations Systems* (New York: Holt, 1958).

3. Bernardo García Díaz, *Un pueblo fabril del Porfiriato, Santa Rosa Veracruz* (Cd. Mendoza, Veracruz: Fondo Mendocino para la Cultura y las Artes, 1997).

4. CV, AC, July 4, 1898.

5. García Díaz, *Un pueblo fabril,* 69.

6. CV, AC, September 5, 1898, and January 15, 1900. CV, AC, February 6, 1899; September 18, 1899; February 16, 1903; April 15, 1907; December 24, 1907; July 11, 1911; April 29, 1913; and March 23, 1920.

7. CV, AC, June 7, 1897; CV, AAG 1899, March 15, 1900.

8. CV, AC, May 22, 1897; CV, AAG 1906, April 2, 1907; CV, AC, October 24, 1906.

9. CV, AC, September 18, 1918.

10. CV, AC, November 5, 1918.

11. CV, AC, August 7, 1928; CV, AAG 1906, April 2, 1907; CV, AC, May 14, 1929.

12. CV, AC, July 4, 1922, and November 29, 1927; CV, October 15, 1929. The taxes that would be deducted were those of land taxes and patents.

13. CD, CR, "Manifestaciones de fincas urbanas a la Receptoría de Rentas del Edo. en Río Blanco," October 1, 1922; CD, CR, "Manifestaciones de fincas urbanas a la Receptoría de Rentas del Edo. en Río Blanco," October 15, 1926.

14. Ana Laura Delgado Rannauro, "El sindicato de Santa Rosa y el movimiento obrero de Orizaba Veracruz" (BA thesis, Universidad Veracruzana, 1977), 85, 89.

15. CV, AC, June 7, 1897; CV, AC, February 21, 1898.

16. Graham W. A. Clark, *Cotton Goods in Latin America* (Washington, D.C.: Government Printing Office, 1909), pt. 1, 26.

17. CV, "Lista de trabajadores." CV, AC, September 7, 1904; July 10, 1905; July 17, 1905.

18. For example, M. Diez y Cia, the owner of the "Río Blanco" and "El Fenix" stores, owned several wooden living quarters for workers close to Santa Rosa from 1907 to 1922. CV, AC, July 25, 1922.

19. Andrew Grant Wood, "¡Viva la Revolución Social! Postrevolutionary Tenant Protests and State Housing Reform in Veracruz, Mexico," in Pineo Ronn and James A. Baer, eds., *Cities of Hope: People, Protests, and Progress in Urbanizing Latin America, 1870–1930* (Boulder, Colo.: Westview Press, 1998), 91.

20. OHMW, interview with Mr. Gonzalo San Juan Hernández by Bety and Pepe, Orizaba, Veracruz, July 20, 1976; "También en Pluviosilla está constituido el Sindicato de Inquilinos que trabajará contra las rentas caras" and "En el Teatro Llave el 2 del presente se nombró al Comité Ejecutivo," *Pro-Paria,* April 9, 1922, 1–4.

21. CV, AAG 1906, April 2, 1907; CV, AC, November 8, 1910; CV, AAG 1911, April 9, 1912; CV, AC, April 6, 1920; CD, CR, RB to MX, May 2, 1924.

22. Roberto Rives Sánchez, *La Constitución Mexicana hacia el siglo XXI* (Mexico City: Plaza y Valdés Editores, 2000), 343.

23. Ley del Trabajo del Estado Libre y Soberano de Veracruz-Llave, January 14, 1918. Gobierno Constitucional del Estado de Veracruz-Llave, *Colección de Leyes: Decretos y Circulares año de 1918* (Orizaba, 1918); CD, CR, RB to Francisco V. Lara, January 24, 1918.

24. CV, AC, November 14, 1917, and March 23, 1920; CV, AAG 1924, June 7, 1924.

25. García Díaz, *Un pueblo fabril,* 83; interview by the author with José Carrasco Abrego, Santa Rosa, Veracruz, June 8, 1998.

26. CD, AC, Fco V. Lara to RB Cidosa, January 24, 1918.

27. Wood, "¡Viva la Revolución Social!," 93.

28. Andrew Grant Wood, *Revolution in the Street: Women, Workers, and Urban Portest in Veracruz, 1870–1927* (Wilmington, Del.: Scholarly Resources, 2001), 30.

29. México, Secretaría de Agricultura y Fomento, Dirección de Estadística, *Tercer censo de población de los Estados Unidos Mexicanos: Verificado el 27 de octubre de 1910* (Mexico City: Dirección de Estadística, 1918).

30. Wood, "¡Viva la Revolución Social!," 94; CD, CR, RB to RB Municipal President, January 10, 1918.

31. CD, CR, RB to RB Municipal President, January 31, 1918; CV, AC, February 21, 1918; CD, CR, RB and SR to Governor, January 26, 1918; CD, CR, letter from RB to Receptor de Rentas of Río Blanco, June 29, 1918.

32. CD, CR, Acta Orizaba, March 22, 1918; CD, CR, Acta del Juzgado 2° Municipal, Nogales, April 12, 1918; "Manifestaciones de fincas urbanas a la Receptoría de Rentas del Edo. en Río Blanco," October 1, 1922.

33. Octavio García Mundo, *El movimiento inquilinario de Veracruz, 1922* (Mexico City: Sep-Setentas, 1976); Wood, "¡Viva la Revolución Social!," 67–87; *El Dictámen,* March 7, 8, 9, and 10, 1922. Cadastral value is the value of property registered before the local authority to serve as the basis for the calculation of property tax; it is generally below market value.

34. Wood, "¡Viva la Revolución Social!," 119–121; *El Dictámen,* February 5, 1922.

35. OHMW, interview with Mr. Gonzalo San Juan Hernández by Bety and Pepe, Orizaba, Veracruz, July 20, 1976.

36. Ibid.

37. Mundo, *El movimiento inquilinario de Veracruz,* 151; *El Dictámen,* July 2 and 4, 1922.

38. Wood, "¡Viva la Revolución Social!," 113. Several articles in *Pro-Paria* were highly critical of this law. See, for example, "Los propietarios de casas de alquiler continúan atropellando inquilinos" January 21, 1928, 1–8, or "Sobre el asunto inquilinario," April 28, 1928, 5–6.

39. CD, Convenio, CIDOSA, SOSRB, October 29, 1924.

40. CD, CR, RB to CIDOSA MX, June 1, 1925.

41. CD, CR, Cámara de Propietarios, Orizaba, Srio José Lama, VP Alberto de la Llave to Cocolapan Administrator, January 27, 1925; and RB to Cámara de Propietarios de Orizaba, January 29, 1925.

42. CV, AAG 1900, March 1, 1901. These figures were even higher if we consider the value of the premises net of depreciation; CV, AAG 1901, April 1, 1902.

43. CD, "Demostración de los productos por arrendamiento de casas y terrenos, adyacentes a la fábrica de Río Blanco," January 8, 1918.

44. Rives, *La Constitución Mexicana.*

45. CD, CR, Gaceta Oficial, 28, March 6, 1923; CD, CR, Ramón Carrillo E. to RB CIDOSA, March 7, 1923, March 18, 1923; RB to Ramón Carrillo E., April 18, 1923; RB to Ramón Carrillo E, May 9, 1923; RB to Ramón Carrillo E., October 27, 1923; RB to Ramón Carrillo E., October 27, 1923; Ramón Carrillo E. to RB CIDOSA, October 29, 1923.

46. Wood, "¡Viva la Revolución Social!," 115.

47. OHMW, interview with Mr. Gonzalo San Juan by Bety and Pepe, Orizaba, Veracruz, July 20, 1975.

48. CD, CR, "Fraccionamiento del terreno Barrio Motzorongo," January 1923.

49. Wood, *Revolution in the Street,* 188–189; Bernardo García Díaz, *La escuela esfuerzo obrero,* Cuadernos del Museo Comunitario de Ciudad Mendoza Veracruz (Ciudad Mendoza: Fomeca, 1998), 2.

50. CD, CR, RB to RB Márquez, May 16, 1924; RCE to CIDOSA MX, May 18, 1924; and CIDOSA MX to RCE, May 19, 1924. This sale was noted in the public registry on August 12, 1925. CD, CR, "Manifestación" CIDOSA makes of mortgages it holds in Río Blanco, Nogales, and Santa Rosa, January 31, 1930.

51. OHMW, interview with Mr. Gonzalo San Juan by Bety and Pepe, Orizaba, Veracruz July 20, 1975.

52. CD, CR, RB, Resident *(Colono)* Payments 1927–1928 and Rent of RB houses and commercial property 1927–1929; CV, AC, September 4, 1928.

53. CV, AC, November 22, 1922.

54. Carrasco Abrego was a CIVSA worker (a welder) in 1974 when he bought one of CIVSA's houses. To pay for it, 18% of his 75 peso weekly wages was deducted. CIDOSA sold a house to Julieta Almeida's father, a Río Blanco worker, in 1965 for 1,500 pesos that he finished paying in 1970. Information is based on the property deeds. Interview by the author with José Carrasco Abrego, Ciudad Mendoza, Veracruz, June 8, 1998; and interview by the author with Julieta Almeida Herrera, Río Blanco, Veracruz, June 8, 1998.

55. CV, AC, January 2, 1897.

56. This tramway line was built by Jiménez partly with a credit from CIVSA (5,000 pesos), which he paid back through freights. CV, Actas del Consejo, April 21, 1897.

57. Until the end of October 1918, José Fuentes continued to appear as the lessee of the store. CV, Caja Santa Rosa, 1900–1918.

58. CD, CR, A. Reynaud to Río Blanco, several letters; CV, CR, Mexico City–Santa Rosa, August 30, 1910.

59. "El siglo del cisnismo," *El Paladín,* May 16, 1907, 1; accounts by Alberto Lara Rojano and Ernesto Casillas Rojas, CEHSMO oral history project, *Historia Obrera* 2, no. 6 (September 1975): 33–34.

60. García Díaz, *Un pueblo fabril,* 67.

61. CV, AC, February 25, 1897.

62. Ibid., and October 25, 1897. That Eduardo Garcín no longer appears as a board member in the General Assembly of 1907 was perhaps caused by the January 7 events. CD, Asamblea General Ordinaria, March 23, 1906, March 22, 1907, and April 3, 1908; Banamex Archive, R. G. Dunn & Co. private reports from August 28, 1899, to January 11, 1904, 97; CD, CR, letters from Víctor Garcín, Grandes Almacenes, to RB, October 23 and November 23, 1906.

63. A description based on the oral accounts of Alberto Lara Rojano, Ernesto Casilla Rojas, and Cecilio Aguilar Gutiérrez, who worked at Río Blanco in 1907 and were interviewed in the 1970s as part of the oral history project of the Centro de Estudios Históricos del Movimiento Obrero Mexicano (CEHSMO). The information obtained is based on excerpts from the interviews published in *Historia Obrera* 2, no. 6 (September 1975): 33–37.

64. CD, CR, Garcín-RB and RB–Garcín, several letters, January–June 1906; CD, CR, April 9, 1906.

65. "El siglo del cinismo," *El Paladín,* May 16, 1907, 1; "Orizaba al vuelo, Río Blanco," April 5, 1907, 2; "Orizaba al vuelo y sus alrededores," *El Paladín,* May 7, 1908, 2.

66. This can be explained if the company store specialized in products bought by the majority of workers in the middle-income range.

67. CV, payrolls, week 6, 1905 (February 3–9), and week 50, 1906 (December 6–13).

68. CD, checkbook stubs for the second semester of 1905 and for the first semester of 1906. For example, check stubs 3509, 3510, 3564, 3472, 3610.

69. The total value of the payroll was 3,000 pesos.

70. CV, CR, Mexico City–Santa Rosa, January 12, 1907.

71. CV, CR, Mexico City–Santa Rosa, August 30, 1910; CV, Caja Santa Rosa, 1900–1918.

72. CV, AC, April 8, 1907; CV, AC, May 24, 1908.

73. AGN, DT, 15/11; Felipe Remolina Roqueñí, *El Artículo 123* (Mexico City: Ediciones del V Congreso Iberoamericano del Deracho del Trabajo y de Seguridad Social, 1974), 69–70.

74. Gobierno de Veracruz, *Colección de leyes y decretos año de 1918,* 189 and 194.

75. "Orizaba al vuelo y sus alrededores, Río Blanco," *El Paladín,* April 9, 1908, 2.

76. "Orizaba al vuelo y sus alrederdores," *El Paladín,* July 1907, 2; "Orizaba al vuelo y sus alrededores, Santa Rosa," *El Paladín,* June 25, 1908, 3.

77. "Orizaba al vuelo y sus alrededores, Santa Rosa," *El Paladín,* June 25, 1908, 3.

78. Ibid.

79. AGEV Caja 99, Exp. 70, 1915 Cocolapam, "Carta de Pedro Baroja, Nicolás Jiménez y Gumersindo Soriano, al Ciudadano Gobernador y Comandante Militar del Estado de Veracruz, Sr. Agustín A. Millán, 25 de diciembre de 1915."

80. OHMW, interview with Mr. Gonzalo García Ortiz by Bernardo García Díaz, Ciudad Mendoza, Veracruz, July 9, 1975.

81. CV, AC, November 23, 1920.

82. CV, CR, letter from C. Maurel to SR, November 10, 1920; CV, AC, January 4, 1921.

83. In 1928 there were seven cooperative stores in the Orizaba Valley. *Pro-Paria,* special edition, January 7, 1928, 2, with photographs of all the stores.

84. "Informe que rinde el Consejo de Administración de Consumo 'Obreros Federados' de los trabajos verificados el 20 de diciembre de 1922 al 25 del presente mes," *Pro-Paria,* July 5, 1924, 2.

85. Advertisement of the cooperative Obreros Federados, *Pro-Paria,* September 23, 1931, 4; August 10, 1929, 8.

86. Ibid., and March 30, 1929; "Proyecto para la Reorganización de la Cooperativa O. Federados," January 21, 1928, 7; "Creación del Departamento de Cooperativas de la CROM," *Pro-Paria,* December 30, 1927.

87. "Sociedad Cooperativa Obreros Ferderados, balcance del activo y pasivo practicado el 30 de Junio de 1928," *Pro-Paria,* July 21, 1928, 1; "Proyecto para la reorganización de la Cooperativa O. Federados," *Pro-Paria,* January 21, 1928, 2, 7, 8.

88. "Demostración práctica de los beneficios que trae el cooperativismo," *Pro-Paria,* March 16, 1929, 8.

89. CV, AC, June 19, 1928.

90. "Fue inaugurado el Banco Cooperativo Obrero de Santa Rosa, Ver," *Pro-Paria,* April 28, 1928, 1–8.

91. OHMW, interview with Mr. Gonzalo García Ortíz by Ana Laura Delgado Rannauro, Ciudad Mendoza, Veracruz, July 9, 1975.

92. Delgado Rannauro, "El sindicato de Santa Rosa," 111–114.

93. See "Memoria que rinde el Jefe Político del Cantón de Orizaba al C. Gobernador del Estado de Veracruz, 9 de marzo de 1895," in Soledad García Morales and José Velasco Toro, eds., *Memorias e informes de jefes políticos autoridades del régimen Porfirista, 1883–1911, Estado de Veracruz* (Xalapa: Universidad Veracruzana, 1997), 282–283.

94. See, for example, Mary Kay Vaughan, *The State, Education, and Social Class in Mexico, 1880–1928* (DeKalb: Northern Illinois University Press, 1982), and Mílada Bazant, *Historia de la educación durante el Porfiriato* (Mexico City: El Colegio de México, 1993).

95. Bazant, *Historia de la educación,* 32–33, 40–41, 86.

96. Moisés T. de la Peña, *Veracruz económico* (Mexico City: Gobierno del Estado de Veracruz, 1946), 2:507.

97. Vaughan, *State, Education, and Social Class,* 122.

98. Ibid., 135.

99. James W. Wilkie, *La Revolución Mexicana* (Mexico City: Fondo de Cultura Económica, 1987), 55.

100. De la Peña, *Veracruz económico,* 501.

101. "Fundación de colegios en Orizaba," *El Paladín,* July 29, 1906, 3; "Rurales obligan a firmar voluntariamente a Obreros," *El Paladín,* August 2, 1906, 2.

102. Gabriel Gavira, *General de Brigada Gabriel Gavira: Su actuación político militar revolucionaria* (Mexico City: A. del Bosque, 1933), 10.

103. OHMW, interview with Mr. Rafael Mendoza by Rosario Dominguez, Orizaba, Veracruz, July 27, 1975.

104. "Orizaba al vuelo, Santa Rosa," *El Paladín,* July 7, 1907, 3.

105. CD, CR, Fco G. Vazquez, head of the Comisión de Instrucción Pública in Nogales to E. Ropiot, Administrator of San Lorenzo, January 3, 1912; CD, CR, San Lorenzo to Ayuntamiento de Nogales, January 4, 1912; CD, CR, Río Blanco to Romero, March 4, 1912.

106. CD, CR, Avelino Bolaños, Consejero de Instituciones para Escolares, Veracruz, to Río Blanco, San Lorenzo, Cerritos, and Cocolapan, January 13, 1916.

107. CD, CR, CIVSA to CIDOSA, February 4, 1916; Ezequiel Pérez Palacios to RB Administrator, September 4, 1918; Ezequiel Pérez Palacios to RB Administrator, October 2, 1918; RB Municipal President to Spitalier, October 15, 1918; Ezequiel Pérez Palacios, to Pedro Durán, January 3, 1919; CV, AC, July 30, 1918.

108. Delgado Rannauro, "El sindicato de Santa Rosa," 78–79, 121.

109. Manuel Reyna Muñoz, *La CROM y la CSUM en la industria textil (1928–1932)* (Mexico City: Universidad Autónoma Metropolitana Unidad Azcapotzalco, 1988).

110. Ibid., 93–95.

111. García Díaz, "La escuela esfuerzo obrero," 4.

112. OHMW, Interview with Mr. Gonzalo San Juan by Bety and Pepe, Orizaba Ver. July 20, 1975.

113. Oral Histories of Mexican Workers, Interview with Mr. Delfino Huerta by Ana Laura Delgado Rannauro, Nogales, Veracruz, August 26, 1975.

114. OHMW, Interview with Mr. Valentín Cueto, Orizaba, n.d.

115. OHMW, Interview with Mr. Gonzalo García Ortíz by Bernardo García, Orizaba Ver., July 9, 1975.

116. Censo y División Territorial del Edo. de Veracruz verificados en 1900, 116–117.

117. "La instrucción pública se difunde brotando de ochocientas y tantas escuelas pero los brotes no llegarán al pueblo" *El Paladín,* February 2, 1908, 2. Letter written as a poem full of satire by "Melchor, Gaspar and Balthasar." They chose these names as an obvious remembrance of the slaughter of January 7, since January 6 is the day of the Three Wise Men.

118. "La instrucción pública abandonada," *El Paladín,* February 9, 1908, 2.

119. Delgado Rannauro, "El sindicato de Santa Rosa," 76.

120. CV, AC, March 4, 1913.

121. CD, CR, MX to RB, August 16, 1923; Natalia Rivera to RB, May 4, 1915; Natalia Rivera, Cerritos, to José Reynayd, RB, January 21, 1915; Durán RB. to Natalia Rivera, February 11, 1915; Natalia Rivera to José Reynaud, February 17, 1915; CD, Cuestionario de Salarios, August 1921.

122. CD, CR, MX to RB, August 16, 1923.

123. CD, CR, Ramonada and eleven others to RB CIDOSA, June 29, 1921 and RB to MX, July 7, 1921; CV, AC, April 26, 1921.

124. CV, AC, September 4, 1917.
125. Delgado Rannauro, "El sindicato de Santa Rosa," 78–79.
126. García Díaz, "La escuela esfuerzo obrero," 5–6. In 1940 Orizaba spent 76.5% of its income in education, Nogales 72.6%, and Río Blanco 65.3%. These numbers compare to the 56% average reported for the forty municipalities of Veracruz. De la Peña, *Veracruz económico,* 508–509; Archivo del Sindicato del Santa Rosa, folio 800, January 3, 1928, quoted by Delgado Rannauro, "El sindicato de Santa Rosa," 121.
127. Delgado Rannauro, "El sindicato de Santa Rosa," 79–80.
128. CV, AC, August 29, 1922. By this time the first four years of elementary school were considered primary school and the next two years, secondary school *(escuela superior).*
129. Delgado Rannauro, "El sindicato de Santa Rosa," 80–81; García Díaz, "La escuela esfuerzo obrero," 10–13; Archivo del Sindicato de Santa Rosa, CR, Elliezer Ollivier to the Sindicato de Santa Rosa, March 20, 1926.
130. Acisclo Pérez Servín was one of Santa Rosa's major education advocates. A textile worker since childhood, he joined the Ejército Libertador del Sur under Zapata, and returned around 1919 to work as a weaver in CIVSA. He was municipal president of Santa Rosa from 1922 to 1923 and president of the pro-school committee of Santa Rosa's union from its inception. In 1926 he was one of the twenty-five workers elected by the general assembly for the committee that would look after the construction of the "América" school. García Díaz, "La escuela esfuerzo obrero," 11–17.
131. Delgado Rannauro,"El sindicato de Santa Rosa," 85.
132. García Díaz, "La escuela esfuerzo obrero," 19–20.
133. Delgado Rannauro, "El sindicato de Santa Rosa," 79–80, and 119–121; García Díaz, "La escuela esfuerzo obrero," 10.
134. Vaughan, *State, Education, and Social Class,* 152; García Díaz, "La escuela esfuerzo obrero," 10.
135. "Hacen mucha falta escuelas," *Pro-Paria,* July 30, 1928, 1, 8.
136. OHMW, interview with Mr. Macario Ventura Ochoa by Ana Laura Delgado Rannauro, Santa Rosa, n.d.; interview with Mr. Delfino Huerta by Ana Laura Delgado Rannauro, Nogales, Veracruz, August 26, 1975; interview with Mr. Rafael Mendoza by Rosario Dominguez, Orizaba, Veracruz, July 27, 1975; interview with Mr. Gonzalo San Juan Hernández by Bety and Pepe, Orizaba, Veracruz, July 20, 1976.

9. The Impact of the Mexican Revolution on CIVSA's Performance

1. CV, AC, April 23, 1899; CV, AAG 1906, April 2, 1907. This fact goes against the idea that Mexican manufacturing firms faced a chronic lack of demand, as stated in Stephen Haber, *Industry and Underdevelopment: The Industrialization of Mexico, 1890–1940* (Stanford: Stanford University Press, 1989).
2. An excellent analysis of the 1907 crisis can be found in Robert F. Bruner and Sean D. Carr, *The Panic of 1907: Lessons Learned from the Market's Perfect Storm* (Hoboken, N.J.: Wiley, 2007).

3. CV, AAG 1908, April 13, 1909; CV, AAG 1909, April 19, 1910.

4. CV, AAG 1911, April 9, 1912.

5. CV, AAG 1912, April 9, 1913.

6. CV, AC, July 8, 1913, November 4, 1913 and December 2, 1913.

7. The Mexican Central Bank was a private bank established on February 15, 1899. It was neither a central bank nor a bank of issue; it acted as a sort of clearing agent for the state banks. United States, National Monetary Commission [Charles Conant], *The Banking System of Mexico* (Washington, D.C.: Government Printing Office, 1910), 41–53.

8. *The Mexican Year Book, 1914* (London: McCorquodale and Co., 1915), 21.

9. CV, AC, January 21, 1913.

10. CV, CR, CIVSA-CCP, December 24, 1913.

11. CV, AAG 1913, April 18, 1914.

12. CV, CR, CIVSA-CCP, January 14, 1914; CV, AC, January 31, 1914, February 7, 1914; CV, AC, October 20, 1914.

13. CV, AAG 1914, July 6, 1915.

14. The adoption of the gold peso meant in practice the adoption of the U.S. dollar as the monetary standard, because gold pesos were considered at a 2:1 exchange rate with the dollar from that year to 1928. CV, AAG 1915, April 29, 1916.

15. For a detailed account of banks' worsening situation in these years, see Noel Maurer, *The Power and the Money: The Mexican Financial System, 1876–1932* (Stanford: Stanford University Press, 2002), 141–159.

16. Ibid., 148.

17. CV, CR, SR-MX, "Nota de Giros Remitidos de Santa Rosa a los Sres. K. Mandell Co.," "Nota de Giros en Dollars en Cartera a Santa Rosa," "Nota Indicando los Clientes que Han Entregado los Valores Sobre Estados Unidos," "Remitidos a K. Mandell Co.," monthly through 1915, 1916, 1917.

18. Aurora Gómez-Galvarriato and Gabriela Recio, "The Indispensable Service of Banks: Commercial Transactions, Industry, and Banking in Revolutionary Mexico," *Enterpise & Society* 8, no. 1 (2007): 68–105.

19. CV, AAG 1916, July 3, 1917.

20. CV, AAG 1917, May 14, 1918.

21. CV, AAG 1918, May 27, 1919.

22. CV, AAG 1919, May 3, 1920.

23. CV, CR, CIVSA-CCP, March 26, 1920, and December 31, 1920.

24. CV, CR, CIVSA-CCP, December 31, 1920.

25. CV, AAG 1921, May 28, 1921.

26. CV, AAG 1920, May 28, 1921.

27. CV, AAG 1921, May 31, 1922.

28. Gómez-Galvarriato and Recio, "The Indispensable Service of Banks."

29. CV, CR, CIVSA-CCP, January 9, 1921.

30. CV, CR, CIVSA-CCP, November 25, 1922, and March 18, 1923.

31. CV, CR, CIVSA-CCP, July 6, 1923.

32. CV, CR, C. Maure to Sres. Maitland Coppel & Co., New York, June 13, 1922; C. Maure to Agency of The Royal Bank of Canada, New York, June 13, 1922; C. Maure

to Sres. K. Mandell & Co., New York, June 13, 1922; C. Maure to First National Bank del Río, Texas, June 14, 1922.

33. CV, AC, March 27, 1928.

34. CV, AAG 1921, May 31, 1922; CV, AAG 1922, May 1, 1923; CV, AAG 1923, June 7, 1924.

35. CV, AC, February 6, 1924; CV, CR, CIVSA-CCP, December 24, 1913, January 4, February 5, and March 24, 1924; CV, AC, January 8 and 29, 1924; CV, AC, March 24, 1924.

36. CV, AAG 1924, March 30, 1925.

37. CV, AAG 1925, April 6, 1926; CV, AAG 1926, April 7, 1927.

38. CV, AAG 1927, May 22, 1928.

39. CV, AAG 1928, June 25, 1929.

40. CV, AAG 1929, June 30, 1930.

41. CV, AC, October 1, 1929.

42. CV, AAG 1930, June 22, 1931.

43. Haber, *Industry and Underdevelopment*, 110–113.

44. The return on assets is calculated by dividing net income by total assets, and the return on equity by dividing net income by total equity. Depreciation was calculated assuming a life span of forty years for buildings, twenty years for machinery, and ten years for furniture and equipment. For further details, see Aurora Gómez-Galvarriato, "The Impact of Revolution: Business and Labor in the Mexican Textile Industry, Orizaba, Veracruz, 1900–1930" (PhD diss., Harvard University, 1999), chap. 7 table 3 and appendix.

45. The dividend yield is calculated by dividing a share's dividend earnings by its market price in a particular year. Haber, *Industry and Underdevelopment*, 111.

46. The average yield of government bonds includes the Bonos de la Deuda Interior, Bonos de la Deuda Consolidada, and the Empréstito of 1899. The average yield of bank stock includes the stock of Banco Nacional de México, Banco de Londres y México, and Banco Central Mexicano. Sources: For government bonds, ibid., 118; for bank stock, Noel Maurer, "Finance and Oligarchy: Banks, Politics, and Economic Growth in Mexico, 1876–1928" (PhD diss., Stanford University, 1997), 18.

47. The annual rate of return is calculated by adding the change in the value of stock from year to year to the dividend paid per year.

48. The internal rate of return (also called yield at maturity) is the required return that results in a zero net present value when it is used as the rate of discount. The net present value is the difference between the present value of the future cash flows and the cost of the investment, discounted by the rate the best alternative investment would provide. An investment should be accepted if the net present value is positive and rejected if it is negative.

49. The rate of return of American corporate bonds in 1900 (returning after 10, 20, and 30 years) of 3.3% was chosen because it was the best rate available for a sufficiently long period of maturity to allow for comparison. U.S. Department of Commerce, *Historical Statistics of the United States* (Washington, D.C.: Government Printing Office, 1975), 1004.

50. CV, AAG 1912, April 9, 1913.

51. From 1984 to 1988 there was a substantial reduction of the tariff fractions subject to import permits. Average ad valorem tariffs went down from 42.5% in December 1985 to 13.8% in December 1987. Carlos Márquez Padilla, "La competitividad de la industria textil," in Fernando Clavijo and José Casar, comps., *La industria Mexicana en el mercado mundial: Elementos para una política industrial* (Mexico City: Fondo de Cultura Económica, 1994), 95–157, 110–111.

52. A similar result is explained in Karl Marx, *Capital* (New York: Vintage, 1977), 1:536, quoted in William Lazonick, *Competitive Advantage on the Shopfloor* (Cambridge, Mass.: Harvard University Press, 1990), 63.

53. Adam Przeworski, *Capitalism and Social Democracy* (Cambridge: Cambridge University Press, 1985), 165.

54. See Aurora Gómez-Galvarriato, "The Political Economy of Protectionism: The Mexican Textile Industry, 1900–1950," in Sebastian Edwards et al., eds., *The Decline of Latin American Economies: Growth, Institutions, and Crises* (Chicago: University of Chicago Press, 2007), 384–386.

55. Mexico, Secretaría de la Economía Nacional [Juan Chávez Orozco], "Monografía Económico-Industrial de la Fabricación de Hilados y Tejidos de Algodón" (Mexico City, 1933), unpublished mimeo, 66.

56. Compañía Industrial de Orizaba, "Segunda ponencia de la Compañía Industrial de Orizaba S.A.," in *Memoria General de la Primera Convención Mexicana de Empresarios Textiles (Rama del Algodón), April 9–12, 1945* (Mexico City: National Advertising Service, 1945), 176–180; and Jesús Rivero Quijano, *La revolución industrial y la industria textil en México* (Mexico City: Joaquín Porrúa, 1990), 2:239–248, 257–262, 279–280.

57. Quijano, *La revolución industrial,* 278.

58. Ibid.

59. Ibid.

60. Mexico, "Monografía económico-industrial," 67.

61. Ibid., 418.

62. Ibid.

63. In England between 1896 and 1914, spinning frames were enlarged in order to maximize effort and at the same time comply with the wage lists. Lazonick, *Competitive Advantage on the Shopfloor,* 163.

64. United Nations, Departamento de Asuntos Económicos, *Productividad de la mano de obra en la industria textil algodonera de cinco países Latinoamericanos* (New York: United Nations, 1951), 14.

65. AGN, DT, 979/3, Saco Lowell Shops to Presidencia de la Convención, August 7, 1926.

66. CV, AC, July 12, 1927.

67. CV, AC, May 14, 1929.

68. Mexico, "Monografía Económico-Industrial," 67; Mexico, Secretaría de la Economía Nacional [Moisés T. de la Peña], *La industria textil en México: El problema obrero y los problemas económicos* (Mexico City: Talleres Gráficos de la Nación), 187–191.

69. Armando Razo, "The Rate of Productivity in Mexico, 1850–1933: Evidence from the Cotton Textile Industry," *Journal of Latin American Studies* 30, no. 2 (1998): 490.

70. Mexico, "Monografía Económico-Industrial," 63.

71. Daniel Cosío Villegas, *La cuestión arancelaria en México* (Mexico City: Ediciones del Centro de Estudios Económicos, 1932), 99.

72. Alberto Pani, "Alocución de bienvenida a los delegados por el Sr. Ingeniero D. Alberto Pani, secretario de industria y comercio," in Mexico, Secretaría de la Industria, Comercio y Trabajo, *Reseña y memorias del Primer Congreso Nacional de Industriales* (Mexico City: Secretaría de Industria, Comercio y Trabajo, 1918), 46.

73. Graciela Márquez, "Protección y cambio institucional en México (1910–1929)," in Rafael Dobado et al., eds., *México y España: ¿Historias económicas paralelas?* (Mexico City: Fondo de Cultura Económica, 2007), 385–389.

74. Increased foreign competition must be part of the reason CIVSA's markup (price/costs) decreased from 96% in the 1904–1908 period to 45% in the 1923–1927 period.

75. Compañía Industrial de Orizaba, "Segunda ponencia," 175.

76. Mexico, Secretaría del Trabajo y Previsión Social [Miguel A. Quintana], *Los problemas de la industria textil del algodón* (Mexico City: Talleres Gráficos de la Nación, 1934), 13–17.

77. CV, AAG, February 26, 1927.

78. "Reglas generales de modernización de la industria textil del algodón y sus mixturas, acuerdo y solicitud relativos a las mimas," *Diario Oficial*, 184, no. 30 (February 6, 195): 4–10.

79. International Bank for Reconstruction and Development, *The Economic Development of Mexico* (Baltimore: Johns Hopkins University Press, 1953), 69; CV, AAG, February 28, 1928.

80. Javier Barajas Manzano, *Aspectos de la industria textil de algodón en México* (Mexico City: Instituto Mexicano de Investigaciones Económicas, 1959), 51.

81. CV, AAG, March 20, 1950; CV, AAG, March 21, 1951.

82. International Bank for Reconstruction and Development, *Economic Development of Mexico*, 69.

83. "Reglas generales," *Diario Oficial*, February 6, 1951.

84. Letter from several firms that were members of the Unión Nacional de Industriales para la Modernización Textil to the president of the Convención Mixta Obrero-Patronal del Contrato Colectivo de Trabajo de la Industria Textil del Algodón y sus Mixturas, in "ACTA de clausura de la Convención Obrero-Patronal, revisora del Contrato Colectivo de Trabajo de Carácter Obligatorio y Tarifas de la Industria Textil del Algodón y sus Mixturas," *Diario Oficial*, 182, no. 43 (October 23, 1950), sec. 2, 5.

85. Compañía Industrial de Orizaba, "Segunda ponencia," 196.

86. Data for the Mexican industry were calculated by CIDOSA; data for the United States and England CIDOSA were obtained from a formal report by the English Textile Commission on a visit to the United States in March–April 1944.

87. Compañía Industrial de Orizaba, "Segunda ponencia," 195.

88. Ibid., 188, 197; Lazonick, *Competitive Advantage on the Shopfloor*, 56.

89. United Nations, *Productividad*, 87.

90. Barajas Manzano, *Aspectos,* 28.
91. Ibid., 44, 67–74, 97–99.
92. This result is similar to that of Przeworski's model of accumulation and legitimation, when the economic militancy of organized wage earners is high. Przeworski, *Capitalism and Social Democracy,* 148–159, 179–196.
93. United Nations, *Productividad,* 87.
94. Barajas Manzano, *Aspectos,* 149.
95. International Bank for Reconstruction and Development, *Economic Development of Mexico,* 69; and United Nations, *Productividad,* 87.
96. Barajas Manzano, *Aspectos,* 31.
97. Ibid., 33.
98. International Bank for Reconstruction and Development, *Economic Development of Mexico,* 69.
99. The United Nations report indicated that the excess of personnel in Brazil's old mills was due to the perpetuation of a traditional organization of labor dating from the end of the nineteenth century or the beginning of the twentieth century, when most of the mills were founded. Because the textile industry developed later in São Paulo than in Rio de Janeiro, restrictions on the organization of labor were less important there. The textile industry developed after the 1930s in Chile and Peru, and these countries had less excess labor and fewer institutional restrictions on reducing it. United Nations, *Productividad,* 1–17, 20, 55, 74, 112.
100. This conclusion supports the views of William Lazonick on the importance of the institutions of social power and workers' power on the relationship between effort and pay. However, it challenges his idea that British entrepreneurs could have taken skills off the shop floor simply by investing in management and following a different managerial strategy. Lazonick, *Competitive Advantage on the Shopfloor.*
101. Susan Wolcott and Gregory Clark, "Why Nations Fail: Managerial Decisons and Performance in Indian Cotton Textiles, 1890–1938," *Journal of Economic History* 59, no. 2 (1999): 421.
102. John Womack Jr., "The Mexican Economy during the Revolution, 1910–1920: Historiography and Analysis," *Marxist Perspectives* (Winter 1978).
103. Haber, *Industry and Underdevelopment,* 122–149.
104. Using the information on mill characteristics available for 1912, a logit model was developed to look for mills' probability of survival in 1920 and 1932. Of the 146 mills that existed in 1912, 106 survived to 1920, and 94 to 1938. Aurora Gómez Galvarriato, "La Revolución y la industria textil del algodón: Un análisis cuantitativo," IX Reunión de Historiadores Mexicanos y Norteamericanos, seminar no. 68, Mexico City, October 1994.
105. Womack, "Mexican Economy."
106. The number of workers was adjusted by their working hours, assuming that the legal shift reductions were put into practice. It does not take into account that the days worked per mill varied widely, with a general trend toward reduction as the recession in the industry after 1926 deepened.
107. Table 9.3, and Stephen Haber, "Financial Markets and Industrial Development: A Comparative Study of Government Regulations, Financial Innovation, and Industrial

Structure in Brazil and Mexico, 1840–1930," in Stephen Haber, ed., *How Latin America Fell Behind: Essays on the Economic Histories of Brazil and Mexico, 1800–1914* (Stanford: Stanford University Press, 1997), 162.

108. Haber, "Financial Markets and Industrial Development"; Aldo Musacchio, Aurora Gómez-Galvarriato, and Rodrigo Parral, "Political Instability and Credible Commitments: The Case of Post-Revolutionary Mexico," paper presented at the conference "Latin American Economies: History and Globalization," UCLA, April 24–25, 2009.

109. Sandra Elena Martínez Aguilar, "Implicaciones del libre comercio sobre la industria textil Mexicana: 1986–1991" (BA thesis, Facultad de Economía, Universidad Nacional Autónoma de México, 1994), appendix, table 12; Gary Gereffi and Jennifer Bair, "En búsqueda del desarrollo integrado en México," *Trabajo* 1, no. 2 (1998): 160; Márquez, "La competitividad de la industria textil," 98–100.

# Archives and Periodicals Consulted

Archives

Archivo General de la Nación, Mexico
Archivo Histórico de Notarías
Archivo General del Estado de Veracruz
Archivo Histórico del Banco Nacional de México
Archivo de la Compañía Industrial de Orizaba S.A.
Archivo del Centro de Estudios de Historia de México, Grupo Carso
Archivo de la Compañía Industrial Veracruzana S.A.
Archivo del Sindicato de Santa Rosa
Oral Histories of Mexican Workers

Journals and Newspapers

*El Correo Español* (Mexico City)
*El Cosmopolita* (Mexico City)
*El Demórcrata* (Mexico City)
*El Diario* (Mexico City)
*Diario Oficial* (Mexico City)
*Excelsior* (Mexico City)
*Gaceta Oficial* (Mexico City)
*El Imparcial* (Mexico City)
*La Lucha Obrera* (Mexico City)
*El Monitor Republicano* (Mexico City)
*El Nacional* (Mexico City)

*El Paladín* (Mexico City)
*Pro-Paria* (Orizaba, Veracruz)
*La Semana Mercantil* (Mexico City)
*El Tiempo* (Mexico City)
*El Universal* (Mexico City)

# Acknowledgments

The making of this book has taken so long that it is wholly interwoven with an important part of my life. It is thus almost an impossible task to include in these lines all those who have contributed to it in one way or another.

John Womack Jr. guided and encouraged this work from its earliest stage. I am grateful to him for showing me the path into the amazing world that this book attempts to describe and walking along with me through all its wonders, providing me the keys to decipher its enigmas. Along the way, he taught me to look at documents with suspicion and insight, to explore further and search in unexpected places, to avoid academic fashions, and to privilege common sense above theories. I thank him for all the time he gave to me within so many bewildering conversations. I am also grateful to him for letting me use all the notes, statistics, and interviews on the textile workers of the Orizaba Valley that he had put together in many years of patient work. This book can be but a small tribute to his generosity, virtue, and erudition.

John Coatsworth's insight, intelligence, and optimism were fundamental for this book to take shape. His practical advice helped me out of many dead-end alleys and showed me the way into fruitful research alternatives. His uncanny ability to read through numbers and connect facts helped me detect mistakes, make new findings, and understand them better. His advice was also invaluable to make my explanations clearer and more interesting.

I am also grateful to Jeffrey Williamson and Claudia Goldin, who guided my way into economic history. With them I learned the basics of the field, and both provided me with invaluable advice to enrich the analysis of some areas of the research that form part of this book. Jeffrey Williamson has continued through all these years inspiring me to finish this project, infusing me with his energy, and opening up new research horizons.

From the very first day I met him at Harvard until today, Emilio Kourí has been there to give me the helpful advice and encouragement I needed. There is no part of this book that has not profited from his knowledge and intelligence. His friendship, commitment, and kindness have been an invaluable treasure for me along the path to the completion of this book. I cannot thank him enough.

I owe deep gratitude to Brodwin Fischer and Graciela Márquez for their companionship and friendship of many years. It has been a privilege to share the way with them. Their insights and queries have helped to shape this book. Their work has been a source of inspiration to me.

I was very lucky to have Bernardo García Díaz as my first guide into the Orizaba Valley. Ever since, we have become partners in the common endeavor of writing the history of the region. His extensive knowledge of the history of the mill towns and their workers, together with his passion for it, has been vital to my work. His generosity and joy for life have been an example for me. I also owe enormous gratitude to Carlos Marichal and Leticia Gamboa. Conversations with them were fundamental to developing and improving several parts of this book, giving me precious comments, encouragement, and friendship.

I cannot imagine the time I spent at Ciudad Mendoza carrying out archival research without the hospitality and friendship of the García Díaz family. Thanks to them I discovered the region, its people, its food, its music, and fell in love with it. Mr. Rubén García Díaz, a wise and virtuous man, and former mechanic of the Santa Rosa mill, taught me more about the working of the mill and the history of the town than any document I could have found. Bernardo, Micaela, Rubén, and Roberto García Díaz and their wonderful family became a family to me. I also express thanks for the hospitality of the Lazcano family at Ciudad Mendoza and of all the engineers and workers who helped me give some order to the factory's archive and explained several technicalities of textile production.

Colleagues who have read portions of the work and have provided guidance, insight, and encouragement include Carlos Bazdresch, Edward Beatty,

Enrique Cárdenas, Gustavo del Angel, Alberto Díaz, Oliver Dinius, Rafael Dobado, Gerardo Esquivel, Stephen Haber, Timothy Leunig, Juliette Levy, Colin Lewis, Clara Lida, Jordi Maluquer, Pablo Martín Aceña, Noel Maurer, Aldo Musacchio, Susie Porter, Gabriela Recio, Luis Ruvalcaba, Carmen Sarasúa, John Scott, Sergio Silva, Kenneth Sokoloff, Mauricio Tenorio, Gail Triner, Angela Vergara, and Andrew Wood. I am indebted to them.

Through the process of this project I have profited from the help of several research assistants. This enterprise has taken so long that some of them are now professors, and many have become dear colleagues and friends. I thank Julieta Almeida, Gabriela Cordourier, Hilda Flores, Ivette Madrid, Lucía Madrigal, Luis Montero, Aldo Musacchio, Rodrigo Parral, Yttze Quijada, and Sergio Silva for their great work, without which this book could not have been finished. I am also thankful to Robert Kovacevic and Isabel Estrada for copyediting my work with care and patience and to my editors at Havard University Press. In spite of the excellent support I received throughout this project from so many people, any remaining inadequacies are, of course, my entire responsibility.

Historical research cannot be conducted without archives. I am grateful to Eduardo and Manuel del Valle for letting me organize and use the Compañía Industrial Veracruzana archive, and to José Torres for opening up the Santa Rosa's Union archive to my research. I also thank the staff of the Archivo General de la Nación, the Lerdo de Tejada Library, the Francisco Xavier Clavijero library from Universidad Iberoamericana, the Banamex historical archive, the Centro de Estudios CARSO, and the Archivo de Notarias del Distrito Federal for their expertise and good will to help me find materials.

I thank the journals and presses that have let me reprint materials previously published with them. Table 1.3 is reprinted from Aurora Gómez-Galvarriato, "Networks and Entrepreneurship: The Modernization of the Textile Business in Porfirian Mexico," *Business History Review* 82 (Autumn 2008): 495, © 2008 the President and Fellows of Harvard College; all rights reserved. Portions of Chapters 2 and 9 are reprinted from Aurora Gómez-Galvarriato, "The Political Economy of Protectionism: The Mexican Textile Industry, 1900–1950," in *The Decline of Latin American Economies: Growth, Institutions, and Crises,* ed. Sebastian Edwards, Gerardo Esquivel, and Graciela Márquez (Chicago: University of Chicago Press, 2007), pp. 366–381; © 2007 by the National Bureau of Economic Research; all rights reserved. Portions of Chapter 8 have been reprinted, with some modifications, from Aurora Gómez-Galvarriato, "From

Company Towns to Union Towns: The Origin and Evolution of Santa Rosa and Río Blanco, Mexico, 1892–1930," in *Company Towns in the Americas: Landscape, Power, and Working-Class Communities,* ed. Oliver J. Dinius and Angela Vergara (Athens: University of Georgia Press, 2011), pp. 45–67; © 2011 by the University of Georgia Press; all rights reserved.

Research for this study was funded by grants from CONACYT, the Social Science Research Council, the Tinker Foundation, the Mexico in Harvard Foundation, and the Harvard Department of History. I am grateful to CIDE for its support throughout this entire project. The semester I spent at the David Rockefeller Center for Latin American Studies as a visiting scholar was vital to the completion of this project.

I have been blessed with a wonderful family, which has been my backbone through life and through the making of this book. Elizabeth Freer, my mother, has been an unconditional support, always giving me a helping hand, a smile, and her love. The passion for work and achievement of Mario Gómez Galvarriato, my father, has been an example to me and a source of strength and endurance. His constant love is a precious asset. My sisters, Elizabeth, Margarita, and Lilian, and Mario, my brother, have knitted with me an invaluable net of love, happiness, and friendship. I have also been blessed with extraordinary friends who have given me companionship, support, and encouragement in the making of this book. In particular I want to thank Blanca Heredia, Ana Magaloni, Judith Mariscal, Lorenza Martínez, and Gabriela Recio for being with me throughout these years.

Finally, I warmly thank my closest family, that which has grown together with this book. Without knowing, my sons, Emiliano and Mario Julian, have granted to this project many hours I could have otherwise spent with them. Fortunately they believe that writing a book is part of everyone's daily chores, so they have never complained. In return, they have loaded me with joy, enthusiasm, and sense of fulfillment.

César, my husband and dear friend, has been an invaluable companion in this trip. He has suffered and rejoiced together with me over every part of this project, helping me to withstand and surmount every problem and to appreciate any accomplishment. Several parts of this book profited from his knowledge, judgment, and clever advice. Without his constant support, patience, and love, this book could never have been written.

# Index

*Note:* Page numbers followed by *f* and *t* indicate figures and tables; page numbers in *italics* indicate photographs.